Al-Arish

SINAI AND
THE RED SEA
COAST

Sharm el-Sheikh

Hurghada

Luxor

Aswan

AROUND CAIRO
See pp158–169

**SINAI AND THE RED
SEA COAST**
See pp216–233

CAIRO AREA BY AREA

CENTRAL CAIRO
See pp68–85

ISLAMIC CAIRO
See pp86–111

**RHODA ISLAND
AND OLD CAIRO**
See pp112–125

GIZA AND HELIOPOLIS
See pp126–139

0 kilometres   140

0 miles   75

EYEWITNESS TRAVEL

EGYPT

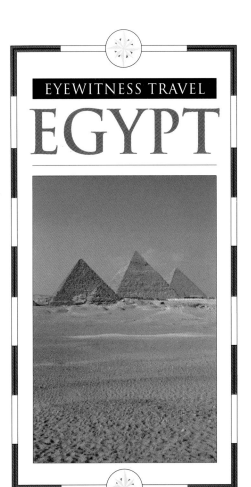

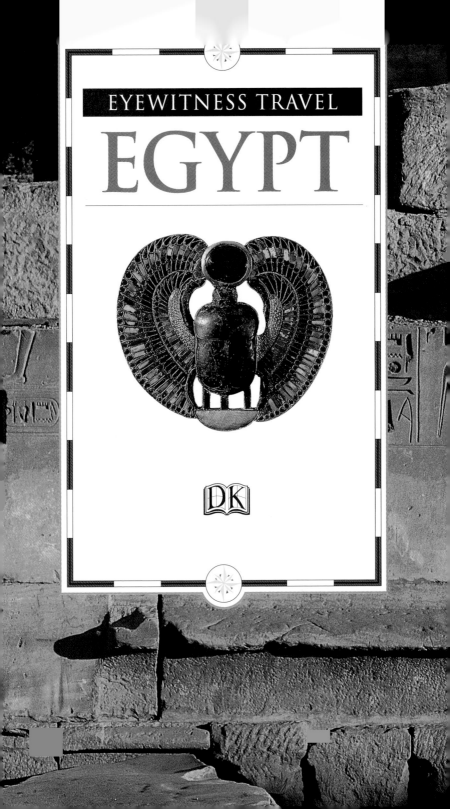

EYEWITNESS TRAVEL

EGYPT

DK

LONDON, NEW YORK,
MELBOURNE, MUNICH AND DELHI
www.dk.com

PROJECT EDITORS Hugh Thompson, Claire Folkard
PROJECT ART EDITOR Jo Doran
EDITORS Liz Atherton, Irene Lyford,
Ferdie McDonald, Marianne Petrou, Martin Redfern
DESIGNERS Emma Rose, Rebecca Milner, Ian Midson,
Sue Megginson, Anthony Limerick
PICTURE RESEARCHERS Monica Allende, Cynthia Frazer,
Katherine Mesquita
MAP CO-ORDINATORS David Pugh, Casper Morris
DTP DESIGNER Maite Lantaron

MAIN CONTRIBUTORS
Jane Dunford, Dr Joann Fletcher, Carole French, Robin Gauldie, Andrew
Humphreys, Kyle Pakka, Richard Williams

MAPS
ERA-Maptec Ltd

PHOTOGRAPHERS
Max Alexander, Jon Spaull,
Peter Wilson

ILLUSTRATORS
Gary Cross, Richard Draper, Claire Littlejohn, Maltings Partnership, Chris
Orr & Associates, John Woodcock

Reproduced by Colourscan, Singapore
Printed in Malaysia by Vivar Printing Sdn. Bhd.

First published in Great Britain in 2001
by Dorling Kindersley Limited
80 Strand, London WC2R 0RL
A Penguin Company

11 12 13 14 10 9 8 7 6 5 4 3 2 1

Reprinted with revisions 2003, 2005, 2007, 2009, 2011

Copyright 2001, 2011 © Dorling Kindersley Limited, London

A CIP CATALOGUE RECORD IS AVAILABLE FROM THE BRITISH LIBRARY.

ISBN 978 1 40535 787 6

THROUGHOUT THIS BOOK, FLOORS ARE REFERRED TO IN ACCORDANCE
WITH EUROPEAN USAGE: THE "FIRST FLOOR" IS THE FLOOR ABOVE
GROUND LEVEL

Front cover main image: Pyramids in Giza

MIX
Paper from
responsible sources
FSC
www.fsc.org   FSC™ C018179

Fertile fields watered by the Nile at Luxor

CONTENTS

HOW TO USE
THIS GUIDE 6

INTRODUCING
EGYPT

DISCOVERING
EGYPT 10

PUTTING EGYPT
ON THE MAP 12

A PORTRAIT
OF EGYPT 14

EGYPT THROUGH
THE YEAR 38

THE HISTORY
OF EGYPT 44

**View from the Cairo Tower looking
at the Radio and TV Union Building**

◁ **A local guide keeping out of the heat of the sun at Luxor Temple in the Nile Valley**

Camel trekking in the desert

SURVIVAL GUIDE

TRAVELLERS'
NEEDS

CAIRO AREA
BY AREA

Fruit stall at Dakhla Oasis showing
the wide variety of produce grown

Colossal foot at the Ramesseum

Ancient Egyptian frieze of lotus
blooms, symbolic of rebirth

SHOPPING AND
ENTERTAINMENT IN
CAIRO **150**

EGYPT AREA
BY AREA

Hanging Church in Coptic Cairo

HOW TO USE THIS GUIDE

This guide helps you to get the most from your visit to Egypt by providing detailed practical information and expert recommendations. *Introducing Egypt* maps the country and sets it in its historical and cultural context. The Cairo section and the five area chapters describe important sights using maps, photographs and illustrations. Features cover topics from food and wildlife to hieroglyphics and mythology. Restaurants and hotel recommendations can be found in *Travellers' Needs*, while the *Survival Guide* has tips on everything from making a telephone call to using local transportation, as well as information on money and other practical matters.

CAIRO AREA BY AREA

The city is divided into three areas, each with its own chapter. A fourth chapter covers the peripheral areas of Giza and Heliopolis. All sights are numbered and plotted on each chapter's area map. Information on each sight is easy to locate as the entries follow the numbering used on the map.

A locator map shows where you are in relation to other areas in the city centre.

All pages relating to Cairo have red thumb tabs.

Sights at a Glance lists the chapter's sights by category: Streets and Squares, Holy Places, Museums, Historic Buildings and Mosques.

1 Area Map
For easy reference, sights are numbered and located on a map. The central sights are also marked on the Street Finder maps on pages 140–49.

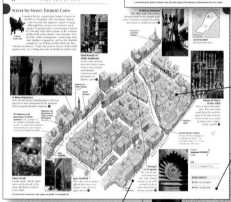

Street-by-Street: Fatimid Cairo

2 Street-by-Street Map
This gives a bird's-eye view of the key area in each chapter.

Stars indicate the sights that no visitor should miss.

Walking routes, in red, take in the area's most interesting streets.

3 Detailed information
City sights are described individually. Addresses and opening hours are given, as well as information on admission charges, guided tours, photography, wheelchair access and public transport.

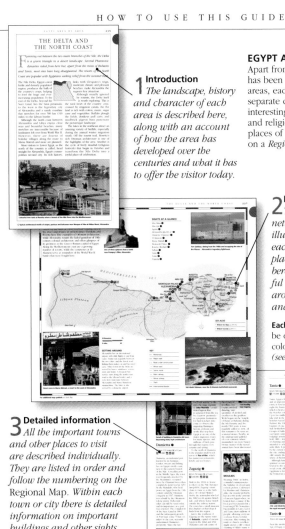

THE DELTA AND THE NORTH COAST

EGYPT AREA BY AREA
Apart from Cairo, the country has been divided into five areas, each of which has a separate chapter. The most interesting cities, towns, ancient and religious sites, and other places of interest are located on a *Regional Map*.

1 Introduction
The landscape, history and character of each area is described here, along with an account of how the area has developed over the centuries and what it has to offer the visitor today.

2 Regional Map
This shows the road network and gives an illustrated overview of each area. Interesting places to visit are numbered, and there are useful tips on getting to and around the region by car and public transport.

Each area of Egypt can be quickly identified by its colour-coded thumb tabs *(see inside front cover).*

3 Detailed information
All the important towns and other places to visit are described individually. They are listed in order and follow the numbering on the Regional Map. Within each town or city there is detailed information on important buildings and other sights.

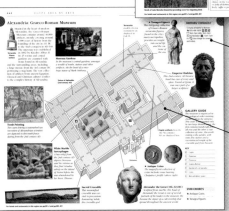

For all major sights, a *Visitors' Checklist* provides the practical information you will need to plan your visit.

4 Egypt's Top Sights
These are given two or more pages. Historic buildings are reconstructed, or dissected to reveal their interiors. Other interesting sights are shown in bird's-eye view, with important features highlighted.

INTRODUCING EGYPT

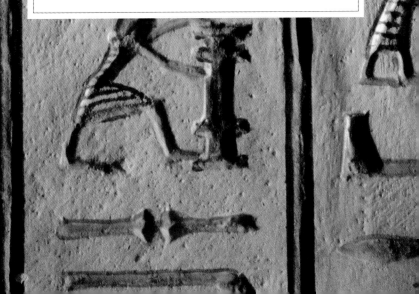

DISCOVERING EGYPT

Few countries can match Egypt's wealth of ancient monuments and temples; the relics of Pharaonic culture have been drawing visitors for centuries. The geographical variety of Egypt means that visitors are spoiled for choice: from the bustle of Cairo to the austere adventure of the

Tutankhamun's gilded fan, Egyptian Museum

Western Desert; from the coral of the Red Sea to the cultural wealth of the Nile Valley temples; from the lush Delta region with its cosmopolitan, cultured city of Alexandria to the endlessly fascinating pyramid fields around Cairo. These pages offer a brief overiew of each region.

The majestic Sphinx on the Giza Plateau, in the suburbs of Cairo

CAIRO

- Mosques and museums
- Wondrous pyramids
- Shopping in the souqs
- Buzzing nightlife

Cairo is a city where ancient and modern are intertwined. As well as the **Pyramids** (see pp128–35), the **Sphinx** at Giza (see p135) and the fabulous **Egyptian Museum** (see pp74–7), there are early Christian churches and Ottoman and Mamluk mosques. The old souqs, alleys and houses are clustered together with modern five-star hotels, shopping malls, restaurants, cinemas and theatres.

The Citadel (Al-Qalaa) (see pp104–7), dating from the 12th century, contains fascinating mosques, museums and battlements which reflect a diverse heritage. Nearby is one of the largest and oldest mosques in Egypt, the

Mosque of Ibn Tulun (see pp110-11), built entirely of mud brick.

The world's oldest bazaar, **Khan al-Khalili** (see p90), sells antiques, textiles, handicrafts and low-quality souvenirs. The city's restaurants offer all types of cuisine and there is a great selection of bars, nightclubs and *sheesha* cafés.

For classical and Arabic music head to the beautiful domed **Opera House** (see p84), a cultural centre with galleries and concert halls.

AROUND CAIRO

- The pyramids at Saqqara
- Lakes and oases
- Ancient Memphis
- Carpet schools

For a day or two's excursion out of Cairo, visitors can take a felucca up the Nile to the **Nile Barrages** at **Qanater** (see p169), a good picnic spot. Heading south out of Cairo, the road leads to **Saqqara** (see pp162–4), the site of the Pyramid of Djoser, which is much older than the Great Pyramids and less crowded. Further down the road are the even more isolated pyramid site of **Dahshur** (see p165) and **Fayoum Oasis** (see p168), Egypt's largest oasis, with its lush vegetation. Closer at hand are the three pyramids of **Abusir** (see p162) and the site of the ancient city of **Memphis** (see p165), with a small museum. After a guided tour around one of the many carpet schools in this area, you might not be able to resist buying a rug.

Camels riding past verdant Fayoum, Egypt's largest oasis

◁ Hieroglyphics on tomb in the Valley of the Kings

THE NILE VALLEY

- **Theban tombs**
- **Luxor and Karnak**
- **The lazy Nile**
- **The dams at Aswan**

For an abundance of tombs and temples, head to **Luxor** *(see pp182–90)* and **Thebes** *(see pp192–203)*. No one can fail to be impressed by the Valley of the Kings, the temples at Karnak and Luxor and the Luxor Museum.

A cruise down the Nile allows you to take in various temples, including **Edfu** *(see pp204–5)*, **Kom Ombo** *(see p205)* and, eventually, **Abu Simbel** *(see pp214–15)*.

Most cruises stop at Aswan *(see pp208–11)*, whose two famous dams (Aswan Dam and High Dam) are extraordinary feats of engineering.

The extraordinary colours of the Red Sea coral reef

The unmistakable sail of a felucca slowly gliding along the Nile

SINAI AND THE RED SEA COAST

- **Beautiful beaches**
- **Spectacular diving**
- **Monasteries and castles**
- **Watersports and golf**

Sun, sea, diving and good food can all be found here. **Sharm el-Sheikh** *(see p226)*, at the southern tip of the Sinai peninsula, has the best choice of hotels, restaurants and nightlife. Naama Bay is good for snorkelling and also boasts many *sheesha* cafés, bars and clubs.

Sinai has much more to offer, however. The Greek

Orthodox **Monastery of St Catherine** *(see pp222–5)* has a fabulous collection of religious icons, while those venturing further up the coast will enjoy the 12th-century Crusader castle on **Pharaoh's Island** *(see p231)*. **Dahab** *(see p230)* is great for diving, sailing and wind-surfing, as is **Hurghada** *(see pp232–3)*, on the west coast of the Red Sea. **Soma Bay** *(see p233)* and **El-Gouna** *(see p233)* offer a tranquil setting, plus top-class spas and golf.

THE DELTA AND THE NORTH COAST

- **Alexandria**
- **Ottoman architecture**
- **Important battlegrounds**
- **Historic Rosetta**

The second city in Egypt, **Alexandria** *(see pp240–47)* was founded by Alexander the Great in the 4th century BC. Little remains of the city's Graeco-Roman architecture, but there is a Mamluk fortress and some Ottoman mosques in the Anfushi area. Although a busy port, the city has a more laid-back Mediterranean feel than Cairo.

To the west of Alexandria is the town of **El-Alamein** *(see p251)*, with its World War II cemeteries and museum. To the east lie **Abu Qir** *(see p250)*, site of Nelson's victory at the 1798 Battle of the Nile, and **Rosetta** (Rashid) *(see p239)*, where the Rosetta Stone was discovered.

THE WESTERN DESERT

- **Verdant oases**
- **Desert treasures**
- **Safari adventure**
- **Berber culture**

A vast expanse of sand and rock, the Western Desert stretches from the Nile west towards the Libyan border. Apart from a few Bedouin desert-dwellers, the area is uninhabited, except for **Kharga** *(see p256)*, **Dakhla** *(see p256)*, **Farafra** *(see p257)*, **Bahariyya** *(see p257)* and **Siwa** *(see p260)* oases, which house a surprising number of ancient Egyptian and Roman temples and medieval forts. Four of these oases are reachable by a looping desert road from Cairo to Asyut and are the main stopping-off points for desert safaris. Siwa, the most remote oasis, offers a great insight into Berber culture.

Ancient ruins in Siwa, a remote oasis in the Western Desert

Putting Egypt on the Map

Sitting on the northeast corner of Africa, with coastlines along the Mediterranean and Red seas, Egypt
borders Libya to the west, Israel to the east and Sudan
to the south. Over 90 per cent of the country is desert
and most of the 82 million population live along the
Nile Valley and in the Nile Delta, with a small percentage living in the oases that dot the barren interior.

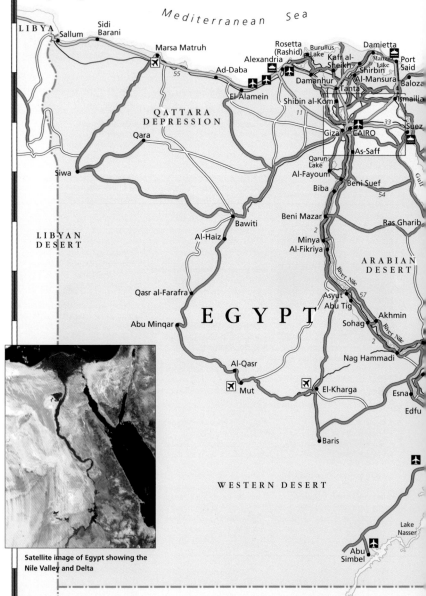

Satellite image of Egypt showing the
Nile Valley and Delta

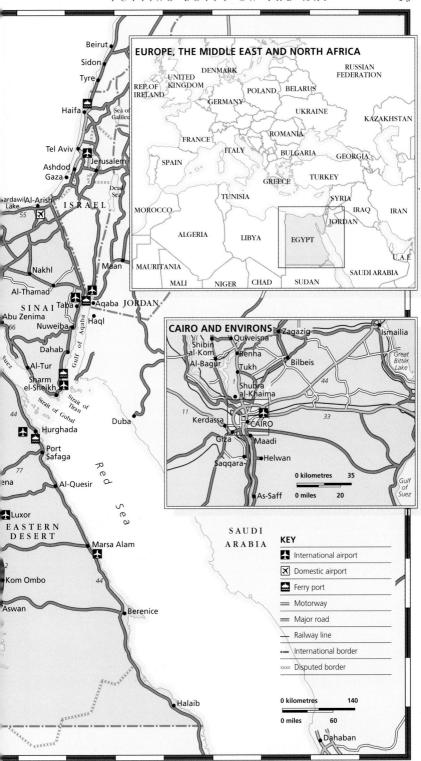

EUROPE, THE MIDDLE EAST AND NORTH AFRICA

REP. OF IRELAND
UNITED KINGDOM
DENMARK
POLAND
BELARUS
RUSSIAN FEDERATION
GERMANY
UKRAINE
KAZAKHSTAN
FRANCE
ITALY
ROMANIA
BULGARIA
GEORGIA
SPAIN
GREECE
TURKEY
TUNISIA
SYRIA
IRAQ
IRAN
JORDAN
MOROCCO
ALGERIA
LIBYA
EGYPT
SAUDI ARABIA
U.A.E.
MAURITANIA
MALI
NIGER
CHAD
SUDAN

Beirut
Sidon
Tyre
Haifa
Sea of Galilee
Tel Aviv
Jerusalem
Ashdod
Gaza
Dead Sea
ardawil Lake
Al-Arish
ISRAEL
55
Nakhl
Maan
Al-Thamad
SINAI
Taba
Aqaba
JORDAN
66
Abu Zenima
Nuweiba
Haql
Dahab
Al-Tur
Gulf of Aqaba
Sharm el-Sheikh
Strait of Tiran
Strait of Gubal
Duba
Suez
44
Hurghada
Port Safaga
Red Sea
ena
Al-Quesir
77
Luxor
EASTERN DESERT
Marsa Alam
SAUDI ARABIA
Kom Ombo
44
Aswan
Berenice
Halaib
Dahaban

CAIRO AND ENVIRONS

Quweisna
Zagazig
Ismailia
Shibin al-Kom
Benha
Great Bitter Lake
Al-Bagur
Tukh
Bilbeis
1
44
Shubra al-Khaima
11
33
Kerdassa
CAIRO
Giza
Maadi
Saqqara
Helwan
Gulf of Suez
As-Saff

0 kilometres   35
0 miles   20

KEY

✈	International airport
⊠	Domestic airport
⛴	Ferry port
━━	Motorway
━━	Major road
───	Railway line
▬▬▬	International border
xxxx	Disputed border

0 kilometres   140
0 miles   60

A PORTRAIT OF EGYPT

Settling along the fertile banks of the Nile, the ancient Egyptians established a magnificent and enduring civilization whose achievements have captured the imagination of the world ever since. Although looking to the future, modern Egypt cannot ignore its glorious past, but the resulting contrasts make it a uniquely fascinating place to visit.

The world's fascination with this country centres on the civilization of ancient Egypt that flourished from around 3000 BC to 30 BC, ruled by approximately 30 dynasties. The river Nile was the powerful force that enabled the ancient Egyptian kingdom to develop. The river's annual cycle of inundation watered the land and replenished the fertile topsoil. This resulted in an agricultural abundance that allowed them to concentrate on developing the knowledge and culture that formed their unique and sophisticated civilization. Over the succeeding millennia, waves of foreign conquerors passed through the country – Persians, Greeks, Romans, crusaders, Arabs and Turks – leaving traces behind in their descendants. Today most Egyptians are classified as being of Eastern Hamitic descent. The once nomadic Bedouin and Berber tribes of the desert are of Arab descent and the third major racial grouping (less than 200,000) is the Nubian community in the south.

Pectoral of Tutankhamun (1336–1327 BC)

DAILY LIFE

Even today, the river Nile remains the lifeblood of Egypt, with around 96 per cent of the population forced by the harsh environment to live in the Nile Delta or Nile Valley.

The fertile Nile Delta, one of the most intensely cultivated areas of the world

◁ Traders negotiating at one of Egypt's lively and fascinating camel markets

Solitary felucca sailing serenely down the tranquil waters of the Nile

The ancient cycle of flooding ended with the completion of the High Dam at Aswan in 1971, forcing the Egyptian *fellaheen* (farmers) to resort to artificial fertilizers. However, it is easy to imagine that life today along the river's edge remains just as it has for thousands of years.

The typical Egyptian rural settlement is a village of between 500 and 10,000 people set amid intensely cultivated fields. Houses are often no more than one or two storeys high and each village also has a mosque or church, and perhaps a colourful pigeoncote, a few shops and an official government building. Most of the inhabitants of smaller villages work in agriculture and the landscape is usually dotted with farmers, wearing the traditional *galabiyya* (long smock), working the green fields or tending their precious animals – buffalo, sheep and goats.

Men chatting in a Cairo coffee house, a popular male Egyptian pastime

The urban population has been expanding rapidly since the 1980s. Increasing pressure on agricultural land and the growth of city-based service industries have led to large numbers of Egyptians moving from the country to urban areas. The buildings in towns and cities are predominantly two-storey houses or higher apartment blocks with flat roofs and balconies, often built close together. The high population density in cities also leads to problems of traffic congestion. Nowhere is this more evident than in Cairo, where there is a constant cacophony of car engines and horns.

Throughout Egypt the family has remained the most significant unit of a patriarchal society. Traditionally, an individual's social identity was closely linked to his or her status in the network of relations. Today families are far more likely to disperse and the ideal of an extended family that lives together is less frequent. However, strong ties with in-laws, grandparents, nieces and nephews and the rest of the family still create a strong social fabric that binds the whole community together.

The *hegab* or headscarf, increasingly worn by Egyptian women

RELIGION AND CULTURE

Underpinning all levels of Egyptian society is a powerful religious faith. Islam is constitutionally established as the official religion and around 90 per cent of the population are Sunni Muslim *(see p91)*, the rest being Christian, mainly of the Coptic church *(see p122)*. However, say to an Egyptian of either faith "I'll see you tomorrow" and the answer will be the same – "Inshallah", which means "if God is willing". For the casual tourist, the many casinos, bars, nightclubs and beach resorts can disguise the fact that Egyptians uphold a fairly conservative mix of traditional and religious values, particularly outside the main cities. Gambling or drinking alcohol in public is frowned upon and Egyptian men rarely wear shorts, except maybe at the beach.

Women, too, are almost always well-covered. In the 1970s, as women gained greater independence and access to education, they swelled the numbers of the non-agricultural workforce and many Muslim women discarded their *hegab* (headscarf). With the wide appeal of Islamist conservatives in the 1990s, women started dressing more modestly and, even in Cairo, increasing numbers are once again covering their heads, with some adopting the *niqab*, the full face covering. However, the number of women in employment has remained at a high level.

Umm Kolthum in concert

Egyptians, governed by outsiders for thousands of years, have only been truly independent since 1952 when Gamal Abdel Nasser removed the last foreign royal and forged a truly Egyptian identity for his people. Despite a climate of political turmoil, this period of Egypt's history was a time of cultural vitality, when Umm Kolthum, the diva of the Arab world, gave concerts for the masses and Naguib

Modern Cairo with the Pyramids of Giza just visible through the evening haze

Negotiating the streets around Midan Ataba in Cairo on a daily bread round

Mahfouz penned his most famous novels. Awarded a Nobel Prize in 1988, Mahfouz single-handedly rejuvenated the Egyptian literary scene. However, few other Egyptian writers have managed to emulate his success. Today, as a result of Egypt's population boom and greater exposure to western music, there is a ready market for home-grown modern pop music. Nevertheless Umm Kolthum's soulful music is as all-pervasive as ever, constantly played in shops and taxis throughout Egypt.

Egypt's cinema had its heyday in the 1940s and 50s when its studios made films for the whole Arab world. Apart from a few independent films which gain a wider exposure during international film festivals, little of merit emerges these days.

POLITICS AND ECONOMICS

After the abolition of the monarchy in 1952, Nasser went on to dissolve all political parties and introduce a new constitution in 1956, declaring the Republic of Egypt. Led by Nasser, the National Union, later the Arab Socialist Union (ASU), became the sole party. In 1971 a new constitution declared Egypt to be "a democratic, socialist state". But it was not until 1977 that the formation of other political parties was allowed. Three years later the ASU was abolished. The next ruling party, the National Democratic Party (NDP) led by Hosni Mubarak, was a direct descendant of Nasser's ASU. Egypt's

Nasser, President of Egypt 1956–70

The modern Nile City Towers complex in Cairo, overlooking the Nile

"dominant party system" allowed a large ruling party to straddle the centre of the ideological spectrum, surrounded by small pressure parties. This limited the possibility for radical reform, but allowed the government to proceed slowly. However, in 2011, following public protests, Mubarak's government was dissolved. The military took over interim rule and Egyptians now hope for a more democratic future.

Ancient tombs lying in the path of a motorway

Egyptian growth has decelerated with the global economic woes. Agriculture is the most important industry. Employing a large amount of the workforce, it feeds much of the country and provides valuable exports, especially the cotton crop. The High Dam project increased arable land and provided a much needed boost to the power supply. However, in the same period, just as much land was swallowed up by industrial and urban development, constantly building over Egypt's celebrated past. Although slowing down, population growth undermines all efforts to foster the economy. Other important sources of income are oil, gas, mining, and of course, tourism. The brutal murder of 58 tourists in 1997 *(see p176)* and the kidnapping of tourists in a remote southern region in 2007 rocked the country, causing visitor numbers to plummet. While the tourist figures are now rising, the government is

A visitor at a Red Sea resort, enjoying Egypt's beautiful beaches and all-year-round sun

aware of the instability and problems that would result from further unrest.

EGYPT TODAY

Given the importance of tradition and religion to Egyptian daily life, it is perhaps surprising that Western technology and lifestyles have steadily gained influence. However, the "benefits" of this cultural invasion are only felt by the select few, due to the seemingly unbridgeable gap between the rich and poor. Films and TV programmes from the West have had a huge impact on Egyptian perceptions, raising expectations and creating resentment among the less well-off. This situation is not always helped by the sight of tourists enjoying luxuries beyond the reach of many Egyptians. Even so, the fascinating mix of ancient monuments, modern culture and the natural hospitality of its people ensure that Egypt's popularity continues to grow.

Discovering Ancient Egypt

Greek historian Herodotus

The magnificence and longevity of the ancient Egyptian civilization has always held a timeless fascination. As early as 1400 BC, King Tuthmosis IV undertook excavations at Giza, and the Greek historian Herodotus left a detailed account of his tour of Egypt in 450 BC. However, modern Egyptology really started with the study of the country commissioned in 1798 by Napoleon. Since then the subject has developed rapidly. In the last 20 years, computers and electron microscopes have begun to replace the pickaxe and shovel.

Napoleon's scholars *amassed the material for the authoritative work* Description de l'Egypte *during the French occupation (1798–1802).*

Jean-François Champollion
(1790–1832), was a French linguist whose brilliant work in deciphering the hieroglyphic script was the single most important event in the development of Egyptology.

Hieroglyphs *were used as early as 3200 BC and are the oldest known writing system. Used primarily in religious contexts, their last datable use was in AD 394 at the Temple of Philae when the script numbered over 6,000 characters.*

Howard Carter *had to carefully remove many layers of solidified perfumes and resins covering Tutankhamun's innermost coffin. The body was protected by several layers of coffins, the last one of solid gold.*

HOWARD CARTER (1873–1939)

Carter trained as an artist and joined the Archaeological Survey of Egypt in 1891. In 1922, he achieved fame when he found King Tutankhamun's tomb, virtually untouched, in the Valley of the Kings.

The treasures *Carter found on opening the tomb were abundant. Most items are on display in the Egyptian Museum (see* pp74–7).

RELOCATION OF ANCIENT TEMPLES

The construction of the Aswan High Dam and Lake Nasser (1960–71) threatened many temples and rock tombs along the Nile with total submersion. Concern over the loss of such archaeological treasures led UNESCO to promote an international relief campaign. Three stages of operations were necessary: a survey of the area, the excavation of sites, and the final movement of as many endangered monuments as was possible. Twenty monuments from Egyptian Nubia and four from the Sudan were carefully dismantled, then reassembled at safe distances from their original sites. The two largest operations involved the Great Temple at Abu Simbel *(see pp214–15)* and the temple complex at Philae *(see p212)*.

Trajan's Kiosk (also known as the Pharaoh's Bedstead) before relocation at Philae

UNDERWATER DISCOVERIES

In 1996, a team led by the French marine archaeologist, Franck Goddio, began to explore the submerged Royal City of Alexandria, where Cleopatra held court. The finds so far include statues, sphinxes, ceramics and the remains of Cleopatra's palace.

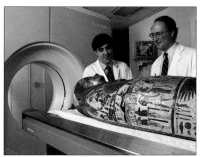

Tutankhamun's death mask, *shown here at the British Museum with Queen Elizabeth II in 1972, was the top exhibit in a display of Carter's finds that toured the major museums of the world rekindling interest in Egypt's rich history.*

ARCHAEOLOGY AND TECHNOLOGY

Egyptology is a relatively young science, but huge advances have been made since Champollion's work opened the door on ancient Egyptian history. Today, Egyptologists are greatly assisted by new technologies, both in the laboratory and in the field – and even under water.

Restoration and preservation work *on ancient artifacts involves skilled and painstaking processes, which have to be conducted in a strictly controlled environment.*

Modern technologies, *such as CAT scanning, radio-carbon dating, DNA and trace element analysis, endoscopy and electron microscopy have all contributed to more accurate dating and a deeper understanding of archaeological finds.*

Hieroglyphics

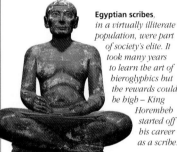

Dating from around 3200 BC, ancient Egyptian hieroglyphics are the world's oldest known writing system. The word "hieroglyph" means "sacred carved letter" and refers to the beautiful pictorial script used by ancient Egyptians to express their religious beliefs and engraved onto nearly every available surface of their monuments. Although pictorial, hieroglyphs convey extremely complex semantic information; they could be read from left to right, right to left or top to bottom. However, when writing on papyrus, the hieroglyphic system was too slow and impractical for everyday use and over the centuries more easily written scripts were developed with the last datable hieroglyphic inscription being at Hadrian's Gate at Philae in AD 394.

Hieroglyph for motion or "to go"

Thoth, *the ibis-headed god of wisdom and patron deity of scribes, is here portrayed holding his sceptre of power or was.*

Egyptian scribes, *in a virtually illiterate population, were part of society's elite. It took many years to learn the art of hieroglyphics but the rewards could be high – King Horemheb started off his career as a scribe.*

THE ROSETTA STONE – CRACKING THE CODE

Until 1822, the ability to read hieroglyphic inscriptions had been lost. It was a black granite stele, discovered in 1799 in Rosetta by Napoleon's army, that held the key. It contained a text in three scripts: hieroglyphic, demotic and Greek. The two main contestants in the race to decipher the symbols were Thomas Young, a British physician and Jean-François Champollion, a gifted French linguist. By 1819, Young was ahead of the Frenchman, translating the demotic text as well as identifying the cartouches of Ptolemy and Cleopatra. However, Champollion was also able to decipher these names and others, compiling an extensive list of symbols. Using this list, he realised that there were separate types of hieroglyphs with different functions and therefore discovered the basis of the writing system used in hieroglyphic texts.

The Rosetta Stone, inscribed by the priests of Ptolemy V (196 BC)

Ptolemaic scribes *raised the number of hieroglyphic symbols from 700 to 6000, in an attempt to keep their knowledge exclusive.*

THE IMPORTANCE OF NAMES

Ancient Egyptians believed that names were as vital to one's existence as the soul. Names held great power and speaking the name of the dead could bring them to life. Therefore, funerary texts often included spells to cause the name of the deceased to be remembered in the afterlife and so ensure eternal life.

The oval cartouche forms a protective wall or enclosure.

Hieroglyphs give the name, "Ramses, beloved of Amun".

Egyptian kings *protected their names within cartouches and increased their chances of eternal life by the sheer number of epithets they possessed.*

This detail of the King List *found at Abydos gives some of Ramses II's names, including "the king of Upper and Lower Egypt, Usermaatre Setepenre, son of Ra, and Ramses, beloved of Amun".*

HIEROGLYPHIC TEXT

Hieroglyphs were a decorative art and ritual pictures, combined with texts, played a vital part in religious ceremonies. Funerary texts were designed to protect the dead and help guide their passage to the underworld. This detail from the funeral texts of the scribe Nebked (c.1400 BC), shows the deceased (his writing kit tucked into his belt) worshipping the god Osiris with his wife and mother.

Hieratic script *was a faster way of writing. Dating from c.2600 BC, it was used for everyday communications until c.600 BC when it was superseded by the even faster demotic or "popular" script.*

TRANSLATING HIEROGLYPHS

Put simply, there are three main types of hieroglyphs. "Phonograms" convey the sounds of the syllables, for example the ancient Egyptian for "son" was spoken *sa* and this is denoted by the duck. "Ideograms" portray the actual object or action, such as a sun on the horizon to indicate "appearance". The final type is "determinatives" which indicate, confirm or modify the meaning of the word to which they are attached, for example, three bars denote a plural. To further complicate matters, many symbols can be either ideograms, phonograms or determinatives. The basket symbol, *neb*, can be a phonogram for "Lord" or simply represent a "basket". Symbols of humans and animals always face the start of the text, indicating the direction the text runs.

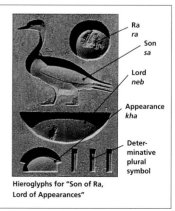

Ra
ra

Son
sa

Lord
neb

Appearance
kha

Determinative plural symbol

Hieroglyphs for "Son of Ra, Lord of Appearances"

Temples and Religious Life

For the ancient Egyptians, the universe was composed of dualities – fertile and barren, life and death, order and chaos – held in a state of equilibrium by the goddess Maat. To maintain this balance, they built enormous temples dedicated to the gods. At the centre of every settlement and devoted to a particular god or set of gods, the "cult" temple served as a storehouse of divine power, maintained by the priesthood for the benefit of all. The temple was also an economic and political centre employing large numbers of the local community and serving as a town hall, medical centre and college.

Statue of a priest praying

Goddess Maat, *the personification of cosmic order and harmony, set the rules by which all kings must govern. Her power regulated the stars, the seasons and humans' relationship with the gods.*

Funerary priest in a leopard skin, performing sacred rituals

A DAY IN THE LIFE OF A TEMPLE PRIEST

Egyptian priests were literally "servants of the god or goddess", responsible for performing the daily rituals that regulated the workings of the universe. The king, although the intermediary between the mortal and the divine, delegated his duties to the high priest of the temple. This priest was then responsible for the most important of the temple rituals – the honouring of the god within its shrine. Twice daily the "cult" statue was bathed and clothed before receiving offerings of food and drink. Incense was burnt and holy water from the sacred lake scattered to show the purity of the offerings. After the essence of the food had been consumed by the gods, the priests were able to eat the actual offerings.

CULT TEMPLE RECONSTRUCTION

As well as housing the deity, the temple complex symbolized the universe. Its architecture represented the fundamental elements of water, sunlight, stars, forests and, inside the depths of the temple, darkness.

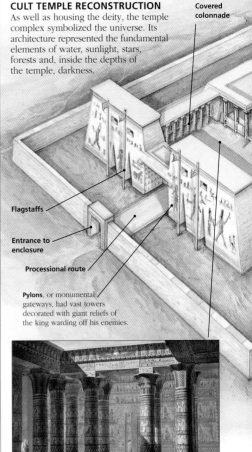

Covered colonnade

Flagstaffs

Entrance to enclosure

Processional route

Pylons, or monumental gateways, had vast towers decorated with giant reliefs of the king warding off his enemies.

The central court, *as depicted in this 19th-century reconstruction of the court at Philae (see p212), was a colonnaded courtyard brightly decorated with reliefs showing the king making offerings to the temple's deities.*

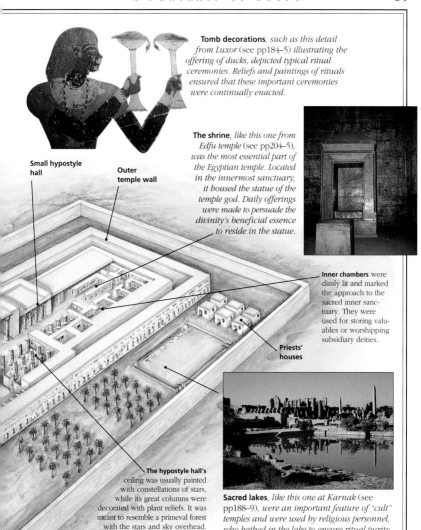

Tomb decorations, *such as this detail from Luxor (see pp184–5) illustrating the offering of ducks, depicted typical ritual ceremonies. Reliefs and paintings of rituals ensured that these important ceremonies were continually enacted.*

The shrine, *like this one from Edfu temple (see pp204–5), was the most essential part of the Egyptian temple. Located in the innermost sanctuary, it housed the statue of the temple god. Daily offerings were made to persuade the divinity's beneficial essence to reside in the statue.*

Small hypostyle hall

Outer temple wall

Inner chambers were dimly lit and marked the approach to the sacred inner sanctuary. They were used for storing valuables or worshipping subsidiary deities.

Priests' houses

The hypostyle hall's ceiling was usually painted with constellations of stars, while its great columns were decorated with plant reliefs. It was meant to resemble a primeval forest with the stars and sky overhead.

Sacred lakes, *like this one at Karnak (see pp188–9), were an important feature of "cult" temples and were used by religious personnel, who bathed in the lake to ensure ritual purity.*

MORTUARY TEMPLES

In addition to the local "cult" temples, each king built a mortuary temple to serve as a place where, following his death, offerings could be made for his soul. The temples were originally attached to the royal tombs of the Old and Middle Kingdoms but by around 1500 BC they had developed into vast, elaborate complexes built at separate locations to the tombs which were now hidden away in secluded desert valleys. The great temples on the West Bank at Luxor are fine examples of New Kingdom mortuary temples. The magnificent Temple of Queen Hatshepsut (see pp196–7) at Deir al-Bahri has one of the most original mortuary temple designs.

The Ramesseum in Thebes (see pp200–1), the mortuary temple of Ramses II

Mythology

Ancient Egyptian religion was a highly complex belief system involving a great number of deities originally based on aspects of the natural world. As these evolved into more cohesive "personalities", each locality developed myths relating to their own particular deities. These myths were many and varied, with even the story of creation having at least three different versions, based on the belief that life first emerged from the waters of chaos as a mound of earth. A number of places claimed to be the original site of this primeval mound and that the first life was created by the gods associated with that particular place, be they the 9 gods of Heliopolis, the 8 gods of Hermopolis or the one god of Memphis.

Household god Bes

Amun, whose name means "the hidden one", became a national deity when Thebes ruled Egypt, in an attempt to unify the country.

CREATION MYTH

This detail from a popular creation myth shows the Egyptian gods in relation to the world. In the beginning there was nothing but the sea of chaos, Nun. Then Atum thought himself into being, sneezing to create Shu and then Tefnut. He caused the seas to recede and called forth all the plants and animals. Shu and Tefnut gave birth to two children: Geb, the earth, and Nut, the sky, who in turn gave birth to the stars.

Nephthys pours the waters of fruitfulness over the earth, where men hoe the land.

Nut, mother of all, swallows the sun each night, giving birth to it again in the morning.

Geb, god of the earth; his bent leg represents the mountains.

OSIRIS, ISIS AND HORUS

One of the most universal Egyptian myths is that of Osiris and Isis. The story has it that Osiris was a king who taught the Egyptians how to live, worship and grow corn. He was murdered by his jealous brother Seth, who cut up the body, scattering it over Egypt. Osiris's beloved wife Isis and her sister Nephthys collected up all the pieces and, with the help of the gods Anubis and Thoth, they put him back together as the first mummy. Isis used her magic to revive him and at the same time conceived a son, Horus, who would avenge his father. Osiris, brought back to life, went down to the underworld to be the lord and judge of the dead.

Statuette of Osiris (centre) with his son Horus and loyal wife Isis

Osiris in a typical pose

THE SUN

Fundamental to the Egyptians, the sun was regarded as the source of all life, conquering the forces of darkness each night before emerging victorious at dawn to repeat the eternal cycle. Worshipped under a variety of names and guises, the sun was most often represented by the falcon-headed god Ra, as well as Atum, Khepri, Harakhty and the Aten sun-disk. The sun god's representative on earth, the king was hailed as the "Son of Ra". When Amun was elevated to supreme deity, for political reasons, his status was validated by linking him with Ra's supremacy to create Amun-Ra, the "King of the Gods".

Khepri *was represented as a dung beetle or scarab. Identified with the sun god Ra, he was said to roll the sun across the sky like a ball of dung.*

Ra-Harakhty *was the combination of two gods: the sky god Horus, whose right eye was the sun and left eye the moon, and the all-powerful sun god Ra.*

Ra, creator of the universe, wears the sun on his brow.

Maat keeps the world in balance.

Shu, jealous of Geb and Nut, stands keeping them apart.

MAJOR GODS

- **Amun**: powerful local Theban deity.
- **Anubis**: jackal-headed god of embalmers.
- **Atum**: creator aspect of the sun god.
- **Bes**: household god of women in childbirth.
- **Geb**: god of the earth.
- **Hathor**: goddess of love, pleasure and beauty.
- **Horus**: falcon-headed god closely identified with each pharaoh.
- **Isis**: goddess of magic.
- **Khepri**: a sun god as a scarab beetle.
- **Maat**: goddess of truth and universal balance.
- **Nekhbet**: vulture goddess of Upper Egypt.
- **Nephthys**: with Isis, protector of the dead.
- **Nut**: goddess of the sky.
- **Osiris**: god of the underworld.
- **Ptah**: creator god and patron of craftsmen.
- **Ra**: pre-eminent form of the sun god.
- **Sekhmet**: lioness goddess of destruction.
- **Seth**: god of chaos.
- **Shu**: god of the air.
- **Tefnut**: goddess of moisture.
- **Thoth**: the ibis-headed god of wisdom.
- **Wadjet**: cobra goddess of Lower Egypt.

Tomb painting showing the worship of the Benu bird

THE BENU BIRD

The Benu bird flew across the waters of Nun at the dawn of creation and saw land first break the water's surface. The Benu bird was identified with the sun and the primeval mound was symbolized by the Benben stone at Heliopolis, thought to be where the sun's first rays touched land. It was the prototype for obelisks whose tips were gold plated – to catch the first rays of the sun.

Obelisk, symbol of first land

Burial Traditions

Wedjat "eye of Horus" amulet

The ancient Egyptians believed in an eternal afterlife and they developed a complex funerary cult aimed at maintaining their life after death. This involved preserving the body of the dead person through a process of mummification so that their soul would live on in their embalmed corpse. The deceased were then supplied with everything they might need in the afterlife before being launched into eternity via a set of elaborate funeral rituals.

Anubis, *the jackal-headed god of embalming, is shown putting the finishing touches to a mummy in this 19th-Dynasty tomb relief.*

MUMMIFICATION TECHNIQUES

The earliest mummies from prehistoric times were probably accidental. True mummification began in the Fourth Dynasty with the development of artificial embalming techniques. Special priests first removed the internal organs of the deceased, leaving only the heart, to be weighed in the afterlife. Then the corpse was dried out with natron and finally wrapped in linen.

Natural mummification *occurred when dead bodies were placed in simple sand graves. The sand absorbed the body's moisture, drying out the corpse and preserving soft tissue.*

Canopic jars *stored the embalmed internal organs of the deceased. The intestines, stomach, liver and lungs had separate jars, which were buried alongside the coffin in the tomb.*

Natron, *a naturally occurring mixture of sodium salts, was packed in and around the body to dry it out artificially. This took 40 days.*

Ramses III, *one of the best preserved of the royal mummies, was discovered in 1881 at Deir al-Bahri. The mummy is now on display in the Egyptian Museum (see* pp74–7).

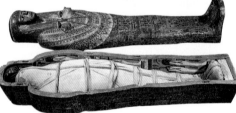

The mummified body *was stuffed with linen and sawdust before being wrapped in tight linen bandages. Finally the wrapped mummy was placed in its painted wooden coffin.*

ANIMAL MUMMIES

The ancient Egyptians believed that all living things contained the divine essence and were, therefore, worthy of respect. In sharing the attributes of the gods they symbolized, animals were venerated as the gods' representatives on earth and mummified after their death. By the Late Period (664–332 BC), animals of all kinds were being mummified and buried in catacombs, from literally millions of ibises and cats to bulls and lions, shrews, snakes and crocodiles.

Ibis mummy

Cat mummy

MUMMY MASKS

A mask was fitted over the head of the mummy to help the dead person's spirit to recognize its body. From the glittering gold masks of pharaohs such as Tutankhamun to the more common painted masks made of *cartonnage* (a sort of papier-mâché), mummy masks were idealized portraits of the deceased.

A mummy mask *showed the face framed by a stylized wig and wide collar.*

Roman portrait masks, *painted on flat wooden panels, were laid over the face of the mummy. The portraits were often painted during the lifetime of the deceased and were more realistic than earlier masks (see p169).*

ACCESSORIES

In addition to significant worldly possessions, the mummy was usually buried with funerary items, including amulets, a set of shabti figures, and a model boat to transport the mummy to Abydos.

Shabti figures *were models of workers placed in the tomb to carry out manual work on behalf of the deceased in the afterlife.*

Amulets *were worn by Egyptians in life and in death to protect the body from evil and to bring good luck.*

A model funerary boat *symbolized the mummy's journey to Abydos, home of Osiris, god of the dead (see p26).*

FUNERARY RITES AND CEREMONIES

At the funeral, relatives left offerings of food and priests performed special funerary rites. These ceremonies and rituals were meant to protect the deceased, ensure a successful journey into the afterlife and sustain them on their way. As further protection, ritual images and texts were placed with the body or used to decorate the tomb.

The Book of the Dead *was a guide through the underworld. The deceased is portrayed here crossing the Lake of Offerings with his gifts.*

The Opening of the Mouth *ritual was performed to the body prior to burial in the belief that this would reactivate the senses, so the deceased would function in the afterlife.*

The Weighing of the Heart *was the final stage in the journey to the afterlife. A jury of gods presided over the ceremony to decide whether the deceased deserved eternal life. The jackal god Anubis weighed the heart against the feather of truth. If the heart was too heavy, it was given to the monster Ammut, who devoured it; only if it balances will the dead live forever.*

Daily Life in Ancient Egypt

Tomb model of man ploughing with oxen

In the hierarchical society of ancient Egypt, the importance of the family was fundamental. Early marriages were encouraged, with the hope of producing children to continue the family line and, importantly, to organize a proper burial. Marriage seems to have required no religious or civil ceremony, but simply involved one partner moving into the home of the other. Youngsters enjoyed a brief period of childhood before taking on adult responsibilities. Education was mainly vocational, with boys often being apprenticed to their fathers.

This family group comprises husband and wife (centre), their son (right) and older male (left).

EGYPTIAN HOUSING

Egyptian houses were built of sun-baked mudbricks and so have not survived well. From the evidence that has been preserved it seems that houses were typically square with a central living room, bedrooms and storerooms and sometimes stairs leading to the roof or to an upper floor. Some even had primitive bathroom suites.

Egyptian houses had basic air-conditioning, provided by small windows and roof vents as shown in this painting from the tomb of 18th-Dynasty scribe Nakht.

The roof vent is designed to catch the cool north breezes.

Small, high windows let in light and breezes, but not the sun.

Soul houses, such as this terracotta example, were included in tombs to house the soul of the deceased. The models demonstrate many features of ancient Egyptian housing and even mirror houses in rural Egypt today.

Cooking would take place outside or in outbuildings.

More complex housing, such as this model town-house, reflected the higher status of the owner.

WORKERS' VILLAGE AT DEIR AL-MEDINA

In a secluded valley on the west bank of the Nile opposite Luxor are the excavated foundations of a village that was inhabited by the craftsmen and labourers who constructed the tombs in the Valley of the Kings. In this early example of urban planning, the houses, arranged in rows, all opened off one central street and were enclosed within an outer wall. A typical house in Deir al-Medina had between 4 and 6 rooms plus a cellar or two for storage. Around the village are the chapels and tombs of the government-employed workers.

The village at Deir al-Medina, founded in the 16th century BC for those working in the Valley of the Kings

Women *often worked and looked after the children. In this 26th-Dynasty tomb relief, a mother with her child sorts fruit in an orchard.*

WOMEN IN SOCIETY

Although their status generally derived from that of their fathers or husbands, women in ancient Egypt enjoyed a relatively high profile. Equal to men before the law, they could own or rent property, engage in business, receive an equal share of inheritances and, in some cases, even rule as pharaoh. Divorce and remarriage were available to them, and if a man divorced his wife, she was entitled to maintenance. Women were expected to manage the household and family, and the poorer ones had to work alongside the men too.

Two women *are depicted in this 30th-Dynasty relief using a tourniquet press to extract the essential oils of lilies for perfume.*

Three noble-women *are seen in this 18th-Dynasty detail, sharing their pleasure in the perfume of lotus blossoms and mandrake fruit.*

WORKING LIFE IN ANCIENT EGYPT

Most of the farmland was owned by the king, the temples and rich individuals. This was farmed by the bulk of the population, who worked either directly for the owner or as a tenant farmer paying large amounts of rent and tax. Slightly better off were the skilled craftsmen, many of whom worked for the pharaoh, the temples or rich nobles. Their crafts included carpentry, jewellery and stone-working. Near the top of the hierarchy was an elite of professionals who ran the country – the scribes *(see p22)*, the priests *(see p24)* and top-ranking officials.

Nile-style farming *is depicted in this painting from the 19th-Dynasty tomb of Sennedjem and Iyneferti. Although portraying the idealized afterlife, it shows the methods used to reap grain, plough and harvest flax.*

The Nile *may have provided fish and fertile soil, but it had its share of risks as well as its rewards. As depicted in this Old Kingdom tomb relief scene, herdsmen had to be mindful of the danger posed to livestock from crocodiles.*

Dairy produce, *as depicted in this tomb relief, played an important part in the diet. Other livestock reared by ancient Egyptian farmers included sheep, goats and even pigs.*

Skilled craftsmen *were usually em-ployed in large workshops or in special communities such as Deir al-Medina.*

Peasant farmers *also supplied most of the labour for large building projects. This was a requirement for everybody except officials. In this tomb painting a team of unskilled workers are making mudbricks.*

Islamic Egypt

Islam was founded by Mohammed, a merchant who was born in around AD 570 in Mecca. At the age of 40 he began to receive revelations of the word of Allah (God) and these were transcribed as the Quran. Mohammed's preachings were not well received in Mecca and, in AD 622, he and his followers fled to Medina. This flight *(hejira)* constitutes year zero in the Islamic calendar. Before he died in AD 632, Mohammed returned to conquer Mecca. The armies of Islam swept through the Byzantine provinces of the eastern Mediterranean, arriving in Egypt in AD 640.

The crescent moon, *a familiar symbol of Islam, has resonances with the lunar calendar, which orders Muslim religious life.*

The Quran, *the holy book of Islam, is regarded as the direct word of Allah. Muslims believe that it can only be fully understood if read in Arabic. It is divided into 114 chapters, or suras, which cover many topics, including matters relating to the family, marriage, and legal and ethical concerns.*

This house *is decorated with pilgrimage scenes, which include a depiction of the great mosque in Mecca. The picture indicates that the house-owner has made the pilgrimage to Mecca.*

Muslims praying outside the Mosque of Sayyidna al-Hussein

THE FIVE PILLARS OF FAITH

Islam rests on the "five pillars of faith". The first of these, the *Shahada*, is a simple declaration that "there is no God but Allah and Mohammed is his Prophet". The second is the set of daily prayers that are supposed to be performed five times a day, facing in the direction of Mecca. The third is fasting during the daylight hours of the holy month of Ramadan. The fourth is the giving of alms. The fifth is *Haj*: at least once in their lifetime all Muslims must, if they are able, make the pilgrimage to Mecca, the birthplace of Mohammed.

VISITING A MOSQUE

Apart from at prayer times and
during the Friday congregation,
most mosques in Egypt are open to
visitors. Very few require an entrance
ticket, but it is customary to give a
tip to the guardian and to the person
who looks after your shoes or
provides a scarf to cover your head
during your visit. Mosques are open
24 hours, but only open to visitors
from 9am–7pm. They close earlier
in winter and during the month of
Ramadan (see also p330).

Arcaded courtyard of the Mosque of al-Azhar, Cairo

Muslim festivals *are relatively
infrequent, with just four major dates
in the calendar (see p39). The most
important of these are* Eid al-Adha,
*marking the time of the pilgrimage
(Haj), and* Eid al-Fitr, *which is held
at the end of Ramadan. Islamic
celebrations tend to be communal
affairs and usually take the form
of great feasts, often held outdoors.*

THE CALL TO PRAYER

A *muezzin* traditionally makes the
call to prayer five times each day
from the balcony of a mosque's
minaret. Today, microphones and
loudspeakers are used to allow the
muezzin to be heard from afar.

Mosques *have been built in a
variety of styles but they all share
some common features. Chief of these
is the* mihrab, *the niche that indicates
the direction of Mecca. Most mosques
also have a* minbar, *from which the
imam delivers his Friday sermon.*

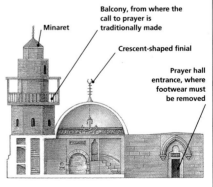

Minaret

Balcony, from where the
call to prayer is
traditionally made

Crescent-shaped finial

Prayer hall
entrance, where
footwear must
be removed

Islamic Architecture

Roof detail on a *madrassa*

The term Islamic architecture refers not only to mosques but also to a wide range of interesting buildings. The styles used were developed primarily under the early Islamic dynasties (the Tulunids, Fatimids and Ayyubids) and reached the height of creativity during the Mamluk era *(see p57)*. Craftsmen from all over the Near East were brought to Egypt to build palaces and mausoleums for rich and vainglorious sultans. They also created public institutions such as hospitals, schools and street fountains, many of which are still in use. The last great period of Islamic architecture in Egypt was under the Ottoman Turks *(see p58)*. Although reserving their best work for the imperial city of Istanbul, the Ottoman legacy includes some impressive structures.

Typical mosque-style building with domes and minarets *(see p93)*

DOMESTIC ARCHITECTURE

Private houses (called *beit* in Arabic) owed their design to both climatic and social conditions. Certain features, such as small windows covered with wooden screens, large airy rooms, shady arcades and fountains, kept the rooms cool. Typically these houses would be partitioned into separate male and female zones, known as the *salamlek* and *haramlek* respectively.

Mashrabiyya screens allowed the women of the house to look out without being seen.

Rooftop wind catchers channelled cool breezes into the rooms below.

The grandest private houses *could rise as high as three or four storeys. They used recurring features such as* ablaq *(striped layers of stone), arcades and fountains.*

Indoor fountains were built into the homes of the wealthy to keep the room temperature down.

The House of Amasyali *is one of numerous examples of the exquisite Ottoman merchants' houses that have survived in the town of Rosetta* (see p239).

Wooden ceilings *were often carved with beautifully intricate geometric patterns and then painted in rich colours.*

A qaa or reception room *typically formed the sumptuous centrepiece of the wealthy merchants' houses.*

SABIL-KUTTAB (FOUNTAIN AND SCHOOL)

Sabils (public fountains) are a typical element of Islamic architecture – some no more than a tap and a trough, some grand like the Sabil-Kuttab of Abdel Katkhuda. The *kuttab* was an open loggia or gallery where teachings of the Quran took place.

Sabil-Kuttab of Abdel Katkhuda *(see p98)*

Tiles painted *with scenes from Mecca were used to decorate some* sabil-kuttabs *in keeping with the religious nature of these buildings.*

MADRASSA (LAW SCHOOL)

A *madrassa* is a Quranic school, where law and theology are taught. Usually a mosque and *madrassa* are one and the same building. Sunni Islam, the variant of Islam followed in Egypt, has four schools of law (Hanafi, Malaki, Shafii and Hanbali), and so typically a *madrassa* will have four separate teaching areas, one for each. These often take the form of *iwans*, which are large arched spaces arranged around a central courtyard.

Fountains existed for the ablutions that had to be carried out before prayer.

Madrassa of Sultan Barquq *(see p97)*

WIKALA (HOTEL)

Also known as a caravanserai, the *wikala* is the precursor of the modern inn. It provided hospitality to the travelling merchant caravans that brought such great wealth to medieval Egypt. Animals were kept on the ground floor, along with goods placed in storage, while upstairs were the lodgings. At night, the whole building was sealed behind a sole gate for security purposes.

The rooms for the travellers overlooked the tiled central courtyard of the *wikala.*

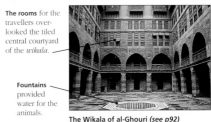

Fountains provided water for the animals.

The Wikala of al-Ghouri *(see p92)*

MAUSOLEUM (TOMB)

Some of the most splendid pieces of architecture in Egypt are mausoleums. Just like the pharaohs before them with their pyramids and immense mortuary temples, medieval sultans sought to glorify themselves in death. This they did by spending lavish amounts on enormous funerary complexes that often incorporated mosques and *madrassas* beside a domed tomb chamber. Inside, the bodies of the dead were laid above ground in a cenotaph marked by a pillar-like headstone. During Ottoman times, soldiers' headstones were frequently decorated with a carved turban.

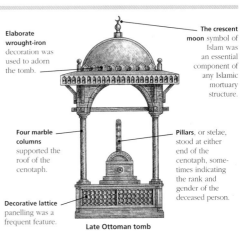

Elaborate wrought-iron decoration was used to adorn the tomb.

The crescent moon symbol of Islam was an essential component of any Islamic mortuary structure.

Four marble columns supported the roof of the cenotaph.

Pillars, or stelae, stood at either end of the cenotaph, sometimes indicating the rank and gender of the deceased person.

Decorative lattice panelling was a frequent feature.

Late Ottoman tomb

The Landscape and Wildlife of Egypt

Although Egypt comprises over 90 per cent desert, it is not a totally barren landscape. A number of plants and animals have developed strategies to cope with extreme temperatures and long periods of drought. Humans, however, are less adaptable and while a tiny percentage lives in desert oases *(see p261)*, 96 per cent live close to water in the green Delta or along the Nile Valley. However, despite plentiful water and rich soil, this land struggles to provide enough food for the rapidly growing population. Around Egypt's coastline the seas teem with marine life and the colourful coral reefs of the Red Sea *(see p227)* are probably the one of the richest natural environments on the planet.

Desert travel, reliant on camels and date palms

DESERTS

The popular image of deserts is of endless seas of sand. However, the rocky interior of Sinai also counts as a desert – strictly defined as an area with less than 25 cm (10 inches) of rainfall a year. Strong winds are also characteristic of the desert, eroding the rocks into bizarre shapes and creating sand which accumulates as slowly moving sand dunes.

Agriculture in the desert oases is vital to the economy of the country, providing large quantities of sugar cane, dates, figs and other fruit and vegetables.

Scorpions are perfectly adapted to the desert environment: they rarely need to drink, as they obtain their fluids from a diet of insects.

Fennec foxes sleep during the day, only leaving their burrows in the cool dusk. Exceptional hearing enables them to catch insects and small mammals in the dark.

Date palms thrive in the rocky desert environment. Growing "with their head in fire and feet in water", they are a sure sign of a hidden water source.

Sinai's red massif rises in places to over 2,000 m (6,700 ft). Criss-crossed with wadis (dry river beds), the area is brought to life by sporadic flooding.

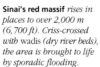

NILE VALLEY AND DELTA

The Nile creates a habitable tract of land never more than 20 km (13 miles) wide from Lake Nasser to the Delta. In the past, floods replenished the soil with rich silt deposits which enabled the land to support a wide range of flora and fauna. The Aswan Dam *(see p211)* ended the floods, making farmers reliant on chemical fertilizers. Today, the Delta is one of the most intensely farmed areas.

Farmland *is irrigated by a complicated system of canals and dykes. The resulting wet croplands provide the ideal environment for cattle egrets, which hunt for frogs, insects and small rodents.*

Acacia *is easily identified along the banks of the Nile by its eye-catching balls of yellow flowers.*

Papyrus, *widely used in ancient times, was all but extinct by the 19th century. It is only grown in a few select areas.*

The Purple Gallinule *is a colourful duck-sized water bird found the length of the Nile. Its long, slender toes enable it to walk on lily pads.*

The Spitting Cobra, *a symbol of Lower Egypt in Pharaonic times, hunts its prey at night in crop fields. It is not usually a danger to humans, but it might attack if threatened, spitting venom accurately at its attacker's eyes.*

COASTAL REGIONS

Egypt's northern coastline is on the Mediterranean Sea where fishing is a key industry. While Egypt's Red Sea and Sinai coastlines also maintain fishing communities, they are far more important as a resource for the tourist industry. These coastlines support several large strips of coral reef *(see p227)* which attract divers from all over the world. A fragile environment, the reefs are under serious threat from overdevelopment of the coastline.

Coral reefs *provide a colourful environment for an equally spectacular array of marine life.*

MANGROVE SWAMPS

The mangrove swamps of the Sinai Peninsula perform an important function protecting the shoreline against erosion and filtering pollutants from the water. The mudflats they create provide a vital environment for crabs and wading birds. Mangroves are able to live in salt water by excreting excess salt via their leaves.

Mangrove swamps fringing the Sinai coastline

EGYPT THROUGH THE YEAR

The Egyptian calendar is crowded with Muslim, Christian, national and local festivals. The dates of these events can be difficult to predict as they are often calculated in different ways. The Islamic calendar is based on twelve 29- or 30-day lunar months, while Egypt's Christian Coptic church uses the

Making sweets in the market

Julian calendar and the solar Coptic calendar. Extra confusion is caused by the frequently changing dates of non-religious events or festivals.

Visitors should confirm the date of the event locally. Whatever the calendar, these are mostly joyous events and a great way to experience Egyptian culture at close hand as both Muslims and Copts often enjoy celebrating *moulids* or festivals together. A wide range of esoteric sports events is staged throughout the year which range from the interesting to the bizarre, from camel racing to long-distance swimming in the Nile at Cairo.

SPRING

Springtime is a pleasant time to visit Egypt. The main visitor attractions such as the Pyramids at Giza, Luxor and Aswan are not too crowded and the temperature has yet to reach the scorching highs of summer. One weather phenomenon that can cause problems is the *khamseen*, a hot, dry wind that blows up from the Sahara Desert in the south. This can turn the air orange with dust and drive everyone indoors.

The main spring festivals are the beginning of the Egyptian New Year in March and the Christian festival of Easter. On the Monday after Easter Sunday, all Egyptians celebrate Sham an-Nessim or the "sniffing the breeze". They go on picnics or hold events outdoors to take in the fresh spring air.

MARCH

Flower Show takes place at the Orman Gardens, Sharia Giza, Giza. Originally a one-day event, it now lasts for over a month.
Feast of the Annunciation *(Mar 23)*. This Coptic feast celebrates the announcement to the Holy Virgin that she was to give birth to Jesus.
Easter is the most important date on the Coptic calendar. The Coptic Pope celebrates Easter Mass at St Mark's Cathedral in Cairo.
Sham an-Nessim, celebrated by both Copts and Muslims, is a day when families enjoy outdoor pursuits and reputed to date from Pharaonic times.

APRIL

Sinai Liberation Day *(Apr 25)*, celebrates Israel's withdrawal from the Sinai Peninsula in 1982.

Coptic Christians celebrating Palm Sunday, a week before Easter

MAY

Labour Day *(May 1)* is a public holiday when most businesses will be closed.
Moulid of St Damyanah *(May 15–20)*, a Coptic festival celebrating one of their important saints.
National Fishing Competition, Sharm el-Sheikh. Top fishermen compete to see who can catch the biggest specimen.
Ragabiyya is a local festival in Tanta. The festival lasts for three days in celebration of the Sufi saint, Sayyid Ahmad al-Badawi, and is held when the Nile rises in late spring.
South Sinai Camel Festival, in the vast desert around Sharm el-Sheikh, raises clouds of dust with the running of the world's bumpiest race, the International Camel Race Competition.

Families celebrating the arrival of spring on Sham an-Nessim

MUSLIM FESTIVALS

Celebrated with great feasts, family gatherings, music and street processions, Muslim festivals are joyous occasions. The largest of the festivals are Eid al-Fitr, which takes place at the end of Ramadan, the month of ritual fasting, and Eid al-Adha, which marks the time of the pilgrimage to Mecca. Other Muslim festivals include the Moulid an-Nabi which celebrates the birth of the Prophet Mohammed, Ras as-Sana, the Islamic New Year, and various saints' name days known as *moulids*.

Cookies for Eid al-Fitr *are traditionally baked in preparation for the three-day feast that marks the end of Ramadan. Food plays an important part of Muslim festivals and preparing it is often a social affair.*

Zikrs *are a feature at moulids, where Sufi sheikhs and their followers chant and sway for hours in an effort to achieve unity with God. A munshi leads with hypnotic singing, and often women both sway and sing.*

ISLAMIC CALENDAR

The Islamic calendar has twelve months, each with 29 or 30 days. Purely lunar based, the Islamic year is around 11 days shorter than that of the Western calendar. Because Islam relies on actual sightings of the crescent moon at a given place, it is difficult to give dates in advance. Local Islamic centres will be able to provide the dates for the current year.

Eid al-Adha This four-day festival marks the time of the *Haj*, or pilgrimage to Mecca.

Ras as-Sana The Islamic equivalent of New Year's Day and quite a low-key affair.

Moulid an-Nabi Birth of the Prophet and one of the major holidays of the year. The streets burst into colour and noise with the celebrations.

Ramadan The ninth month of the Muslim calendar when most Muslims observe a degree of fasting and abstinence. The *iftar,* or breaking of the fast, occurs every evening when the sun sets.

Eid al-Fitr The end of Ramadan and the signal for a joyous, three-day feast.

Eid al-Fitr *is a happy celebration marking the end of Ramadan. During the festivities, which usually last for three days, new clothes are worn and gifts are exchanged.*

Religious holidays *provide the perfect opportunity for family gatherings. Muslim celebrations often centre around the enjoyment and sharing of food and picnics are therefore a popular choice.*

Donkey trekking in the heat of summer, Valley of the Kings, Luxor

SUMMER

From June to August the temperature in Egypt climbs to unbearable levels in Upper Egypt, although the sites are often less crowded and hotel accommodation is plentiful. Many Egyptians choose to holiday on the North Coast where the temperature is slightly cooler. The Red Sea coastal resorts, although also very hot, have beautiful, clear water in which visitors can keep themselves cool. In the summer heat and smog, Cairo can get very uncomfortable and there are fewer interesting festivals.

JUNE

Ahlan Wa Sahlan Belly Dance Festival *(end Jun)*, Cairo. Performances and classes by some of the world's best belly dancers accompany a competition.
Evacuation Day *(Jun 18)* celebrates the departure of the British Forces from the Canal Zone in 1956 and the start of the Egyptian Republic.

JULY

International Shopping and Tourism Festival, Sharm el-Sheikh *(Jul)*. In an effort to boost tourism during the scorching summer months,

discounts are offered in shops, hotels and restaurants.
Revolution Day *(Jul 23)* commemorates the 1952 coup which toppled the puppet monarchy *(see p62)*.
Shopping and Tourism Festival, Cairo *(Jul–Aug)*.

AUGUST

Nile Festival Day or Wafaa an-Nil, Cairo. This is a series of processions, parades and sporting competitions which take place on the Nile.
Arab Music Festival, Cairo. The Opera House hosts the best in Arab music.

AUTUMN

Autumn brings cooler weather to Egypt and a proliferation of events and festivals. While some of these are obvious attempts to boost tourist revenues, the best can be truly magical events that are well worth making the effort to go to. However, it is worth noting that the time of year some of these events take place is liable to change at the whim of the Egyptian authorities so check nearer the time.

COPTIC FESTIVALS

Christmas, Epiphany, Easter and the Annunciation are the main Christian festivals of the year and all are celebrated by Copts, with Easter being the most important. Saints' days also feature strongly and, as with Islamic feasts, they are usually celebrated with a lively moulid. The main saints' days include the Moulid of St Damyanah, the Feast of the Apostles Peter and Paul and various moulids of the Virgin and St George which take place throughout August. The spring festival of Sham an-Nessim is celebrated by both Muslims and Christians with family picnics of painted eggs and salted fish.

Pope Shenouda III, *the patriarch of the Coptic Christian church, presides over important religious ceremonies and events.*

COPTIC CALENDAR

While some Coptic festivals correspond to the Julian calendar, others rely on the solar Coptic one. This calendar has 13 months, 12 of 30 days each and an intercalary month at the end of the year of 5 or 6 days, depending whether it is a leap year or not.

Easter This is the most important date in the Coptic calendar. However, it can differ by up to a month from the date of the Orthodox church's festival.

Coptic festivals *are primarily religious affairs with celebrations centred around church services for the young and old.*

A colourful pageant at the Arabian Horse Festival, Az-Zahraa

SEPTEMBER

Alexandria Film Festival, Alexandria. This festival features more home-produced films than the very popular Cairo festival.
Arabian Horse Festival, Az-Zahraa. Egypt holds two horse festivals. The other is held at Sharkeya in the Delta during September.
International Folkloric Festival, Ismailia, attracts energetic tribal performances from all over the world.

OCTOBER

Aida Opera, Giza. This spectacular Egyptian-themed extravaganza was written by Verdi for the opening of the Suez Canal. Performed in front of the pyramids, this is a very popular production.
National Day (Armed Forces Day) *(Oct 6)* is a day of parades, fly-bys and non-stop patriotic songs and films.
The Battle of El-Alamein Commemoration *(Oct 24)*, with services conducted by former Allied and Axis countries, remembers those that died in the campaigns in North Africa during World War II.
Sun Festival of Ramses II, Abu Simbel *(Oct 22)*. On this day, and again in February, the sun reaches 55 m (185 ft) into the inner chamber of the Temple of Ramses and illuminates the statues inside.

Moulid of Sayyid Ahmed al-Badawi, Tanta. Egypt's largest festival, up to two million revellers attend this week-long celebration at the end of the cotton harvest.
National Liberation Day *(Oct 23)* and the **Suez Victory Day** *(Oct 24)* are popular celebrations of Egypt's martial past.
Pharaoh's Rally (International Egypt Rally), is a gruelling 3,100-km (1,900-mile) motor vehicle race through the Egyptian deserts. Major car manufacturers and competitors come from all over the world to participate.

NOVEMBER

International Fishing Competition, Sharm el-Sheikh. These competitions are staged at several of the Red Sea resorts.
Luxor National Day *(Nov 4)* is combined with a commemoration of the discovery of the Tomb of Tutankhamun in 1922.
Cairo International Film Festival, Cairo, is an often chaotic festival which shows the best of world cinema. However, its popularity is partly due to the fact that it is the only time that Egyptians get to see uncensored films.
The Pharaonic Race, Cairo. This 100-km (62-mile) run started in 1977, inspired by a similar race by royal soldiers in the 7th century B.C.

One of the cultural highlights of the Egyptian calendar, Verdi's spectacular opera, Aida

WINTER

Winter brings some slight relief from the heat and, in Cairo and Alexandria and along the North Coast, even the odd shower of rain. The days are still sunny and warm but the nights can be quite cold, especially in desert areas. It also brings the start of the tourist season and a large influx of foreign visitors seeking winter sun and a glimpse into the fascinating, civilization of ancient Egypt. Cruise tours and hotels in Upper Egypt tend to get busy during this period and prices increase accordingly.

DECEMBER

Alexandria Mediterranean Biennale (for artists) brings Mediterranean artists together for an exchange of cultural and artistic ideas, featuring exhibitions and activities.

The organized chaos of the International Book Fair, Cairo

JANUARY

New Year's Day *(1 Jan)* is a widely-celebrated public holiday.
Coptic Christmas *(7 Jan)*. On this day, Copts through-out Egypt dress up in their Sunday best, visit their relatives and feast together. It is not an official public holiday, but many Egyptian Copts take this day off.
Epiphany *(19 Jan)*, a Coptic celebration of the revelation of Jesus's divinity after his baptism by John.
International Egyptian Marathon, Luxor. As many as 2,000 competitors brave the heat to take part in this run around Luxor.
The International Nile Regatta, Alexandria. Organized by the Egyptian Rowing Federation, this event attracts teams of young and more experienced rowers from all over the world.
The Belly Dancing World Cup takes place each year in the Taba Heights resort in Sinai. There are competitions for advanced dancers, as well as workshops for beginners, lectures and classes.
International Cairo Biennale, *(Dec–Feb)*, this major cultural event in the Middle East features contemporary art shows, concerts, film and installations.
Cairo International Book Fair, Nasr City. Ostensibly for the book trade, this event also attracts regular book lovers and Cairenes simply looking for a day out among the fast food stalls. During the event a bus service departs for Nasr City from Midan Tahrir.

FEBRUARY

Sun of Ramses Festival *(22 Feb)*. This festival celebrates one of the two days in the year (the other is in October) when the sun's rays penetrate the sanctuary of Ramses's Great Temple at Abu Simbel.

Competitors in the International Egyptian Marathon, Luxor

The Climate of Egypt

Snorkelling in the Red Sea

Egypt's weather is predominantly hot, sunny and very dry. The only rain that falls regularly is on the North Coast during winter, but this is under 100 mm (4 inches) a year. There are two seasons – May to October, the hot season, and November to April, the cool season. In general, it is warm all the year round, although the deserts can get cold during winter nights. The most striking meteorological phenomenon is the *khamseen*, a dry wind during April and May that causes sandstorms.

THE DELTA AND THE NORTH COAST

°C				
	23	30	28	
	15	23	20	18
				11
☼	10	12	9	7
☂	3 mm	- mm	5 mm	48 mm
month	Apr	Jul	Oct	Jan

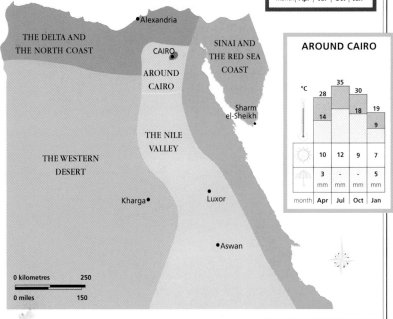

Alexandria

THE DELTA AND THE NORTH COAST

CAIRO

SINAI AND THE RED SEA COAST

AROUND CAIRO

Sharm el-Sheikh

THE NILE VALLEY

THE WESTERN DESERT

Kharga

Luxor

Aswan

0 kilometres	250
0 miles	150

AROUND CAIRO

°C				
	28	35	30	
	14		18	19
				9
☼	10	12	9	7
☂	3 mm	- mm	- mm	5 mm
month	Apr	Jul	Oct	Jan

THE WESTERN DESERT

°C				
	37	42	37	
	20	23	21	21
				5
☼	11	12	11	10
☂	- mm	- mm	- mm	- mm
month	Apr	Jul	Oct	Jan

THE NILE VALLEY

°C				
	34	40	35	
	18	25	19	24
				8
☼	9	10	8	7
☂	- mm	- mm	- mm	- mm
month	Apr	Jul	Oct	Jan

SINAI AND THE RED SEA COAST

°C				
	26	32	30	
	16	25	23	21
				10
☼	11	12	11	10
☂	- mm	- mm	- mm	- mm
month	Apr	Jul	Oct	Jan

THE HISTORY OF EGYPT

gypt's history has been crucially influenced by its environment. When lack of rain forced the early nomadic inhabitants to migrate towards the Nile Valley, the fertile floodplain gave birth to a nation that produced some of the most important achievements in human history and established a culture that would remain largely unchanged for over 3000 years.

Although the beginning of Egyptian history is generally given as 3100 BC, human activity in the Predynastic Period can be traced back many thousands of years before this date. The Sahara Desert used to be a green and fertile savannah, home to a nomadic population who hunted the wildlife they portrayed in rock drawings (petroglyphs). Archaeologists have also discovered that cattle-herders in Nabta Playa in the Western Desert built stone-circle calendars dating from 8000 BC.

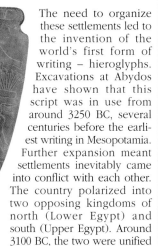

King Narmer's Palette c.3100 BC

The way of life of these early peoples remained much the same for around 4000 years, but as the climate became increasingly arid, the population left the growing areas of desert (*deshret* or red land) for the banks of the river Nile where the annual flooding sustained a region of great fertility (*kemet* or black land). The excavation of their settlements has revealed the rapid development of a sophisticated culture of mud-brick houses and workshops, together with primitive temple structures.

The need to organize these settlements led to the invention of the world's first form of writing – hieroglyphs. Excavations at Abydos have shown that this script was in use from around 3250 BC, several centuries before the earliest writing in Mesopotamia. Further expansion meant settlements inevitably came into conflict with each other. The country polarized into two opposing kingdoms of north (Lower Egypt) and south (Upper Egypt). Around 3100 BC, the two were unified for the first time into a single state. This event was commemorated on the cosmetic slate palette of King Narmer (sometimes known as Menes), found at Hierakonpolis. The palette is possibly the most important historical document from the whole of Egyptian history, recording the creation of the world's first nation state. The dramatic pose as he is about to smash the skull of his defeated foe became the standard way to portray Egypt's kings throughout the next 3,000 years.

TIMELINE

Pots from 4000– 3000 BC

10,000 BC	5000 BC	4500 BC	4000 BC	3500 BC	3000 BC

8000 BC Early human settlement of Nabta Playa in Western Desert builds huge sculptures and a stone-circle calendar

3400 BC Egypt's oldest temple built at Hierakonpolis

3250 BC Invention of hieroglyphs – world's first script

10,000 BC Nomadic population of Sahara draw petroglyphs of the animals they hunt

Earliest known human sculpture

c. 4000 BC Earliest known human figure sculpted in Africa, at Neolithic settlement in western Delta

3100 BC Political unification of Egypt by King Narmer. Memphis becomes the capital city

◁ **Graeco-Roman mosaic showing the flooding of the Nile, Egypt's temples and its fabled wildlife**

THE OLD KINGDOM
(3100–2180 BC)

The power base of the Old Kingdom was established at Memphis, the first capital of a united Egypt. This was strategically located where Upper Egypt meets Lower Egypt at the apex of the Delta close to modern Cairo. Whereas the earliest kings chose Abydos as their funeral site to reflect their southern origins, later rulers preferred to be buried close to their new capital in its necropolis, Saqqara. The site of Egypt's earliest pyramid (c.2650 BC), Saqqara is also home to many stone *mastaba* (bench-shaped) tombs built for members of the royal court and beautifully decorated. The king was seen as the living incarnation of the god Horus and his court sought to be buried close to his divine power.

Statue of King Khafre protected by the falcon god Horus

King Narmer's successors managed to suppress any outside threat to Egypt's stability whilst organizing the country into 42 provinces or *nomes*. These were administered by means of a highly efficient bureaucracy of officials. The great wealth created through a carefully organized system of taxation – based on the collection and redistribution of Egypt's abundant grain supplies – was also used to fund ambitious building schemes. This culminated in the massive pyramid complexes of the Old Kingdom god-kings such as Djoser, Sneferu, Khufu and Khafre. The organization required for such huge projects helped to unify the nation, while the vast numbers of skilled craftsmen involved meant that art and technology developed at a rapid pace.

Of all the pyramid-building pharaohs, Sneferu was the greatest, building three such structures, including the first true pyramid at Dahshur. It was only with techniques perfected by Sneferu that his son Khufu was able to construct the largest of all Egypt's pyramids at Giza around 2589 BC.

Eventually centuries of pyramid-building, together with a series of poor harvests, severely depleted the economy. This led to a decline in royal power, which was reflected in the small size of the later pyramids built at Abusir and Saqqara. The incredibly long reign of Pepi II (2278–2184 BC), only added to the problem and with the pharaoh seen as a feeble old man, royal authority was further undermined. After an incredible

The Pyramids at Giza, magnificent symbols of the divine power of the early Egyptian kings

TIMELINE

Figurine from a unified Egypt fashioned in c.2900 BC

2665 BC The world's oldest stone monument, the step Pyramid of King Djoser, built at Saqqara

2613–2589 BC Reign of King Sneferu, builder of 3 pyramids at Dashur and Meidum

2900 BC	2800 BC	2700 BC	2600 BC	2500 BC

2686 BC Oldest surviving mudbrick building built by King Khasekhemwy at Hierakonpolis

c.2589 BC The Great Pyramid of Khufu (Cheops) built at Giza

c.2558 BC Pyramid of Khafre (Chephren) built at Giza. Its complex includes the oldest surviving temple in Egypt

94 years on the throne Pepi II was succeeded by Egypt's first female pharaoh Nitocris, but despite being remembered as "the bravest and most beautiful" of her time, it was too late to reverse the decline in royal fortunes.

FIRST INTERMEDIATE PERIOD, MIDDLE KINGDOM AND SECOND INTERMEDIATE PERIOD (2180–1550 BC)

As royal power declined, officials began to relocate to their home provinces. No longer reliant on the king, they created their own small kingdoms maintained with private armies. As the country gradually fragmented, central authority finally broke down into anarchy and the First Intermediate Period began c.2180 BC.

The lack of overall authority is clearly expressed in provincial and rather "idiosyncratic" art styles typical of local trends. The breakdown of social order is also reflected in the literature – "All is ruin...men kill their brothers...blood is everywhere".

The remnants of royal power relocated to Herakleopolis, at the entrance to the Fayoum Oasis, and attempted to rule through the forging of alliances with the southern regions. However, any temporary unity was shattered when Thebes formed an independent monarchy. Civil war and fierce fighting between neighbouring tribes tore the whole country apart.

Statue of Montuhotep II, Theban founder of the 11th Dynasty

After a long and bitter struggle the powerful Theban warlord Montuhotep II conquered the north to reunite the country under the 11th Dynasty. His reign took Egypt from the chaos of the First Intermediate Period into the stability of the Middle Kingdom (c.2055 BC). Thebes now grew into a major metropolis, home to skilled craftsmen who created new art styles at a rate not seen since the Age of the Pyramids. The old trade routes and mines were reopened and expansionist policies prevailed. Although the office of pharaoh would never again reach the absolute divinity of earlier times, the Theban monarchy restored royal power as growth in revenue led to a resumption of building projects. The greatest new structure was Montuhotep's imposing funerary complex built at Deir al-Bahri which, 500 years later, would serve as the prototype for Hatshepsut's temple.

Model of the private army of the Governor of Asyut (c.2000 BC)

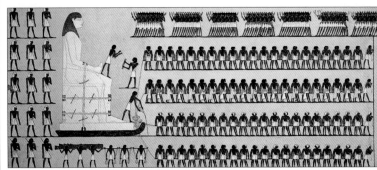

Teams of workers dragging a huge stone statue, from the Middle Kingdom tomb of Djehutyhotep (c.1850 BC)

The kings of the 12th Dynasty, which lasted from c.1985–1795 BC, moved the royal residence back to the traditional capital, Memphis, in order to be closer to the centre of the country. They continued with ambitious building projects, and the art and literature of this time is regarded as the "classic" period of Egyptian culture. Pharaohs such as Senusret III and Amenemhat III constructed impressive pyramids at Saqqara, Dahshur, Lahun and Hawara, where they were buried alongside their relatives with beautiful jewellery made of gold, amethyst, carnelian and lapis lazuli.

Successful military campaigns expanded Egypt's borders, whilst at home the crown centralized its authority by removing power from provincial governors and replacing these governors with a vast bureaucracy of loyal officials. Many of these officials were migrants from nearby Palestine

Sphinx bearing the face of Amenemhat III

who had settled peacefully in northern Egypt and had been gradually absorbed into Egyptian society over a period of about 150 years. By infiltrating the government they took advantage of the instability caused by a series of short-lived rulers during the 13th and 14th Dynasties. In 1650 BC, these settlers, referred to as the Hyksos (Rulers of Foreign Lands), finally assumed control.

This marks the beginning of the Second Intermediate Period, when Egypt was once again divided geographically. Based in their northern capital Avaris, the Hyksos formed an alliance with Nubia to help them to control southern Egypt, where the native Egyptian opposition to foreign rule had organized itself in Thebes. The country was once again subject to intermittent civil war until the Theban warlord Seqenenre Taa II and his sons Kamose and Ahmose finally drove the Hyksos out of Egypt to reunite the Two Lands.

TIMELINE

1965 BC Assassination of Amenemhat I and accession of his son Senusret I	*Statue of Senusret III*	**1795–1725 BC** Unstable 13th Dynasty of 70 kings	**1750–1650 BC** Minor rulers of the 14th Dynasty

1900 BC	1800 BC	1700 BC

1874–1855 BC Reign of Senusret III	**1799–1795 BC** Reign of Egypt's second female ruler Sobekneferu	
1855 BC Senusret III and his family buried at Dahshur	*Middle Kingdom Horus head pendant*	

THE NEW KINGDOM
(1550–1070 BC)

With the reunification of north and south, the New Kingdom began. This is Egypt's "Golden Age", when a series of unrelenting warrior pharaohs turned the country into the most powerful empire in the ancient world. The expulsion of the Hyksos was followed by vigorous military campaigns as far north as the river Euphrates and as far south as Nubia. The enormous wealth amassed from foreign tribute was channelled into massive building projects in and around Thebes, with successive monarchs trying to outdo their predecessors. The magnificent temple of Karnak – the cult centre of the local Theban deity Amun – was embellished by successive pharaohs, built as Amun was linked with the sun-god Ra to create Amun-Ra, "King of the Gods". Meanwhile, pharaohs built huge funerary temples for themselves on the west bank of the Nile, and were buried in spectacular rock-cut tombs in the Valley of the Kings, designed to ensure their eternal afterlife.

As the first king of the New Kingdom, Ahmose continued his family's military successes and established a pattern for his successors. His son Amenhotep I followed in his father's footsteps by pacifying Nubia. He also founded a village for royal tomb builders at Deir al-Medina,

Tuthmosis III making offerings to Amun-Ra, the national deity during the New Kingdom

Statue of Hatshepsut as a bearded pharaoh

where both he and his mother and co-ruler Ahmose-Nofretari were worshipped long after their deaths.

Then began the succession of the Tuthmosis pharaohs: men born to minor wives of the king who strengthened their claims to the throne by marrying into the female royal line. Tuthmosis II was succeeded by his wife and half-sister Hatshepsut, the most familiar of Egypt's female pharaohs, who is often portrayed in statues as a bearded pharaoh. Her successor, Tuthmosis III, the so-called "Napoleon of Ancient Egypt", expanded the Egyptian Empire into Asia Minor and as far as the Euphrates. His son Amenhotep II, a great warrior like his father and an accomplished athlete, consolidated Egypt's control over the vassal states of Asia Minor. Their foreign conquests created the wealth used so wisely by the greatest of all the pharaohs, Amenhotep III. Known as "the Magnificent", his peaceful 38-year reign marks the height of Egypt's cultural and artistic achievement.

| 1650 BC Palestinian Hyksos take power | c.1560 BC Theban warlord Seqenenre Taa II killed fighting the Hyksos | c.1500 BC Valley of the Kings becomes royal burial ground | Head of Tuthmosis III | 1458–1425 BC Tuthmosis III campaigns as far as the Euphrates |

| 1600 BC | 1500 BC | 1400 BC |

| 1550 BC Seqenenre Taa II's younger son Ahmose drives the Hyksos out of Egypt and becomes the first ruler of the 18th Dynasty | 1525 BC Amenhotep I founds royal tomb builders' village of Deir al-Medina | 1473–1458 BC Reign of Hatshepsut | 1390–1352 BC Peaceful reign of Amenhotep III, "the Magnificent" |

The Egyptian Pharaohs

The ancient Egyptians dated events to the particular year in the reign of a king or pharaoh (regnal dating). It was a Ptolemaic scholar, Manetho, who later sorted the kings into dynasties, a system still used today along with ancient king lists, astronomical records and modern archaeological dating methods. The resulting chronology is, however, neither fixed nor complete and liable to change.

EARLY DYNASTIC PERIOD

3100–2890 BC		2890–2686 BC	
IST DYNASTY		**2ND DYNASTY**	
Narmer	3100	Hetepsekhemwy	2890
Aha	3100	Raneb	2865
Djer	3000	Nynetjer	
Djet	2980	Weneg	
Den	2950	Sened	
Anedjib	2925	Peribsen	2700
Semerkhet	2900	Khasekhemwy	2686
Qaa	2890		

aka Amenhotep IV *(see p 175)*   † aka Amenophis
* denotes female pharaoh   ‡ aka Sesostris

FIRST INTERMEDIATE PERIOD

2181–2125 BC	2160–2055 BC
7TH & 8TH DYNASTIES	**9TH & 10TH DYNASTIES**
	HERAKLEOPOLITAN
During this unstable period of ancient Egyptian history there were numerous ephemeral kings. The weakening of centralized power led to the establishment of local dynasties.	Kheti
	Merykare
	Ity
	11TH DYNASTY
	(THEBES ONLY)
	Intef I 2125–2112
	Intef II 2112–2063
	Intef III 2063–2055

MIDDLE KINGDOM

2055–1985 BC	1985–1795 BC
11TH DYNASTY	**12TH DYNASTY**
ALL EGYPT	Amenemhat I 1985–1955
Montuhotep II 2055–2004	Senusret I ‡ 1965–1920
Montuhotep III 2004–1992	Amenemhat II 1922–1878
Montuhotep IV 1992–1985	Senusret II ‡ 1880–1874
	Senusret III ‡ 1874–1855
	Amenemhat III 1855–1808
	Amenemhat IV 1808–1799
	Sobekneferu* 1799–1795
"Block" statue from the 12th Dynasty	Overlaps in dates indicate periods of co-regency

NEW KINGDOM

1550–1295 BC		1295–1186 BC		1186–1069 BC	
18TH DYNASTY		**19TH DYNASTY**		**20TH DYNASTY**	
Ahmose	1550–1525	Ramses I	1295–1294	Sethnakhte	1186–1184
Amenhotep I †	1525–1504	Seti I	1294–1279	Ramses III	1184–1153
Tuthmosis I	1504–1492	Ramses II	1279–1213	Ramses IV	1153–1147
Tuthmosis II	1492–1479	Merneptah	1213–1203	Ramses V	1147–1143
Tuthmosis III	1479–1425	Amenmessu	1203–1200	Ramses VI	1143–1136
Hatshepsut*	1473–1458	Seti II	1200–1194	Ramses VII	1136–1129
Amenhotep II †	1427–1400	Siptah	1194–1188	Ramses VIII	1129–1126
Tuthmosis IV	1400–1390	Tawosret*	1188–1186	Ramses IX	1126–1108
Amenhotep III †	1390–1352			Ramses X	1108–1099
Akhenaten #	1352–1336			Ramses XI	1099–1069
Nefertiti					
Smenkhkare*	1338–1336				
Tutankhamun	1336–1327				
Ay	1327–1323				
Horemheb	1323–1295				

Bracelet of Queen Ahotep, mother of Ahmose, first king of the 18th Dynasty

Head of Ramses III, who built the great mortuary Temple at Medinat Habu

LATE PERIOD

672–525 BC		525–359 BC		404–c.380 BC		380–343 BC	
26TH DYNASTY		**27TH DYNASTY**		**28TH DYNASTY**		**30TH DYNASTY**	
(Saite)		**(Persian Period 1)**		Amyrtaios	404–399	Nectanebo I	380–362
						Teos	362–360
Necho I	672–664	Cambyses	525–522	**29TH DYNASTY**		Nectanebo II	360–343
Psamtek I	664–610	Darius I	522–486	Nepherites I	399–393		
Necho II	610–595	Xerxes I	486–465	Hakor	393–380		
Psamtek II	595–589	Artaxerxes I	465–424	Nepherites II	c.380		
Apries	589–570	Darius II	424–405				
Ahmose II	570–526	Artaxerxes II	405–359				
Psamtek III	526–525						

One of the stone sphinxes from Luxor Temple, carved with the face of Nectanebo I

OLD KINGDOM

2686–2613	2613–2498 BC	2494–2345 BC	2345–2181 BC
3RD DYNASTY	**4TH DYNASTY**	**5TH DYNASTY**	**6TH DYNASTY**
Sanakht 2686–2667	Sneferu 2613–2589	Userkaf 2494–2487	Teti 2345–2323
Djoser 2667–2648	Khufu 2589–2566	Sahure 2487–2475	Userkare 2323–2321
Sekhemkhet 2648–2640	Djedefre 2566–2558	Neferirkare 2475–2455	Pepi I 2321–2287
Khaba 2640–2637	Khafre 2558–2532	Shepseskare 2455–2448	Merenre 2287–2278
Huni 2637–2613	Menkaure 2532–2503	Raneferef 2448–2445	Pepi II 2278–2184
	Shepseskaf 2503–2498	Nyuserre 2445–2421	Nitocris* 2184–2181
		Menkauhor 2421–2414	
		Djedkare 2414–2375	
		Unas 2375–2345	

The Pyramids at Giza, built in the 4th Dynasty

	1795–1650 BC	1650–1550 BC	1650–1550 BC
	13TH DYNASTY	**15TH DYNASTY**	**17TH DYNASTY**

SECOND INTERMEDIATE PERIOD

	1795–c.1725	**(HYKSOS)**	In addition, several kings ruled from Thebes including the following:

14TH DYNASTY

Salitis
Khyan c.1600
Apepi c.1555
Khamudi

1750–1650

Minor rulers probably contemporaneous with the previous dynasty.

16TH DYNASTY

1650–1550

Minor Hyksos rulers contemporary with the 15th Dynasty.

Intef
Ta I
Seqenenre Taa II c.1560
Kamose 1555–1550

Limestone relief of Senusret I from the Temple at Karnak

THIRD INTERMEDIATE PERIOD

			LATE PERIOD
1069–945 BC	945–715 BC	818–715 BC	747–656 BC
21ST DYNASTY	**22ND DYNASTY**	**23RD DYNASTY**	**25TH DYNASTY**

21ST DYNASTY	22ND DYNASTY	23RD DYNASTY	25TH DYNASTY
Smendes 1069–1043	Sheshonq I 945–924	Several continuous lines of rulers at Herakleopolis Magna, Hermopolis Magna, Leontopolis and Tanis including the following:	Piy 747–716
Amenemnisu 1043–1039	Osorkon I 924–889		Shabaqo 716–702
Psusennes I 1039–991	Sheshonq II c.890		Shabitqo 702–690
Amenemope 993–984	Takelot I 889–874		Taharqo 690–664
Osorkon the Elder 984–978	Osorkon II 874–850		Tanutamani 664–656
Siamun 978–959	Takelot II 850–825	Pedubastis I 818–793	
Psusennes II 959–945	Sheshonq III 825–773	Sheshonq IV c.780	
	Pimay 773–767	Osorkon III 777–749	
	Sheshonq V 767–730		
	Osorkon IV 730–715	**24TH DYNASTY**	
		Bakenrenef 727–715	

Silver coffin of Psusennes I from Tanis

	PTOLEMAIC PERIOD		
343–332 BC	332–305 BC	305–80 BC	80–30 BC
PERSIAN PERIOD 2	**MACEDONIAN DYNASTY**	**PTOLEMAIC DYNASTY**	**PTOLEMAIC DYNASTY (CONT.)**

PERSIAN PERIOD 2	MACEDONIAN DYNASTY	PTOLEMAIC DYNASTY	PTOLEMAIC DYNASTY (CONT.)
Artaxerxes III		Ptolemy I 305–285	Ptolemy XI 80
Ochus 343–333	Alexander the Great 332–323	Ptolemy II 285–246	Ptolemy XII 80–51
Arses 338–336	Philip Arrhidaeus 323–317	Ptolemy III 246–221	Cleopatra VII* 51–30
Darius III	Alexander IV 317–305	Ptolemy IV 221–205	Ptolemy XIII 51–47
Codoman 336–332		Ptolemy V 205–180	Ptolemy XIV 47–44
		Ptolemy VI 180–145	Ptolemy XV 44–30
		Ptolemy VII 145	
		Ptolemy VIII 170–116	
		Ptolemy IX 116–107	
		& (second reign) 88–80	
		Ptolemy X 107–88	

Alexander the Great in Egyptian headgear

Egypt becomes part of the Roman Empire in 30 BC (see pp56–7)

With the death of Amenhotep III in 1352 BC, the succession passed to his son Akhenaten *(see p175).* His mismanagement of the political situation, relocation of the capital to Akhetaten (modern Tell al-Amarna) and attempts to overturn the traditional religious hierarchy destabilized Egypt and brought the country close to ruin. Akhenaten's successor, probably his wife

Philistines, one of the "Peoples of the Sea", being taken prisoner by Egyptians, from Ramses III's mortuary temple at Medinat Habu

Nefertiti, restored order by returning the seat of power to Thebes and re-establishing the traditional religion. The reign of Akhenaten's son Tutankhamun was largely devoted to restoring internal stability before trying to reverse Egypt's fortunes abroad. But it took the military prowess of Horemheb, who had worked his way up from scribe to general and finally king, to restore the country to its former greatness. The last king of the 18th Dynasty, he soon began recovering Egypt's empire. This military policy was continued by the rulers of the 19th Dynasty, which began in 1295 BC. Under Seti I, Egypt regained much of her prestige abroad, whilst at home the monarchy's reputation was consolidated and enhanced by

Bust of Queen Nefertiti, 18th Dynasty

great new building projects such as Karnak's hypostyle hall *(see pp188–9)* and Seti's temple at Abydos. Seti was succeeded by his son Ramses II – also known as Ramses the Great – whose 66-year reign saw royal construction on a massive scale. Huge monuments, including the awesome Great Temple of Abu Simbel *(see pp214–15),* were erected in a deliberate effort by Ramses to impress his subjects and preserve his reputation for posterity.

Ramses was succeeded by his son Merneptah, and four more pharaohs in less than 20 years. In c.1186 BC, Sethnakhte inaugurated the 20th Dynasty; nine kings followed, all named Ramses. The greatest of these was Ramses III, who successfully defended Egypt's northern borders against repeated invasions by Libyans and settlers from the Mediterranean region – the so-called "Peoples of the Sea". But his weak successors could not sustain his victories, and foreign infiltration grew rapidly. With internal disorder and social unrest, even the royal tombs were ransacked. The New Kingdom finally collapsed in 1070 BC.

TIMELINE

1279–1213 BC Reign of Ramses II

c.1274 BC Ramses II claims victory over the Hittites at the Battle of Qadesh

1070 BC Fall of New Kingdom. Egypt divided between north and south

747–656 BC Nubians conquer Egypt and rule as 25th Dynasty

| 1300 BC | 1150 BC | 1000 BC | 850 BC |

1352–1336 BC Reign of Akhenaten. Relocation of capital to Akhetaten

Collar of Tutankhamun

1070 BC Kings rule from Tanis in the Delta, with Theban priests in control of the south

945–924 BC Sheshonq I, thought to be "Shishak" from the Old Testament, invades Israel

THIRD INTERMEDIATE PERIOD, LATE PERIOD AND PTOLEMAIC PERIOD (1070–30 BC)

The New Kingdom gave way to four centuries of disunity and foreign infiltration, known as the Third Intermediate Period. Egypt was again divided between north and south: the south remained under the control of the semi-royal high priests of Thebes, while the monarchy was located in the north and ruled from Tanis in the eastern Delta.

Egypt was further fragmented by the Libyan invasion of the western Delta, but in 747 BC the country was united by the Nubians, who managed to hold onto power for over a century, ruling as the 25th Dynasty.

Alexander the Great

The Late Period began with the Assyrian invasion of Egypt in 669 BC. The Assyrians meant to rule the country through their vassal king Nekau then Psamtek of the western Delta city Sais, but Psamtek outmanoeuvred his former masters and the 26th "Saite" Dynasty saw a brief flowering of native Egyptian culture.

Hopes of a permanent revival were, however, cut short by the Persians' invasion in 525 BC. Two hundred years of Persian domination was only interrupted by the short-lived 30th Dynasty – the last native Egyptian rulers. Finally the Macedonian king Alexander the Great "liberated" Egypt from the Persians and founded his new capital Alexandria on the Mediterranean coast, followed by the Ptolemaic Period.

On Alexander's death in 323 BC, his most trusted general assumed power, and over the next three centuries (305–30 BC) 14 of Ptolemy's successors and namesakes ruled from their capital Alexandria. The Ptolemies were accepted by the native Egyptians because they ruled as traditional pharaohs and built temples, such as Edfu, Dendara and Philae, in deliberate imitation of ancient Egyptian design. They also embellished Alexandria, which became the most important city of the ancient world. The last of the Ptolemies, Cleopatra VII, inherited the throne in 51 BC. Her 21-year reign briefly restored Egyptian greatness in the face of the expansionist ambitions of Rome. Her suicide marks the notional end of ancient Egypt, as the country finally became a Roman province.

Ptolemy V, wearing traditional Pharaonic clothing, making offerings to the sacred Buchis bull

669 BC Ashurbanipal of Assyria invades Egypt

Female mummy head from Late Period

332 BC Alexander the Great conquers Egypt and founds Alexandria

323 BC Death of Alexander in Babylon and burial of his body in Egypt

30 BC Egypt becomes Roman province

51–30 BC Reign of Cleopatra VII

700 BC · **550 BC** · **400 BC** · **250 BC** · **100 BC**

664–525 BC Native Egyptian renaissance under 26th "Saite" Dynasty

525 BC Invasion by Persian King Cambyses

380–343 BC 30th Dynasty, the last native Egyptian rulers

305 BC Ptolemy I establishes Ptolemaic dynasty, ruling from Alexandria

Coin of Cleopatra

Cleopatra VII (69 BC–30 BC)

Perhaps the most familiar of ancient Egyptian figures, the real Cleopatra is hidden beneath centuries of misinformation. Most of the detail about her is supplied by Roman sources who waged a propaganda war against her. To them she was the ruler of a decadent eastern culture who seduced two of Rome's generals in order to sieze the Roman Empire. In fact, Cleopatra was an educated Macedonian Greek, who had one child with Julius Caesar and three during her 11 years with Mark Antony. These two men used Egypt's wealth for their imperial ambitions as much as she used their military might to assure her position.

Cleopatra's cartouche

Ptolemy I (305–285 BC) *ruled Egypt after his close friend Alexander the Great died, founding a dynasty that lasted nearly 300 years.*

ORIENTALIST PAINTING OF CLEOPATRA

Part inspired by reliefs on temple walls, part by a confusion of the exotic and the erotic, this painting by Alexandre Cabanel (1823-89) misrepresents Cleopatra in seductive Pharaonic attire.

This Classical bust *is probably a more realistic representation of Cleopatra. She was portrayed in Pharaonic dress on the walls of temples such as Dendera (see p179) to re-inforce her position in the eyes of her subjects as the rightful heir to the great pharaohs.*

This Ptolemaic papyrus *bears Cleopatra's signature. Although fluent in seven languages, including Egyptian, she used Greek for official documents.*

EGYPT AND ROMAN EXPANSION

Rome's expansion from the 4th to the 1st century BC was fuelled in part by the need for ever-increasing quantities of grain. Grain's importance to the ancient economies is somewhat analogous to the value of oil to modern economies. Thanks to its efficient Greek administration, Egypt's vast grain harvests made it incredibly wealthy and a threat to Rome if the country fell into the wrong hands. Therefore the Romans knew they had either to ensure Egypt's ruler was sympathetic towards them, or annex the country. At first, Egypt avoided being absorbed by Rome through a skilful combination of bribery and diplomacy – on different occasions, Julius Caesar and Mark Antony were paid large sums of money to restore the throne of Egypt to Cleopatra's father, Ptolemy XII. When Cleopatra and her brother were installed on the throne in 51 BC, Rome expected simply to add Egypt to their empire.

KEY

■ *Rome 300 BC*

■ *Rome 51 BC*

□ *Ptolemaic Kingdom 51 BC*

CLEOPATRA AND ROME

In 51 BC, Cleopatra and Ptolemy XIII, her brother, were named co-rulers of Egypt. When they fought for sole control, Rome sent Julius Caesar to settle the dispute. He put Cleopatra on the throne and formed a close relationship with her. Three years after Caesar's murder, Mark Antony paid a visit to Cleopatra seeking funding for his expeditions. They became lovers and when Antony handed Roman territories over to Egypt in 34 BC, Rome, at Octavian's urging, declared war on Cleopatra.

Julius Caesar, after moving Cleopatra to Rome, was killed by Republicans who feared that, under her evil influence, he wanted to return Rome to monarchy.

Mark Antony *was derided by Rome for his lack of self control towards Cleopatra. Forced to marry the sister of Octavian, he later returned to his Egyptian lover.*

Octavian, *with the prize of the Roman Empire at stake, decided to fight Antony at sea near Actium, off the coast of Greece.*

At the Battle of Actium (31 BC) *the two fleets quickly clashed, opening up a gap in Octavian's formation. Seeing her chance, Cleopatra headed for Egypt closely followed by Antony. His men, thinking him a deserter, defected to Octavian. A year later Octavian's army routed Antony's troops and marched on Alexandria.*

The African asp *is a cobra, which, as the uraeus snake, protected the pharaoh in this world and the next. It is possible, therefore, that Cleopatra did in fact choose to die by snake bite.*

THE ENDURING APPEAL OF CLEOPATRA

The appeal of Cleopatra's story is magnified by her tragic death: defeated by Octavian and believing reports that Antony was dead, Antony committed suicide; Cleopatra realising all was lost then took her own life. As told by Roman writers, this tale of sex, power, greed and ultimately tragedy proved irresistible for artists from the Renaissance, Shakespeare and Hollywood.

Shakespeare's play *was based on Plutarch's Lives (c.AD 75), the Roman account most sympathetic to Cleopatra.*

Hollywood films *such as Cleopatra, starring Liz Taylor and Richard Burton used grand sets and outrageous outfits and did not let historical accuracy ruin a good story.*

Eye makeup *was one detail Hollywood did not get wrong, except that it was worn by both sexes. Ancient Egyptians used ground minerals mixed with water and stored in tubes.*

FROM CHRIST TO MOHAMMED

Egypt was now a province of mighty Rome, whose emperors established themselves as the successors of the pharaohs. As Christianity spread throughout the Roman Empire, its Egyptian adherents, known as Copts, came into conflict with the Roman authorities. Even when Christianity was adopted as the official religion of the Eastern half of the now divided Roman Empire in 323 AD, there were differences in theology, and the Copts were mercilessly persecuted.

The Eastern Romans, later known as Byzantines, remained largely unchallenged in power until in the 7th century they were confronted by a new force sweeping up from Arabia. Following the teachings of the Prophet Mohammed, the army of Islam defeated the Byzantines in battle and entered Egypt. Ignoring Alexandria, the Arab army, led by the general Amr Ibn al-Aas, marched on the fortress of Babylon-in-Egypt near to the old capital of Memphis. After a brief siege it surrendered and Amr settled his men just to the north, where he founded a new city known as Fustat.

Egypt became a province of an already vast Islamic empire ruled first from Damascus (the Umayyad dynasty), then from Baghdad (the Abbasids). Ahmed Ibn Tulun, an administrator sent from Baghdad, decided to declare the territory independent. His mosque still stands but his dynasty did not outlive him long; his son was assassinated and rule from Baghdad reimposed.

Salah ad-Din al-Ayyubi (1138–93), the scourge of the European Crusaders

In AD 969 Egypt was seized by the Fatimids from Tunisia. They built a new city north of Fustat, encircled by fortified walls and containing palaces, great mosques and plazas. They called their new city Al-Qahira, "The Victorious", a name later corrupted by European tongues to "Cairo". Their reign in Egypt lasted for barely more than 200 years, until it was brought to an end in 1171 by the arrival of a Syrian warrior-general, Salah ad-Din al-Ayyubi, known in English as Saladin. In Cairo, Salah ad-Din expanded the city walls and added a fortress that survives as today's Citadel (*see pp104–7*). A hero of the Arab world, who recaptured Jerusalem from the European Crusaders, Salah ad-Din's role in Egyptian history is, however, overshadowed by the dynasty that succeeded him, a warrior caste called the Mamluks.

Detail of a manuscript showing Mamluk cavalrymen in training (1348)

TIMELINE

30 BC–395 AD Roman Period	*Roman mummy portrait from 4th century AD*	**451** Egypt's Coptic church splits from Eastern Christianity at the Council of Chalcedon
		527 St Catherine's Monastery founded in Sinai

AD 1	150	300	450	600	75

394 End of ancient Egypt as Roman Empire accepts Christianity as official religion and closes all temples

640 Islamic army under Amr Ibn al-Aas invades and conquers Egypt

19th-century lithograph of Sultan Baybars I (c.1265) executing Christians who refuse to convert to Islam

SLAVES AND SOLDIERS

The word "Mamluk" means "one who is owned," and reflects their origins as slaves brought to Egypt to be palace guards. Their service was rewarded by land and eventual freedom. By the middle of the 13th century the Mamluks were the most powerful force in the land, and were able to claim Egypt for themselves.

The Mamluks retained the slave system, and whoever had the largest slave army installed himself as sultan at the top. There was no hereditary lineage, instead it was succession by the strongest. Once in power, there remained constant challenges, and only the exceptionally able and ruthless survived.

The Mamluks prided themselves on their martial skills and were known particularly for their masterful horsemanship. From their base in Cairo they fought victorious campaigns throughout Palestine and Syria, completing the job begun by Salah ad-Din by finally evicting the Crusaders from the Holy Land in 1291. They governed Jerusalem and Damascus, and carved out an empire that extended north as far as eastern Turkey. With these territories came control of East-West trade. The taxes raised on spices, perfumes, silks and dyes made Cairo one of the richest cities in the world. This wealth remains evident in the legacy of superb architecture left behind from this time, built with fine marble panelling, intricate ivory-inlaid woodwork, and carved stone ornamentation.

Mamluk monopolies forced Europe to seek alternative routes to the East, and when, in 1498, Vasco da Gama rounded the Cape of Good Hope, the fortunes of Egypt were dealt a crippling blow. Worse still, the Ottoman Turks from their capital of Constantinople were eroding the Mamluks' empire from the north. Sultan Qansuh al-Ghouri (1501–16) rode out to meet this new threat. His Mamluk army was defeated, and the following year the Ottoman Turks entered Cairo to take control of Egypt.

Magnificent interior of the Mosque of Qaitbey (1475), built with money raised by taxes

	969 Fatimids found the city of Al-Qahira, forerunner of modern Cairo	**1250** Mamluks accede to power	**1468–96** Reign of Qaitbey, enthusiastic patron of architecture

Mamluk tile from the 15th century

900	**1050**	**1200**	**1350**	**1500**

876–9 Construction of the Mosque of Ibn Tulun

1171 Salah ad-Din becomes ruler of Egypt

Mamluk jacket (c.13th century)

1516 Al-Ghouri's Mamluk army defeated by Ottomans, who take control of Egypt

The defeat of the Mamluks by Napoleon's army during the 1798 Battle of the Pyramids

OTTOMAN RULE

Under Ottoman rule, Egypt ceased to be the centre of the Mediterranean world and Cairo became just one of numerous provincial capitals ruled from Constantinople. The Turkish sultan Selim "the Grim", so called for his habit of executing his advisers, ruled Egypt and the Mamluks lived on as lords or *beys* still wielding considerable power.

The Ottoman empire reached its peak during the reign of Suleiman the Magnificent, but his death in 1566 heralded a long era of decline for the empire. A succession of weak Ottoman sultans enabled the Mamluks to re-emerge in the mid-17th century as the most powerful force in Egyptian politics. However, internal rivalry and bloody feuding prevented them

Sultan Selim I (1467–1520), also known as Selim "the Grim"

from exploiting power to the full. At the same time, economic decline and recurrent outbreaks of plague further weakened the country.

EUROPE "DISCOVERS" EGYPT

In 1798 Egypt was invaded by a French army under the command of Napoleon Bonaparte. With France and Britain at war, Napoleon saw the occupation of Egypt as a way of threatening British rule in India. The French defeated the Mamluks at the Battle of the Pyramids but this success was short lived. Napoleon's fleet was destroyed at Abu Qir *(see p250)* by the British Navy, led by Admiral Nelson. A declaration of war by the Ottoman sultan followed, and by 1801 the French expedition had come to an end. Their legacy is

TIMELINE

1520–66 Reign of Suleiman the Magnificent

1566 Death of Suleiman the Magnificent

1650 Mamluks re-emerge as a powerful force

1550   1600   1650

1528 Egypt's first Ottoman mosque (Suleiman Pasha) built at the Citadel

Suleiman the Magnificent

1623 First overt rebellions in Egypt against rule from Constantinople

the *Description de l'Egypte*, an exhaustive scientific study of the country which encouraged many other writers and artists to visit Egypt.

MOHAMMED ALI AND HIS HEIRS

In the resulting power vacuum, the Mamluks, Ottoman troops and a contingent of Albanian mercenaries locked horns in a struggle for power which was won, in 1805, by Mohammed Ali, commander of the Albanians. To consolidate his position he eliminated the threat of the Mamluks by inviting the leading *amirs* to a banquet and having them massacred on the way home. He then began to transform Egypt into an industrialized nation. Bringing agriculture under state control, he built textile plants, shipyards and munitions factories to supply his new Western-style army. After a series of military victories in Greece, Arabia and the Sudan, Mohammed Ali threatened the Ottoman sultan, but was forced to back down after the British intervened and he died in 1849.

Mohammed Ali in negotiations with the British, following his threat to overthrow the Ottoman sultan

Two successors followed before Khedive Ismail acceded to power. He was determined to transform Egypt into a modern nation and introduced the first national postal service, extending railroad networks throughout the country. His greatest achievement was to preside over the opening of the Suez Canal in 1869 *(see pp60–61)*.

19th-century advertisement showing Europeans at Giza

Such projects were funded by loans from European banking houses at exorbitant rates of interest. As the national debt rose, Ismail was forced to sell the majority of Suez Canal shares to the British and the French.

In 1882, Egyptian army officers led by Colonel Ahmed Orabi staged popular uprisings in an attempt to establish a more independent regime. The breakdown in local order led the British to send in the warships, shelling Alexandria and landing an army of occupation which routed Orabi's forces at Tell al-Kebir.

The 1811 massacre of the leading Mamluk *amirs* ordered by Viceroy Mohammed Ali

1719 Plague decimates the population of Egypt

1798 Egypt invaded by Napoleon

1805 Mohammed Ali wins control of Egypt

1882 British troops occupy Egypt

1700	1750	1800	1850

1707 Mamluk power struggle reaches new heights in Cairo

Napoleon Bonaparte

1822 Translation of hieroglyphs by French scholar Champollion

1869 Khedive Ismail opens the Suez Canal

Khedive Ismail

The Construction of the Suez Canal

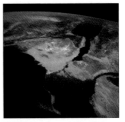

As early as the 7th century BC, the ancient Egyptians had connected the Nile and Red Sea with an east-west canal. A north-south canal, slicing through the Isthmus of Suez to connect the Mediterranean with the Red Sea was first considered in the Middle Ages by Venetian merchants. At the end of the 18th century, Napoleon's engineers took up the idea but **Statue of** dropped it when they mistakenly calculated **Ferdinand** that one sea was 10 m (33 ft) higher than the **de Lesseps** other. The canal project was taken up by Ferdinand de Lesseps, the French consul to Egypt, who received the go-ahead during the reign of Khedive Said. Construction began on 25 April 1859.

This impressive *satellite picture shows how the Suez Canal separates Africa (Egypt) from Asia (Sinai).*

THE CANAL ROUTE

This 19th-century painting by Albert Rieger shows how the Suez Canal utilizes lakes as passing places for shipping – Lake Manzila at its northern end, Lake Timsah, and the Bitter Lakes at the mid-point of the canal. This route is 163 km (101 miles) in length.

Rosetta branch of the Nile

Cairo

The Bitter Lakes provided a natural passing point for shipping.

Suez remains the most important of Egypt's ports.

Ferdinand de Lesseps *(1805–94) was a French diplomat descended from a long line of civil servants. It took him 20 years to receive approval for his canal plans.*

DIGGING THE SUEZ CANAL

At the outset, the building of the canal was largely carried out by hand, but acquiring the 20,000 workers needed each month proved extremely difficult. In addition, fatalities were high, running at about 200 per year, and work was periodically halted by waves of infectious diseases, such as cholera. After five years of construction, the Egyptian government discontinued its supply of unhappily drafted peasant labour and work continued with the use of mechanical diggers and a smaller number of labourers. It took ten years to plough through the 96 km (60 miles) of lake and 64 km (40 miles) of land, but finally, in March 1869, the waters of the Mediterranean flowed into the basins of the Bitter Lakes finally bringing into existence a new sea route between Europe and Asia.

Construction *of the canal began in a manner that recalled the great building projects of ancient Egypt. Hampered by a lack of drinking water, huge numbers of labourers worked in awful conditions, aided only by camels with baskets.*

The Cairo Marriott Hotel, *built along the lines of Spain's Alhambra as a palace for Empress Eugénie of France, was one of the extravagant projects designed for the opening of the canal.*

BUILDING BOOM

The construction of the Suez Canal inspired a building boom in Cairo where grand new buildings, such as the Khedival Apartments on Sharia Emad al-Din, were constructed to house the various dignitaries invited for the opening celebrations. An opera house was erected for their entertainment and a palace (now the Marriott Hotel) built for the guest of honour Empress Eugénie, wife of Napoleon III of France. A tree-lined road, still in use today, was also laid for the Empress's visit to the Pyramids. The canal also resulted in the founding of three new towns – Port Said, Ismailia and Suez.

Ismailia was the headquarters of the Suez Canal Company.

Lake Timsah

Lake Manzila

Port Said is the Mediterranean gateway to the canal.

Inaugural celebrations *for the canal began on 17 November 1869. Khedive Ismail, escorting the French Empress Eugénie and Austro-Hungarian Emperor Franz Josef in this painting by Mahmoud Said, offered weeks of lavish hospitality to visiting dignitaries.*

The opera Aida *was written by Giuseppe Verdi for the canal opening. However, it was not completed in time and another Verdi opera, Rigoletto, was performed in its place.*

THE SUEZ CRISIS

The cost of building the canal and financing the accompanying lavish celebrations bankrupted Egypt. Ismail was forced to sell his shares and full ownership passed to the French and British who kept control over the canal for the next 80 years. When, in the wake of Egyptian independence, President Nasser nationalized the canal in 1956, Britain and France, in collusion with Israel, invaded the canal zone in an attempt to take it back by force. In the face of widespread international condemnation they were forced to retreat, leaving the canal in Egyptian hands.

President Gamal Abdel Nasser (1918–70)

British troops at Port Said during the 1956 invasion

Early 20th-century photograph of members of the British elite at Shepheard's Hotel in Cairo

BRITISH OCCUPATION

When Egypt's soaring national debt rendered the country unable to repay British loans, Britain invaded. The occupation, motivated by the need to protect British interests in the Suez Canal, was intended as a temporary policing measure. Although the *khedives*, the heirs of Mohammed Ali, remained on the throne, all real power was held by the British.

With the outbreak of World War I in 1914, Britain took an even firmer hold on Egyptian affairs. The demands of the British war effort fell hard on the country's peasants and popular discontent spread. At the end of the war, Egyptian demands for autonomy, led by nationalist leader Saad Zaghloul, were curtly dismissed, causing the 1919 rebellion. The violence of the rebellion forced Britain to proclaim the end of its protectorate and recognize Egypt as an independent state with a hereditary monarch, King Fuad I, sixth son of Khedive Ismail. Despite

Nasser receives a hero's welcome after the successful coup of 1952

the king, Britain still controlled Egypt's legal system, communications, foreign policy and the Suez Canal. During World War II, Egypt was vital to British war aims. At El-Alamein the Eighth Army under Montgomery repulsed Rommel's Afrika Korps, changing the course of the war in North Africa.

1952 REVOLUTION

At the conclusion of the war, the British withdrew most of their soldiers from the country, but new forces in Egyptian politics were demanding nothing less than full independence. The disaster of the 1948 War, in which the Egyptian army was defeated by the newly-formed state of Israel, contributed to the mood for independence. Fuad's son, King Farouk, who was rumoured to have made a fortune by selling faulty equipment to Egyptian troops, was blamed for the disaster. In 1952 Egyptian anger resulted in "Black Saturday", when European businesses in central Cairo were torched by rampaging mobs. Six months of rioting and political instability followed until, on 23 July, a group calling itself the Free Officers, led by Gamal Abdel Nasser, seized power in a bloodless coup. The monarchy was deposed, King Farouk went into exile and Mohammed Neguib, an army general, became prime minister, commander-in-chief and, later, president. He was deposed in 1954 by Nasser, who succeeded him first as prime minister,

TIMELINE

	1919 Nationwide anti-British riots	**1922** King Fuad I is made king by the British	**1942** Battle of El-Alamein, a turning point in Allied fortunes in WWII	**1956** Newly elected as president, Nasser provokes Suez Crisis	
1900		**1920**		**1940**	**1960**

Howard Carter exiting the tomb of Tutankhamun

1922 Howard Carter discovers tomb of Tutankhamun

1935 King Farouk succeeds his father, King Fuad I

1952 Free Officers seize power, paving the way for an independent republic

then in 1956 as president. Nasser's ideology of socialism, allied with Arab nationalism, made him a hero to the masses. During the Suez Crisis of 1956 he took on the combined forces of Britain, France and Israel, who invaded following Nasser's announcement of his intention to nationalize the Suez Canal. The invaders were forced to withdraw after intervention by the United Nations and America.

This golden era for Nasser was brought to an abrupt end in 1967, with the shattering defeat of Egypt in the Six Day War with Israel. Nasser died a broken man three years later.

Former US President Bill Clinton and ousted President Mubarak during the Middle East peace talks in 2000

SADAT AND MUBARAK

Nasser's successor, Anwar Sadat, rejected his socialist policies and sought private and foreign investment. On 6 October 1973, he launched a surprise attack on Israeli lines along the Suez. This early success, though quickly reversed, paved the way for peace talks that culminated in the signing of the Camp David peace treaty in 1979. Sadat was assassinated in 1981 by Islamic extremists. His successor, Hosni Mubarak, inherited an ailing economy and recovery was slow. For much of his reign Egypt was ostracized by the other Arab nations because of its peace with Israel. In the 1990s and 2004 and 2005, Egypt was hit by Islamist-inspired violence, including fatal attacks on tourists. Visitor numbers fell, damaging the economy, though the situation was stabilised. The country maintains a cool peace with Israel and plays a key role as a peace broker in the Middle East crisis.

However, in 2011 extensive anti-government riots and demonstrations forced Mubarak to step down as president. The military dissolved parliament and took over the running of Egypt. The military regime will be in place until elections begin later in 2011.

Lasers and fireworks illuminate the Giza Pyramids on Millennium night

1967 Defeat by Israel in the Six Day War

Anwar Sadat (1918–81)

1988 Egyptian novelist Naguib Mahfouz wins Nobel Prize for Literature

2000 International coverage of Millennium celebrations at the Pyramids

2011 President Mubarak resigns after anti-government protests

1980   2000   2020

1970 Nasser dies and is succeeded by Anwar Sadat

1981 Sadat is assassinated and succeeded by Hosni Mubarak

Naguib Mahfouz

1999 Egyptian scientist Ahmed Zewail wins Nobel Prize in Chemistry

2005 President Hosni Mubarak re-elected following landslide victory in multi-candidate election

CAIRO
AREA BY AREA

Cairo at a Glance

Cairo is one of the most densely populated cities in the world. Though its suburbs have spilled over onto the Nile's west bank, its top attractions lie on the eastern bank. Central Cairo is the heart of the modern city and boasts some fine 19th-century architecture. Gezira and Rhoda islands, cooled by the Nile, seem quieter than the centre, while Old Cairo's Roman and early Christian history predates the capital itself. Islamic Cairo is the highlight of the city; its minarets and domes, bazaars and alleyways recall scenes from *1001 Nights*. Further afield, the suburb of Heliopolis spreads northeast, while Giza and the Pyramids lie to the west.

Cairo Tower

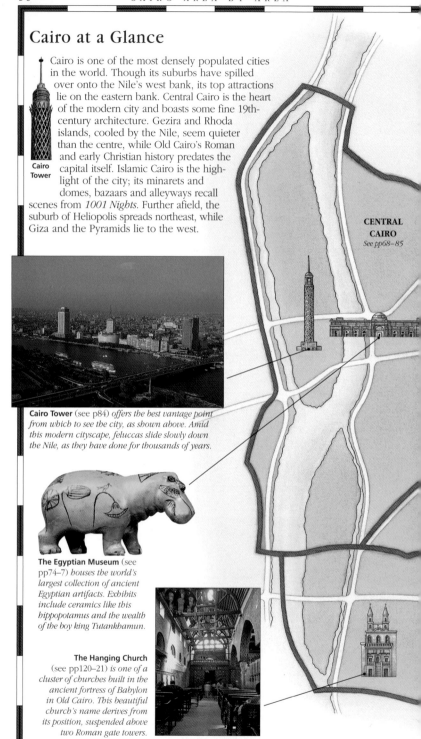

CENTRAL CAIRO
See pp68–85

Cairo Tower (see p84) *offers the best vantage point from which to see the city, as shown above. Amid this modern cityscape, feluccas slide slowly down the Nile, as they have done for thousands of years.*

The Egyptian Museum (see pp74–7) *houses the world's largest collection of ancient Egyptian artifacts. Exhibits include ceramics like this hippopotamus and the wealth of the boy king Tutankhamun.*

The Hanging Church (see pp120–21) *is one of a cluster of churches built in the ancient fortress of Babylon in Old Cairo. This beautiful church's name derives from its position, suspended above two Roman gate towers.*

◁ Surrounded by the domes of Fatimid Cairo, the minaret of the Madrassa and Mausoleum of Sultan Qalawun

Khan al-Khalili (see pp88–90) *is an Aladdin's cave of spices, perfumes, jewellery and souvenirs. The bazaar spills over into the nearby areas which, dotted with some superb Mamluk architecture, have buzzed with similar commercial activity since the Middle Ages.*

The Mosque of al-Azhar (see p91), *at the heart of the Fatimid capital of "Al-Qahira" (Cairo), has been a centre for Islamic scholarship and teaching for more than a thousand years.*

ISLAMIC CAIRO
See pp86–111

0 metres	900
0 yards	900

The Citadel (see pp104–7) *was built by Salah ad-Din in the 12th century and crowned with the Mosque of Mohammed Ali 700 years later. This stone fortress dominates Cairo's eastern horizon.*

RHODA ISLAND AND OLD CAIRO
See pp112–125

The Mosque of Ibn Tulun (see pp110–11) *is known for its unusual spiral minaret. Its size and simple geometric shapes give it an air of tranquillity which contrasts nicely with the eclectic collection of the nearby Gayer-Anderson House.*

CENTRAL CAIRO

When Ismail (*see p59*) acceded to power in 1863, Cairo was an almost medieval city with a street plan little changed in 500 years. But the khedive, educated in France, set about transforming his capital into a modern, fashionable city that could compare with Paris. Rather than try to impose order on the existing city, he

Sculpture outside Opera Complex

chose to drain the marshy flood plains between it and the Nile and start again. His creation is the heart of Central Cairo. Fine 19th-century European architecture – albeit battered and worn – is the backdrop to thoroughly Middle Eastern streetlife, with the placid Nile offering a refuge from the noise and crush of people and cars.

SIGHTS AT A GLANCE

Areas, Streets & Squares
Corniche el-Nil ⑬
Garden City ⑫
Midan Opera and
  Midan Ataba ⑦
Midan Ramses ⑥

Midan Tahrir ②
Sharia Qasr el-Nil ⑤
Sharia Talaat Harb ④
Zamalek ⑲

Museums & Historic Buildings
Abdeen Palace Museum ⑨
American University in Cairo ③
Beit as-Sennari ⑩
Cairo Tower ⑰
Egyptian Museum pp74–7 ①
Mahmoud Khalil Museum ⑮
Manial Palace ⑭

Mausoleum of Saad
  Zaghloul ⑪
Museum of Islamic Art ⑧
Opera House Complex ⑯

Walks
River Promenade ⑱

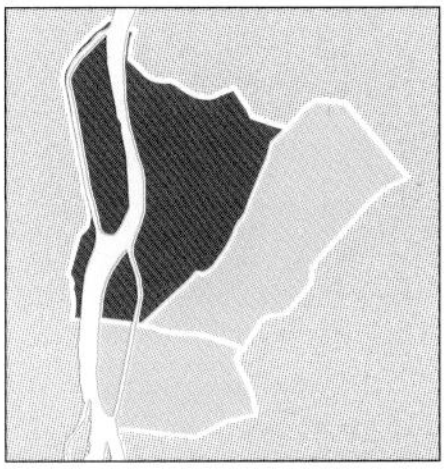

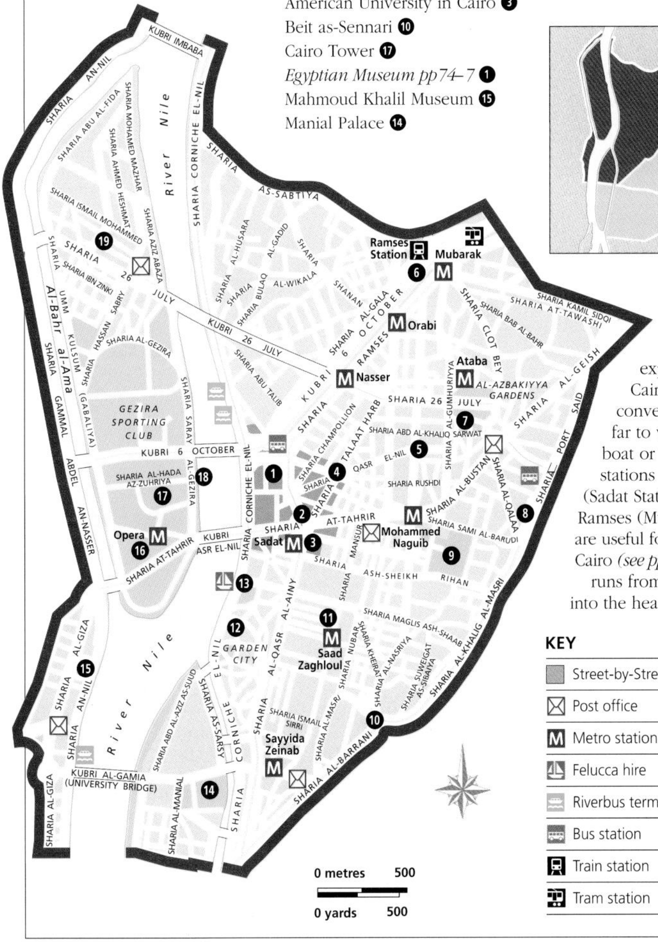

GETTING AROUND
Walking is the best way to experience Central Cairo, and taxis are convenient if it is too far to walk. The riverboat or the Metro, with stations at Midan Tahrir (Sadat Station) and Midan Ramses (Mubarak Station), are useful for getting to Old Cairo (*see pp346–7*). A tram runs from Midan Ramses into the heart of Heliopolis.

KEY
▨	Street-by-Street map *pp70–71*
⊠	Post office
Ⓜ	Metro station
🛥	Felucca hire
▭	Riverbus terminal
🚌	Bus station
🚉	Train station
🚋	Tram station

◁ The faded grandeur of a typical apartment balcony near Midan Ataba (*see p78*)

Street-by-Street: Around Midan Tahrir

Overrun by traffic and far from pretty, Midan Tahrir is the hub of Central Cairo and was the site of extensive public protests against the government in 2011. All routes lead here and most visitors become very familiar with its Brutalist landmarks: for example the Mogamma, home to 18,000 bureaucrats. Brighter spots include the dusky pink Egyptian Museum, the Arab League Building and the elegant curve of façades between Sharia Qasr el-Nil and Sharia Talaat Harb – the location of airline offices, travel agents, souvenir shops and cafés.

Ramses Station

SHARIA CHAMPOLLION

SHARIA RAMSES

Bus Station

KUBRI 6 OCTOBER

Zamalek

Central Cairo
Cairo's bustling modern centre is flanked to the west by the tranquil waters of the Nile.

CORNICHE EL-NIL

★ Egyptian Museum
The museum has the greatest collection of Pharaonic treasures in the world and is one of Cairo's most popular sights **1**

The Nile Ritz-Carlton Hotel
(see p73), built in 1959, was Egypt's first modern hotel. It was orginally named the Nile Hotel.

Gezira

```
0 metres        130
0 yards         130
```

KEY

– – – – Suggested route

STAR SIGHTS

★ Egyptian Museum

Corniche el-Nil
This boat-lined boulevard is wide and shady and the city's favourite place for an evening stroll **13**

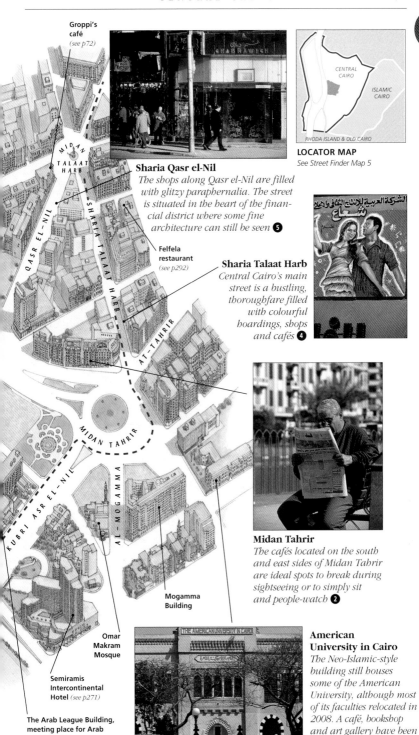

Groppi's café
(see p72)

LOCATOR MAP
See Street Finder Map 5

CENTRAL CAIRO

ISLAMIC CAIRO

RHODA ISLAND & OLD CAIRO

Sharia Qasr el-Nil
The shops along Qasr el-Nil are filled with glitzy paraphernalia. The street is situated in the heart of the financial district where some fine architecture can still be seen **5**

Felfela restaurant
(see p292)

Sharia Talaat Harb
Central Cairo's main street is a bustling, thoroughfare filled with colourful hoardings, shops and cafés **4**

Midan Tahrir
The cafés located on the south and east sides of Midan Tahrir are ideal spots to break during sightseeing or to simply sit and people-watch **2**

Mogamma Building

Omar Makram Mosque

Semiramis Intercontinental Hotel *(see p271)*

The Arab League Building, meeting place for Arab world leaders.

American University in Cairo
The Neo-Islamic-style building still houses some of the American University, although most of its faculties relocated in 2008. A café, bookshop and art gallery have been created **3**

Two Cairenes, dressed in traditional garments called *galabiyyas*, in Midan Tahrir

Egyptian Museum ●

See pp74–7.

Midan Tahrir ●

Map 5 B4. Ⓜ *Sadat.*

Midan Tahrir was not always the dauntingly urban square that it is today. Until the 19th century, the area was a swampy plain, flooded each summer by the Nile. When Khedive Ismail (1863–79) came to power, however, he had the land drained as part of his grand scheme to transform Cairo by building a European-style city of tree-lined boulevards and grand public squares.

The Qasr el-Nil (Palace of the Nile) was built beside the river, fronted by an extensive plaza named Midan Ismailia (Ismail's Square). However, Ismail's glory was short-lived: his ambitious scheme drained not only the swamps, but also the state coffers, as Egyptian debt to European lenders spiralled out of control.

In 1882, the British stepped in to take control *(see p59)*, requisitioning Qasr el-Nil as their headquarters, and later as the barracks for their army of occupation. Overcrowded with Allied soldiers during World War II, the building gained a reputation for the remarkable tenacity of its bedbugs. The barracks were evacuated at the end of the war and the palace was demolished. In 1959, the Nile Hotel was built on the site – the first modern international hotel to be built in Egypt. The 1952

revolution saw all traces of the old regime wiped away, including the name of Ismail, and the largest square in the city was reincarnated as Midan Tahrir (Liberation Square).

Midan Tahrir is the closest Cairo gets to having a centre, and several major airlines have their offices here, along with tourist agencies, the Omar Makram Mosque which serves as a venue for state funerals, and the enormous monolithic structure of the Mogamma Building. Housing around 18,000 civil servants. The square was the rally point for protesters in early 2011 *(see p63)*.

American University in Cairo ●

Qasr al-Ainy, Midan Tahrir. **Map** 5 B4. Ⓜ *Sadat.* ◯ *8:30am–5pm Sun–Thur, 10:30am–5pm Sat.*

The American University in Cairo (AUC) has its roots in this attractive Neo-Islamic building, although most faculties relocated in 2008 to a state-of-the-art campus in the outlying area of New Cairo. Attending the private AUC is Egypt's equivalent of an Ivy League education and beyond the means of most Egyptians.

The historic downtown building houses a branch of the AUC bookstore, a café and

Flags fly above the Neo-Islamic façade of the American University

the Margo Veillon Gallery for Contemporary Egyptian Art. Regular lectures and discussions are held on the campus, and non-students are welcome to attend. Visitors are admitted on proof of identity.

Shar Hashamaim Synagogue, near Sharia Talaat Harb

Sharia Talaat Harb ●

Map 5 C3. Ⓜ *Sadat.*

Running from Midan Tahrir to Midan Orabi, Sharia Talaat Harb is quintessential modern Cairo. Its pavements are permanently crowded and the road is jammed with horn-honking traffic. As you walk along, music blares from cars on one side and shops on the other, while the air is heavy with car fumes mingled with the smells of cooking and incense. Rising above this pandemonium is some grand architecture, especially around Midan Talaat Harb, where Parisian-style buildings dwarf the statue of Talaat Harb, founder of the National Bank.

On the square is **Groppi's**, a tearoom that once supplied confectionery to the royalty of Great Britain; the only clues to its more glamorous past are the delightful, spangly mosaics around the entrance. More memories of a golden era now past are evoked by the Art Deco lines of the

PARIS BY THE NILE

Inspired by Baron Haussmann's plans for the modernization of Paris in the mid-19th century, Khedive Ismail turned to foreign architects to realize his dream of a modern Cairo. Drawing on Renaissance, Baroque and even Gothic styles, their buildings were adorned with wrought-iron grilles, plaster mouldings, carved foliage, cherubs and angels, plus some local flavouring in the form of scarabs and sphinxes. Later buildings began to take more account of Egypt's heritage, incorporating Islamic motifs such as striped stonework and crenellations. Downtown streets, including Qasr el-Nil and the intersecting Mohammed Farid and Emad ad-Din, still contain a wealth of these beautiful buildings.

Kubri Qasr el-Nil (Qasr el-Nil Bridge), part of the European-style Cairo planned by Khedive Ismail

Metro Cinema, which opened in 1939 with *Gone With the Wind*. It now screens low-budget action movies – fun to attend for the experience of Egyptian cinema-going, where the bad guys are dispatched to a round of applause.

Little mention is made, in the current climate of Arab-Israeli tension, of Egypt's own Jewish community. However, in Sharia Adly (which joins Sharia Talaat Harb beside the Metro Cinema) the Babylonian-style Shar Hashamaim Synagogue is evidence of their historical presence. You must show your passport in order to enter.

Talaat Harb terminates in another elegant square, named after the nationalist politician Ahmed Orabi who sought political reform in 1881. Off to the east is pedestrianized Sharia Alfy, full of small bars and restaurants, including the excellent Alfy Bey *(see p290).*

Sharia Qasr el-Nil ❺

Map 5.C3. **M** *Sadat.*

A frenetically busy shopping street running in front of the Nile Ritz-Carlton Hotel in Midan Tahrir to Midan Opera, Qasr el-Nil is taken up almost exclusively with shop windows that display the brightest and gaudiest of goods. The streets on either side of Sharia Qasr el-Nil traditionally constituted Cairo's financial district. At the junction with Sharia Sherif is the National Bank of Egypt building. Here, too, is the Bourse, or stock exchange, which is enjoying a new lease of life since the government undertook a programme of privatization in the late 1990s.

Statue of Mustafa Kamel overlooking his square

The boom in trading was reflected in a renovation programme that covered a 60,000-sq m (645,000-sq ft) section of downtown Cairo. The area around the Bourse has been pedestrianized and many of the roads are now paved. These walkways are also furnished with 19th-century-style lamp posts, along with flower beds, greenery and palm trees. Some of the buildings in this area have also been renovated, including the lovely Trieste Insurance Building on the corner with Sharia Sherif. This was designed by the Italian architect Antonio Lascaic (1856–1946), who was responsible for many of central Cairo's most beautiful Belle Epoque buildings.

Sharia Qasr el-Nil crosses over Midan Mustafa Kamel, named after the founder of the Egyptian Nationalist Party, formed in 1907. Kamel was an early opponent of British occupation and his statue looks out over the square.

Sharia Qasr el-Nil continues past some jewellers' shops and a few outlets selling street signs (you can have your name put on one) to emerge on Sharia al-Gumhuriyya. This leads into Midan Opera *(see p78),* which was once one of Cairo's grandest squares, but is now occupied by a vast car park and the derelict Continental-Savoy hotel.

Small fruit stall set up in an alleyway off Sharia Talaat Harb

Egyptian Museum ❶

Gold bracelet from Tanis

Founded by a Frenchman, Auguste Mariette (1821–81), Egypt's first national museum of Pharaonic antiquities opened in 1863. It outgrew two homes before settling in these premises in 1902. More than 120,000 items are on display here, with another 150,000 stored in the basement. Pride of the collection are the artifacts from Tutankhamun's tomb, but there are great pieces from every period of ancient Egyptian history, from the Narmer Palette, dating from around 3100 BC, through to the Graeco-Roman Fayoum Portraits of the 2nd century AD. Some of these items may be transferred to the new Grand Egyptian Museum, currently under construction at Giza and due to open in 2013.

GALLERY GUIDE

The museum has two floors and confusingly the rooms on each floor are numbered the same. Artifacts on the ground floor are organized in a roughly chronological order, running clockwise from the entrance and atrium, while the first-floor collection is arranged by themes. The central hall houses large monumental statuary and the annexe in the basement houses the Children's Museum.

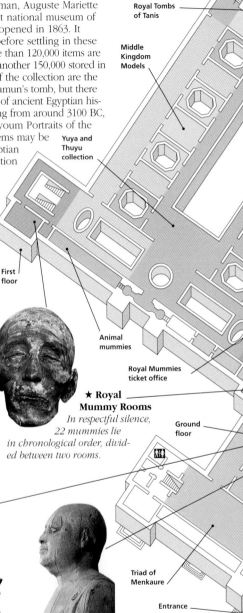

Royal Tombs of Tanis

Middle Kingdom Models

Yuya and Thuyu collection

First floor

Animal mummies

Royal Mummies ticket office

★ **Royal Mummy Rooms**
In respectful silence, 22 mummies lie in chronological order, divided between two rooms.

Ground floor

Triad of Menkaure

Entrance

Prince Rahotep and Nofret
These life-like limestone statues (c.2620 BC) were found in their mastaba (tomb-chapel) near the Meidum Pyramid (see p168).

STAR EXHIBITS

- ★ Tutankhamun Galleries
- ★ Royal Mummy Rooms
- ★ Amarna Room
- ★ Statue of Ka-Aper

★ **Statue of Ka-Aper**
This skilfully carved statue's eyes have rims made of copper, whites of opaque quartz and corneas of clear rock crystal, drilled and filled with black paste.

★ **Tutankhamun Galleries**
This life-sized gold mask is just one in a collection of 1,700 items from the tomb of the boy king.

VISITORS' CHECKLIST

Midan Tahrir, Cairo. **Map** 5 B3.
Ⓜ *Sadat.* 🚌 🚐 *to Midan Tahrir.* **Tel** *(02) 2578 2448, (02) 2578 2452.* ◯ *9am–6:30pm Thu–Tue (last admission 4:45pm); 9am–2pm Wed (last admission noon); 9am–5pm Ramadan.* 🎟 🔌 📷 🍴 🛍 📱 🚻 *Left luggage facilities available.* 📷

The Fayoum Portraits are remarkably lifelike studies of Egyptians from the Graeco-Roman period.

Ancient Egyptian Jewellery
Made with beads of gold and lapis lazuli, this c.11th-century BC necklace is one of several examples of the royal jewellers' exquisite skill.

Tutankhamun's Throne
On the back of the lavishly decorated throne is this portrayal of Tutankhamun and his wife under the rays of Aten, the sun.

★ **Amarna Room**
During Akhenaten's 15-year rule, not only was the old religion abandoned (see p175) but also its art. A new style developed which depicted figures with elongated heads (as in this bust of the king) and protruding bellies.

Colossus of Amenhotep III and Queen Tiye

KEY

🟦 Old Kingdom		🟦 Tutankhamun Galleries	
🟦 Middle Kingdom		🟦 Royal Mummy Rooms	
🟦 New Kingdom		🟦 Middle Kingdom Models	
🟦 Late Period/Graeco-Roman		🟦 Miscellaneous exhibits	
🟦 Coffins and Sarcophagi		🟦 Non-exhibition space	

Exploring the Egyptian Museum

Tuya's golden funeral mask

While not particularly large, the museum is densely packed with artifacts and anybody with more than a passing interest in ancient Egypt will need more than one visit to take everything in. When the museum is busy, long queues can form outside the room holding Tutankhamun's funeral mask. To view the mask at some leisure, it is best to visit the museum just as it opens or late in the afternoon and make straight for the Tutankhamun Galleries, visiting the rest of the museum afterwards. Independent guides tout for business at the entrance to the museum and, as the labelling inside is sparse, it may be worthwhile hiring one.

Her jewellery is on display on the second floor. The room also contains an alabaster canopic chest that was used to store the internal organs of the deceased. The chest was found in Hetepheres's tomb at Giza, with the remains of its contents still visible.

Wall frieze, known as the Meidum Geese, painted on plaster (c.2620 BC)

OLD KINGDOM

All the museum's great pieces of monumental statuary are on the ground floor. These start in the museum's atrium with King Djoser's empty-eyed statue carved in limestone nearly 5,000 years ago. It was discovered at Saqqara (see pp162–4) in his *serdab*, a small sealed room beside his Step Pyramid. Other Old Kingdom highlights on the ground floor include a statue of Khafre, builder of the middle pyramid at Giza, in Room 42. He is seated on his throne with the wings of the falcon god Horus wrapped protectively around his head, symbolizing the divine sanction of the king's rule (the term *pharaoh* was rarely used before 1500 BC). Also in Room 42, the wooden figure of Ka-Aper, a 5th-Dynasty official, puts his left foot forward in a stylized pose that suggests movement and, along with his gleaming eyes, brings the statue to life. Further examples of the vitality of the ancient artists are exhibited in Room 32 in the lifelike, seated statues of

Prince Rahotep and Princess Nofret, whose real hairline can be seen poking out from under her wig, and in the Meidum Geese panels, which were discovered at Fayoum (see p168). Room 37 contains a touchingly personal collection of alabaster ornaments and bedroom furniture, including a golden four-poster bed, an armchair and a jewellery box all of which belonged to Hetepheres, the mother of Khufu, builder of the Great Pyramid.

MIDDLE KINGDOM MODELS

The daily life of the less-exalted ancient Egyptian is well illustrated in rooms in the west wing, which hold finely detailed 11th-Dynasty models of domestic scenes. The models provide a wealth of detailed information about Egyptian life, as well as reflecting an interest in factual artistic representation. Room 22 holds an exquisite rendering in cedar wood of Senwosret I. Its companion statuette (wearing the red crown of lower Egypt) is housed in the Metropolitan Museum of Art in New York.

Model servant girl (c.2010 BC)

NEW KINGDOM

Ancient Egypt's New Kingdom represented an artistic golden age, but many of the

18th-Dynasty relief of Amenhotep III riding over bound Nubian captives

best pieces are housed at the Luxor Museum *(see p187)*. However, Room 11 holds the painted limestone face of Hatshepsut from her mortuary temple in Thebes, and Room 3 contains fine arti-facts from Amarna, the short-lived capi-tal of the 'heretic king' Akhenaten *(see p175)*. Here, the sleek muscular forms of traditional Pharaonic art are replaced by swollen bellies and almost cartoon-like elongated faces. This is particularly evident on a set of reliefs showing the sun god, Aten, whose solar rays end in hook-like hands. One of the notable exceptions to this style is an unfinished, sculpted head of Nefertiti, Akhenaten's wife, which is stunning in its human beauty.

Head of Queen Nefertiti (c.1340 BC)

TUTANKHAMUN GALLERIES

The Tutankhamun Galleries fill the upper floor's east and north wings. Entering via the southeast stairs, visitors pass the two life-size statues of the young king that stood guard at the entrance to his tomb. Out of the 5,000 items discov-ered, some 1,700 are on display, ranging from board games and hunting imple-ments to couches and beds and, of course, the fabulous

Tutankhamun's carved throne inlaid with gold and ebony

death mask. A glass cabinet is filled with some of Tutankha-mun's *shabtis*. These were small effigies of the deceased that were buried with the body to carry out any tasks that the deceased might be asked to do in the afterlife. In all, 413 *shabtis* were found in the tomb; one for each day of the year, plus foremen. Nearby is the dazzling royal "lion" throne, named after the golden lion heads and legs on each side. Aside from the craftsmanship, this throne is of great interest in that it reveals influences of the "Amarna period" when the Aten cult still thrived *(see p175)*. The Aten sun-disk and rays resemble reliefs from Amarna, and the phar-aoh's name from this peri-od, Tutankhat-en, is inscribed on the back of the throne. In the north wing is the alabaster canopic chest holding four jars with Tutankhamun-head stoppers. Room 3 holds Tutankhamun's solid gold death mask and the two inner coffins, one of gilded wood set with semi-precious gems, the other solid gold. The king's body lies in its tomb in the Valley of the Kings on the west bank of the Nile.

ROYAL MUMMY ROOMS

There is a separate fee to see the mummies, which is paya-ble at the ticket desk at the top of the southeast stairs. This allows the experience of coming face to face with some legendary kings such as Tuthmosis II, Seti I and the mighty Ramses II. The good condition of the bodies belies the fact that they all died more than 3,000 years ago. The beak-nosed face of Ramses II barely resembles his sleek bust downstairs in the New Kingdom galleries.

MISCELLANEOUS EXHIBITS

In addition to the human mummies, the museum holds a fascinating collection of ani-mal mummies in Rooms 52 and 53 (upstairs). The ancient Egyptians revered certain animals, for example the ibis and baboon were sacred to the god Thoth and cats sacred to Bastet. In the regions where these cults thrived, great numbers of these mummified creatures have been unearthed.

Across the hall, in Room 43, are 18th-Dynasty funerary artifacts from the tomb of Yuya and Tuya, the great grandparents of Tutankha-mun. Discovered in 1905, the beautiful sarcophagi and other lustrous items here are unde-servedly ignored by most visitors. Better known are the Graeco-Roman funerary paintings known as Fayoum Portraits, after the oasis where many of them were found *(see pp168–9)*; Room 14 (upstairs) contains a collection of these haunting faces, along with some of the mummies to which they were attached.

One of Tutankha-mun's gilded fans

Two galleries devoted to the Royal Tombs of Tanis and Ancient Egyptian Jewellery contain some of the muse-um's finest small pieces. Tanis was a major city in the Delta during the 21st and 22nd Dynasties *(see p239)*. In 1939 archaeologists found a series of intact royal tombs that held a marvellous haul of death masks, coffins and jewellery. One of the items, the coffin of Shashanq II is interesting not just for its striking hawk's head but also because it is made of solid silver. Rare in Egypt, silver had to be imported, making it a highly prized commodity. The Children's Museum is in an annexe beneath the main building and displays statues, miniatures and some impres-sive creations made of Lego.

Midan Ramses **6**

Map 2 D3. M *Mubarak.*

Marking the northernmost extent of central Cairo, Midan Ramses is the gateway to the city. In ancient times, when the river followed a different course, a port here served the Pharaonic city of Heliopolis. When Salah ad-Din (Saladin), ruler of Egypt, refortified Cairo in the 12th century, he built a great gate here, the Bab al-Hadid, or Iron Gate, which remained standing until 1847, when it was demolished to make way for the new railway station.

Mahattat Ramses (Ramses Station) is still Cairo's main rail terminus and the place to catch trains for most destinations, although Giza Railway Station is also in use *(see pp342–3)*. The **Egyptian National Railway Museum**, housed at the eastern end of the station, has a fascinating collection of engines, carriages and models.

The 11m- (36ft-) high colossus of Ramses II, found at Mit Rahina near Memphis *(see p165)* in 1882, stood in the square for more than 50 years. The red granite statue was restored in 1955 and erected here, becoming one of the city's most imposing landmarks. In 2006 the 3,200-year-old statue was moved in a carefully orchestrated 10-hour journey to its new home on the Giza plateau, where Cairo's Grand Egyptian Museum is currently under construction.

🏛 **Egyptian National Railway Museum**
Midan Ramses. **Map** 2 D3.
M Mubarak. **Tel** (02) 2576 3793.
◯ 8am–2pm daily. 🖼

Midan Opera and Midan Ataba **7**

Map 6 D2 & E2. M *Ataba.*

In just five months in 1868, labour gangs constructed a completely new opera house for the inaugural celebrations marking the opening of the Suez Canal. To mark the occasion, the Italian composer Giuseppe Verdi had been commissioned to write a new opera, *Aida*, but he was unable to finish it in time, so the new Cairo Opera House opened instead with a performance of Verdi's *Rigoletto*.

Modelled on Milan's La Scala and built entirely of wood, the Opera House was the loveliest landmark in central Cairo – until it was burnt to the ground in 1971. A less lovely multistorey car park was built on the site, but the square is still known as Midan Opera. In the middle of the paved plaza is a statue of Ibrahim Pasha (1789–1848), general and viceroy of Egypt, who successfully campaigned in Syria in 1832–3.

Just beyond Midan Opera is Midan Ataba, which forms a dividing point between so-called "European" Cairo to the west and the old medieval city, known as Islamic Cairo, to the east. From this point, the streets get narrower, the buildings smaller and more decrepit. The square itself can be a knot of snarled traffic, but

Ibrahim Pasha's statue, Midan Opera

Clothes stall in front of mosque in Midan Ataba

in the surrounding streets are various markets. To the northwest is a small area of secondhand bookstalls; there is a clothing market to the northeast, electronics to the southeast and, in the southwest, a few stalls sell cards and stationery. The latter run, appropriately enough, in front of the central post office, an old building with an attractive courtyard and an annexe where the **National Postal Museum** is housed. Egypt was one of the first countries in the world to issue stamps (1866). The museum is small, but there is a lot crammed into the space, including models of carriages and delivery bikes, old mail boxes and a vast collection of stamps.

Also on Midan Ataba is the **Cairo Puppet Theatre**, which puts on regular colourful puppet shows for children and adults.

🏛 **National Postal Museum**
Midan Ataba. M Ataba. **Tel** (02) 2391 0011. ◯ 10am–2pm Sat–Thu.

🎭 **Cairo Puppet Theatre**
Midan Ataba. M Ataba. **Tel** (02) 2591 0954. ◯ Oct–May: show at 11am Tue–Sun, also 6:30pm Thu & Fri.

Museum of Islamic Art **8**

Sharia Port Said. **Map** 6 E3. M Bab al-Khalq. **Tel** (02) 2390 9930. ◯ 9am–4pm daily (9am–3pm Ramadan). 🖼

Often overlooked by the crowds that throng the Egyptian Museum, this museum

Former Tiring department store designed by Oscar Horowitz in 1911, Midan Ataba

contains some beautiful pieces of medieval decorative art salvaged from the houses, mosques and palaces of Islamic Cairo at the instigation of Khedive Tawfiq. Most striking of all are the large *mashrabiyya* screens, which are constructed of thousands of individual pieces of wood. Still seen today in many old buildings, such screens shaded rooms from the sun while admitting cooling breezes. They were also important as they allowed the women of the house to look out without being seen.

The museum houses other examples of creative wood-working taken from mosques around the city, including huge ivory-inlaid doors, carved friezes and a fine 14th-century *minbar* (pulpit).

Three ornamental fountains provide the best examples of another speciality of Egyptian craftsmen – inlaid stone and marble-work. These pieces, dating from the Mamluk and Ottoman periods, would have decorated the reception halls of rich merchants' houses. Look out, also, for enamelled glass lamps; these beautiful objects, many of them decorated with stylized Arabic lettering, would have

been suspended by chains from the ceilings of mosques. Other exhibits include Persian and Turkish ceramics, illuminated manuscripts and books, and carpets and rugs. The museum has been renovated and is a true highlight among Cairo's many attractions.

Cannon yard of the Abdeen Palace Museum

Abdeen Palace Museum ❾

Sharia Abd ar-Raziq. **Map** 6 D4. Ⓜ *Mohammed Naguib.* **Tel** *(02) 2391 0130.* ◔ *9am–3pm Sat–Thu (10am–1pm Ramadan).* 🎟

Abdeen is a former royal palace, part of which is now open to the public as a museum that embraces several collections. These include displays of weaponry, presidential gifts, royal acquisitions and silver plates.

From the time of Salah ad-Din in the 12th century, Egypt was ruled from the safety of the Citadel (*see pp104–7*), but tradition was broken 700 years later by Khedive Ismail, who

A manuscript in the Museum of Islamic Art

ordered a European-style residence to be built on the edge of his new city. Designed by the French architect Rousseau, the 500-roomed palace was begun in 1863 and took over ten years to complete. Over the years, it was constantly remodelled and expanded, with the addition, in the 1930s, of a Byzantine throne room.

Following the overthrow of King Farouk in 1952, the Abdeen Palace was vacated, but later put to its present use as a venue for receiving visiting heads of state.

In the late 1980s, President Mubarak ordered that the palace be restored. The work took longer than anticipated because the palace was hit by the 1992 earthquake. The museum was inaugurated by the president in 1998.

Entered via neat gardens at the rear of the palace, the museum occupies a complex of unadorned halls; the more extravagantly decorated state rooms remain off-limits to the public. A lot of space is given over to the collection of guns, swords and daggers, many of which were gifts to Egypt's various khedives, kings and presidents. There are also displays of medals and other decorations, as well as a room of awards and gifts presented to President Mubarak. A silver-ware section contains a display of silver, crystal and *objets d'art* belonging to the family of Pasha Mohammed Ali.

Centrally located in the museum is the fountain court-yard, where the fountain is surrounded by the busts of Mohammed Ali, Khedive Ismail and King Fuad I.

Entrance to Abdeen Palace, museum and gardens

Beit as-Sennari ⑩

Harat Monge, off Sharia Khayrat.
Map 4 D2. Ⓜ *Saad Zaghloul.*

Napoleon invaded Egypt in
1798, bringing with him an
army of scientists, scholars
and artists to establish a French
cultural base in the country.
Over the next few years, they
carried out the first European
study of Egypt and published
their findings in the *Description
de l'Egypte (see p20)*.

This *beit* (house), which
was built in 1794 for Ibrahim
Katkhuda as-Sennari, an
occultist from Sudan, was
requisitioned by Napoleon
and housed many of his
artists during the occupation.
It has some fine wooden
mashrabiyya screens, an
attractive court-
yard and
well-preserved
rooms. Extensive
renovation works
have been com-
pleted, and it is
hoped that the
building will
open in the future
as the Institute for
Applied Arts, with
displays of glass-
ware, textiles,
pottery and other
work by local artists.

**Side view of *mashrabiyya* bay on
first floor of Beit as-Sennari**

Mausoleum of Saad Zaghloul ⑪

Sharia Mansour. **Map** 5 B5.
Ⓜ *Saad Zaghloul.*

Saad Zaghloul (1853–1927)
spent most of his life trying to
get the British out of Egypt.
He became a national spokes-
man for self-rule and held the
post of prime minister for a
time. Zaghloul was highly
respected, even by the foreign
governors he opposed, and
shortly after his death this vast
mausoleum was erected in his
honour. Built of granite, the
mausoleum's design echoes
that of a Pharaonic temple,
with an outward-curving
cornice and entrance flanked
by two great lotus pillars.

**Elegant, curving façade of a building in Garden
City flanked by tree-lined pavements**

It is also possible to visit
Zaghloul's house, **Beit al-
Umma** (House of the Nation),
which is just a short distance
west. Most of the rooms have
been preserved with Zaghloul's
original furnishings and
belongings still in place.

> 🏛 **Beit al-Umma**
> Sharia Darih Zaghloul. Ⓜ *Sadat.*
> 🕙 10am–5pm Tue–Sun. 📷

Garden City ⑫

Map 5 A5. Ⓜ *Sadat.*

Garden City, one of the most
attractive and tranquil of
Cairo's quarters, was created
by the British in the early
years of the 20th century as
a leafy green suburb, where
officers and administrators
could pretend they were still
living in rural England, far
from the dusty, dry streets

of Cairo. The roads
were designed to
curve and wind like
country lanes but,
instead of England's
oaks and beeches,
leafy coverage was
provided by native
palms, rubber and
mango trees.

As well as housing
the British, the villas
of this exclusive
suburb were home
to Egypt's most
prominent doctors,
lawyers, bankers
and politicians.

Today, Garden
City suffers from an
onslaught of concrete high-
rise buildings, but it remains
a very desirable address: the
British, American and several
other embassies are located
here. Garden City still offers a
welcome respite from the hustle of Cairo, however, and a
walk through the area reveals
a wonderfully eclectic array of
architecture, including the
building known as **Grey
Pillars** – the British Army's
headquarters in Egypt during
World War II. This can still be
seen on Sharia as-Suraya.

Corniche el-Nil ⑬

Map 5 A4. Ⓜ *Sadat.*

Although it is one of the
city's busiest highways, the
Corniche el-Nil is also where
Cairo comes to relax. In a city
chronically short of public
green spaces, this is as close

View across the Nile from the Corniche north of Rhoda Island

◁ **Shaira Romses and Kubri 6 October winding their way into the heart of Downtown Cairo**

as it gets to a park. Each evening, the wide pavements of the Corniche are packed with promenading families, roaming college kids, and young lovers, all enjoying the pleasant water-borne breezes and the sense of open space that the river provides.

An even better way to enjoy the river is on a *felucca*, one of the small triangular-sailed boats used on the Nile since antiquity. The boats (which can be hired by the hour) and their captains gather at various landing stages, including one opposite the Semiramis Hotel and another at Dokdok, opposite the northern tip of Rhoda Island. Lazily scudding about the river while the sun drops towards the skyline makes for a calming end to a hectic day of sightseeing.

Regnault's painting of a fleeing Mamluk, in the Manial Palace

Manial Palace ⑭

Sharia al-Saray, Rhoda. **Map** 3 B2. **Tel** (02) 2368 7495. M Sayyida Zeinab. ◯ 9am–4pm daily. 📷

Located on the northern tip of the island of Rhoda is the Manial Palace, a former royal residence. It it open to the public, although parts of it may be closed for renovation, so check ahead. The palace was built for Prince Mohammed Ali Tawfiq, a descendant of Egypt's famed ruler Mohammed Ali, and the uncle of King Farouk. It was constructed between 1899 and 1929 and is a curious ensemble of

five separate buildings in a variety of Islamic styles. Beside the mock-Medieval gateway is a Moorish tower attached to the Turkish-tiled Mosque of Mohammed Ali. Nearby, the Hunting Museum has a somewhat grim display of over 300 mounted gazelle heads strung along its narrow gallery.

The eccentrically contrived design extends to the interiors. The Main Residence is a series of rooms decorated in a mixture of styles. The Syrian room has an elaborately painted wooden ceiling, an Ottoman room is furnished with turquoise ceramics from Anatolia, while the Egyptian corner has windows featuring *mashrabiyya* screens. Also included among the valuable displays is a painting of a Mamluk and his mount leaping over the Citadel walls. The painting, by Henri Regnault (1843–71), hangs in the Blue Salon, and depicts an alleged incident that took place during Mohammed Ali's suppression of the Mamluks' 1826 revolt.

Behind the residence, through the banyans, palms and Indian rubber trees, is the Throne Hall, complete with red carpet, sunburst ceiling and portraits of the prince's illustrious forebears. While Prince Mohammed Ali Tawfiq never attained the throne, he was able to hold his own court here.

Detail of Mohammed Ali Mosque, Manial Palace

Mahmoud Khalil Museum ⑮

1 Sharia Kafour, off Sharia Giza. **Map** 3 A1. **Tel** (02) 3748 2142. M Dokki. ◯ 10am–5pm Tue–Sun. 📷

It may come as a surprise to learn that Cairo has a fine collection of Impressionist paintings. They were amassed by Mohammed Mahmoud Khalil (1876–1953), a devout Francophile and patron of the arts, and an important figure on the political scene during the 1930s and 40s. Khalil bequeathed his art collection to the state, along with the house – a beautiful late-19th-century Parisian-style mansion overlooking the Nile.

Khalil's paintings were removed when the house was taken over as the official residence during Sadat's term as Egyptian president (1970–81). In the early 1990s, after the assassination of Sadat, however, the house was refurbished and returned to the public domain. The paintings on show include works by Degas, Ingres, Monet, Pissarro, Renoir, Sisley and Toulouse-Lautrec. Pride of place goes to Gauguin's *La Vie et la Mort* and Van Gogh's *Genêts et Coquelicots*. No longer on display is Van Gogh's *Poppy Flowers*, which was stolen in 2010.

Façade of Cairo's Mahmoud Khalil Museum

Sculpture in the grounds of the Opera House Complex

Opera House Complex ⓰

Sharia at-Tahrir, Gezira. **Map** 1 A5. Ⓜ *Opera.* **Tel** *(02) 2739 0144.*

A gift to Egypt from Japan, the Opera House Complex was opened in 1988, replacing the original Opera House, which burned down in 1971 *(see p78)*. At the heart of the complex is the **New Cairo Opera House**, where a busy programme of classical music and dance, including visits from international performers such as the Bolshoi Ballet, is staged *(see pp310–13)*.

Situated across the lawn, the **Museum of Egyptian Modern Art** displays the work of Egyptian artists since 1908. One who deserves far greater recognition than he is currently given is Mahmoud Said (1897–1964), whose use of warm, glowing colours and subject matter of dignified, proud *fellaheen* (peasants) is reminiscent of the Mexican artist Diego Rivera (1886–1957). Several of Said's paintings are displayed in the museum. There

are two more art galleries within the grounds: the Nile Gallery and the Hanager Gallery, which both host changing exhibitions of contemporary work.

> 🏛 **Museum of Egyptian Modern Art**
> Opera House Complex, Gezira.
> Ⓜ *Gezira.* **Tel** *(02) 2736 6667.*
> ◷ *9am–2pm, 5–9pm Tue–Sun.* 🌐

Cairo Tower ⓱

Sharia Hadayek el Zuhreya. **Map** 1 A5. Ⓜ *Opera.* **Tel** *(02) 2736 5112.* ◷ *9am–midnight daily.* 🌐

The southern half of Gezira (the Arabic word for "island") is almost completely flat, making it the ideal site for the 185-m (610-ft) Cairo Tower, which affords excellent views of the city and is beautifully lit at night. Built in the late 1950s, the tower takes the form of a latticework tube that fans out slightly at the top, supposedly in imitation of the lotus blossom. From the top, it is possible to make out the easternmost extent of Cairo, where the dark grey buildings run up against the cliff face of the Muqattam Hills. To the west, the Pyramids mark the limits of the city and the start of the desert, while below the Nile flows north to the Mediterranean, slicing Cairo in two.

The best time to go up the tower is at sunset, when millions of lights twinkle into life, accompanied by the haunting evening call to prayer.

River Promenade ⓲

Gezira. **Map** 1 B5. Ⓜ *Opera.*

Created in the late 1990s, Gezira's river promenade is a wide paved avenue down by the Nile, with fine views of the central city skyline opposite. The promenade starts at the foot of the elegant Qasr el-Nil Bridge, which was designed and built by Dorman Long & Co., the British architects responsible for Australia's Sydney Harbour Bridge.

Between the promenade and the main road is the small, neat **Andalusian Garden**, with lawns, benches and an obelisk from Heliopolis. A small admission charge keeps out the crowds, and it makes for a restful break. On the street beside the garden, *hantours* (also called *caleches*) wait for hire. A quick spin in one of these horse-drawn black carriages is a fine way to see the island – but expect to pay inflated

Horse-drawn carriage (hantour) for hire on the River Promenade

prices for the pleasure. Moored off the promenade is a string of former Nile cruisers, most of which have now been converted into upmarket floating restaurants and bars *(see pp290–95).*

Zamalek ⓳

Gezira. **Map** 1 A3. 🚗

Occupying the northern half of Gezira, Zamalek is a well-to-do residential district. The main thoroughfare Sharia 26 July, which runs diagonally through the area, is the best place to come for European-style comforts. Simonds makes a classic venue for a coffee or an orange juice, and Maison Thomas does great pizza and desserts. European newspapers and magazines are sold at local news stands

View from Rhoda Island of New Cairo Opera House and Cairo Tower

Entrance to Cairo Marriott Hotel, formerly the Gezira Palace

and there are a couple of well-stocked supermarkets, plus several bars which attract a mixed Egyptian and expat crowd. Zamalek's most prominent landmark is the twin orange towers of the Cairo Marriott. This atmospheric and luxurious hotel *(see p270)* was built around the palace created for Empress Eugénie of France when she attended the opening of the Suez Canal in 1869. It has an attractive garden terrace, open to non-residents, which is an excellent spot for lunch or a beer.

Tucked away behind the Cairo Marriott is a small 19th-century, Islamic-style villa, now home to the **Islamic Ceramics Museum** and **Gezira Arts Centre**. This little-visited museum displays exquisite ceramics from Egypt, Iran, Morocco and Andalusia, while the Arts Centre, located in the basement of the same building, hosts changing exhibitions by contemporary artists. To the north of the island, the quiet, orderly streets are a treasure trove of splendid villas and mansion blocks in a variety of styles, from Gothic to Baroque to Arts and Crafts. Many of the finest properties here are embassies, but the **Greater Cairo Library** is open to visitors. This is now Egypt's main resource for information about its capital and contains many interesting books, maps, documents and surveys relating to the history of the city.

🏛 **Islamic Ceramics Museum and Gezira Arts Centre**
1 Sharia Sheikh al-Marsafi. *Tel* (02) 2737 3298. ⭕ 10am–2pm, 5–9pm daily. 📷

🏛 **Greater Cairo Library**
15 Sharia Mohammed Mazhar. *Tel* (02) 2736 2278. ⭕ 10am–2pm & 4–10pm Sat–Thu.

HOUSEBOATS

On the narrow stretch of water separating Zamalek from the Nile's western bank sits a small flotilla of tatty, two-storey wooden houseboats. They are all that remains of the floating neighbourhood that once lined the river from the city's southern edge to the north. The community flourished in the early 20th century when, supplied with gas, electricity, fresh water and telephones, the boats provided homes or served as cafés, casinos and nightclubs. In 1943, on a houseboat owned by belly-dancer Hekmat Fahmy, a German spy, John Eppler, was arrested. The episode formed the basis of Ken Follett's thriller *The Key to Rebecca*. Most boats are now private residences although a couple are garish cafés.

One of the houseboats moored near 15th May Bridge

Looking south from 15th May Bridge towards high-rise buildings lining the waterfront in west Zamalek

ISLAMIC CAIRO

Sacks of spices in Khan al-Khalili

Following their conquest of Egypt in 641 AD, the Muslims built their city, Al-Fustat, on what is now the southern border of modern Cairo. Successive dynasties established their own capital, each one further to the northeast of the old, until Salah ad-Din built the impressive Citadel (*Al-Qalaa*) on a rocky spur and settled the capital's location. During the Mamluk era which lasted from 1250 to 1517, a wealth of mosques, mausoleums and Islamic buildings were added. Today, Islamic Cairo's maze of narrow, congested streets teems with life, challenging the senses with its unique blend of sights, sounds and smells, and vivid glimpses of the past. Most mosques are open to non-Muslims, and the majority do not charge an entrance fee.

SIGHTS AT A GLANCE

Mosques and Historic Buildings
Al-Azhar Park 28
Al-Ghouri Complex 7
Bein al-Qasreen 8
Beit as-Suhaymi 13
Beit Zeinab Khatoun
  and Beit al-Harawi 5
The Citadel pp104–7 22
Dervish Theatre 25
Mosque of al-Aqmar 12
Mosque of al-Azhar 4
Mosque of al-Hakim 15
Mosque of ar-Rifai 24
Mosque of as-Salih Talai 20
Mosque of Ibn Tulun pp110–11 27
Mosque of Sayyidna al-Hussein 3
Mosque of Sultan Hassan 23
Northern Cemetery 17
Qasr Beshtak 9
Sabil-Kuttab of Abdel
  Katkhuda 11
Sabil-Kuttab of Qaitbey 26
Sharia al-Muizz
  li-Din Allah 14
Wikala of al-Ghouri 6

Bazaars and Markets
Carpet Bazaar 18
Khan al-Khalili 1
Sharia Muski 2
Tentmakers' Market 21

Museums
Textile Museum 10

Walls and Gates
Bab Zuweila 19
Northern Walls and Gates 16

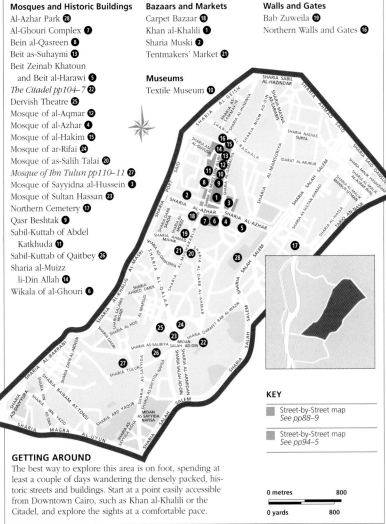

KEY

▨	Street-by-Street map *See pp88–9*
▨	Street-by-Street map *See pp94–5*

0 metres   800

0 yards   800

GETTING AROUND
The best way to explore this area is on foot, spending at least a couple of days wandering the densely packed, historic streets and buildings. Start at a point easily accessible from Downtown Cairo, such as Khan al-Khalili or the Citadel, and explore the sights at a comfortable pace.

◁ Dominating the skyline of Islamic Cairo, the silver domes of the Mosque of Mohammed Ali in the Citadel

Street-by-Street: Around Khan al-Khalili

Stall on Al-Muizz li-Din Allah

Any exploration of Islamic Cairo begins at the medieval bazaar of Khan al-Khalili, the commercial heart of the quarter. The original Khan area lay between Al-Muizz li-Din Allah and Midan Hussein but today it encompasses a wider area made up of several markets selling everything from souvenirs to spices. Traders line the streets all the way to the old city gates, but the bazaar's narrow alleyways are at their densest and most beguiling in the original Khan area. The quarter's mosques, houses and palaces offer an escape from the incessant sales pitches.

Mosque of al-Ashraf Barsbey
Built in 1423, this mosque boasts a beautifully-carved wooden pulpit, inlaid with ivory.

Al-Muizz li-Din Allah
This narrow thoroughfare was for centuries the main route through the medieval city of Cairo.

Pedestrian overpass

★ **Al-Ghouri Complex**
The mosque-madrassa and mausoleum complex of Al-Ghouri is housed in twin striped buildings and boasts a unique, red-chequered minaret ❼

Egyptian Pancake House
(see p291)

Mosque of Abu Dahab

KEY

 Suggested route

Wikala of al-Ghouri
This wikala *or caravanserai is Cairo's best preserved example of a medieval merchants' hostel. It is now a cultural centre that hosts whirling dervish performances* ❻

STAR SIGHTS

★ Mosque of al-Azhar
★ Khan al-Khalili
★ Al-Ghouri Complex

★ Khan al-Khalili
Filled with glittering paraphernalia, this bazaar is Cairo at its most magical. The lanes of the original Khan area are lined with shops selling everything from waterpipes and handicrafts to silks and spices ❶

Medieval gates

LOCATOR MAP
See Street Finder Map 2

0 metres	50
0 yards	50

Mosque of Sayyidna al-Hussein
The holiest site in Cairo, this mosque is said to contain the head of Hussein, grandson of the Prophet Mohammed. Built in 1870 on the site of a 12th-century mosque, it is off-limits to non-Muslims ❸

SIKKET AL-BADESTAN

MIDAN HUSSEIN

Fishawi's coffee house *(see p90)*

Sharia Muski
This busy market street is where Cairenes come for serious bargains on everything from wedding dresses to plastic furniture and children's toys ❷

SHARIA AL-AZHAR

Pedestrian underpass

★ Mosque of al-Azhar
Founded in AD 970, this mosque and centre for Islamic study is one of the oldest in the city. It displays a mix of architectural styles including this 18th-century Gate of the Barbers ❹

One of two medieval, carved stone gates in Khan al-Khalili

Khan al-Khalili ❶

Map 2 F5. 🚌 or taxi to Midan al-Hussein. ◯ daily (most shops closed Sundays).

Built in 1382 by Garkas al-Khalili, Master of Horses to Sultan Barquq, Khan al-Khalili is one of the biggest bazaars in the Middle East. This is the oriental bazaar of fable, where gold, silver, brass and copper goods glitter enticingly in the cave-like interiors, and sacks overflowing with exotic spices fill the air with their pungent scents. Its maze of narrow, canvas-covered alleyways is crammed with shops selling a huge variety of goods. Here, too, traditional Egyptian crafts, such as dyeing, carving and sewing, are practised as they have been for centuries.

Khan al-Khalili is, of course, also a major tourist attraction. Hordes of tourists arrive here, by the coachload, to haggle and stock up on the kitsch trinkets and souvenirs that are sold in nearly every shop in the main part of the bazaar.

The bazaar grew up around several *khans* (also known as *wikalas*), which served as both warehouses and lodgings for travelling merchant caravans. Most have been swallowed up by later structures, but a few remain. On a side street off Sharia Muski, stairs lead to the upper level of the **Wikala of Silahdar** (1837), where the former living quarters can be made out, ranged around the central courtyard. Two carved stone gates in the Badestan area, added during the reign of Sultan al-Ghouri (1501–16), are the oldest surviving part of Khan al-Khalili.

Apart from exploring and haggling, the bazaar's other great attraction is **Fishawi's**, located in an alley one block in from Midan al-Hussein. Open day and night for the past 200 years, it is possibly Cairo's oldest coffee house and is crammed with small copper-topped tables, while huge antique mirrors line the walls. Here, patrons puff on *sheeshas* (waterpipes) and sip mint tea round the clock.

For further information on shopping in Egypt and Cairo, see Shopping in Cairo (*pp150–51*) and What to Buy (*pp306–7*).

Apple vendor in the bustling street market of Sharia Muski

Sharia Muski ❷

Runs between Midan Ataba and Midan al-Hussein. **Map** 6 F3, 2 F5.

In a city that is bursting at the seams, Sharia Muski is possibly the single most crowded street of all. Before Sharia al-Azhar was bulldozed through the area in the mid-20th century, Muski was the main route between Khan al-Khalili and downtown Cairo. The street is crammed with budget-end clothing emporia and bargain-basement market stalls that are piled high with synthetic goods: clothing that is guaranteed to bobble and fade; wedding outfits, plastic toys and garden furniture. At the Khan al-Khalili end of the street, clothing gives way to perfume and "antiques" but, just before Midan al-Hussein, there is one last glorious burst of glitzy glamour in the form of outfitters selling lavishly decorated belly-dancing outfits.

The sounds that fill Sharia Muski are as much part of the experience as the goods on display. The sales patter of the stall-keepers, the warning cries and hisses of barrow-men as they push through the crowds, drink vendors selling liquorice water, all contribute to the lively character of the street.

Mosque of Sayyidna al-Hussein ❸

Midan al-Hussein. **Map** 2 F5. 🚫 to non-Muslims.

This is the most important mosque in all Egypt, so sacred that only Muslims are allowed to enter. Hundreds come here to pray each day, and as many as 10,000 on Fridays. Replacing an earlier 12th-century mosque, it was built in 1870 and is reputed to shelter one of the holiest relics of Islam – the head of

Brass and leather goods for sale in Khan al-Khalili

Domes and minarets of Mosque of al-Azhar seen from Zeinab Khatoun

Al-Hussein, grandson of the Prophet Mohammed. After the Prophet's death in AD 632, control of the caliphate was assumed by the Umayyad clan. The Prophet's son-in-law Ali, claiming to be the natural successor, took up arms and was killed. His son, Al-Hussein, led a revolt but died in AD 680 at the battle of Kerbala, Iraq, where the rest of his body is said to lie. Islam is still divided into followers of Al-Hussein (Shiites) and Sunnis, who hold the Umayyads to be the true successors to Mohammed.

During the annual ten-day Moulid of Al-Hussein and other feast days, thousands throng Midan al-Hussein to enjoy the fair and join in the festivities.

Mosque of al-Azhar ❹

Sharia al-Azhar. **Map** 2 F5. ⬛ daily. ⬤ for noon prayers Fri. 📷

Just southwest of Midan al-Hussein is one of Cairo's most venerable institutions. Al-Azhar was founded in AD 970 as the main mosque and centre of learning for the city that had just been built by the new Fatimid rulers from North Africa. Though the Fatimids were swept from power some 200 years later, their mosque and university remained central to religious and political life in Egypt.

Today, the Sheikh of al-Azhar is the highest religious authority in the land and the university the most revered

centre of learning in the Sunni Islamic world. Although now housed in several modern campuses around the country, including a separate faculty for women, the university continues to provide free education and board for Muslim students from all over the world. They come to study the Quran and Islamic law along with other traditional subjects such as grammar, logic and rhetoric.

Since a reorganization of Al-Azhar in 1961, faculties have been formed for the study of medicine, agriculture, engineering and commerce.

Little remains of the original structure of the mosque, which now exhibits a mix of styles from different periods. The double-arched **Gate of the Barbers**, where students traditionally had their heads shaved, dates from the mid-18th century. Visitors now enter through this gate, which leads into an enclosure flanked by two *madrassas* (places of study). Both *madrassas* date to the early part of the 14th century; the one on the left is usually open and is worth visiting to see the beautifully ornate *mihrab* (niche indicating the direction of Mecca).

In the centre of the mosque is the main *sahn* (courtyard), which dates as far back as Fatimid times. Although classes are no longer held here, small circles of students still come

to sit in the peace and shade of its arcades to memorize their Quranic texts, much as they have done for centuries.

Before entering the mosque, women must cover their heads; no admission will be granted to anyone with bare legs.

Beit Zeinab Khatoun and Beit al-Harawi ❺

Harat al-Azhar. **Map** 2 F5. ⬛ 9am–5pm daily. 📷

Running between the south-wall of Al-Azhar Mosque and a long, low, medieval *wikala*, a narrow alley leads to a small garden square. Projecting into the square on its northern side is Beit Zeinab Khatoun, an Ottoman-era house (*beit*) originally built in 1486 and restored in the 1990s. On the southern side of the square is the restored Beit al-Harawi, built in 1731 as the home of a rich Cairo merchant.

Both houses are beautiful examples of the sophisticated domestic architecture that once filled the city. Beit al-Harawi, in particular, contains some fine *mashrabiyya* (carved wooden screens) and elegant painted ceilings. Built around central courtyards, both houses are designed to stay as cool as possible with their airy rooms, shaded stone floors and interior fountains.

The houses are open to visitors during the day and, since being restored, also operate as cultural centres, where regular performances of music and theatre are staged (*see pp308–11*).

Wooden *mashrabiyya* screen covering the window of Beit Zeinab Khatoun

Tapestry of women carrying water, an example of the craft items on sale in the Wikala of al-Ghouri

Wikala of al-Ghouri ❻

Off Sharia al-Azhar. **Map** 2 F5.
🕐 8am–5pm daily. 📷

Also known as *khans* or caravanserais, *wikalas* were hostels used by merchants arriving in caravans from North Africa, Arabia and the east. As well as rooms, they provided stables, storage space and a place where merchants could trade. *Wikalas* were typically rectangular in shape with a central courtyard and a main gate that could be locked at night. During the Mamluk era, Cairo's golden age, some of the city's *wikalas* were up to four or five storeys high. Unfortunately, none of these have survived. The finest remaining example is the Wikala of al-Ghouri, which dates from the early 17th century and is three storeys high. It boasts a fine courtyard and beautiful *mashrabiyya* (carved wooden screens) on the upper floors. Parts of the building serve as an arts and crafts centre, with rooms converted into artists' studios and shops. The courtyard is used as a concert hall, theatre and venue for the free Whirling Dervish performances that take place on Monday, Wednesday and Saturday nights *(see below)*.

Carpenter at work in the Wikala of al-Ghouri

Al-Ghouri Complex ❼

Sharia al-Muizz li-Din Allah. **Map** 2 F5.
Tel (02) 2511 0472. **Mosque**
🕐 9am–midnight daily. **Mausoleum**
🕐 9am–5pm daily. 🌙 11:30am–1:30pm Fri. 📷

One of the finest buildings in Cairo, the Al-Ghouri Complex is made up of twin, boldly striped black-and-white buildings situated opposite each other across a narrow market street. Dating from 1505, the structure was constructed by Qansuh al-Ghouri, the last of the powerful Mamluk sultans, who ruled between 1501–16 and died at the hands of the Ottoman Turks. The sultan's body was never recovered from the battlefield and his mausoleum, the building on the east side of the complex, was used for his short-lived successor, Tumanbey. The Al-Ghouri's four beautifully renovated floors and courtyards deserve exploration. The interiors are stunning, although the stairs up to the roof are not for the faint of heart. Opposite the mausoleum, on the west side of the complex, is the Al-Ghouri Mosque and Madrassa offering fine views from its rooftop. Of particular note is the mosque's unique square minaret which is topped by five bulbs. A replica of the 18th century wooden roof that linked the two buildings recreates the covered area that once housed the city's silk market.

WHIRLING DERVISHES

Cairo's Whirling Dervishes are members of the Mawlaiyya sect of Sufis, followers of a semi-mystical branch of Islam. Sufis were originally associated with poverty and self-denial and wore rough woollen clothes next to their skin – the name Sufi originates from *suf*, the Arabic for wool. Sufis aspire, through meditation, recitation, dance and music, to attain union with God. The Whirling Dervishes, so called because of their ritual spinning dance, offer a rare glimpse of this otherwise underground phenomenon. The group performs thrice-weekly at the Wikala of al-Ghouri. Questions of authenticity aside, the show is a marvellous spectacle. Dancers turn like spinning tops while a line of musicians create a hypnotic pulse, tossing their heads jerkily from side to side. Performances are popular, so it is recommended that you pick up a free ticket at 6:30pm and return at 8pm for the start. See p308 for more details.

Whirling Dervishes performing their mesmerising dance ritual

Fine architectural detail at the three-storey Wikala of al-Ghouri

Minarets and Domes

One of the greatest achievements of Cairo's medieval artisans was the decorative carving of stone surfaces, seen at its best on the city's myriad minarets and domes. The craft flourished under the Mamluk dynasty (1250–1517) during which time minarets evolved from short, stubby towers, with little decorative detail, to slender, elegant spires boasting carved balustrades and stalactites. The stone domes of the city's mausoleums are also a

Crescent moon symbol

characteristic of Mamluk architecture, beginning their development in the early 14th century and reaching their zenith in the latter part of the 15th century. Originally small and plain, domes rapidly progressed to vast structures adorned, in the first instance, with a simple rib pattern followed by zigzags and finally explosions of star patterns and floral arabesques. The flourishing of this art form was brought to an abrupt end by the Ottoman invasion.

MINARETS

These elegant towers, attached to Cairo's mosques, fall broadly into three categories: the square-based towers of the Fatimid period, the lavish three-tiered spires of the late-Mamluk era and the pencil minarets of the Ottoman Turks.

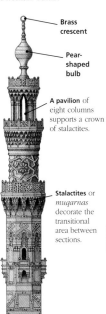

Brass crescent

Pear-shaped bulb

A pavilion of eight columns supports a crown of stalactites.

Stalactites or *muqarnas* decorate the transitional area between sections.

This three-tiered *spire, adorning the Mosque of Qaitbey (see p102), displays the elaborate decorative stonework typical of late Mamluk minarets.*

Pepperpot caps adorn these early, square-based minarets.

This external staircase is a unique feature of the Mosque of Ibn Tulun.

The minaret of *the AD 879 Mosque of Ibn Tulun (see pp110–11) was inspired by the great Mosque of Samarra in Mesopotamia.*

Simple wooden railings and modest stalactite decoration were favoured by the Ottomans.

This simple minaret *of the 1528 Mosque of Suleiman Pasha (see p107) has typical Ottoman styling such as a pointed cap and little decorative detail.*

STONE DOMES

Developed by the Mamluks, decorating domes became an increasingly sophisticated art form.

The dome *of Madrassa Sultaniya (c.1370) in the City of the Dead (see p103) has a rib design.*

This cupola, *in the City of the Dead, illustrates the progression to a more elaborate zigzag pattern.*

The dome *of the Mosque of Qaitbey (1474) combines geometric and floral designs in its decoration.*

Street-by-Street: Fatimid Cairo

Founded by the conquering Fatimid dynasty in AD 969 as "Al-Qahira" (the Victorious), Islamic Cairo became the imperial capital of Egypt. Although they created an extensive royal quarter of grand palaces and mosques hidden by towering walls, little remains of the Fatimids' architectural achievements. Later dynasties recycled the earlier monuments, constructing their own displays of grandeur, such as the Mamluk complexes on al-Muizz li-Din Allah and fine Ottoman residences. Today, the narrow streets of this small quarter serve as a living museum of medieval architecture.

A horse-drawn cart

Sabil-Kuttab of Abdel Katkhuda
In the centre of what was once Cairo's main street is one of many sabil-kuttabs (structures with fountains) in Islamic Cairo ⓫

Madrassa of Sultan Barquq
(see p97)

Textile Museum

★ Bein al-Qasreen
Once the site of two Fatimid palaces, Bein al-Qasreen is now dominated by the minarets of three grand Mamluk complexes ⓼

Madrassa and Mausoleum of Sultan an-Nasr Mohammed
(see p96)

The Madrassa and Mausoleum of Sultan Qalawun is an example of the ambition of Mamluk architecture. As well as the madrassa and mausoleum it also houses an ancient hospital *(see p96)*.

BEIN AL-QASREEN

SHARIA BEIT AL-QADI

MIDAN BEIT AL-QADI

Khan al-Khalili

Glass Goods
Locally made "Muski" glassware can be found in the alleys off Sharia al-Muizz li-Din Allah.

Qasr Beshtak
This 14th-century palace affords fine views over Islamic Cairo from its upper storeys ⓽

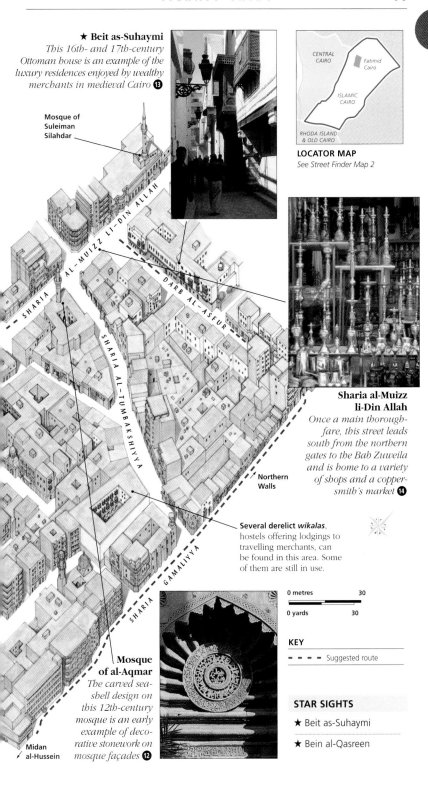

★ **Beit as-Suhaymi**
*This 16th- and 17th-century
Ottoman house is an example of the
luxury residences enjoyed by wealthy
merchants in medieval Cairo* **13**

Mosque of
Suleiman
Silahdar

LOCATOR MAP
See Street Finder Map 2

CENTRAL
CAIRO

Fatimid
Cairo

ISLAMIC
CAIRO

RHODA ISLAND
& OLD CAIRO

SHARIA AL-MUIZZ LI-DIN ALLAH

DARB AL-ASFUR

SHARIA AL-TUMBAKSHIYYA

SHARIA GAMALIYYA

**Sharia al-Muizz
li-Din Allah**
*Once a main thorough-
fare, this street leads
south from the northern
gates to the Bab Zuweila
and is home to a variety
of shops and a copper-
smith's market* **14**

Northern
Walls

Several derelict *wikalas*,
hostels offering lodgings to
travelling merchants, can
be found in this area. Some
of them are still in use.

0 metres		30
0 yards		30

KEY

- – – – Suggested route

**Mosque
of al-Aqmar**
*The carved sea-
shell design on
this 12th-century
mosque is an early
example of deco-
rative stonework on
mosque façades* **12**

Midan
al-Hussein

STAR SIGHTS

★ Beit as-Suhaymi

★ Bein al-Qasreen

Detail of inscription and motifs in the Mausoleum of Sultan Qalawun

Bein al-Qasreen ❽

Sharia al-Muizz li-Din Allah. **Map** 2 F4.

Bein al-Qasreen, which translates as "between the two palaces," is the local name for the stretch of Sharia al-Muizz li-Din Allah that runs immediately to the north of Khan al-Khalili. The name is a testament to the tenacity of history in Cairo, because the two palaces to which it refers ceased to exist more than 600 years ago. Facing each other across a busy public square, the two palaces formed the splendid centrepiece of Al-Qahira (the Victorious), the original Fatimid city, which was founded in AD 969.

Subsequent dynasties replaced them with buildings of their own, but the area was always reserved for only the grandest of building projects.

Today, Bein al-Qasreen is lined on the western side by a sequence of spectacular façades, belonging primarily to three early Mamluk religious complexes. The most southerly is the **Madrassa and Mausoleum of Sultan Qalawun**, which also happens to be the oldest of the three, having been completed in 1279. Three hundred Crusader prisoners took part in its construction, which was completed in

only 13 months. The Christian involvement may account for its almost Gothic façade. Inside, a long, dark corridor separates the *madrassa*, on the left, from the mausoleum, on the right. The latter is one of the most spectacular and stunning interiors in Cairo. Inspired by Jerusalem's Dome of the Rock, it has an octagonal arrangement of columns, two pairs of which are massive granite pillars that originated in some Pharaonic structure. The walls are covered in vivid geometric mosaics tracing the name "Mohammed" in florid strokes. Lavish amounts of gold gleam as they are picked out by the coloured rays of sunlight filtering through countless stained-glass windows.

View across the rooftops to the balconies on the minaret of the Madrassa of Sultan Barquq

Despite the sumptuous restored interior, the complex as a whole receives few visitors, which adds to its charm. Built as part of the complex set back from the street, is a *maristan* or hospital which treated the sick for free and amazingly, over 700 years later, still operates as a clinic.

Continuing north, adjoining the Qalawun complex is the lower, less expansive façade of the **Madrassa and Mausoleum of Sultan an-Nasr Mohammed**. It was erected between 1299 and 1304 by a sultan who, despite being deposed twice, fought back to regain the throne on both occasions and reigned for a total of 42 years. During this time, he endowed Cairo with over 200 buildings, the best known of which is his mosque at the Citadel *(see pp104–7).*

NAGUIB MAHFOUZ

1966 novel by Naguib Mahfouz

The West was introduced to the work of writer Naguib Mahfouz (1911–2006) in 1988, when he won the Nobel Prize for Literature. Mahfouz grew up in the back streets of Islamic Cairo, and his work was greatly influenced by the neighbourhoods and people of his youth. His best-known work is *The Cairo Trilogy*, a vast work spanning the generations of one family. Each title in the trilogy takes its name from a particular locale: the first, *Bein al-Qasreen*, was translated as *Palace Walk*. The award of the Nobel Prize rekindled opposition to Mahfouz's earlier novel *Children of the Alley*, which caused uproar when it was serialized in *Al-Ahram* in 1959. In 1994 the author was attacked near his home, receiving injuries that affected his physical ability to write.

Dome and minaret in Bein al-Qasreen

Sultan an-Nasr's monument in Bein al-Qasreen has also been restored and now houses a mosque, madrassa and tomb. The exterior boasts a detailed North African-style stuccowork covering the minaret and the Gothic black and white doorway. The latter was removed from a church in Acre (now Akko, Israel) and re-erected in Cairo to mark the final defeat of the Crusaders by the Mamluks in the Holy Land in 1291.

The northernmost building in Bein al-Qasreen is the **Madrassa of Sultan Barquq**, built around 1384–6. While a *madrassa* does not appear to be noticeably different from a mosque on the outside, it is actually a school for teaching Islamic law. Barquq's complex, has four doors, each intricately decorated with bronze, leading off the main courtyard to four separate sets of classrooms and student cells – one for each of the schools of Islamic law. The mausoleum, just off the prayer hall, resembles an ornate jewellery box, with marbled walls under a lovely gilded dome. It is not Barquq but rather his daughter who lies here: the sultan is buried in the Northern Cemetery (*see pp102–3*).

The three complexes that make up Bein al-Qasreen make an excellent break from the hustle and bustle of the market streets all around. They are especially magical after dark, when the lighting is dim and atmospheric.

C Madrassa and Mausoleum of Sultan Qalawun
Map 2 F4. ☐ 9am–9pm daily.

C Madrassa and Mausoleum of Sultan an-Nasr Mohammed
Map 2 F4. ☐ 9am–9pm daily.

C Madrassa of Sultan Barquq
Map 2 F4. ☐ 9am–9pm daily.

Qasr Beshtak ❾

Sharia al-Muizz li-Din Allah.
Map 2 F4. ☐ daily. ● 11:30am–1:30pm Fri. ☑

Qasr Beshtak or Beshtak Palace is easy to miss: from the outside it presents just a plain, two-storey façade, decorated with a few small *mashrabiyya* windows. However, a narrow alleyway on the left leads to a courtyard with steps leading up to an impressive reception hall, complete with a marble floor and inlaid panelling.

Beshtak was a powerful emir in the 14th century, a notorious rake who married the sultan's daughter and accrued great wealth and influence. His palace, which was built in 1334, was the sumptuous venue for fabulous balls.

During the Mamluk era, however, great wealth and influence was a dangerously double-edged sword, and so it was almost inevitable that a jealous rival succeeded in having Emir Beshtak arrested and executed, at the same time seizing all his possessions.

From what is now the roof of the palace (but which used to be just the second storey of five), there is an excellent panoramic view of Islamic Cairo, looking down Sharia

Mashrabiyya screens on the façade of Qasr Beshtak

al-Muizz li-Din Allah and over the rooftops to the impressive collection of minarets and domes around the Citadel.

The second-floor chamber (*qaa*), with its *mashrabiyya*-screened galleries, stained-glass windows and gilt and painted wood panelling is a fine example of a private chamber of the period.

The entrance ticket for the Qasr Beshtak also includes admission to the Sabil-Kuttab of Abdel Katkhuda (*see p98*).

RECYCLING HISTORY

Since Pharaonic times, the rocky Muqattam Hills to the east of Cairo have been quarried for stone. However, it was often found to be more convenient to use materials from closer to hand – in particular, from other buildings. Throughout history, Cairo has been shaken by earthquakes that have reduced great swathes of the city to rubble. Just as frequently, succeeding dynasties have not been above dismantling the existing monuments and reusing the materials for new ones. The Mausoleum of Qalawun, for example, is supported on red granite pillars of Pharaonic origin, while the Mosque of an-Nasr Mohammed at the Citadel (*see pp104–7*) has a courtyard arcade that is made up of oddments of Roman and Coptic columns and capitals. Most striking of all, though, are the blocks embedded in the interior corridors and rooms of the Northern Walls, which are carved with ancient Egyptian gazelles, hippos and figures – clear evidence of the fact that the stone for these fortifications was scavenged from the ruins of the ancient city of Memphis.

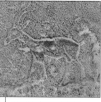

Pharaonic carving on Cairo's Northern Walls

Textile Museum ⑩

Sharia al-Muizz li-Din Allah.
Map 2 F4. ◯ *9am–7:30pm daily (to 9:30pm in summer).* 🏷

Housed within a restored *sabil-kuttab* (a school built around a fountain), this museum presents the 7,000 year old history of weaving in Egypt. On display are pieces of linen from the time of the pharaohs, including shrouds and the decorated bandages used to wrap mummies. The vibrant designs of the Coptic weaving tradition, whose geometric patterns and floral motifs were incorporated by Islamic artists, are showcased. Immense black and golden woven coverings made for the *kaba'a* in Mecca (the structure at the centre of the mosque), which were produced in Egypt up until the 20th century, are impressive. The museum is, as yet, a relatively undiscovered place and a quiet respite from the hustle of nearby Khan al-Khalili.

Sabil-Kuttab of Abdel Katkhuda ⑪

Sharia al-Muizz li-Din Allah.
Map 2 F4. ◯ *daily.* ◑ *11:30am–1:30pm Fri.* 🏷

Islamic Cairo is dotted with odd-shaped buildings with large windows covered by lacy grilles and what looks like a water trough where the windowsill should be. The *sabil*, or fountain, was kept full of fresh water and copper

Carved stone stalactites between ribbed arches on Mosque al-Aqmar

cups were attached to the grille so that passers-by could help themselves to a drink. Wealthy warlords and nobles would build a *sabil* to curry favour with both the city populace and their god above.

On an upper floor was often a terrace open to the breezes on three sides, which was set aside for the teaching of the Quran and known as a *kuttab*. Thus a *sabil-kuttab* provided two things commended by the Prophet Mohammed – water for the thirsty and spiritual enlightenment for the ignorant.

Built in 1744, this structure has been carefully renovated. Faïence tiles depicting Mecca adorn the lower floor, while the upper floor is decorated with carved wooden pillars and beams. The exterior of the building has some fine "joggling" – panels of different coloured blocks of marble fitted together like a jigsaw.

Mosque of al-Aqmar ⑫

Sharia al-Muizz li-Din Allah.
Map 2 F4. ◯ *daily.* ◑ *for noon prayers Fri.*

The name of the Mosque of al-Aqmar (the Moonlit Mosque) was supposedly inspired by the luminous quality of its grey stone. These days, coated in centuries of Cairo grime, the mosque does anything but shine. Nevertheless it is an architectural gem.

The mosque was built in 1125 by one of the last Fatimid caliphs, and is the oldest stone-built mosque in Egypt (earlier buildings were made of brick faced with plaster). The layout of the mosque is interesting as it uses an outer wall of varying thickness to realign the interior, reconciling the conflicting geometry imposed by the street plan and the direction of Mecca. The façade also displays the earliest use of decorative features that were later to become popular under the Mamluks, such as the sculpted stone "stalactites" (*muqarnas*) and carved ribbing in the hooded arch.

Beit as-Suhaymi ⑬

19 Darb al-Asfar, off Sharia al-Muizz li-Din Allah. **Map** 2 F4. ◯ *9am–5pm daily.* ◑ *for noon prayers Fri.* 🏷

Beit as-Suhaymi is really two houses, one built in 1648 and the other in 1796, joined to create a structure of almost palatial proportions. Its traditional design means entry is gained through a right-angled passage (which ensured complete privacy) into a central courtyard. Originally this would have had been filled with copious greenery ranged around a fountain.

The rooms on the ground floor comprise the *salamlek*, an area reserved for men; those on the upper floor form part of the *haramlek*, for women and the family. Here, the effect of the stained glass and painted ceilings combined with the dappled light from the *mashrabiyya*-covered windows is entrancing. These large wooden screens overlook the courtyard, filtering sunlight and cool breezes inside as well as allowing the women to observe the goings-on below without themselves being seen.

"Joggling" on southern facing arch of Sabil-Kuttab of Abdel Katkhuda

For hotels and restaurants in this region see pp268–71 and pp290–96

Stalls setting up along Sharia al-Muizz li-Din Allah

Some of the restored decoration is sumptuous, particularly in the ground floor *qaa* or reception room, which features intricate paintwork and a polychrome marble fountain set into the floor. The Beit hosts free music concerts every Sunday at 8pm.

Sheesha pipe manufacturer on Sharia al-Muizz li-Din Allah

Sharia al-Muizz li-Din Allah ⑭

Map 2 F5.

Al-Muizz li-Din Allah was the Fatimid caliph who conquered Cairo in AD 969. This street was the former main thoroughfare of medieval times, entering the city through the southern gate of Bab Zuweila and

exiting out of Bab al-Futuh to the north. Over the centuries, buildings have encroached on its width and it is no longer very grand, but it is still vital and busy. Lined with stalls, at Khan al-Khalili it is home to the coppersmiths' market and an assortment of workshops. Further along are shops selling a miscellany of coffee-house equipment such as tin-topped tables and *sheeshas*.

Mosque of al-Hakim ⑮

Sharia al-Muizz li-Din Allah. **Map** 2 F4. ⬜ *daily.* ⬤ *for noon prayers Fri.*

Al-Hakim, the third Fatimid caliph (997–1021), was one of the most notorious rulers in Egyptian history. He ruled from the age of eleven and had his tutor murdered when he was fifteen. Infamous for his

Unique style of minaret at the Mosque of al-Hakim

bizarre laws and arbitrary acts of violence, he proceeded to burn areas of Cairo, when people objected to the substitution of his name for Allah at Friday prayers. He was also a virulent misogynist and banned the manufacture of women's shoes in order to keep them indoors.

The mosque that bears his name was actually started by his father, but completed by Hakim in 1013. Since that time it has been variously used as a prison for captured Crusaders, as a stable by Salah ad-Din, a warehouse by Napoleon and a boys' school. After a somewhat heavy-handed restoration during the 1980s, it gleams with polished marble and glitzy golden chandeliers. The minarets are the only original features of the mosque.

Northern Walls and Gates ⑯

Sharia al-Galal. **Map** 2 F4. ⬜ *daily.* ⬤ *11:30am–1:30pm Fri.*

The medieval city of Cairo was completely walled with at least ten huge gateways, but only a short northern section of the ramparts and two gates now remain, as well as one other gate to the south, Bab Zuweila *(see p103)*. The two northern gates, the square-towered Bab an-Nasr (Gate of Victory) and the rounded Bab al-Futuh (Gate of Conquests), were built in 1087 and later strengthened by Salah ad-Din.

Steps in the gate towers lead into a vaulted corridor running the whole length of the wall, through which mounted guards could ride. The passage is lit by daylight filtering through arrow slits. These were widened to accommodate cannons in 1789 when Napoleon garrisoned troops within the walls. Evidence of their stay remains in the names the French gave to the towers, which they painted over the doorways.

Intricate Mamluk designs on the Mosque of
Qaitbey's minaret, Northern Cemetery

Northern Cemetery ⑰

East of Sharia Salah Salem.
🚌 🚌 102, 103 from Midan Tahrir.

On the edge of the city,
across the six-lane Salah
Salem highway, the Northern
Cemetery (al-Qarafah) is not
just a place of burial, it is home
to the living too. While several
magnificent funerary com-
plexes dominate the area, a lot
of the more modest, low-rise
tombs double as family homes.
   By the end of the 14th
century, Cairo's population
may have numbered 500,000,
making it the largest urban
centre in the world. Land was
at a premium, so the Mamluk
sultans looked beyond the city
walls for the building space to
match their egos. The great
mausoleums they built here
rank as some of their finest
achievements. Best of these
is the **Mosque of Qaitbey**,
completed in 1474. A beautifully proportioned structure,
with a simple but dazzling
sunlight-infused interior, it is
topped by the most elegant of
minarets and intricate carved
stone domes. The Qaitbey
mosque features on the
Egyptian one pound note.
   Further south, down the
sandy main street, a stone wall
encloses the **Complex of
Sultan Ashraf Barsbey**. Much
of this has been lost over the
centuries but the central
mosque remains, topped by
a beautiful dome carved with
interlocking stars. If the door
is unlocked, it is worth

looking at the
fine marble floor
and the ivory-
inlaid *minbar*.
   Further north
lies the fortress-
like bulk of the
**Mausoleum of
Ibn Barquq**. This
was built by the
son of the
Barquq whose
complex sits on
Bein al-Qasreen
(see p96). The
building is quite
unique in being
perfectly sym-
metrical with
two domes and two minarets.
It served as a *khanqah*, a
monastery for Islamic mystics
called Sufis *(see p92)*, and has
rows of small cells ranged
around the courtyard. Beneath
the twin domes are tomb
chambers, one for the women,
one for the men, with bright,
painted ceilings. It is possible
to get up onto the roof and
climb the minarets.
   The best route to the cemetery is to walk east for ten
minutes along Sharia al-Azhar
from the Khan al-Khalili area.

C Mosque of Qaitbey
Sharia Sultan Qaitbey.
🔵 daily. 🔵 for noon prayers Fri.

**C Complex of Sultan Ashraf
Barsbey**
Sharia Sultan Qaitbey. **Map:** 4 D2.
🔵 daily. 🔵 for noon prayers Fri.

C Mausoleum of Ibn Barquq
Sharia Sultan Qaitbey. **Map:** 4 D2.
🔵 daily. 🔵 for noon prayers Fri. 🔵

Carpet Bazaar ⑱

Sharia al-Muizz li-Din Allah. **Map** 6 F3.

Khan al-Khalili's markets
continue south of Sharia al-
Azhar, where tourist trinkets
give way to items that the
locals might want to buy. The
alleyways east of the Al-Ghouri
Complex *(see p92)* are home to
the Carpet Bazaar. Here, rugs
of coarse wool or camel hair
are sold, either striped in
varying shades of beige and
brown, or featuring colourful,
stylized images of birds, camels
and country scenes.
   Back on Sharia al-Muizz li-
Din Allah, just south of the
Al-Ghouri Complex, are two
tarboush workshops, making
the hat better known in the

Northern Cemetery, including dome of Sultan Ashraf Barsbey Mosque

◁ View through the morning mist over Islamic Cairo

West as a fez. Once common street wear, they are now a parody of their former elegant self, sported only by a few waiters and restaurant staff.

Courtyard of Mosque of Sultan al-Muayyad, by Bab Zuweila

Bab Zuweila ⑲

Sharia Ahmed Mahir. **Map:** 6 F4.
🞌 8:30am–5pm daily. 🖼

Bab Zuweila is the sole remaining southern gate of the city walls of Fatimid Cairo. It was built in the late 11th century. In Mamluk times, it was from the platform of Bab Zuweila that the sultan would watch the start of the annual pilgrimage to Mecca. This was also the site of executions, and the heads of criminals were displayed on top of the walls. This bloody habit persisted until the 1800s: after the 1811 Citadel massacre (see p59), the heads of the slain Mamluks were mounted on spikes here.

The towering minarets that soar over the gate were added when the adjacent **Mosque of Sultan al-Muayyad** was built in 1415. It is possible to climb the minarets for one of the best views of the city.

Across the entrance to Bab Zuweila is the Sabil-Kuttab Nafisa al-Bayda, a splendid building that combines a water dispensary with a school for orphans.

🄲 **Mosque of Sultan al-Muayyad**
Sharia Ahmed Mahir. **Map:** 6 F4.
🞌 daily. 🞌 for noon prayers Fri.

Mosque of as-Salih Talai ⑳

Sharia Ahmed Mahir. **Map:** 6 F4.
🞌 daily. 🌑 for noon prayers Fri.

The last of the Fatimid mosques of Cairo, the Mosque of as-Salih Talai was built in 1160. It was the first mosque to be built on an upper storey, resting on top of a layer of shop units. However, over the centuries, through the gradual accumulation of rubbish and dirt, the street level has risen by some 3 m (10 ft), so the mosque is now at ground level and the shops are in the basement.

The façade has five pointed arches, while the interior reveals columns with florid capitals taken from pre-

Appliqué motif from the Tentmakers' Market

Islamic sites. The prayer hall walls are decorated with superb stained-glass windows. The mosque also features a splendid *minbar* (pulpit), which was donated in 1300 by amir Baktimur al-Jugandar.

Tentmakers' Market ㉑

Sharia al-Khaimiyya. **Map:** 6 F4.

Leaving the Fatimid city via Bab Zuweila, the old main street runs south, passing through a venerable covered market known in Arabic as Sharia al-Khaimiyya, or the Street of the Tentmakers. This covered market was built in 1650 by Radwan Bey, who was in charge of the annual pilgrimage to Mecca. It is here that at one time a huddle of small workshops produced the brightly coloured printed fabrics that adorned the caravans bound for Mecca. Similar decorative material is now used in the large pavilions frequently seen around Cairo. These are erected for events such as weddings and funerals and the opening of new businesses. Huge rolls of the mainly blue or orange cloth are sold at the small, open-fronted kiosks that line the dimly lit street. These places also stitch detailed appliqué work, usually in workshops nearby.

LIVING WITH THE DEAD

Death has always been a significant part of Egyptian life. Even when the country abandoned Pharaonic beliefs, becoming first Coptic and then Islamic, practices such as visiting the dead were maintained. Most family tombs included a room where visitors could eat and rest and even stay overnight. Inevitably, the city's home-less took to occupying these tombs, some as early as the 14th century. Today, the Northern (and Southern) Cemeteries contain a mixture of tombs and homes, as well as tombs that are homes, where the living and the dead coexist side by side.

Children playing amongst the tombs in the Northern Cemetery, sometimes known as the "City of the Dead"

The Citadel ⓶

Home to Egypt's rulers for almost 700 years, the Citadel (Al-Qalaa) is today one of the most popular tourist sites in Cairo. Originally founded in 1176 by the famed Muslim commander Salah ad-Din (also known as Saladin), its mosques, museums and battlements reflect a diverse heritage. Divided into three sections, the Citadel's main tourist area is in the Southern Enclosure, where the Mosque of an-Nasr Mohammed (the Citadel's only surviving Mamluk structure) is dwarfed by the 19th-century Mosque of Mohammed Ali. The upper terraces of the Citadel offer spectacular views over the city.

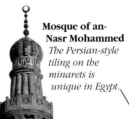

Mosque of an-Nasr Mohammed
The Persian-style tiling on the minarets is unique in Egypt.

Police Museum
Entered via a mock-Gothic gateway, the museum traces the gory history of Egyptian crime and punishment.

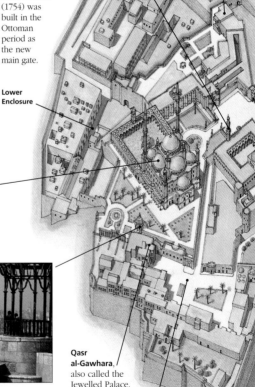

Bab al-Azab (1754) was built in the Ottoman period as the new main gate.

Lower Enclosure

★ **Mohammed Ali Mosque**
Built in a wholly Turkish style between 1830 and 1848, this mosque has nevertheless become a symbol of Cairo.

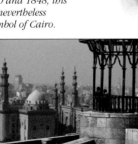

★ **Views over Cairo**
Superb views of the city's minarets and domes are afforded from the Citadel's fortifications. In the foreground here is the Mosque of Sultan Hassan.

Qasr al-Gawhara, also called the Jewelled Palace, is now a museum depicting the court life of Mohammed Ali.

Southern Enclosure

THE HIPPODROME

Now a large roundabout known as Midan Salah ad-Din, the area to the west of the Citadel walls was once the Hippodrome, an important site in medieval Cairo. Created by An-Nasr Mohammed as a cavalry training ground, this was where the Mamluks – renowned for their feats of horsemanship – practised complex military manoeuvres. Equestrian games were also frequently held here, including horse-racing and polo.

19th-century engraving of Bab al-Azab and the Hippodrome area

VISITORS' CHECKLIST

Sharia Salah Salem.
Map 4 F2. 🚌 🚐 **Tel** (02) 2512 1735. 🕐 summer: 8am–4:30pm daily; winter: 8am–4pm daily (museums close 1 hour earlier). 📷

The upper ramparts, entered at ground level, can be explored, offering views across the Citadel.

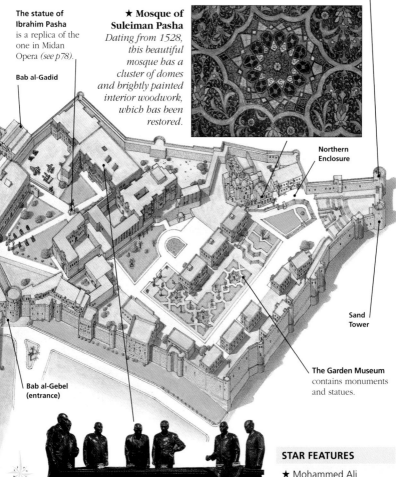

The statue of Ibrahim Pasha is a replica of the one in Midan Opera *(see p78).*

Bab al-Gadid

★ **Mosque of Suleiman Pasha**
Dating from 1528, this beautiful mosque has a cluster of domes and brightly painted interior woodwork, which has been restored.

Northern Enclosure

Sand Tower

The Garden Museum contains monuments and statues.

Bab al-Gebel (entrance)

Military Museum
Once the Harem Palace of Mohammed Ali, the museum has displays of weapons, uniforms and decorations, and a scale model of the Citadel.

STAR FEATURES

★ Mohammed Ali Mosque

★ Mosque of Suleiman Pasha

★ Views over Cairo

Exploring the Citadel

Although its main attraction is the Mohammed Ali Mosque, the Citadel has a great many other features worthy of attention. This fortified complex serves as a museum of Islamic architecture, with numerous fine examples of Mamluk and Ottoman-era mosques and fortifications from the time of Salah ad-Din (1171–91). With four separate museums also enclosed within its walls, a visit to the Citadel can occupy the best part of a day. Visitors should be aware that certain parts of the complex are out of bounds, notably the lower enclosure leading down to the Bab al-Azab gate.

Arcaded courtyard of the Mosque of an-Nasr Mohammed

Detail of a water fountain in the Mosque of Mohammed Ali

Mosque of Mohammed Ali

Dominating the eastern Cairo skyline, the Mohammed Ali Mosque is a relative newcomer, having been constructed as recently as the mid-19th century. It was erected on the orders of the reformist ruler Mohammed Ali, who is regarded as the founder of modern Egypt. When he came to power in 1805, Egypt was a backwater province of the Ottoman empire. By the time of his death in 1849, however, the country was once again a regional superpower.

Mohammed Ali's imposing mosque was a grand gesture that was meant to echo the great imperial mosques of the Ottoman capital. It is modelled along classic Turkish lines, with a great central dome and two towering, yet slender, minarets. The ornate clock in the courtyard near the entrance to the mosque was a gift from King Louis-Philippe of France, in exchange for the obelisk in the Place de la Concorde in Paris. The clock was damaged on delivery and has yet to be repaired. Mohammed Ali's body lies in a marble tomb to the right on entering the vast space of the prayer hall.

Mosque of an-Nasr Mohammed

When Mohammed Ali came to power, the greatest threat to his authority came from the Mamluks, former overlords of Egypt who were still a force to be reckoned with. In addition to his infamous massacre of 500 Mamluks at the Citadel in 1811 (see p59), Mohammed Ali ordered all the Mamluk structures in the Citadel to be destroyed. This one mosque survived because it had been put to use as a stable.

Situated just behind the Mosque of Mohammed Ali, this simple structure is all that remains of a massive building programme undertaken by Sultan an-Nasr Mohammed (1294–1340), whose *madrassa* and mausoleum stand on Bein al-Qasreen (see p96).

Built between 1318 and 1335 as a congregational mosque, where everyone gathered to pray, the building has two unique, corkscrew minarets with bulbous finials, covered with faïence tiles in a fashion more Persian than Egyptian.

There are two entrances to the mosque: one is in the form of a three-lobed arch and was used by soldiers, while the other arch was used exclusively by the Sultan.

Although many of the columns within the arcaded courtyard were salvaged from Pharaonic, Roman and Byzantine buildings, they nevertheless blend together surprisingly well.

The marble panelling that once graced the mosque's courtyard was removed by Sultan Selim I in 1517 and sent to Constantinople.

A view of the Mosque of Mohammed Ali, within the Citadel walls

🏛 Police Museum

Built on top of the former Mamluk-era Lion's Tower – so-called because of the statues of big cats at the base of the building – this small museum illustrates the history of Egyptian policing through the ages. Exhibits include uniforms and weapons, a small display on political assassinations and accounts of infamous Egyptian criminals, including Raya and Sakina *(see box, below)*. Included in the museum is the small row of cells that were in use as recently as 1983. Among their last inhabitants were President Sadat's assassins, held here while awaiting trial in 1981. The museum terrace offers some of the best views over the city.

Statue of a lion at the entrance of the Police Museum

🏛 Military Museum

Built by Mohammed Ali in 1827, this was the residence of the Egyptian royal family until 1874, when Khedive Ismail moved into the newly built Abdeen Palace *(see p79)*.

The building served as a military hospital during British occupation in World War II but it became a military museum when control of the Citadel reverted to Egypt in 1946.

Displays include uniforms, weaponry and dioramas of battles. Some of the palatial interiors are impressive, especially the superb *trompe l'oeil* in the main salon.

🇨 Mosque of Suleiman Pasha

This mosque was built in 1528 by Suleiman Pasha, who ruled Cairo after the Turks defeated the Mamluks in 1517. It was the first of many Ottoman mosques to be built in Egypt and, though modest in scale, it is one of the most charming. On the underside of the domes is some exquisitely painted decoration inspired by Turkish tiling. There are also some fine examples of traditional

Mihrab (prayer niche) and *minbar* (pulpit) in Mosque of Suleiman Pasha

inlaid marblework. In the mosque is a small mausoleum with tombs marked by turban-like headstones. These mark the burial places of Ottoman military officers, who were known as Janissaries.

🏯 Towers, Gates and Walls

Punctuated by towers and gates, the Citadel walls extend for over 3 km (2 miles). The former main gate, the Bab al-Azab, has been closed for decades and entrance is now through the Bab al-Gebel (Mountain Gate), created in 1786. The enormous vaulted portal of the Bab Al-Gadid (New Gate) was built in 1826 by Mohammed Ali.

The oldest parts of the walls are those around the northern enclosure. Fortifications here date back to the Ayyubid era. Salah ad-Din built the original walls and all the small half-

round towers (1171-93). These were strengthened in the early 13th century by his successors, who also added most of the larger towers. It is possible to visit the interiors of Salah ad-Din's two eastern-most towers, Burg al-Haddad and Burg al-Ramla.

🏛 Other Museums

Al-Gawhara Palace was built by Mohammed Ali in 1814 to house his administration and as a place to receive guests. The former Audience Hall now serves as a museum and is crammed with furniture, portraits and life-sized models of Mohammed Ali and other monarchs and their courtiers. **The Seized Museum**, which is currently closed, contains stolen Pharaonic, Coptic and Islamic works of art which were retrieved from dealers on the black market.

RAYA AND SAKINA – SISTERS IN NOTORIETY

Egypt's most infamous criminals, sisters Raya and Sakina, were tried and hanged in 1921 for the murders of 17 young women. The sisters lived in the poorest quarter of Alexandria where, with the connivance of their husbands, they ran a string of brothels. Their victims were picked up in the market place, lured back to one of their houses and strangled. The motive was money: only girls wearing expensive-looking jewellery were selected. The eventual arrest of Raya and Sakina occurred after a policeman became suspicious of the strong smell of incense emanating from Raya's home. He ordered a search that led to the discovery of the corpses. Since then, the grisly murders have provided lasting inspiration for writers, dramatists and film-makers, and Raya and Sakina have become part of popular Egyptian mythology.

Raya   **Sakina**

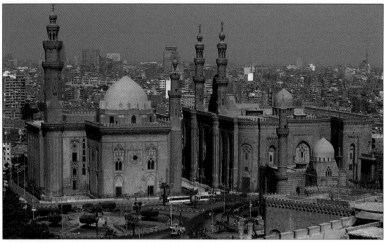

Mosque of Sultan Hassan (*left*) and Mosque of ar-Rifai (*right*) seen from the Citadel

Mosque of Sultan Hassan ㉓

Midan Salah ad-Din. **Map** 4 E2.
🕗 *8am–4:30pm daily.* 🕌 *for noon prayers Fri.* 📷

One of the most interesting of the capital's mosques, this is also Cairo's finest example of early Mamluk architecture. The mosque overlooks what were the fields of the Hippodrome (now Midan Salah ad-Din), across from the precipitous walls of the Citadel. The dimensions of this massive structure are truly staggering: 150 m (492 ft) long, with walls 36 m (118 ft) high, the tallest minaret rising to 68 m (223 ft).

The construction of the mosque was funded with money from the estates of people who had died in the Black Death (which struck Cairo in 1348). This policy increased the unpopularity of the sultan, An-Nasr Hassan, who was already renowned for his greed. Building work began in 1356 and five years later, in 1361, one of the minarets collapsed, killing hundreds of people. By the end of 1361, two years before his mosque was completed, Hassan had been murdered. Despite the unhappy history of Hassan's grand monument, the interior of the mosque is overwhelming. Through a magnificent portal, a dimly lit corridor leads to a

high-walled central courtyard. On the four sides of the courtyard are great, recessed arches, known as *iwans*, which were formerly used for teaching. Each *iwan* was devoted to one of the main schools of Sunni Islam.

At the rear of the eastern *iwan*, situated to the right of a particularly beautiful *mihrab* or niche, a bronze door leads to the mausoleum. The largest in Cairo, it was never occupied by the sultan, whose body was not recovered. However, the mausoleum was used for the burial of two of his sons. Tickets for the mosque are sold at a kiosk outside. The exterior gates are locked outside of visiting hours.

Detail of wall and steps from the Mosque of Sultan Hassan

Mosque of ar-Rifai ㉔

Midan Salah ad-Din. **Map** 4 E2.
🕗 *8am–4:30pm daily.* 🕌 *for noon prayers Fri.* 📷

Separated from the Mosque of Sultan Hassan by a pedestrian street, the Mosque of ar-Rifai has a similar scale and symmetry but 450 years separate them.

Founded in 1819, this mosque was not completed until 1912. Its patron was Princess Khushyar, mother of the Europhile Khedive Ismail, who intended the mosque as a tomb for her family. Built in a pseudo-Mamluk style, with decoration copied from existing period mosques, the result is rather clumsy compared with the Mosque of Sultan Hassan. The over-wrought interior is filled with glitzy tombs of members of the royal family, including Farouk, the last king of Egypt. Also buried here is the last shah of Iran, who found refuge in Egypt after fleeing Khomeini's Islamic revolution in 1979.

Directly in front of the mosque is the **Mosque of Amir Akhur**, a building distinguished by its *ablaq* banding of red and white stone, its imposing dome and double minaret finial.

🄲 **Mosque of Amir Akhur**
Midan Salah ad-Din. **Map** 4 F2.
🕗 *daily.* 🕌 *for noon prayers Fri.*

For hotels and restaurants in this region see pp268–71 and pp290–96

Dervish Theatre

Sharia as-Suyufiya. **Map** 4 E2.
⬜ *daily.* 🎟️

In the gardens behind the
Mosque of Hassan Sadaqa
(also known as Sunqur Sadi)
is a restored 19th-century
theatre. It is accessed from a
small courtyard garden, which
is reached via a door on the
right of the façade of the
mosque, in Sharia as-Suyufiya.
Its circular, polished-wood
stage is surrounded by a two-
storey gallery. The theatre was
built by an order of Mevlevi
Dervishes, who extended the
complex to include a hostel
(*khanqah*). The Dervishes
(*see p92*) are Sufis, who follow a spiritual offshoot of
Islam, and who believe that
their whirling dance leads to
oneness with Allah. From the
theatre, you can go down into
the beautiful mausoleum
containing the tomb of
Hassan Sadaqa, for whom
the mosque was built.

Part of a complex dating
from 1321, the Mosque of
Hassan Sadaqa is distiguished
by fine stuccowork on its
minaret and dome, visible
from the street. The complex
originally included a
monastery (*ribat*), which was
replaced by the theatre.

🅒 **Mosque of Hassan
Sadaqa**
Sharia as-Suyufiya. **Map** 4 E2.
⬜ *daily.* ● *for noon prayers Fri*

A view of the interior of the Mosque of Sultan Hassan

Sabil-Kuttab of Qaitbey

Sharia as-Saliba. **Map** 4 E2.

Just 200 m (650 ft) west of
Midan Salah ad-Din, at the
western end of Sharia as-Saliba,
is the huge, block-like structure
of the 15th-century Sabil-Kuttab
of Qaitbey. Now restored and
in use as a library, this old
Quranic school is notable for
the fine marble-inlay on its
western façade.

Qaitbey was a ruthless sultan
who started life as a slave-boy
to the previous sultan. He built
some of Cairo's most beautiful
monuments, including his
spectacular mosque in the
Northern Cemetery (*see p102*).

Further west, Sharia as-Saliba
passes between the **Mosque**

of **Sheikhu** on the right and
the **Khanqah of Sheikhu** on
the left. These 14th-century
buildings are still in use. A
khanqah is a Sufi hostel,
where the sheikh resides,
teaching his disciples.

Also on Sharia as-Saliba, a
short walk straight ahead
takes you to Midan Sayyida
Zeinab – a good place to get a
taxi back to the centre.

🅒 **Mosque and Khanqah
of Sheikhu**
Sharia as-Saliba. **Map** 4 E2.
⬜ *daily.* ● *for noon prayers Fri.*

Mosque of Ibn Tulun

See pp110–11.

Al-Azhar Park

Sharia Salah Salem. **Map** 2 F5.
Tel (02) 2510 3868. ⬜ *daily.* 🎟️

Providing panoramic views of
Islamic Cairo from its lush,
landscaped gardens, this
74-acre park was created by
the Aga Khan Trust for Culture. Once a derelict mound
of rubble between the eastern
edge of the 12th-century
Ayyubid city and the 15th-
century Mamluk "City of the
Dead", Al-Azhar Park now
boasts orchards, cultural
venues and restaurants. An
800-year-old Ayyubid city
wall, built by Salah ad-Din
and discovered as work on
the park began, is undergoing
continued excavations.

DECORATIVE MAMLUK MOTIFS

The buildings created between 1250 and 1517, in the time
of the Mamluk sultans, represent the pinnacle of Islamic art
in Egypt. A fusion of the building traditions of the Near East,
they blend Armenian stonework with North African stucco,
Byzantine golden mosaics, and Syrian polychrome marble
inlays. It is the latter that provide the most striking element.
Created by painstakingly cutting small pieces of different
coloured stone and fitting
them together like a jigsaw
puzzle, the intricate ornamentation forms incredibly
complex geometric patterns
that are completely abstract
in character. Repetitive
and hypnotic, it has been
suggested that the colourful
decoration aided prayer by
heightening the viewers'
sensory experience.

Detail of the marble inlay on the
Sabil-Kuttab of Qaitbey

Mosque of Ibn Tulun ㉗

Decorative motif on arch

One of the largest and oldest mosques in the country, Ibn Tulun was built between AD 876 and AD 879 by an Abbasid governor sent from Baghdad to rule Egypt. Called a "Friday Mosque", its open-air courtyard is large enough to hold the whole male congregation of the district for prayers on the holiest day of the week. Built entirely of mudbrick, the mosque is surrounded by an outer courtyard, which was meant to act like a moat and keep the secular city at bay. This, and its curious spiral minaret, make it unique in Egypt. Contrasting with the geometric simplicity of the mosque, the maze of rooms in the nearby Gayer-Anderson House is filled with a diverting collection of artifacts.

★ Mihrab
A niche indicating the direction of Mecca, this mihrab dates back to the 13th century. Next to it is the minbar, or pulpit, one of the finest in Egypt.

Gayer-Anderson House

Lectern
Called a dikka in Arabic, the wooden platform, in line with the mihrab, is used for Quranic recitations and calls to prayer inside the mosque.

Entrance

Outer Courtyard

Arcades
Running around the courtyard, the arcades (riwaq) provide shade for worshippers. The largest, on the southeast side, is five columns deep and serves as the mosque's prayer hall. Quranic verses are inscribed along the whole length of the ceiling in the arcade.

STAR FEATURES

★ Mihrab

★ Spiral Minaret

★ Fountain

GAYER-ANDERSON HOUSE

This charming museum is the legacy of John Gayer-Anderson, a British officer serving in Cairo. In the 1930s, he lovingly restored two adjacent 16th- or 17th-century houses. Lavishly decorated with *mashrabiyya* screens and marble inlays, they were further ornamented by a vast amount of interesting and often intriguing orientalia. He also added a room, decorated in lacquer and gold, taken from a 17th-century house in Damascus. The cumulative effect of all these items makes the museum one of the most magical places to visit in Cairo.

Reproduction bust of Nefertiti

VISITORS' CHECKLIST

Sharia Salibah. **Map** 4 D2.
8am–5pm daily. **Gayer-Anderson House** *Tel* (02) 2364 7822. 9am–4pm daily.
noon–1:30pm Fri (mosque & museum).

Inner courtyard or *sahn*

★ **Fountain**
The original had a beautiful gilded dome but this collapsed in AD 968. The current dome is a 13th-century replacement.

Pointed arches are inscribed with geometric designs.

The windows have ornately decorated stucco grills, no two of which are the same.

Outside staircase

★ **Spiral Minaret**
Inspired by the tower at the Great Mosque of Samarra in Iraq, Ibn Tulun's minaret is an easy climb, rewarded by excellent views of the city.

Crenellations
The design of these brick-built crenellations is supposed to have been inspired by ranks of standing soldiers.

RHODA ISLAND AND OLD CAIRO

For several centuries following the decline of the old Pharaonic religions and before the arrival of Islam, Egypt was a predominantly Christian country. Alexandria was then the country's capital, while Cairo had yet to be founded. Around the 6th century AD the site of the city consisted of little more than a Roman fortress beside the Nile, guarding a crossing point on the route between the ancient Egyptian cities of Heliopolis and Memphis. When Arab general

Virgin icon in Hanging Church

Amr Ibn al-Aas set up camp in its shadow and built a capital nearby, he was placing the marker for the future foundation of Cairo. Known today as Old Cairo (Misr al-Qadima), this ancient part of the city contains a bastion of Egyptian Christianity, known as Coptic Cairo, and many historic churches. The area also takes in the southern tip of the island of Rhoda, site of the Nilometer which has been used to measure the height of the river Nile since Pharaonic times.

SIGHTS AT A GLANCE

Holy Places
Ben Ezra Synagogue ③
Church of St Barbara ④
Church of St Sergius and St Bacchus ⑤
Coptic Convent of St George ⑥
Greek Orthodox Church of St George ①
Hanging Church ⑦

Monastery of St Mercurius ⑩
Mosque of Amr Ibn al-Aas ⑨
Tomb of Suleiman al-Faransawi ⑪

Archaeological Sites
Fustat ⑧

Museums & Historic Buildings
Coptic Museum ②
Nilometer ⑫

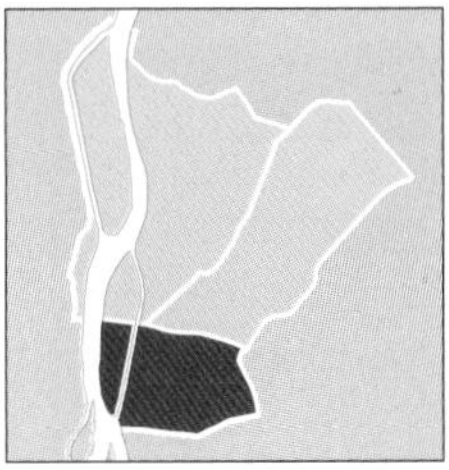

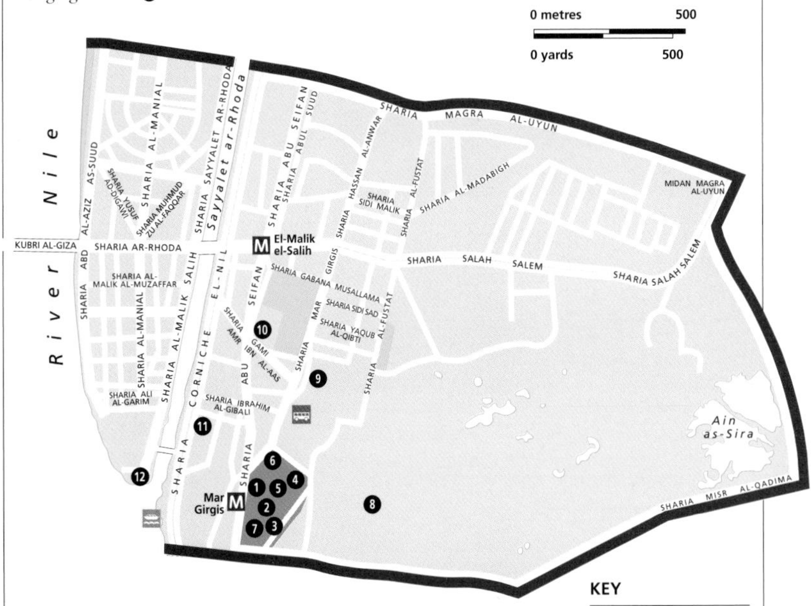

0 metres 500
0 yards 500

GETTING AROUND

Old Cairo is most easily reached by Metro; Mar Girgis station is just four stops south of Midan Tahrir (Sadat Metro). River buses to Old Cairo depart from a point below the Corniche in front of the Radio and TV Union Building. From the landing stage, it is only a short walk to Coptic Cairo, the oldest part of the modern-day city.

KEY

	Street-by-Street See pp114–15
Ⓜ	Metro station
	Bus station
	Riverbus terminal

◁ **A haven of peace and tranquillity among the high-walled cobbled alleyways of Coptic Cairo**

Street by Street: Coptic Cairo

Coptic Museum window panel

Coptic Cairo is the modern name for the oldest part of the city. The compound lies within the walls of the 3rd-century AD Roman fortress of Babylon and is a haven of quiet, narrow lanes and ancient holy places. Separate entrances, leading to the Coptic Museum and the Hanging Church, are located between two round Roman towers, against which the Nile once lapped before it shifted course. A third, stepped entrance to the north leads along a sunken alley to the rest of the churches, the synagogue and the cemeteries. Conservation work is ongoing in various locations across Coptic Cairo.

Coptic Convent of St George
While not allowed inside, visitors can re-enact the persecution of Palestinian St George, famed for his dragon slaying, and be wrapped in chains ❻

Greek Orthodox Church of St George
Coptic Cairo is also home to some other significant Christian sights. The Greek Orthodox Church of St George is built upon the Northern Roman Tower and is flanked by a cemetery ❶

Subterranean entrance to compound

SHARIA MAR GIRGIS

Coptic Convent of St George

Greek Orthodox Cemetery

Entrance to Coptic Museum

Greek Orthodox Church of St George

Church of St Sergius & St Bacchus

Mari Girgis Station Ⓜ

Entrance to Hanging Church

OLD ROMAN TOWER

Coptic Museum

Hanging Church

★ **Coptic Museum**
Artifacts here trace the origins of Christian art in the Near East. The building itself is beautiful, especially the older, southern wing. There is also a lovely garden and a small café ❷

★ **Hanging Church**
This most beautiful of Cairo's churches has an ornately decorated interior consisting of three barrel-vaulted, wooden-roofed aisles, ivory inlaid screens and a finely carved marble pulpit ❼

KEY

	Built-up area
	Roman wall
—	Railway line
Ⓜ	Metro station

Church of St Barbara

Dedicated to the saint who was beaten to death by her father for trying to convert him to Christianity, St Barbara's is one of Egypt's largest and finest churches. There is a domed apse behind the altar with seven steps decorated in bands of black, white and red marble **4**

LOCATOR MAP
See Street Finder Map 3

0 metres	50
0 yards	50

COPTIC CEMETERY

The Nuptial Hall was part of a church first founded in AD 681.

Ben Ezra Synagogue

This is Egypt's oldest synagogue and it has been heavily restored. Ben Ezra is a testament to the ancient and significant presence of Jews in this region **3**

Amr Ibn al-Aas Mosque

Church of St Barbara

Ben Ezra Synagogue

Church of St Sergius and St Bacchus

Since this, the oldest church in Coptic Cairo, was built, ground levels have risen. It is now entered down some steps. Legend says that the Holy Family sheltered in a cave below the altar **5**

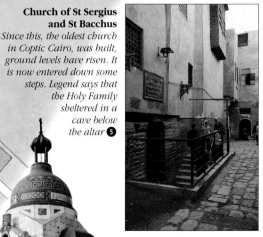

CATHOLIC CEMETERY

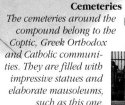

Cemeteries

The cemeteries around the compound belong to the Coptic, Greek Orthodox and Catholic communities. They are filled with impressive statues and elaborate mausoleums, such as this one.

STAR SIGHTS

★ Coptic Museum

★ Hanging Church

A 7th-century painting in the Coptic Museum depicting the Virgin Mary and the infant Jesus flanked by apostles

Greek Orthodox Church of St George ❶

Coptic Cairo compound. **Map** 3 B5.
Ⓜ *Mar Girgis.* ◯ *9am–4pm daily.*

Long before the Crusaders carried tales of his legendary exploits back to Europe, St George was venerated throughout the Christian Middle East as Mar Girgis. He is said to have been a Roman legionary who defied a decree by the Emperor Diocletian outlawing the worship of Christ and was martyred for his beliefs in the 3rd century.

There has been a church dedicated to St George on or near the site since at least the 10th century, but today's striking round structure dates only

Worshippers attending church in Coptic Cairo

to the beginning of the 20th century. The circular form of the church echoes the shape of the 1st century AD Roman gate tower on top of which it was built. Follow the sign to the small Church of the Sleeping Mary; below is a crypt dedicated to the Holy Family who reputedly sheltered there.

Coptic Museum ❷

Coptic Cairo compound. **Map** 3 B5.
Ⓜ *Mar Girgis.* **Tel** *(02) 2362 8766.*
◯ *9am–5pm daily.* 🖼

Largely built in 1947, this charming museum houses the finest collection of Coptic art in the world. The building itself has undergone extensive renovation since suffering earthquake damage in 1992, and boasts elaborately painted wooden ceilings, elegant *mashrabiyya* windows, and a garden courtyard.

The exhibits date back to Egypt's Christian era and both Pharaonic and Islamic influences are evident in the artifacts on display. Early exhibits carry motifs and symbols, such as *ankhs* and Horus-like falcons, that are recognizably ancient Egyptian. Elsewhere, carved capitals from an early Coptic cathedral in Alexandria display a mastery of stone carving that would later come to fruition during the era of the Mamluks. A 6th-century Coptic stone pulpit resembles the stairs and

shrine of the pyramid complex at Saqqara *(see pp162–3)*, and also prefigures the *minbars* found in all Cairo mosques. Still more fascinating are the crudely painted depictions of Mary suckling Jesus, which directly echo images found all over Egypt of Isis nursing Horus. Many of the pieces are also Classical in inspiration, a legacy of Alexander's Ptolemaic dynasty and Roman rule.

On the upper floor are the finely woven textiles for which the Copts were once famous.

Carved stone capital, Coptic Museum

There are also lavishly embroidered silk garments, icons, and what is claimed by some to be the oldest book in the world, the 1,600-year-old Coptic book of the Psalms of David.

Ben Ezra Synagogue ❸

Coptic Cairo compound. **Map** 3 B5.
Ⓜ *Mar Girgis.* ◯ *9am–4pm daily.*

Jewish history in Egypt dates back to the era of the Old Testament and the stories of Moses and the persecution by the pharaohs. After the Roman expulsion of Jews from Jerusalem in the first century AD, Alexandria became the world's most important centre of Judaism. As recently as the early 20th century the Jewish community in Egypt remained significant and prominent. This changed dramatically with the creation of Israel in 1948. Those Jews that had not already left by choice were forced out of Egypt when the country went to war against the newly formed Jewish state. Monuments to the long history of the Jews in Egypt are few and, of these, Ben Ezra is the oldest. Legends link it with Moses but in fact the synagogue was formerly a church, built in the 8th century. Around 300 years later the church was destroyed and the site and its ruins given to Abraham ben Ezra, a 12th-century rabbi of Jerusalem.

Repairs in the 19th century unearthed hundreds of Hebrew manuscripts from the synagogue's intact *geniza*, or treasury. In Egypt any paper bearing the name of God had to be preserved and this has resulted in a legacy of thousands of documents dating largely from the 11th and 12th centuries. Together, they amount to a minutely detailed chronicle of life in medieval Cairo.

The synagogue underwent extensive renovation in the 1980s and although it is no longer used for worship it is in a pristine state.

Church of St Barbara ❹

Coptic Cairo compound. **Map** 3 B5.
Ⓜ *Mar Girgis.* ◯ *9am–4pm daily.*

This church was named after an early Christian martyr who lived in the 3rd century AD. Daughter of a merchant, she was killed by her father for trying to convert him to Christianity. Occupying the site of an earlier church dedicated to St Cyrus and St John, the church of St Barbara was built in the 11th century and is one of the largest and finest in Egypt. It boasts a beautiful 13th-century iconostasis, or sanctuary screen, of wood inlaid with finely carved

Carved 13th-century iconostasis in the Church of St Barbara

ivory. There is also a series of striking icons, dating to around 1750, depicting Jesus, Mary, two archangels and various saints and apostles.

Church of St Sergius and St Bacchus ❺

Coptic Cairo compound. **Map** 3 B5.
Ⓜ *Mar Girgis.* ◯ *9am–4pm daily.*

This is perhaps Egypt's most famous church, owing its reputation to the widely held belief that the Holy Family sheltered in a cave here during

their "Flight into Egypt" *(see p123)*. The cave is preserved as a crypt, but it often floods with underground water.

Whatever the truth of the Holy stopover, the church is likely to be the oldest existing structure within the fortress, with foundations dating back to the 5th century AD. Rebuilt and reconstructed many times, most of the fabric of the building dates to between the 10th and 12th centuries.

Coptic Convent of St George ❻

Coptic Cairo compound. **Map** 3 B5.
Ⓜ *Mar Girgis.* ◯ *9am–4pm daily.*

This convent dates back at least as far as the 15th century when it was written about by the Arab chronicler Al-Maqrizi. Nuns still live at the convent but visitors are permitted to enter the Great Hall where there is a shrine with a famed icon of St George. The hall is currently being renovated.

The convent is also known for its unusual chain-wrapping ritual still practised by the nuns. The chains symbolize the persecution of St George.

The shrine dedicated to St George in the Coptic Convent of St George

Hanging Church ❼

**Icon of
St George**

Dedicated to the Virgin Mary, this church
is popularly called the "Hanging" or
"Suspended" Church (Al-Muallaqa in Arabic)
because it was built on top of the Water
Gate of the old Roman fortress of Babylon.
The original structure was built possibly
as early as the 4th century AD, but it was
destroyed and rebuilt in the 11th century.
Expansion and reconstruction has gone on
ever since, making it difficult to date precisely
any specific part of the church. A marble pulpit and the
inlaid ivory screens that hide the three altar areas date
from between the 10th and 13th centuries. Despite its
venerable nature, the church is still used for regular public
services, which are held every Friday and Sunday morning.

Outer Porch
*Decorated with
geometrical and floral
designs, the porch dates
from the 11th century.*

Carved Frieze
*The church incorporates some fine old
decoration, but this frieze of Christ
flanked by angels and many of the
earliest pieces are now housed in the
nearby Coptic Museum (see p116).*

The inner courtyard has
souvenirs for sale, such
as crosses, CDs and
painted papyri.

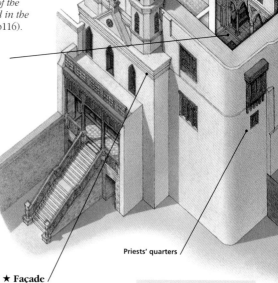

Priests' quarters

★ Façade
*Surmounted by its distinctive
twin bell towers, the whole
front section is a relatively
recent addition, dating only
from the 19th century.*

STAR FEATURES

★ Façade

★ Sanctuary Screen

◁ **Detail from the interior of the dome in the Coptic Museum**

★ Sanctuary Screen

Carved from cedarwood and delicately inlaid with ivory, the central screen that shields the main altar is the finest of its kind in Egypt.

VISITORS' CHECKLIST

Coptic Cairo compound, Sharia Mar Girgis. **Map** 3 B5. M Mar Girgis. from Midan Tahrir. from Maspero terminal. **Tel** (02) 2363 6305. 9am–5pm daily. 8–11am Fri, 7–11am Sun. **www**.coptic-cairo.com

Icons of St George, the Virgin and John the Baptist also adorn the walls.

Barrel-vaulted roof supported on columns

Top of the screen adorned with icons

Pulpit

Made of marble and dating from the 11th century, the exquisite pulpit rests on 13 columns representing Christ and his disciples.

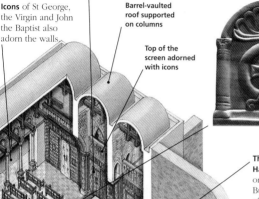

The Chapel of Takla Haymanot was part of the original 4th-century church. Built in one of the bastions of the Water Gate, it honours the patron saint of Ethiopia.

Roman Towers

The towers belonged to the southwestern bastion of the original Roman fortress of Babylon and date from the 1st century AD.

Interior of Church

Three barrel-vaulted roofs are supported on columns with Corinthian capitals, indicating that they were recycled from earlier buildings.

Coptic Christianity

The word "Copt" is a corruption of the Arabic *Qibti*, which is derived from the Greek word *Aegyptios*, meaning "Egyptian". According to tradition, St Mark, one of the 12 Apostles, introduced Christianity into Egypt in the first century AD. Alexandria was one of the first five patriarchates – branches of the Christian church headed by patriarchs claiming descent from the Apostles – and by the 4th century, Christianity was the official religion of Egypt. Egyptian Christians split from the orthodox church after the Council of Chalcedon proclaimed, in AD 451, the dual human and divine nature of Christ. Dioscurus, patriarch of Alexandria, refused to accept this definition, believing only in Christ's divinity.

The ankh, *symbol of eternal life in ancient Egypt, is transformed into a Christian cross.*

Dating from *c.1400 BC, this sculpture of Isis with the infant Horus is an image akin to later depictions of the Virgin Mary and the infant Christ. This, along with the ankh and the belief in the afterlife, are some of the more obvious parallels between the ancient Egyptian religion and Christianity, and may explain the ease of Egypt's conversion to the new religion.*

POPE SHENOUDA III

The 117th patriarch of the Coptic church, Pope Shenouda III, and several Coptic priests attend midnight mass at St Mark's Cathedral in Cairo. The Pope was once a monk at Wadi Natrun (*see p169*), from where the Coptic pope is traditionally chosen.

The Coptic language, *shown here on an early engraving, has its origins in ancient Greek and Egyptian hieroglyphics. Copts claim to be direct descendants of ancient Egyptians. The Coptic language is still used today in religious ceremonies.*

Boutros Boutros-Ghali (see p63), *the former UN Secretary-General, is an internationally renowned Copt. Always an economically powerful minority, Copts have long provided an educated elite in Egypt, filling many of the country's important posts.*

THE HOLY FAMILY IN EGYPT

According to biblical tradition, the Holy Family fled to Egypt to escape Herod's "massacre of the innocents". Coptic tradition links their visit to several sites. At Matariyya, a north-eastern suburb of Cairo, the Virgin's Tree is a gnarled sycamore under which Mary is said to have rested. In Coptic Cairo *(see pp116–17)*, part of the Church of St Sergius and St Bacchus is a cave in which the family supposedly dwelt, while the town of Asyut *(see p176)* is the southernmost point associated with their route.

The Flight into Egypt by Jean-Léon Gérôme (1824–1904)

Monks, *like this one from the Monastery of St Anthony in the Eastern Desert, still wear traditional black robes and a hood with distinctive gold embroidery. Today, monasticism is experiencing a renaissance and attracting many new recruits.*

St Anthony's Monastery (see p232) *represents the beginning of the Christian monastic tradition. It was later followed by Coptic monasteries like Wadi Natrun (see p169) and St Catherine's in Sinai (see pp222–5).*

This is a typical *Egyptian town in Middle Egypt, dominated by a Coptic church and surrounded by fertile fields. There are approximately 8 million Copts – 10 per cent of Egypt's population – and most live in Middle Egypt. Despite the odd claim and counter-claim, Copts and Muslims live harmoniously side by side.*

Fustat ⑧

Sharia Ain as-Sirah. **Map** 3 C5.
Ⓜ *Mar Girgis.*

Fustat represents almost 1,400 years of Egyptian history. When the armies of Islam, led by their general Amr ibn al-Aas, conquered Egypt in AD 640 they chose not to occupy any of the existing cities of Alexandria, Memphis or Karnak. Instead they set up camp immediately north of the Roman fortress of Babylon beside the Nile.

In time the canvas city was replaced by one of mudbrick and stone but was still known as Fustat, meaning "tent". It flourished and became Egypt's first Islamic capital. Under the Fatimid dynasty (969–1171), however, the new rulers built their own city further to the north *(see pp94–5)* and in 1168 put Fustat to the flame rather than risk its capture by the Crusaders. From the 13th to the 16th century, the Mamluks used the area as a rubbish dump and today it is a vast wasteland. Once inhabited by thousands of people who earned a living as potters and rubbish-collectors, now only a few remain on the outskirts. To archaeologists it is a treasure chest waiting to be opened – an ancient city preserved under the garbage of hundreds of years.

Fustat is the location for a new National Museum of Egyptian Civilization, which opened in 2011. The museum overlooks Ain el Seera lake.

A pottery on the edge of Fustat, Egypt's first Islamic city

Mosque of Amr ibn al-Aas ⑨

Midan Amr ibn al-Aas. **Map** 3 B4.
Ⓜ *Mar Girgis.* ⃝ *daily.* ● *to non-Muslims at prayer times.* 🗎

Named after the general who conquered Egypt for Islam in AD 640, the original Mosque of Amr ibn al-Aas was the first place of Islamic worship in Egypt and therefore the first mosque on the continent of Africa.

According to contemporary accounts, the mosque was a basic building of mudbrick walls, unpaved floor and a palm-thatch roof supported on palm columns. It had no *mihrab*, courtyard or minaret, but it was large enough to hold Amr's army at prayer. Apart from the site, however, nothing of the original remains in the present mosque, which is a patchwork of countless rebuildings and restorations. It is said that no two of its 200 or so columns are the same. The earliest existing parts date to the 9th century, when the original mosque was rebuilt, almost doubling in size. However, other areas, such as the entrance, were reconstructed as recently as the 1980s.

The mosque has retained an air of simplicity, in keeping with its humble origins and it still fills each day for prayers with a devout congregation. Visitors to the mosque are welcome at other times.

Monastery of St Mercurius ⑩

Sharia Abu Seifan. **Map** 3 B4.
Ⓜ *Mar Girgis.* ⃝ *9am–5pm daily.* 🗎

To the northwest of the Mosque of Amr ibn al-Aas is a complex consisting of three churches and a convent. Surrounded by a high wall, the compound is entered via a small doorway off the main street. This leads to a narrow, sunken alleyway that connects the various buildings. The monastery complex was reputedly named after a martyred Roman legionary and dates from the early 6th century, but it has been destroyed and rebuilt on at least four occasions.

Relief painting, Church of St Mercurius

The main building in the complex is the **Church of St Mercurius**, which in its current form dates back to 1176. It was destroyed in the blaze when the Fatimid overlord Vizier Shawar ordered Fustat to be razed to the ground.

The church is now a repository of fine early Coptic art with unique wall paintings, an extraordinary collection of icons and a fine wooden altar canopy. A flight of stairs in

Façade and entrance to the Mosque of Amr ibn al-Aas

Ornate ironwork exterior of the Tomb of Suleiman al-Faransawi

the north aisle of the church leads down to a small crypt where, in the 4th century, the ascetic St Barsum the Naked is said to have spent the last 20 years of his life with only a snake for company.

The **Church of the Holy Virgin** and the **Church of St Shenouda** are both open to visitors but the **Convent of St Mercurius**, also part of the complex, is still inhabited by nuns and is off limits.

Tomb of Suleiman al-Faransawi ⑪

Sharia Mohammed Fouad Galal. **Map** 3 B5. Ⓜ *Mar Girgis.*

A small cast-iron tomb in a residential square, this is one of the most unusual monuments in Cairo, built in the 19th century in honour of an extremely unusual man.

Suleiman "the Frenchman" (originally a soldier named Joseph Sèves) was a veteran of Napoleon's campaigns who came to Egypt to train the armies of the viceroy Mohammed Ali *(see p59)*. It is said that the Frenchman, who died in 1860, was so despised by his conscripts that they would shoot at him during target practice. Sèves later converted to Islam, taking the name Suleiman, and was rewarded with the honorary title "Pasha" following Egypt's successful campaigns against Greece and Syria. A statue of Suleiman mounted on his horse used to stand in Downtown Cairo on what was Sharia Suleiman Pasha. During the 1952 Revolution

the statue was consigned to the Citadel and the street renamed in honour of the Egyptian nationalist and banker, Talaat Harb.

Nilometer ⑫

Sharia al-Malik Salih. **Map** 3 B5. Ⓜ *Mar Girgis.* 🕐 *9am–4pm daily.* 📷

Until the construction of the dams at Aswan, Egyptian life was governed by the annual flooding of the Nile. Most years, its waters rose to swamp the river valley, then retreated, leaving behind richly fertile deposits of alluvial soil. Occasionally, however, the floods failed to cover the whole agricultural area and this resulted in low crop yields and sometimes famine. In order to forecast what kind of harvest a particular year might bring,

Nilometer on Rhoda Island showing the simple calibration used to predict the floods

the ancient Egyptians constructed a series of Nilometers, one of which is cut into the bedrock of the island of Rhoda. It takes the form of a deep, square pit containing an octagonal column, marked off with graduations. Water was let in through three channels – these are now blocked up but are still visible. At the annual meter-reading ceremony, a sufficiently high level of water would be greeted by festivities, while a shortfall would trigger anxious prayers.

Although there is evidence that a Nilometer has been here since Pharaonic times, in its existing form it dates from the 9th century – hence the elaborate Islamic inscriptions adorning the walls. Set over the Nilometer is a small Ottoman kiosk with a distinctive conical cap, dating from the 19th century. Decorating its wooden ceiling are some impressive painted arabesques.

Adjacent to the Nilometer is the **Umm Kolthum Museum**, dedicated to the revered Egyptian singer and worth a visit. The nearby **Rococo Monasterly Palace**, built in the 1850s, holds occasional classical concerts during the winter.

UMM KOLTHUM: THE VOICE OF EGYPT

For much of the 20th century Umm Kolthum was the greatest living cultural icon not just in Egypt, but in the whole of the Arab world. She began singing with her father at weddings in the villages of the eastern Delta around 1910. Astonished by the strength of her voice, friends and family encouraged her to move to Cairo and establish her career. From the 1930s onwards for almost the next 40 years the whole of the country came to a standstill on one Thursday night each month when her concert would be broadcast live on national radio to audiences of millions. During this time she also recorded over 300 songs and appeared in countless films. When she died in 1975 her funeral was the biggest ever witnessed in Cairo. She remains inescapable today; her music is played constantly in coffeehouses and taxis, her voice providing a powerful soundtrack to any visit to Egypt.

Umm Kolthum, Egypt's favourite singer

GIZA AND HELIOPOLIS

Giza and Heliopolis are two Cairo suburbs that are not only geographically opposed, they also epitomize two extremes of Egypt's history. Giza, in the southwest, is famed for its ancient monuments. The Sphinx, usually dated to around 2500 BC and the earliest known monumental sculpture, stands guard over the Pyramids at Giza, and their attendant Queens' pyramids, temples, and tombs. The Pyramids are the only one of the Seven Wonders of the Ancient World to survive. Even the accompanying circus of camel and horse rides, souvenir and soft drinks vendors, persistent beggars and the nightly Sound and Light show do not diminish their splendour. In the diagonally opposite suburb of Heliopolis, history moves on to the late 19th century and Baron Edouard Empain, the entrepreneur whose vision inspired this garden city in the desert. Built in a mixture of European and Moorish styles, Heliopolis attracted wealthy Egyptians to its leafy grandeur. Although it is no longer separate from Cairo, visitors still come to enjoy its stylish architecture, restaurants and nightlife.

Moorish detail from a façade in Heliopolis

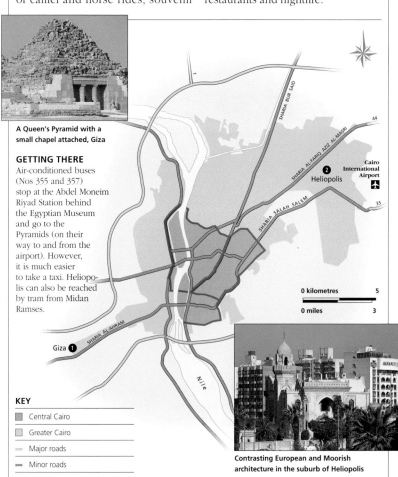

A Queen's Pyramid with a small chapel attached, Giza

GETTING THERE

Air-conditioned buses (Nos 355 and 357) stop at the Abdel Moneim Riyad Station behind the Egyptian Museum and go to the Pyramids (on their way to and from the airport). However, it is much easier to take a taxi. Heliopolis can also be reached by tram from Midan Ramses.

SHARIA BUR SAID

SHARIA AL FARIQ AZIZ AL-MASRI

44

Cairo International Airport

② Heliopolis

SHARIA SALAH SALEM

33

Giza ①

SHARIA AL-AHRAM

Nile

0 kilometres 5

0 miles 3

KEY

Central Cairo

Greater Cairo

Major roads

Minor roads

Contrasting European and Moorish architecture in the suburb of Heliopolis

◁ **The Sphinx, carved from an outcrop of soft limestone, in front of the Pyramid of Khafre at Giza**

The Giza Plateau ●

Nearly 5,000 years ago, Giza became the royal burial ground (necropolis) for Memphis, capital of Egypt. In less than 100 years, the ancient Egyptians built the three pyramid complexes to serve as the tombs for their dead kings. After the king's death, his body was brought by boat to the valley temple for preparation before being taken up the causeway and buried under, and in some cases within, the pyramid. The mortuary temples were maintained for many years afterwards with priests making daily offerings to the dead god-king. The king's close family and the royal court were buried in satellite pyramids and stone tombs called *mastaba* nearby, seeking to share in the king's power in death, as they had in life.

Pyramids of Giza
Three successive generations built these monumental structures during the 4th Dynasty of the Old Kingdom (2686–2181 BC).

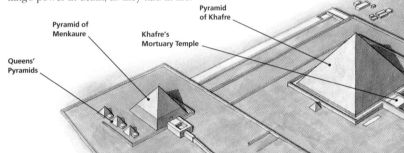

Pyramid of Khafre

Pyramid of Menkaure

Khafre's Mortuary Temple

Queens' Pyramids

GIZA PLATEAU RECONSTRUCTION

The funerary complex included the main pyramid, covered in white limestone, various satellite pyramids and a mortuary temple joined by a causeway to a valley temple.

Causeway

Pyramids of Menkaure and Khafre
While Khafre's Pyramid is nearly as grand as that of his father, Khufu, the Pyramid of Menkaure, Khafre's successor, is much smaller, hinting perhaps at a decline in power and commitment or simply a change in priorities.

Tomb of Khentkawes
This was the last major tomb built at Giza. Queen Khentkawes, daughter of Menkaure, probably gave birth to a new dynasty that moved its necropolis to Abu Sir.

STAR SIGHTS

★ The Great Pyramid

★ The Sphinx

MEANING OF THE GIZA PYRAMIDS

Archaeologists agree that pyramids served as monumental structures for the burial of kings. They were topped with gold-covered pyramidions (pyramid-shaped capstones) which caught the first rays of the sun and their shape perhaps symbolized the mythical, primeval mound of creation (see p26). However, because the exact purpose of some of the rooms and shafts of the Giza Pyramids is unknown, the fact that some air shafts point towards important constellations, that the southeast corners lie on a near perfect diagonal and that their sides align with true north inspires many to look hard for fanciful explanations. However, such alignments are simply consistent with ancient Egyptian funerary beliefs that the king's soul would rise up to join the "eternal stars".

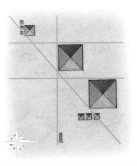

Mastaba tombs were built in the 4th and 5th Dynasty.

Boat pit

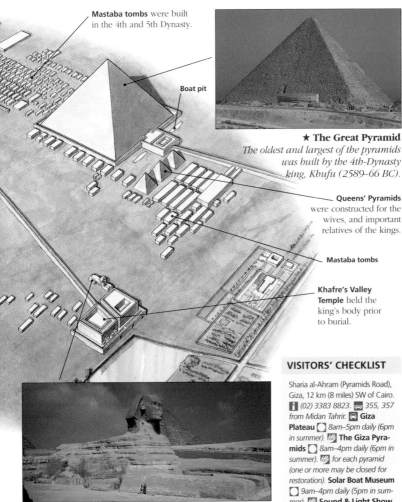

★ The Great Pyramid
The oldest and largest of the pyramids was built by the 4th-Dynasty king, Khufu (2589–66 BC).

Queens' Pyramids were constructed for the wives, and important relatives of the kings.

Mastaba tombs

Khafre's Valley Temple held the king's body prior to burial.

★ The Sphinx
Guardian of the Giza Plateau, the leonine Sphinx is known to the Arabs as Abu al-Hol, the "father of terror".

VISITORS' CHECKLIST

Sharia al-Ahram (Pyramids Road), Giza, 12 km (8 miles) SW of Cairo. (02) 3383 8823. 355, 357 from Midan Tahrir. **Giza Plateau** 8am–5pm daily (6pm in summer). **The Giza Pyramids** 8am–4pm daily (6pm in summer). for each pyramid (one or more may be closed for restoration). **Solar Boat Museum** 9am–4pm daily (5pm in summer). **Sound & Light Show** 6:30pm, 7:30pm, 8:30pm in winter (2.5 hours later in summer).

The Giza Plateau: The Great Pyramid

The facts of Khufu's Pyramid, commonly referred to as the Great Pyramid, are staggering. It is estimated to contain over two million blocks of stone weighing on average around 2.5 tonnes, with some stones at the base weighing as much as 15 tonnes. Until the 19th century it was the tallest building in the world. Yet for such a vast structure the precision is amazing – the greatest difference in length between the four 230-m (756-ft) sides is only 4 cm (2 inches). The construction methods and exact purpose of some of the chambers and shafts are unknown, but the fantastic architectural achievement is clear.

Statue of Khufu (Cheops)
Khufu's only surviving statue is this 7.5-cm (3-inch) high ivory figure from Abydos, now kept in the Egyptian Museum.

The Queen's Chamber probably held a statue representing the *ka* or life-force of the king.

The **"air shafts"** may have been symbolic paths for the king's soul to ascend to the stars.

Queens' Pyramids
These three small pyramids were built for members of the king's family, although the actual identity of the occupants is unknown.

Underlying bedrock

★ King's Chamber
Probably emptied 600 years after being built, the chamber, despite holding only a lidless sarcophagus, was often broken into by treasure seekers.

Unfinished underground chamber

★ Great Gallery
Soaring nearly 9 m (30 ft) high, this is thought to have been used as a slipway for the huge blocks that sealed the passageway.

STAR FEATURES

★ King's Chamber

★ Great Gallery

◁ **The Pyramids at Giza set in a timeless desert landscape**

RECONSTRUCTION OF THE KING'S CHAMBER

Built to protect the chamber, the stress-relieving rooms also hold the only reference to Khufu in the pyramid – graffiti, from the time of construction, stating the names of the gangs who built the pyramid - one such name being "How powerful is the great White Crown of Khufu".

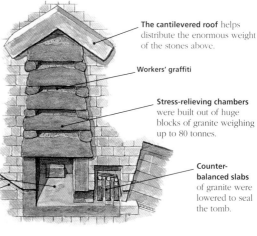

The cantilevered roof helps distribute the enormous weight of the stones above.

Workers' graffiti

Stress-relieving chambers were built out of huge blocks of granite weighing up to 80 tonnes.

Counter-balanced slabs of granite were lowered to seal the tomb.

King's Chamber

The "air shaft" would have been closed off by the outer casing.

This vertical shaft probably served as an escape route for the workers.

Entrance
The original entrance is now blocked and visitors use a lower opening made by the Caliph Maamun in AD 820.

THE DEVELOPMENT OF PYRAMIDS

It took the ancient Egyptians around 400 years to progress from mudbrick mastaba to smooth-sided pyramid. The last stage, from stepped to "true" or smooth-sided pyramid took only 65 years. In this time each pyramid was a brave venture into the unknown. Rarely in the history of mankind has technology developed at such a rate.

The Red or North Pyramid, at Dahshur (c.2600 BC)

Mastaba
Around 3000 BC the sandy mounds of the graves of the upper echelons of society were formalized into low, box-like mastabas.

Stepped pyramid (c.2665 BC)
A more impressive memorial was made by putting six stone mastabas on top of each other (see King Djoser's Pyramid pp162–3).

Prototype pyramid (c.2605 BC)
The first smooth-sided pyramid was achieved by filling in the steps of a stepped pyramid (see Meidum Pyramid p168). This was followed by purpose-built, smooth-sided pyramids.

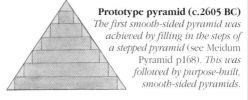

Exploring the Giza Plateau

For preservation purposes, each of the pyramids is closed for a spell on a rotating basis and the number of visitors allowed inside is limited. Early morning is therefore the best time to visit, before the heat and crowds become unbearable; it is also worth a trip in the evening for the kitsch but spectacular Sound and Light Show. It can get hot and airless inside the pyramids so clambering inside is not recommended for claustrophobics or the unfit. Camel owners tout expensive rides between the monuments but the area is compact enough to get around on foot.

Egyptian offering camel rides or simply a photo opportunity

The space-age shape of the Solar Boat Museum

🏛 Solar Boat Museum

On the south side of the Great Pyramid sits the pod-shaped, Solar Boat Museum. This holds a full-size ancient Egyptian boat discovered in pieces in 1954, lying in a pit beside the pyramid. Experts spent 14 years putting its 1200 pieces together again using only ancient Egyptian materials of wooden pegs and grass rope.

It is called a solar boat by archaeologists because it resembles the vessels seen in tomb paintings in which the sun-god makes his daily trip across the heavens. It is not clear whether the boat was buried for the sun-god or for the pharaoh's own journey across the heavens. Marks on the wood suggest that the boat had been sailed before being buried. It might have served as a funerary barque, carrying the body of Khufu from Memphis to his

tomb at Giza. A similar unexcavated boat in a nearby pit can be inspected in situ by camera for an additional fee.

⌂ Pyramid of Khafre

The base of the Pyramid of Khafre (also called Khephren), is just 15 m (50 ft) shorter than the Great Pyramid, while in height there is a difference of only 3 m (10 ft). Today, however, Khafre's pyramid appears the larger by virtue of being built on higher ground, and because its summit remains intact. This summit is the only area that retains the limestone casing that originally covered all three pyramids. The rest was taken by the medieval rulers of Cairo who used it for their own monuments.

The interior is simpler than that of the Great Pyramid. It has two descending passageways converging and leading to a single tomb chamber. Whereas Khufu's tomb chamber sits high up inside the structure, Khafre's is dug deep into the bedrock beneath his pyramid. There

Idu, guardian of the burial complexes

is little to see except the king's granite sarcophagus. Khafre's mortuary temple still has parts of a small sanctuary and a courtyard, and sections of the 500-m (550-yard) granite-lined causeway are still visible.

⌂ Pyramid of Menkaure

The last pyramid built on the Giza Plateau, the pyramid of Menkaure (also known as Mycerinus) has a base area less than a quarter of that of its two neighbours. Some attribute this to a reduction in the power of the king. However, others point to a change in priorities; the size of the pyramid has been reduced but its valley and mortuary temples are larger and more elaborate. This can perhaps be viewed as the start of a process that eventually saw pyramids abandoned, in favour of secret, rock-cut tombs with separate large funerary temples.

In the 12th century one of Cairo's sultans attempted to dismantle this pyramid. After eight months the project was abandoned, merely having achieved the vertical scar visible on the north face.

Inside, a passageway descends from the entrance to an antechamber decorated with a stylized false-door motif. Beyond that is another antechamber, from where a passage leads down to the tomb chamber carved from

The Sphinx and Pyramid of Khafre viewed from the edge of the plateau

For hotels and restaurants in this region see pp268–71 and pp290–96
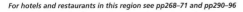

the bedrock. Its barrel-ceiling is carved from a giant granite roof slab. A beautifully decorated sarcophagus was discovered here in the early 19th century but it was lost at sea while being shipped to the British Museum in London.

⋔ The Sphinx

Standing guard at the approach to the Pyramid of Khafre, the Sphinx is the earliest known monumental sculpture of ancient Egypt. Archaeologists date it to around 2500 BC, crediting Khafre as the inspiration. It stands 20 m (66 ft) high with an elongated body, outstretched paws and a royal headdress framing a fleshy face, possibly that of the king himself. It is carved from an outcrop of natural rock, augmented by shaped blocks around the base, added during repeated renovations from the 18th Dynasty onwards.

Although it is often written that the Sphinx's nose was shot off by the Mamluks, Ottomans or Napoleon's French army, it was in fact lost some time before the 15th century. Originally the Sphinx also had a stylized false beard, symbol of royalty, but that too fell off. A piece taken from where it lay on the sand is now held by the British Museum in London.

Directly in front of the statue are the remains of the Sphinx Temple, closed to the public. Access to the area around the Sphinx is gained via the adjacent Valley Temple of Khafre, one of the oldest surviving temples in Egypt. At the time the pyramids were built, during the annual Nile flood, the waters came up to the edge of the Giza Plateau. Khafre's Valley Temple stood on a quay and served as a gateway to the pyramid, connected by a long, mostly covered, causeway. Buried in the sand, this was discovered by Auguste Mariette in 1852 and traces of it can still be seen today. The other two pyramids had similar complexes but their temples are not so well preserved.

The historic Mena House Hotel, at the edge of the Giza Plateau

Around the Giza Plateau

There are also several tombs worth a visit. The mastaba tombs near Khufu's Queens' Pyramids include the 6th-Dynasty **Tombs of Qar and Idu**. Qar was a high ranking official in charge of maintaining the pyramids and their associated ceremonies and his son, Idu, was the royal scribe. These have reliefs and statues of the deceased. The nearby tomb of Khufu's son **Khufu-khaf** has some perfectly preserved reliefs, while the tomb of Khafre's wife **Meresankh III** is intriguing. Its painted reliefs show Meresankh, a priestess dressed in the leopardskin usually associated with male priests, while her mother, the blonde-haired Hetepheres III, wears a dress with pointed shoulder pads.

After the dusty heat of the plateau, it makes a nice end to the day to have a drink at the luxurious **Mena House Hotel** and to contemplate the Pyramids as they take on the colour of the setting sun.

CLIMBING THE GREAT PYRAMID

At one time, a complete visit to the Great Pyramid entailed not only an exploration of the passages within, but a clamber to the top as well. A 1902 guidebook to Egypt describes how it was done: "Assisted by two Bedouins, one holding each hand, and, if desired, by a third (no extra payment) who pushes behind, the traveller begins the ascent of the steps". Once up there, many commemorated their climb

19th-century photograph of tourists climbing the Great Pyramid

by carving their names in stone. A recent archaeological project has been cataloguing each block of the pyramid. The graffiti noted includes the will of someone who climbed to the top and committed suicide and the names of two lovers carved together for all eternity. As early as 1840 writers complained about the excessive amount of graffiti. This is no longer an issue as since the 1980s, climbing the pyramids has been forbidden, although some people still try. This has been done as much to protect the monuments as to prevent injury and even death to climbers.

A Walk Through Heliopolis ❷

Hindu motif from Baron's Palace

A product of the visionary ambitions of a wealthy Belgian entrepreneur, Baron Edouard Empain (1852–1929), Heliopolis was built in the first decade of the 20th century. It was designed by a team of European and Egyptian architects as a self-contained garden city in the desert to the northeast of Cairo, linked to the centre by a tram system. Known in Egypt as Masr al-Gedida (New Cairo), Heliopolis has since been swallowed up by the expanding capital, but still retains some of its extraordinary original architecture. A magnet for wealth, this elegant, leafy suburb has good shops, restaurants and nightlife.

Around Uruba Palace

The walk begins where the bus or tram from Cairo swings left beside the high walls of the Uruba Palace ①. Formerly the Heliopolis Palace Hotel, one of the grandest hotels in the African continent, this is now the official residence of the Egyptian president and entry is strictly forbidden. Be careful not to wave your camera around, either, as it is not permitted to photograph the buildings. The palace's distinctive, drum-shaped wing once housed a magnificent ballroom.

Diagonally opposite the palace, at the junction of Sharia al-Ahram and Sharia Ibrahim Laqqany, is the venerable L'Amphitrion ②, a bar/restaurant that is as old as Heliopolis itself. The

SIGHTS ON WALK

L'Amphitrion ②
Baron's Palace ⑥
Basilica ⑤
Le Chantilly ⑧
Normandy Cinema ④
Sharia Baghdad ⑦
Sharia Ibrahim Laqqany ③
Uruba Palace ①

On the terrace of the L'Amphitrion cafeteria, Heliopolis

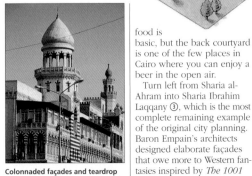

Colonnaded façades and teardrop turrets in Sharia Ibrahim Laqqany

food is basic, but the back courtyard is one of the few places in Cairo where you can enjoy a beer in the open air.

Turn left from Sharia al-Ahram into Sharia Ibrahim Laqqany ③, which is the most complete remaining example of the original city planning. Baron Empain's architects designed elaborate façades that owe more to Western fantasies inspired by *The 1001 Nights* than to any authentic Islamic architectural traditions. This particular street has a wonderful sweep of arcades with Moorish arches and balconies, punctuated by pretty little towers and turrets.

TIPS FOR WALKERS

Sarting point: *Sharia al-Ahram.*
Length: *4 km (2.5 miles).*
Duration: *1.5 hours.*
Getting there: *Airport bus No. 356 from the bus station behind the Egyptian Museum, trams from Midan Ramses, or taxi.*

For hotels and restaurants in this region see pp268–71 and pp290–96

The Baron, a train enthusiast, was also responsible for what was then a state-of-the-art electric tramway connecting his satellite city to central Cairo. Trams still rattle up the middle of Sharia al-Ahram, but now they are Eastern European models rather than the quaint double-deckers of old.

Turning right from Sharia Ibrahim Laqqany into Sharia Sayyid Abdel Wahid and right again, return to Sharia al-

Baron Empain's Byzantine-style Basilica, modelled on Istanbul's Aya Sofya

Ahram where, a little further along, on the left, is the Normandy cinema ④. Operating as an open-air auditorium during the summer months, the cinema screens Egyptian movies and the very occasional English-language film.

Basilica to Sharia Baghdad

Continuing up Sharia al-Ahram, the distinctive central arch of Empain's Basilica ⑥ can be seen straight ahead, serving as a reminder that Heliopolis was built by and for (Christian) Europeans. Empain and his family are buried in a crypt within the Basilica, which is designed in a highly stylized Byzantine manner, in order to resemble the Hagia Sofia church in Istanbul.

Turning right at Shahid Tayyar Nazih Khalila, a ten-minute walk leads to the most magnificent of follies, known as the Baron's Palace (Qasr al-Baron) ⑦. Built in 1910, this was Baron Empain's Cairo residence and, for reasons unknown, he had it designed to resemble a Hindu temple. The French architect, Alexander Marcel, based his design on a temple at Angkor Wat in Cambodia. Its sandstone exterior is covered with carved animals, Hindu symbols and gods. Legend has it that the building originally had a revolving tower, which allowed the owner to follow the sun throughout the day. The palace has been empty for decades and despite the fact that the building has been renovated, sadly, the palace and its grounds are closed to visitors.

Return to central Heliopolis along Sharia Abd al-Salaam Zaky, turning left onto Sharia Baghdad ⑧, which, like Sharia Ibrahim Laqqany earlier, contains a wealth of fantasy Oriental architecture. About halfway along, on the left, is Le Chantilly *(see p295)* ⑨, a Swiss-style restaurant and an excellent place to stop for a meal or a beer on the shady back terrace.

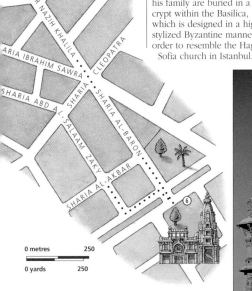

KEY

••• Walk route

▨ Tram stop

= Tram route

Carved sandstone façade of the Baron's Palace

CAIRO STREET FINDER

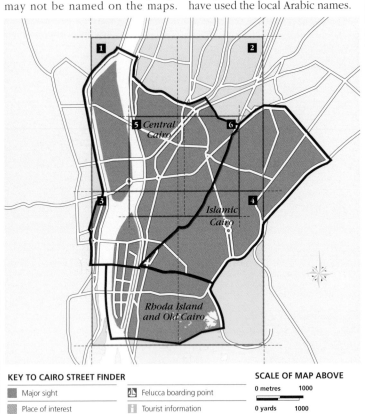

The map below shows the areas of the city covered by the *Street Finder*. The maps include the major sightseeing attractions and railway, bus and Metro stations. Map references are given for Cairo's restaurants *(see pp290–96)*, hotels *(see pp268–71)*, entertainment venues *(see pp152–3)* and shopping venues *(see pp 150–51)*. Some of Cairo's small streets and alleyways may not be named on the maps.

Sightseeing in Cairo

Some monuments have two names: one in Arabic and often a commonly used English-language form. What we call the Citadel, taxi drivers sometimes know only as *Al-Qalaa*. Refer to the Survival Guide for guidance on taxis *(see p344)*. In this guide and on the following maps, where there is a well-recognized English name, we have used it; otherwise we have used the local Arabic names.

Central Cairo

Islamic Cairo

Rhoda Island and Old Cairo

KEY TO CAIRO STREET FINDER

▨	Major sight	⚓	Felucca boarding point
▨	Place of interest	ℹ	Tourist information
▨	Other important building	✚	Hospital
🚉	Railway station	▣	Police station
🚌	Bus station	✉	Post office
🚋	Tram station	☾	Mosque
Ⓜ	Metro station	✝	Church
🚖	Taxi rank	✡	Synagogue
🚤	River taxi		

SCALE OF MAP ABOVE

0 metres   1000
0 yards   1000

SCALE OF MAPS 1–4

0 metres   200
0 yards   200

SCALE OF MAPS 5–6

0 metres   200
0 yards   200

◁ **Cairo at night – view from the Cairo Tower looking south down the Nile over the Opera House Complex**

Street Finder Index

Because of different preferences in the transliteration of Arabic into English, our spellings of street and place names may differ from those on street signs – which, of course, also carry Arabic script.

Note that the word "Sharia" denotes a street. Other Arabic words used here include "Midan" (a square), "Bab" (a gate), "Beit" (a house), "Kubri" (a bridge) and "Qasr" (a palace).

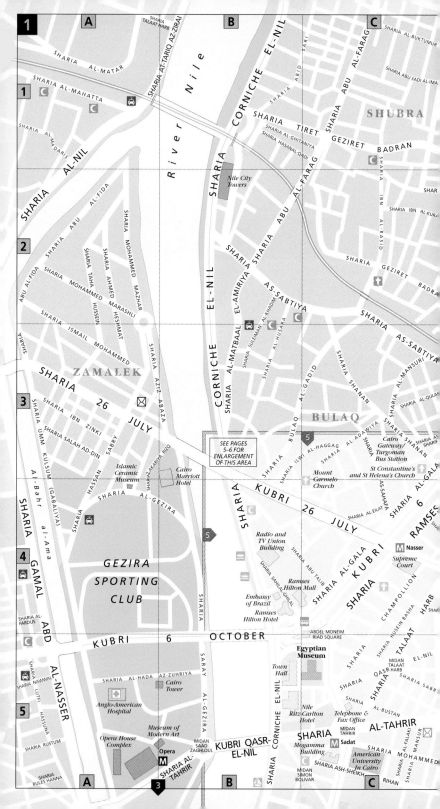

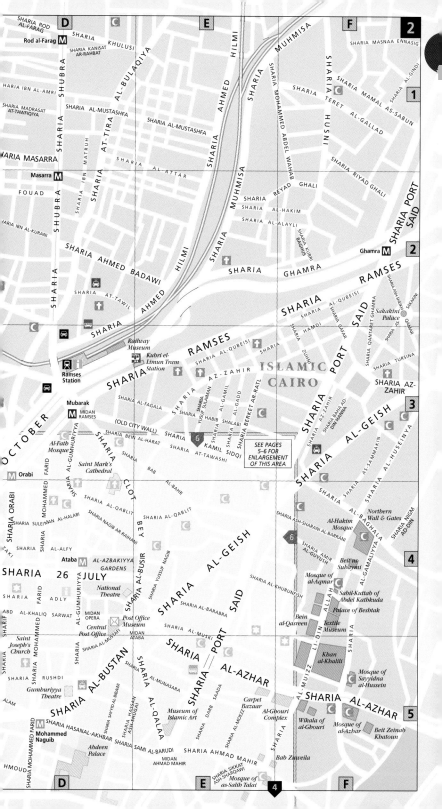

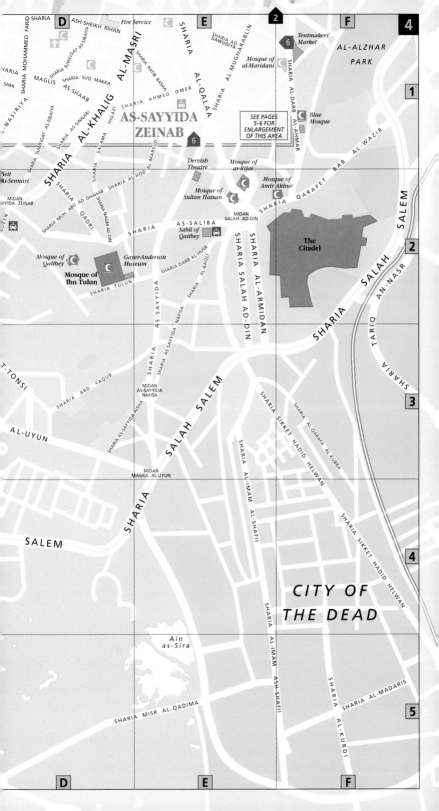

D ASH-SHEIKH RIHAN Fire Service **E** **2** **F** **4**

SHARIA MOHAMMED FARID SHARIA

SHARIA SUWEIDAT AS-SIBAYA

AL-MASRI

SHARIA AD
DAWUDIYA

Tentmakers'
Market

AL-ALZHAR
PARK

SHARIA AS-SINNARI

SHARIA RATIB BASHA

SHARIA AL-MUGHARABLIN

SHARIA AL-DARB

1

SHARIA AL-KHALIG

SHARIA AL-QALAA

SHARIA AHMED OMER

Mosque of
al-Maridani

SHARIA AL-AHMAR

SHARIA SUYIGGAT AS-SIBAYA

MAGLIS
AS-SHAAB

SHARIA SUQ MAKKA

SHARIA SAMI

SHARIA HIGAZI

SALAMA

**AS-SAYYIDA
ZEINAB**

SEE PAGES
5–6 FOR
ENLARGEMENT
OF THIS AREA

Blue
Mosque

BAB AL-WAZIR

Beit
As-Sennari

SHARIA QADRI

SHARIA AL-HOD

SHARIA AL-MARSUD

Dervish
Theatre

Mosque of
ar-Rifai

Mosque of
Amir Akbur

SHARIA QARAFET

MIDAN
YYIDA ZEINAB

SHARIA MUH. ABU AD DHAHAB

SHARIA NAGM AD-DIN

Mosque of
Sultan Hassan

SHARIA

AS-SALIBA

MIDAN
SALAH AD-DIN

SHARIA AL-ARMIDAN

**The
Citadel**

SHARIA SALAH

SHARIA QADRI

Mosque of
Qaitbey

Gayer-Anderson
Museum

SHARIA DARB AL-HUSR

Sabil of
Qaitbey

2

**Mosque of
Ibn Tulun**

SHARIA TULUN

SHARIA AS-SAYYIDA

SHARIA AL-BAQLI

SHARIA SALAH AD-DIN

TARIQ AN-NASR

SHARIA

SHARIA AS-SAYYIDA NAFISA

MIDAN
AS-SAYYIDA
NAFISA

3

T-TONSI

SHARIA ARD YAQUB

SHARIA AS-SAYYIDA-AISHA

SALEM

AL-UYUN

SALAH

MIDAN
MAGRA AL-UYUN

SHARIA AL-IMAM AL-SHAFII

SHARIA SIKKET HADID HELWAN

SHARIA AL-QARAFA AL-KUBRA

SALEM

SHARIA

4

SALEM

SHARIA SIKKET HADID HELWAN

**CITY OF
THE DEAD**

SHARIA AL-IMAM ASH-SHAFII

SHARIA AL-MADARIS

Ain
as-Sira

SHARIA AL-KURDI

SHARIA MISR AL-QADIMA

5

D **E** **F**

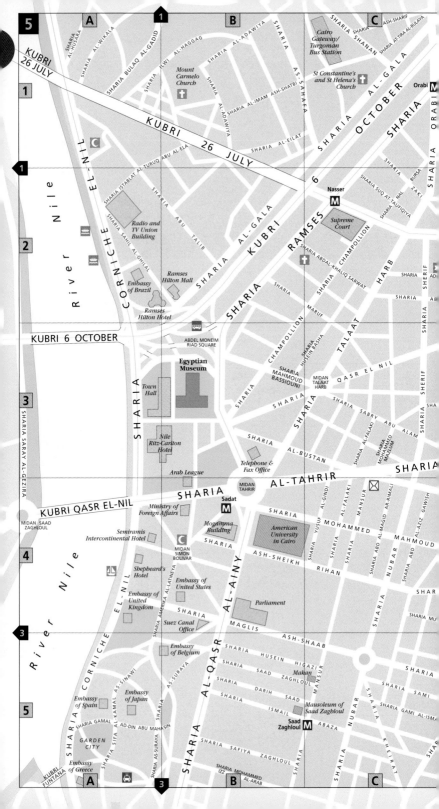

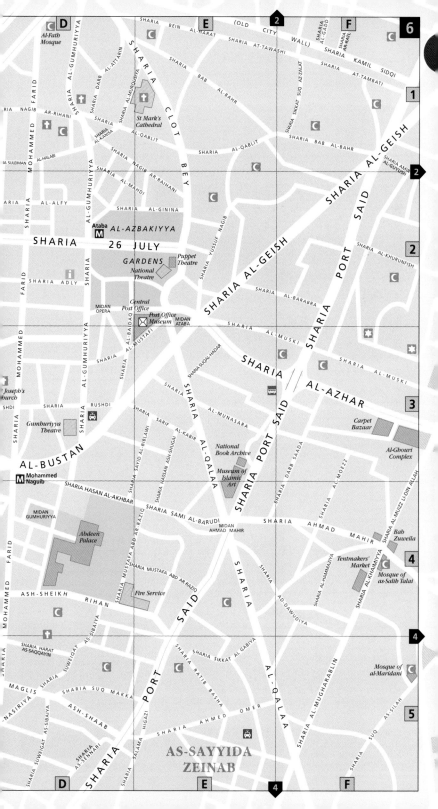

SHOPPING IN CAIRO

The hardest thing about shopping in Cairo is knowing when to stop. Souqs, or markets, sell all manner of goods. Khan al-Khalili is the best known: here you will be able to buy jewellery, statues, papyrus and many other items. Artisans such as coppersmiths and glass-makers tend to be gathered together, which helps keep prices low. Alternatively, shop in a modern mall. Here you will find many Western-style shops with recognizable brand names, but prices will be higher. Haggling, usually acceptable in the big shops, is vital in the souqs. Start at below half the asking price and go up in small amounts.

One of the many stalls in the Khan al-Khalili market

SOUQS AND MARKETS

Khan al-Khalili *(see p90)* is a large area of souqs and workshops. Bordering it on its west side is **Sharia al-Muizz li-Din Allah** *(see pp98–9)*, where you will find coppersmiths, goldsmiths, perfumes, spices and carpets. Sections of this wide alley are unofficially named according to the goods on offer: Souq al-Nahhasin (Coppersmiths' Market), Souq al-Sagha (Goldsmiths' and Jewellers' Market) or Souq al-Attarin (Spices Market). Al-Muizz li-Din Allah becomes Sharia al-Khaimiyya, site of **Souq al-Khaimiyya** (Tentmakers' Market) *(see p103)*. The **New Khan al-Khalili** is a market within a market, in the form of a miniature shopping mall in the heart of the souq.

Wikalit al-Balah (Dates Market) is close to the Nile, between Kubri 26 July and the Conrad International Hotel. Everything is sold here – from fruit to car parts – and prices for textiles, curtains and lace are the lowest in Cairo.

MALLS

The **Four Seasons** has designer brands. **Arkadia Mall** and **Citystars** are vast and glitzy malls with many outlets. Others include the **Ramses Hilton Annexe**, **Four Seasons First Mall** and **Nile City Towers**.

Sheesha pipe

SOUVENIRS

Most "papyrus" souvenirs are actually machine-printed banana stalk. For the genuine article, head to one of the reputable stores in a high-end hotel or to **Al-Ghouri Papyrus Art**. **Dr Ragab's Papyrus Institute** gives you an insight into papyrus's history and manufacture.

You can purchase *sheesha* pipes from **Al Tarbiaa** or, much cheaper, from workshops in Khan al-Khalili. The **Old Shop Gallery** in Khan al-Khalili sells antiques.

HANDICRAFTS

You will always get a good deal at hard-to-find workshop **El-Eraki**. Workshops

are also the best places to buy mother-of-pearl boxes, since the artisans will be keen to show you their best work. Muski glass can be found at **Afnan**, in New Khan al-Khalili and other malls; for the rarer red Muski glass, head to **Saed Abd El-Raouf**. Good-quality *mashrabiyya* ornamental woodwork can be found at the workshop of **El Osta Hussein**. For quality leather goods, head downtown to **Vero Chic** and **Silver Eagle**.

MUSICAL INSTRUMENTS

Most music shops are on and around Sharia Mohammed Ali (al-Qalaa), south of Midan Ataba. Instruments for sale include the *rababa*, a sort of fiddle, and the *oud*, a round-bodied stringed instrument. Good shops to visit are **Abdel Ghafar** and **Gawharet El Fan**.

JEWELLERY

The Souq al-Sagha in Khan al-Khalili is thick with jewellers. Try **Mohamed Amin, Atlas Jewellery** or **Azza Fahmy**. Gold and silver are sold by weight: the shopkeeper will weigh the item and quote a price. This is only a starting price to haggle around.

A dazzling array of silver jewellery on display in a market

TEXTILES

For belly-dancing costumes, try **Saad Hassan Bazaar**, in Khan al-Khalili. Traditional Bedouin jewellery, crafts and costumes can be found at **Nomad**. If you are in search of appliqué, head to the Souq al-Khaimiyya (Tentmakers' Market), and to the **Fattoh Sons** and **El Khiamiah Star** stores in particular.

One of the oldest and largest conventional places to purchase carpets and rugs in Khan al-Khalili is **El Kahhal Carpets**. Here you can spend hours taking tea with the owner while every carpet in the shop is displayed for you.

SPICES AND PERFUMES

Spices and herbs make excellent gifts to bring back home from Egypt. Head to Khan al-Khalili for the widest selection at the best prices.

Perfume shops such as **Al-Haroun Bazaar** sell quality perfumes and aromatic oils and you will get a good deal if you haggle hard.

The colourful range of spices for sale at a market in Cairo

DIRECTORY

MALLS

Arkadia Mall
Corniche el-Nil, Bulaq.
Map 1 B2.

Citystars Mall
Stars Centre, Heliopolis.

Four Seasons First Mall
Sharia al-Giza, Giza.

Four Seasons Nile Plaza
Corniche el-Nil,
Garden City.
Map 3 B1.

Nile City Towers
Corniche el-Nil, Boulaq.
Map 1 B2.

Ramses Hilton Annexe
1115 Corniche el-Nil,
Downtown
Map 5 B2.

SOUVENIRS

Al-Ghouri Papyrus Art
(upstairs, beside Wikala al-Ghouri), Sharia al-Azhar.
Map 2 F5.
Tel (02) 2512 5859.

Al Tarbiaa
51 Ramses Hilton Annexe.
Map 5 B2.
Tel (02) 2575 2399.

Dr Ragab's Papyrus Institute
Houseboat on Corniche el-Nil, Giza.
Tel (02) 3571 8675.

Old Shop Gallery
7 Khan al-Khalili.
Map 2 F5.
Tel (02) 2787 0378.

HANDICRAFTS

Afnan
25A El Batal Ahmed Abdel Aziz, Mohandiseen.
Tel (02) 3304 2563.
Other branches:
Arkadia Mall,
New Khan al-Khalili,
Ramses Hilton Annexe.

El-Eraki
55 Sharia Mossadak,
Dokki.
Tel (02) 3337 0646.

El Osta Hussein
22 Tabozada (off Sharia Mohammed Ali/Al-Qalaa).
Map 6 E4.
Tel (02) 2291 9858.

Saed Abd El-Raouf
8 Khan al-Khalili.
Map 2 F5.
Tel (02) 2593 3463.

Silver Eagle
18 Sharia Adly,
Downtown. **Map** 5 D2.
Tel (02) 2393 6704.

Vero Chic
19 Sharia Talaat Harb,
Downtown. **Map** 5 C3.
Tel (02) 2393 1895.

MUSICAL INSTRUMENTS

Abdel Ghafar
39 Sharia al-Bustan,
Bab el-Louk.
Tel (02) 2794 4948.

Gawharet El Fan
160–168 Sharia
Mohammed Ali (Al-Qalaa),
Al-Ataba. **Map** 6 E4.
Tel (02) 2391 5243.

JEWELLERY

Atlas Jewellery
10 Sharia Khan al-Khalili.
Tel (02) 2590 6139.

Azza Fahmy
15C Sharia Taha Hussein,
Zamalek. **Map** 1 A2.
Tel (02) 2735 8531.

Mohamed Amin
5 Sharia Taha Hussein,
Zamalek. **Map** 1 A3.
Tel (02) 2736 4375.

TEXTILES

El Kahhal Carpets
Khan al-Khalili.
Map 2 F5.
Tel (02) 2590 9128.

El Khiamiah Star
Bab Zuweila. **Map** 6 F4.
Tel (02) 2510 6388.

Fattoh Sons
Bab Zuweila. **Map** 6 F4.
Tel (02) 2512 8853.

Nomad
14 Sharia Saray al-Gezira,
Zamalek. **Map** 1 B4.
Tel (02) 2736 1917.

Saad Hassan Bazaar
Sharia Gouhar al-Kaad
(off Midan al-Hussein),
Khan al-Khalili.
Tel (02) 2588 0834.

SPICES AND PERFUMES

Al-Haroun Bazaar
Garden City House Hotel,
1101–1103 Corniche el-Nil, Garden City.
Map 5 A4.
Tel (02) 2794 7534.

ENTERTAINMENT IN CAIRO

Cairo is a big, bustling city, with plenty to keep you occupied. Be aware that Cairenes are night owls, often not dining until 11pm and then partying on until morning. For a predominantly Muslim city, there is a surprising number of bars, particularly in upmarket districts such as Zamalek, catering mainly to the young and the expat community. The Cairo Opera House is the venue for Arabic music, classical opera and ballet. The Al-Ghouri Complex puts on regular shows of whirling-dervish dancing, and you can find displays of belly dancing in many places, though the standard varies.

A colourful performance of whirling-dervish dancing

INFORMATION AND LISTINGS

Your hotel concierge should be able to suggest a range of entertainment options. The listings in local publications will help with any specialized interests, such as classical or jazz music, art exhibitions, theatre or cinema. Get a copy of *Al-Ahram Weekly*, the local newspaper, the glossy monthly *Egypt Today* or the funky free *iCroc* guide for detailed listings (www.icroc.com). Last-minute changes of programme or venue are possible so call ahead.

BELLY DANCING

Belly-dancing shows are held twice weekly in some of the larger hotels – including, the **Aladin Club** at the Cairo Sheraton and the **Haroun al-Rashid** at the Semiramis Interconti-nental. Alternatively, embark on a dinner-and-belly-dancing cruise. The **Nile Maxim** is the best, and you have a choice of two sessions: 8–10pm or 10pm–midnight. Less touristy are the many clubs along the Pyramids Road in Giza and Sharia al-Alfy, Downtown. **Sheherazade**, in Downtown, has a good local flavour.

WHIRLING DERVISHES

Whirling-dervish dancing developed from a religious rite connected with Sufism. Sufis claim that the centuries-old dizzying dance produces a state of trance that brings protagonists closer to God. Wonderfully intense, colour-ful displays can be seen at the **Wikala al-Ghouri**, just south of the Al-Azhar mosque, on Monday, Wednesday and Saturday nights at 8pm. There is no charge for entry, but collecting a ticket at 6:30pm is recommended.

CLASSICAL AND ARABIC MUSIC

The huge, domed **Cairo Opera House** complex in Gezira is the home to most classical

A classical quintet performing at the Cairo Opera House

music, in the form of the Cairo Symphony Orchestra and the Cairo Opera. There are regular performances in the Main Hall, the Small Hall and the Open-Air Theatre. Look also for performances at **Beit al-Harawi**, the **Goethe Institute Gardens** at Midan al-Missaha in Doqqiand the **Gumhuriyya Theatre**, just south of Al-Ataba.

JAZZ AND ROCK MUSIC

The **Cairo Jazz Club** is the main venue for jazz, electronic, funk and Oriental music. It also offers good food and drink, not to mention a hip ambience that makes it popular with young bar-hoppers. Down-town's **After 8** is a smokey den that features local talent. Jazz events are also held at the various venues within the Cairo Opera House. Most of the big hotels have live music in their bars and cafés too. The **Jazz Bar** at Kempinski Hotel in Garden City is an especially good venue.

BARS AND NIGHTCLUBS

There is no real centre to the nightlife in Cairo, so a night out on the town usually involves taxi-hopping from bar to restaurant to nightclub. Wednesdays and Thursdays tend to be the busiest nights.

The **Sherlock Holmes** in the Ramses Hilton is a quiet English-style pub, and the **Promenade Café** at the Cairo Marriott Hotel is a good place to enjoy a beer and a *sheesha*. Most top-end hotels have roof-top bars with great vie ws of the city, though less well-heeled Cairenes prefer the terrace bar of the **Odeon Palace Hotel**, where the beer is much cheaper.

Two restaurants in Zamalek, **La Bodega** and **L'Aubergine**, have trendy bars that stay open late.

Some of the best nightclubs are at the big hotels – for example, **Club 35** at the Four Seasons First Residence and **The Bar** at the Four Seasons Nile Plaza, which is open until 3am. For dancing under the stars, try the floating restaurants moored up at

Zamalek: **Le Pacha 1901** and the **Moon Deck on the Blue Nile**. Younger clubbers prefer to gather at **Purple** on the Imperial floating restaurant moored near the Marriott Hotel. The upmarket club **Tamarai**, in the Nile City Towers, offers an extremely glamorous night out. There's an outdoor terrace, and the bar serves excellent cocktails.

OTHER ENTERTAINMENT

There is no denying that the **Sound and Light Show** held against the stunning backdrop of the Giza Pyramids is impressive. Travellers with children may enjoy a visit to **Cairo Zoo**, while the **Pharaonic Village**, also at Giza, involves a boat trip and a wide choice of museums, historic reconstructions and activities.

DIRECTORY

BELLY DANCING

Aladin Club
Sheraton Cairo Hotel Towers and Casino, Midan el-Gala, Doqqi. **Map** 3 A1.
Tel (02) 3336 9700.
www.starwoodhotels.com/sheraton

Haroun al-Rashid
Semiramis InterContinental, Corniche el-Nil, Downtown. **Map** 5 A4.
Tel (02) 2795 7171.
www.intercontinental.com

Nile Maxim
Sharia Saray al-Gezira (opposite Cairo Marriott Hotel), Zamalek.
Map 1 B4.
Tel (02) 2632 5917.

Sheherazade
Sharia Alfy Bey, Downtown. **Map** 2 D4.

WHIRLING DERVISHES

Wikala al-Ghouri
off Sharia al-Azhar, Islamic Cairo. **Map** 2 F5.

CLASSICAL AND ARABIC MUSIC

Beit al-Harawi
Harat al-Azhar, Islamic Cairo. **Map** 2 F5.
Tel (02) 2735 7001.

Cairo Opera House
Sharia at-Tahrir, Gezira.
Map 1 A5.
Tel (02) 2739 0114.

Goethe Institute
13 Sharia Hussein Wassef Midan al-Missaha, Doqqi.
Tel (02) 3748 4501.

Gumhuriyya Theatre
12 Sharia al-Gumhuriyya, Downtown. **Map** 6 D3.
Tel (02) 2390 7707.

JAZZ AND ROCK MUSIC

After 8
6 Sharia Qasr el-Nil, Downtown. **Map** 5 B3.
Tel (010) 339 8000.

Cairo Jazz Club
197 Sharia 26th July, Mohandiseen.
Tel (02) 3345 9939.

Jazz Bar
Kempinski Hotel, 12 Sharia Ahmed Ragheb, Corniche el-Nil, Garden City. **Map** 3 B1.
Tel (02) 2789 0000.
www.kempinski.com

BARS AND NIGHTCLUBS

L'Aubergine
5 Al-Sayyid al-Bakri, Zamalek. **Map** 1 A3.
Tel (02) 2738 0080.

The Bar
Four Seasons Hotel Cairo at Nile Plaza, 1089 Corniche el-Nil, Garden City.
Map 3 B1.
Tel (02) 2791 7000.
www.fourseasons.com/caironp

La Bodega
157 Sharia 26th July, Zamalek. **Map** 1 A3.
Tel (02) 2735 6761.

Buddah Bar
Sofitel El Gezira Hotel, 3 Sharia Thawra, Zamalek.
Map 3 A1.
Tel (02) 2737 3737.

Club 35
Four Seasons First Residence, 35 Sharia al-Giza. **Map** 3 A3.
Tel (02) 3573 1212.

Moon Deck
Blue Nile (boat), 9A Saray al-Gezira, Zamalek.
Map 5 A3.
Tel (02) 2735 3114.

Odeon Palace Hotel Bar
6 Abdel Hamid Said (off Sharia Talaat Harb), Downtown. **Map** 5 C2.
Tel (02) 2576 7971.

Le Pacha 1901
Saray al-Gezira, Zamalek.
Map 5 A3.
Tel (02) 2735 6730.

Promenade Café
Cairo Marriott Hotel, Sharia Saray al-Gezira, Zamalek. **Map** 1 B3.
Tel (02) 2735 8888.

Purple
Imperial Restaurant (boat), Saray al-Gezira, Zamalek.
Map 1 B4.
Tel (02) 2736 5796.

Sherlock Holmes
Ramses Hilton, 1115 Corniche el-Nil, Downtown. **Map** 5 A2.
Tel (02) 2577 7444.
www.hilton.com

Tamarai
Nile City Towers, Rhod al-Farag. **Map** 1 B2.
http://tamarai-egypt.com

OTHER ENTERTAINMENT

Cairo Zoo
Sharia Mourad, Giza.
Tel (02) 3570 8895.

Dr Ragab's Pharaonic Village
3 Sharia el-Bahr el-Aazam, Giza.
Tel (02) 3571 8676.

Sound and Light Show
The Pyramids, Giza.
www.soundandlight.com.eg

EGYPT
AREA BY AREA

Egypt at a Glance

Most of Egypt's great Pharaonic monuments
lie along the Nile Valley, but visitors should not
ignore the variety of sights and activities on
offer elsewhere. From the vast desert expanses
to the biblical scenery of the rocky Sinai interior,
Egypt fully engages the senses. For those who
need to be near the sea, the north coast is lined
with Mediterranean-influenced cities
and beaches, while the
resorts and dive centres
on the Red Sea coast
allow access to the
stunning coral reefs.

The Bent pyramid at Dahshur *(see p165)*
in the pyramid fields around Cairo

**THE DELTA AND THE
NORTH COAST**
(pp234–51)

**AROUND
CAIRO**
(pp158–69)

Statue in the Graeco-Roman
Museum gardens in
Alexandria *(see pp240–47)*

**THE WESTERN
DESERT**
(pp252–61)

Siwa *(see p260)*, the most isolated of Egypt's oases and a
living antiquity in the midst of the Western Desert

Farmer working in the well-watered fields
around Dakhla Oasis *(see p256)*

| 0 kilometres | 150 |
| 0 miles | 100 |

◁ Man riding a camel beside the Nile with view of Luxor on the opposite bank

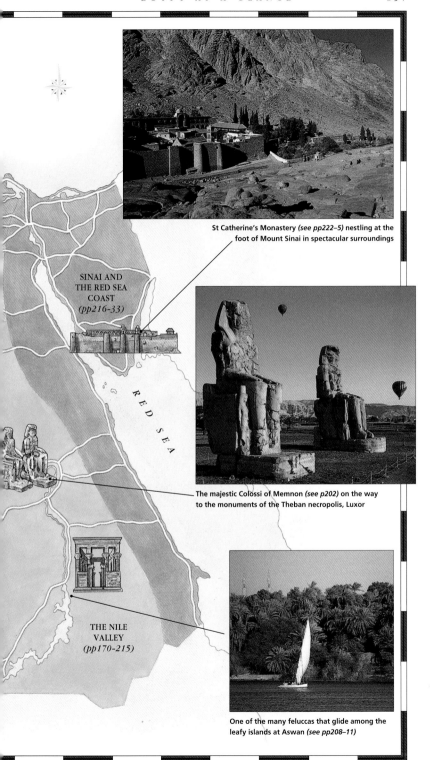

St Catherine's Monastery *(see pp222–5)* nestling at the foot of Mount Sinai in spectacular surroundings

**SINAI AND
THE RED SEA
COAST**
(pp216-33)

R E D   S E A

The majestic Colossi of Memnon *(see p202)* on the way to the monuments of the Theban necropolis, Luxor

**THE NILE
VALLEY**
(pp170-215)

One of the many feluccas that glide among the leafy islands at Aswan *(see pp208–11)*

AROUND CAIRO

*D*esert expanses around the modern capital offer escapism in many forms. Cairenes flock to the greenery of Fayoum and Qanater, while visitors can explore millennia of human ingenuity and achievement in the glorious monuments of Egypt's Old Kingdom burial sites and the monastic retreats of early Christians.

The ruins of Memphis, a religious and commercial centre of vast importance nearly 4,000 years before the birth of Egypt's present capital, are situated on the left bank of the Nile about 30 km (19 miles) south of Cairo. One of the main necropolises of Memphis, Saqqara is rich in fascinating sites: prototype pyramids; tombs with the earliest known examples of Pharaonic decorative writing; the mysterious Serapeum, an underground tomb dedicated to the sacred Apis bulls, and some of the deepest burial chambers in Egypt. Other ancient burial sites nearby include Abusir, where a cluster of pyramids built for the principal 5th-Dynasty pharaohs is located on the edge of the desert, and remote Dahshur, home to several stone and mudbrick pyramids including the intriguing Bent Pyramid. West of the Delta region, between Alexandria and Cairo, are the monasteries of Wadi Natrun. Valued by the ancient Egyptians as a source of *natron*, the salt used during mummification, Wadi Natrun became, in the Roman era, a bolt hole for persecuted Christians, and later a centre of monasticism. Of several monasteries here, Deir as-Suriani, Deir Abu Makar and Deir Anba Bishoi are the most beautiful.

Fayoum is famed for its abundant fruits and vegetables, fragrant flowers and orange blossom. Its vast salt lake hosts a rich population of waterfowl. The area is renowned for its prehistoric remains and has numerous Ptolemaic and Roman archaeological sites. To sail along the Nile from Cairo to the gardens of Qanater is another favourite excursion of city residents.

Boating on the lake at Wadi Rayyan, a popular leisure activity for modern Cairenes

◁ The Step Pyramid and vast funeral complex of Djoser, a 3rd-Dynasty king, in the desert at Saqqara

Exploring Around Cairo

When the hustle of Cairo gets too much, it is easy to slow down the pace a little by visiting one of the many interesting sights outside the capital. Saqqara attracts far fewer visitors and covers a larger area than the Pyramids at Giza and so rarely feels crowded, while the pyramid fields of Abusir and Dahshur are often practically deserted. Pharaonic remains are also dotted throughout Fayoum Oasis, although most make the trip for the lush vegetation. The other option for grassy spaces and trees is to sail down the Nile to Qanater, but this is so popular at the weekends that it is often just as congested as the city everyone is looking to escape. For real peace and quiet the best option, as the early Christians discovered, is to head out into the desert. Wadi Natrun is one of the founding sites of monasticism and the monks, although on holy retreat, are gracious when receiving visitors.

View of the mortuary temple and pyramid of Sahure at Abusir

Farmers tending their sheep near Memphis, the first capital of ancient Egypt

GETTING AROUND

Abusir, Saqqara, Memphis and Dahshur all lie on the same road; unfortunately, it is not served by public transport and the only option is to hire your own. Most hotels in Cairo can arrange a taxi or, even better, a car and driver for the day. Birqash camel market is only really accessible by car or taxi, too. Buses for Wadi Natrun and Fayoum depart from the Cairo Gateway bus station (formerly known as Turgoman Station).

Alexandria

WADI NATRUN **8** 🏛 **11**

Medinet el Sadat

10

Gebel Qairani

Bahariyya Oasis

Wadi al Hitan

Birket Qarun   Sanh

Qarun   **FAYOU**

El Shawashna

Tubhar

Wadi Rayyan

Abu Gandir

El Gharaq el Sultani

0 kilometres   25

0 miles   15

SIGHTS AT A GLANCE

Abusir ❶
Birqash ❻
Dahshur ❹
Fayoum ❺
Memphis ❸
Nile Barrages (Qanater) ❼
Saqqara pp162–4 ❷
Wadi Natrun ❽

Date palms at Fayoum Oasis, inspiration for Pharaonic columns

KEY

═══ Motorway

▬▬ Major road

═══ Minor road

– – Track

═══ Main railway

—— Minor railway

SEE ALSO

- *Where to Stay* pp271–2

- *Where to Eat* p296

The Red Pyramid at Dahshur, so called because of
ancient red graffiti found inside

Abusir ❶

Off Hwy 27, 27 km (17 miles) S of Cairo. 🚗 🚌 8am–3pm daily. 📷

The cluster of four 5th-Dynasty pyramids at Abusir has not aged as well as the Giza complex *(see pp28–9)*. Instead, the site's appeal comes from its location at the edge of the desert and the fact that few tourists ever venture here.

Only the northernmost and best-preserved **Pyramid of Sahure** can be entered, though this is not recommended for claustrophobics. The pyramid is fronted by a mortuary temple, which has partially reconstructed walls with reliefs of sea voyages and scenes of the king hunting. To the left, the **Pyramid of Nyuserre** is badly dilapidated but has the most complete causeway linking its valley and mortuary temples. Further south is the **Pyramid of Neferirkare**. The brother and successor of Sahure, Neferirkare died while his pyramid was still being constructed, so it was hastily completed with a facing of perishable mudbrick. This has since crumbled away to reveal a six-stepped stone inner core, similar to Djoser's pyramid at Saqqara. Finally, to the southwest lies the unfinished **Pyramid of Neferefre**, still being excavated by Czech archaeologists.

Abusir has also been the site of two major archaeological finds. In the 19th century, a famed set of Old Kingdom papyri, describing schedules of ceremonies and festivals, was discovered. Then, in 1998, a team of Czech archaeologists found the undisturbed tomb of a 6th-century BC Egyptian priest, Iufaa, containing Iufaa's mummy and hundreds of artifacts such as amulets and *shabtis (see p29)*.

The pyramids of Abusir on the edge of the desert

Saqqara ❷

A mounted policeman

Saqqara is one of the richest archaeological sites in Egypt. Its monuments span 3,000 years, from the earliest ancient Egyptian funerary structures to Coptic monasteries. Saqqara developed as the royal necropolis for the Old Kingdom capital of Memphis, just to the west. As Memphis grew, so did this city of the dead until it covered an area of 7 km (4 miles), north to south. While Saqqara continued to be used as a burial site for officials for a time, it was eventually abandoned and, apart from Djoser's pyramid, lay buried under sand for centuries. Then, in 1851, Auguste Mariette discovered the Serapeum, since when regular finds continue to be made at Saqqara.

Step Pyramid of Djoser at Saqqara, built by the architect Imhotep

🏛 Step Pyramid of Djoser

The centrepiece of the Saqqara necropolis is the Step Pyramid of Djoser, the prototype for all other pyramids. This remarkable structure was built for 3rd-Dynasty King Djoser by his architect, the high priest Imhotep, in the 27th century BC and is currently undergoing extensive exterior conservation work. This pyramid marks an unprecedented leap forward in the history of world architecture. Until then, Egyptian royal tombs had been underground rooms covered with low, flat, mud-brick *mastabas (see pp130–1)*. The great innovator Imhotep chose to use stone rather than mud-brick, and to build not just one *mastaba* but six, one on top of the other, with each additional layer smaller than the one beneath it. The vast enclosure surrounding the step pyramid marked yet another major achievement. Bounded by a finely cut limestone wall originally 10.5 m (34 ft) high, this complex included vast open courts, pavilions, shrines and chapels.

A part of the ancient wall has been restored in the south-east corner, and this provides the entrance to the enclosure. A colonnaded corridor of 40 pillars, ribbed in imitation of palm stems, leads

Frieze of cobras, Saqqara

into the Great South Court, where things to look out for include a restored section of wall bearing a frieze of cobras. Some of the oldest known examples of tourist graffiti, dating from the 12th century BC, can be seen preserved under perspex in buildings east of the pyramid. On the north side of the pyramid, there is a life-size painted statue of Djoser in a *serdab*, a stone box designed to allow the dead king's *ka* (spirit) to interact with the living world. The statue is a replica – the original is in Cairo's Egyptian Museum *(see p76)*. The excellent Imhotep Museum has six galleries with pieces found both here and at Abusir. One gallery is dedicated to the French archaeologist Jean-Philippe Lauer who died in 2001 having devoted 75 years to restoring these monuments.

Pyramid of Unas

Unas was the last king of the 5th Dynasty. His tomb is covered with vertical columns of hieroglyphic text designed to protect the king in the afterlife. These so-called Pyramid Texts are the earliest known examples of decorative writing in a Pharaonic tomb chamber. They later formed the basis

Pyramid Texts in the chambers of the Pyramid of Unas, Saqqara

of the New Kingdom Book of the Dead *(see pp28–9)*. Unfortunately, deterioration caused by too many visitors means that the pyramid is now closed to the public.

More than 200 *mastabas* and tombs line the causeway running east of the pyramid. Many of them are beautifully decorated and open to visitors.

VISITORS' CHECKLIST

Off Hwy 27, 44 km (27 miles) S of Cairo. 🚌 or tour from Cairo. ◯ 8am–4pm daily. 📷

Persian Tombs

Some of the deepest underground burial chambers discovered in Egypt, the Persian Tombs, are situated immediately south of the Pyramid of Unas. A spiral staircase leads down from a wooden hut to the final resting places of three Persian noblemen. Psamtik, Djenhebu and Pediese were all officials of the 27th Dynasty. Colourful inscriptions on the walls of the tombs reveal that Psamtik was chief physician of the pharaoh's court and Djenhebu was a famous Persian admiral. Pediese was Psamtik's son and held various official titles.

MAP OF SAQQARA

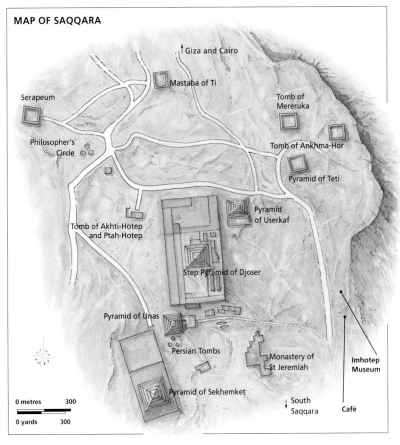

Giza and Cairo

Mastaba of Ti

Serapeum

Tomb of Mereruka

Philosopher's Circle

Tomb of Ankhma-Hor

Pyramid of Teti

Tomb of Akhti-Hotep and Ptah-Hotep

Pyramid of Userkaf

Step Pyramid of Djoser

Pyramid of Unas

Persian Tombs

Monastery of St Jeremiah

Imhotep Museum

Pyramid of Sekhemket

South Saqqara

Café

0 metres   300

0 yards   300

Pyramid of Teti

The pyramid of Teti, who was the first king of the 6th Dynasty, looks like nothing more than a mound of rubble. However, it is worth visiting for its burial chamber, which contains the king's well-preserved giant basalt sarcophagus. The ceiling of the chamber is decorated with carved stars, and the walls are inscribed with sections of Pyramid Texts. Though found in several pyramids on the Saqqara site, this is currently the only place where these ancient funerary writings are accessible to the public.

Statue of Mereruka emerging from a false door in his tomb at Saqqara

Tomb of Mereruka

An extensive complex of 33 chambers, the tomb of Mereruka, Teti's son-in-law, is one of the highlights of Saqqara. The tomb has some magnificent wall paintings, including a marsh scene with Mereruka hunting among birds, fish and hippos, and in another chamber a scene showing tax evaders being punished. The largest hall, which has a stone ring at its centre for tethering sacrificial animals, contains a life-size statue of Mereruka striding forward from a false door.

Tomb of Ankhma-Hor

A short walk from Mereruka's tomb is the tomb of Ankhma-Hor, also referred to as the "Physician's Tomb" because of its fascinating wall reliefs depicting surgical operations.

These include surgery being performed on a man's toe and, apparently, a circumcision, as practised in the 6th Dynasty.

Serapeum

Saqqara's strangest monument is the eerie underground burial chamber of the sacred Apis bulls. The Serapeum consists of a series of long, dark passageways lined with side chambers, which house 25 giant granite sarcophagi. Weighing up to 70 tons each, the sarcophagi once contained the mummified corpses of the Apis bulls. Seen as an incarnation of Ptah, god of Memphis, the Apis bulls were looked after by priests. When they died they were buried with great ceremony in the rock-cut, subterranean galleries of the Serapeum. The catacombs were begun by Amenhotep III (1390–52 BC) and remained in use until 30 BC. They are currently closed to the public.

When Auguste Mariette discovered the site in 1851, he found that all the tombs had been broken into and pillaged except for one. Inside was a sarcophagus containing a mummified bull, now in the Agricultural Museum in Cairo.

Mastaba of Ti

East of the Serapeum, the Mastaba of Ti is the tomb of a court official who served three kings during the 5th Dynasty. Its wall paintings are unrivalled for the wealth of information they provide about everyday life in Old Kingdom Egypt. The far chamber has the best reliefs and also three slits in the wall revealing Ti's statue in its *serdab*. This was a room for the deceased's statue in which his spirit or *ka* resided.

Philosopher's Circle

This grouping of statues, near the Serapeum, was set in place by the Ptolemaic Greeks. The circle of figures includes Plato and Homer, although most are in a very poor condition. The circle was originally designed as an adjunct to a temple built by the last truly Egyptian pharaoh, Nectanebo, in the 4th century BC. The temple has long since disappeared, leaving the philosophers sitting alone.

Statue in the Philosopher's Circle, built by the Ptolemies at Saqqara

Environs

Beginning 2 km (1 mile) south of the main complex, **South Saqqara** is a field of smaller, dilapidated pyramids built by pharaohs Pepi I, Pepi II, Djedkare and Merenre. Pepi II's pyramid contains some fine examples of hieroglyphic text. Nearby, the Mastabat al-Faraun, or "Pharaoh's Bench", is a large monolithic mortuary complex of a 4th-Dynasty king. Hiring a horse, donkey or camel from near the Serapeum is the best way to reach these secluded southern sites.

An agricultural scene from the Mastaba of Ti, Saqqara

Palm groves at Memphis, covering the site of the ancient city

Memphis ❸

Off Hwy 27, 47 km (29 miles) S of Cairo. 🚌 from Cairo.

The ancient city of Memphis was the capital of Egypt during the Old Kingdom and most of the Pharaonic period. It is thought it was founded in about 3100 BC by King Menes, the ruler responsible for uniting Upper and Lower Egypt. Situated at the head of the Nile Delta, this majestic city con-trolled important overland and river routes. While Thebes (the site of modern-day Luxor) became the ceremonial centre of Egypt during the New Kingdom, Memphis was still an important administrative and commercial centre until well into the Ptolemaic era. There are countless descriptions of the city in Classical texts from Greek writers and historians such as Plutarch and Strabo. In the 5th century AD, the historian Herodotus described Memphis as a "prosperous city and cosmopolitan centre". The extent and grandeur of the city's necropolis, centred on Saqqara, give some indication of how large and prosperous Memphis must once have been. Sadly, there is little remaining evidence of this former glory. The city has

almost completely vanished. Its magnificent temples and palaces were torn down and pillaged by foreign invaders from the Romans onwards, and the ruins were then buried under the alluvial mud deposited by the annual flooding of the Nile. Palm groves, cultivated fields and villages now cover the site of this once impressive city.

What little has been discovered at Memphis is gathered together in a small open-air **Museum** in the village of Mit Rahina. The showpiece is a colossal limestone statue of Ramses II, which lies, truncated at the knees, in a viewing pavilion. The statue's more complete twin once stood in Midan Ramses but was moved in 2006 to somewhat cleaner Giza (see p78). In the garden there are more statues of Ramses II and an 18th-Dynasty sphinx, at 80 tons the largest calcite statue ever found. The garden also contains several calcite slabs, on which the sacred Apis bulls were mummified before being buried in nearby Saqqara.

Giant calcite sphinx at Memphis

Museum
⬜ daily. 📷

Dahshur ❹

Off Hwy 27, 64 km (40 miles) S of Cairo. 🚌 from Cairo. ⬜ 8am–4pm daily (to 5pm in summer). 📷

Dahshur is a remote desert pyramid field of great significance in the history of pyramid building. The two Old Kingdom pyramids at the site were constructed by 4th-Dynasty king Sneferu (2613–2589 BC), father of Khufu, the builder of the Great Pyramid (see pp130–31). Chronologically they come after Saqqara and Meidum and before Giza and Abusir. The **Bent Pyramid** is considered to be Egypt's first proper pyramid because until this time pyramids were stepped, like Djoser's at Saqqara. The prevailing theory is that the pyramid is bent because once it began to rise the whole structure became unstable and so it had to be completed at a shallower slope. Unusually for pyramids dating from this period, much of its outer limestone casing is still intact, giving a good impression of what it must once have been.

Not happy with his Bent Pyramid, in the thirtieth year of his reign Sneferu began construction of the northern **Red Pyramid**, so called because of its ancient red graffiti. Second in size only to the Great Pyramid, it can be entered via a passage on the north face. At the foot of a long shaft are three chambers, two of which have corbelled ceilings – where the arch is formed by a series of steps.

The two smaller pyramids at Dahshur date from the Middle Kingdom, when there was a revival in pyramid building and are badly dilapidated.

Sneferu's Bent Pyramid at Dahshur with much of its outer limestone casing still visible

Fishermen mending their nets on the shores of Lake Qarun, Fayoum

Fayoum ❺

Off Hwy 27, 100 km (62 miles) SW of Cairo. 🏯 *2 million*. 🚌 *from Cairo*. ℹ️ *Governorate Building, Medinat al-Fayoum (084) 6342 313*.

Just an hour-and-a-half's drive from Cairo, Fayoum is Egypt's largest oasis and a popular escape for the smog-choked inhabitants of the big city. They avoid the ugly, modern town of Medinat al-Fayoum (Fayoum City), the oasis's administrative centre, and head instead for the heart of the area, **Lake Qarun**.

This tranquil lake, which existed in antiquity, was linked to the Nile by a series of canals built by the 12th-Dynasty pharaoh Amenemhat III. The area later became a favoured Pharaonic vacation spot.

The Greeks knew the area as Crocodilopolis, named after the reptiles in the lake, which they worshipped. Remains of crocodile temples can be seen at **Kom Aushim**, once the 3rd-century BC city of Karanis, north of Medinat al-Fayoum on the road to Cairo. Some of the objects found on the site are exhibited at the nearby museum. Although the crocodiles are long gone, Lake Qarun is home to an amazing variety of birds. As well as the indigenous species, there are also many migrants and winter visitors.

The ancient Egyptians were aware of bird life throughout the country, which they recorded here in friezes on tomb walls – most famously the Meidum Geese, now in Cairo's Egyptian Museum *(see pp76–7)*.

Birding opportunities also exist at **Wadi Rayyan**, a stunning bit of land reclamation, in which excess water from the oasis has been channelled into the desert to create lakes and waterfalls among the dunes. The lakes are well stocked with fish and are a major nesting ground for birds, as well as a big draw for picnicking daytrippers.

Of the pyramid sites around the Fayoum oasis, two are worth visits – but only by keen pyramid-ologists: the **Pyramid of Hawara** and the **Pyramid of Meidum**. Within Fayoum, **Wadi al-Hitan** is a remote valley where whale skeletons dating back 40 million years were discovered

The inner core of the Meidum Pyramid at Fayoum

in 1902. The site is so important that it is now a UNESCO World Heritage Site. The area is accessible by 2WD vehicles and can be undertaken as a daytrip from Cairo. Alternatively, accommodation is available in nearby Tunis.

🏯 **Kom Aushim**
30 km (18 miles) N of Medinat al-Fayoum. 🚌 🔵 *daily*. 🎫

🏊 **Wadi Rayyan**
45 km (28 miles) SW of Medinat al-Fayoum. 🚗 🔵 *daily*. 🎫

🏯 **Pyramid of Hawara**
12 k (7 miles) SE of Medinat al-Fayoum. 🚗 🔵 *daily*. 🎫

🏯 **Pyramid of Meidum**
32 km (20 miles) NE of Medinat al-Fayoum. 🚉 *to Al-Wasta, then taxi*. 🔵 *daily*.

🏯 **Wadi al-Hitan**
60 km (35 miles) SW of Wadi Rayyan. 🔵 *daily*. 🎫

Birqash Camel Market ❻

Off Mansuriyya Canal Road, 30 km (18 miles) NW of Cairo. 🚌 *from Cairo*. 🔵 *mornings*. 🎫

Contrary to what many might think, the camel is not indigenous to Egypt: it was probably introduced to Egypt by the Persians or the Ptolemies in the 6th century BC. Having since proved themselves indispensable, camels are now brought up to Egypt in their thousands from western Sudan. Most are taken to Birqash, Egypt's largest camel market. Hundreds of camels are sold every morning, but trade is at its briskest on Fridays. The sound of the animals bawling competes with traders' haggling voices, and the smell is truly awful.

Camels and traders at the daily Birqash camel market

◁ Camels, cattle and other livestock on sale at the Birqash camel market

Nile Barrages (Qanater) 7

16 km (10 miles) N of Cairo. 56,000. Corniche el-Nil, in front of Arab Television Building. from Cairo.

The Nile divides into its eastern Damietta and western Rosetta branches at Qanater, where the main attraction is the Nile Barrages, built to control the flow of water to Lower Egypt. Work on the barrages began in 1834, under Mohammed Ali, and was completed in 1863, when it was discovered that they were ineffectual. The barrages were abandoned until 1883 when a group of British engineers, led by Sir Colin Scott-Moncrieff, finally completed the work.

View across Deir Anba Bishoi monastery at Wadi Natrun

Nile Barrages at Qanater, where the two branches of the river fork

Today the Nile Barrages are surrounded by gardens and are popular with picnickers. Although busy at weekends, Qanater is a pleasant destination for day trips from Cairo, the journey by river bus taking approximately two hours.

Wadi Natrun 8

Off Desert Hwy, 100 km (62 miles) NW of Cairo. from Cairo.

Just west of the Delta region, Wadi Natrun was valued by the ancient Egyptians as a source of the salt deposit natron, a vital ingredient in the mummification process (see p28). Later, during the Roman era, the valley's isolation made it an ideal retreat for early Christians escaping Roman

persecution. Initially these monks and hermits lived in caves, but over the years they built many monasteries, of which only four remain today.

The monasteries are easily reached from Cairo by bus, which terminates at the small village of Bir Hooker. All four are surrounded by high, mud-brick walls and resemble desert fortresses. Within the fortified keep of **Deir Anba Bishoi** (the Monastery of St Bishoi), are a well, kitchens, church and storerooms large enough to hold provisions for a year. The church is believed to hold the body of St Bishoi, perfectly preserved in a sealed tube on the altar. He is also commemorated at the Monastery of the Syrians, **Deir as-Suriani**, whose main church (dedicated to St Mary) is built over a cave where St Bishoi is believed to have received a vision of Christ. A bigger draw are the icons and wall paintings, some of which date back to the 8th century.

A little to the north is **Deir al-Baramus**, where the bodies of two sons of the Roman emperor Valentinus are reputed to be buried in a crypt below one of its five churches. 20 km (12 miles) to the southeast is **Deir Abu Makar**, the most secluded of the monasteries; permission to visit must be arranged in advance. Each monastery has a full complement of monks, who will show visitors around and may provide a simple meal, for which a small donation should be offered.

THE FAYOUM PORTRAITS

Although Fayoum is visited by few tourists, many know the name because of the Fayoum Portraits. Several of the portraits, which have been exhibited throughout the world, were discovered here. Some of the earliest ever examples of portraiture, these eerily lifelike faces with their wide staring eyes date back to the Graeco-Roman period. What makes the portraits particularly haunting is that these are funerary artifacts, painted on wooden boards during the subject's lifetime then, at death, laid over the face of the mummified corpse. Many portraits are now on display to the public at the Egyptian Museum (see pp74–5).

Portrait of an Egyptian dating from 3rd century AD, found at Fayoum

THE NILE VALLEY

E gypt has been described as the "gift of the Nile" because without the river the whole country would be a barren desert. Instead, a narrow and verdant strip of cultivated land cuts through the arid country. In ancient times, a great civilization flourished along the river's banks and the incredible wealth of temples and tombs left behind makes the Nile Valley the greatest open-air museum in the world.

For Egypt's *fellaheen* (farmers), the Nile is as central to life today as it was to the farmers and fishermen depicted in the Pharaonic tombs dotted along the valley. For thousands of years the annual flooding of the Nile deposited fresh, fertilizing silt on the surrounding land. Once the flood subsided, the peasants built irrigation channels, planted their crops and waited for the harvest. Though the construction of Aswan's High Dam in the 1960s put an end to the annual inundation, many of Egypt's farmers still live in simple, mudbrick villages and cultivate the precious fertile belt using the same age-old methods.

Since the 19th century, visitors have come to the Nile Valley to gaze in awe at the countless treasures that have been excavated along the banks of the river. Most of the ancient monuments here were rediscovered after being buried for centuries under sand and debris. As a result, some have been preserved in amazing condition.

In addition to the magnificent monuments, the Nile itself is part of the region's attraction. The traditional feluccas, with their distinctive white sails, are part of the Nile Valley landscape as they dart between cruise ships gliding up and down the river between Luxor and Aswan.

Tourism remains the region's main industry. Despite the setback caused by a series of attacks on foreign tourists in the 1990s, visitors continue to flock to the Nile Valley to experience the sense of living history found along the banks of this majestic river – the lifeblood of Egypt.

Villager in Luxor *(see pp184–7)*, setting out his vegetable stall with crops grown in the fertile Nile Valley

◁ View of the Aga Khan Mausoleum *(see p210)* from across the other side of the Nile at Aswan

Exploring the Nile Valley

Most visitors to the Nile Valley head for the tourist magnet of Luxor, where the magnificent Luxor and Karnak temples and the Theban necropolis are the major attractions. Further south, the beautiful ancient garrison town of Aswan is a relaxing place to stay and a good base for exploring the temples on the banks of Lake Nasser, including the stunning Abu Simbel. The sheer number of ancient monuments in the Nile Valley can be overwhelming and to enjoy the region fully it is a good idea to combine sightseeing with a felucca trip on the Nile or a visit to the colourful souqs of Luxor and Aswan.

SIGHTS AT A GLANCE

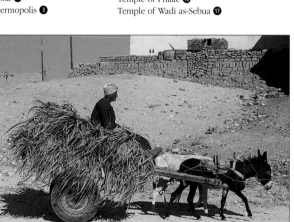

Donkey and cart, a traditional mode of transport for Nile farmers

GETTING AROUND

Luxor and Aswan have airports served by regular international and domestic flights and Abu Simbel has daily domestic flights. Trains run frequently between Cairo, Luxor and Aswan, stopping at major towns. However, the current political situation means that care should be taken if visiting sites between Cairo and Luxor *(see p176)*. The road from Cairo to Aswan is good, and buses and service taxis operate between the main cities. Dendara and Abydos are best visited on a day trip from Luxor, and Abu Simbel can be reached by air or road from Aswan. Many cruises operate between Luxor and Aswan, and on Lake Nasser. A felucca trip may appeal to the more adventurous, while a dahabiya boat is one of the best ways to travel in luxury *(see pp322–5)*.

The graceful Kiosk of Trajan on the enchanting island of Philae, near Aswan

A selection of exotic spices on sale in Aswan's famous souq, one of the most colourful markets in Egypt

KEY

▬▬	Major road
═══	Minor road
▬▬	Scenic route
▭▭	Main railway
--	Track
▬▬	International border
▪ ▪	Disputed border

SEE ALSO

- *Where to Stay* pp272–7
- *Where to Eat* pp296–8

0 kilometres   100

0 miles   50

Map labels:

Port Safaga
ishna   Qena
8 DENDARA
Qift
Quesir
9 LUXOR & THEBES
El-Rizeiqat
ESNA 10
El-Mahamid
El-Kanayis
Marsa Alam
EDFU 11
Nile
Silwa Bahari
12 KOM OMBO
13 DARAW
W. el-Kharit
14 ASWAN
15 TEMPLE OF PHILAE
Berenice
TEMPLE OF KALABSHA 16
Eastern Desert
Lake Nasser
17 TEMPLE OF WADI AS-SEBUA
8 TEMPLE OF AMADA
Wadi Allaqi

Minya ❶

Al-Minya governorate, 245 km (152 miles) S of Cairo. 🚶 *200,000.*
🚉 🚌 ℹ️ *Governorate Building, Corniche el-Nil (086) 2371 521.*

Situated on the west bank of the Nile, the regional capital Minya was a wealthy centre of the cotton industry in the early 20th century. Today it is a semi-industrial city, although it still feels distinctly rural. With its green squares, pretty, tree-lined corniche and run-down Italian villas built by cotton magnates, Minya is a pleasant place to simply wander around. Unfortunately, the surrounding countryside's association with Islamic militants and the relatively high police presence mean that few tourists now venture here. However, Minya makes an excellent base from which to explore historical sites such as Beni Hasan. The tourist office is keen to encourage people to come to the town and will help arrange tours to the sites, although the police may insist on escorting visitors.

Beni Hasan ❷

Al-Minya governorate, 20 km (12 miles) S of Minya. 🚌 *to Abu Qirkis, then ferry.* ⭕ *daily.* 🎫

Carved into limestone hills on the east bank of the Nile, the rock tombs of Beni Hasan date from the Middle Kingdom (2055 to 1650 BC).

The necropolis belonged to military and regional rulers who, in a clear assertion of their growing independence, chose to be buried in their own *nome* (province) rather than close to the king at Saqqara *(see p162).* With their deeper shafts and more elaborate layout and decoration than earlier *mastabas*, these tombs mark a transition in style between the Old and New Kingdoms.

Only a handful of the 39 tombs are open to the public but the vivid murals on some of the walls reveal much about life in the Middle Kingdom. Among the most beautiful is the **Tomb of Khnumhotep** (No.3), which shows Khnumhotep, a 12th-Dynasty regional governor, hunting with a throwstick and fishing with spears. The **Tomb of Amenemhat** (No.2) is decorated with desert hunting scenes, while wall paintings in the **Tomb of Kheti** (No.17) depict many aspects of rural life, including wine-making. The wrestling scenes in the **Tomb of Baqet** (No.15) are precursors of the battle reliefs found in New Kingdom tombs.

Tall granite columns, which once supported a Coptic basilica, amid the ruins of Hermopolis

Hermopolis ❸

Al-Minya governorate, 8 km (5 miles) N of Mallawi. 🚌 *to Al-Ashmunein.* ⭕ *daily.* 🎫

Believed by ancient Egyptians to be one of the sites of creation, the city of Khmun was the cult centre of Thoth, god of writing and wisdom. The city was later renamed Hermopolis Magna by the Ptolemies, who associated their own god Hermes with Thoth. Standing out among the rather scant remains are 24 huge **columns** from a Christian basilica and two **sandstone baboons** of Amenhotep III from his original Thoth temple.

Sandstone baboon from Amenhotep III's Thoth temple

Environs
The ancient city's vast necropolis, **Tuna al-Gebel**, lies to the southwest. Thousands of mummified baboons and ibises, animals sacred to Thoth, once filled the labyrinth of catacombs here. A

The Tomb of Kheti (No.17) in Beni Hasan with detailed scenes of daily life during the Middle Kingdom

For hotels and restaurants in this region see pp272–7 and pp296–8

short walk further south is the "City of the Dead", where streets lined with chapels and tombs lie semi-buried in sand dunes. Most remarkable is the family tomb of Petosiris, high priest of Thoth in the 4th century BC, which resembles a small temple. It is decorated with detailed reliefs featuring an unusual blend of Greek and Egyptian art. The Tuna al-Gebel necropolis bordered on Akhetaten (see below) and a boundary stele showing Akhenaten and his family is visible just to the north of the tombs.

🏛 **Tuna al-Gebel**
7 km (4 miles) SW of Hermopolis.
🕐 8am–4pm daily. 📷

Relief showing wine-pressing in the Tomb of Petosiris, Tuna al-Gebel

Tell al-Amarna ❹

Al-Minya governorate, 12 km (7 miles) SW of Mallawi. 🚌 to Deir al-Mawas, then ferry. 🕐 7am–4pm daily (to 5pm in summer). 📷

The remains of the city of Akhetaten, built by the rebel pharaoh Akhenaten and his wife Queen Nefertiti, lie at a site known today as Tell al-Amarna. The site, which once stretched an impressive 15 km (9 miles) north to south and boasted magnificent temples and palaces, is now almost desolate but the sense of history and romance remains.

The widely dispersed ruins are spread around a desert plain bounded by the Nile to the west and surrounded by cliffs. South of the landing stage at At-Till, a cemetery covers part of what was once the **Great Temple of Aten**. In contrast to traditional Egyptian temples which had darkened sanctuaries (see pp24–5), this temple had a roofless sanctuary, designed to allow the rays of the sun-

god Aten to flood in. To the south is the **Small Temple of Aten**. Better preserved are the remains of Nefertiti's **Northern Palace**, to the north of At-Till. Here, the remains of some mosaics can still be seen on the floor of summer residence.

The highlights of Tell al-Amarna are the two sets of cliff tombs at either end of the city. Of the **Northern Tombs**, 3 km (2 miles) north of At-Till, one of the finest is the **Tomb of Huya** (No.1), Superintendent of the Royal Harem and Steward to Queen Tiye, Akhenaten's mother. This fascinating tomb is carved with royal banquet scenes, including one that shows the queen wining and dining with her son and his family. In the highly decorated **Tomb of Mery-Re I** (No.4), Akhenaten is shown presenting Mery-Re I with the high priest's golden collar. Reliefs depicting Akhenaten and the Great Temple on the eastern wall of the tomb give an indication of what the city must have looked like during its brief period of glory. Grouped in clusters, 8 km (5 miles) south of At-Till, the **Southern Tombs**

Relief of Nefertiti and her daughter praying to the sun-god Aten, in Cairo's Egyptian Museum

are less accessible but equally rewarding. The **Tomb of Ay** (No.25), Akhenaten's vizier, is considered the finest tomb in Tell al-Amarna. The wall paintings show Ay and his wife receiving ceremonial golden collars from Akhenaten and Nefertiti, watched by a crowd of cheering onlookers. The well-preserved **Tomb of Mahu** (No.9) contains reliefs of Mahu carrying out his duties as Akhenaten's chief of police. Malawi has a small museum exhibiting finds from across the Al-Minya area.

AKHENATEN THE HERETIC

In the 14th century BC, Amenhotep IV turned his back on Thebes and the practice of worshipping several gods to establish a religion based on the worship of just one god, Aten, god of the sun disc. He changed his name from Amenhotep to Akhenaten, meaning servant of Aten, and built a huge city dedicated to Aten at Akhetaten. The city was the capital of Egypt for 14 years but, when Akhenaten died, Thebes was re-established as the capital by Akhenaten's son-in-law and successor Tutankhamun. Akhetaten was destroyed on the order of the priests of Karnak who were determined to eradicate all trace of the heretical pharaoh's new religion.

The rebel pharaoh Akhenaten

Asyut ⑤

Asyut governorate, 110 km (68 miles)
S of Minya. 🏚 *280,000.* 🚉 🚌
ℹ️ *Sharia ath-Thawra (088) 2305 110.*

Convent of the Holy Virgin, built into the cliffs at Dirunka, near Asyut

In Pharaonic times Asyut
was capital of the 13th *nome*
(province) and centre of the
cult of Wepwawet, the wolf-
headed god and avenger of
Osiris. At the crossroads of
caravan routes to the Western
Desert oases and across the
Sahara, the city has a long
history as a centre of trade.
Until the mid-19th century,
slaves who had survived the
torturous "Forty Days Road"
from Darfur in Sudan were
sold here alongside camels in
Egypt's biggest slave market.

Today Asyut is the largest
city in Upper Egypt and has
the third largest university in
the country. Known for its
carpet making,
Asyut remains
the region's
main agricultural
trading centre.
The area is also
associated with
the Virgin Mary.
In August 2000,
the Virgin was
reportedly seen
above St Mark's
Church. For a few months
afterwards there were reports
of lights around the church
towers and many thousands
flocked to see them. The
apparitions have now ceased.

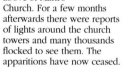

Icon showing the Holy Family in
the Convent of the Holy Virgin

Environs
Coptic Christians believe that
Mary, Joseph and the baby
Jesus sheltered in caves at
Dirunka, 12 km (7 miles)

southwest of Asyut. They
were escaping from King
Herod, who had ordered the
killing of all baby boys under
the age of two in Bethlehem.
A large convent, the **Convent
of the Holy
Virgin**, was
built nearby.
During the
annual Moulid
of the Virgin,
held between 7
and 22 August,
around 50,000
pilgrims flock
here to see
icons paraded
around the cave-church.

Another place held sacred
by Christian Copts is the
Burnt Monastery (Deir al-
Muharraq). This is situated on
the edge of the desert, 5 km
(3 miles) outside Al-Qusiya, a
small town 42 km (26 miles)
north of Asyut. The Holy
Family is said to have lived in
a cave here for a month and
it is thought that the church

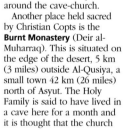

built over it was the first in
Egypt. What is now the
church's altar stone once
blocked the entrance to the
cave. The annual moulid,
which is held here between 21
and 28 June, attracts many
thousands of visitors.

A further 7 km (4 miles)
west of the monastery are the
Tombs of Mir, a burial ground
dating from the Old and
Middle Kingdoms.

⋔ **Convent of the Holy Virgin**
12 km (7 miles) SW of Asyut. 🚗
from Asyut.

⋔ **Burnt Monastery**
47 km (29 miles) N of Asyut. 🚌 🚗
to Al-Qusiya, then a local taxi.

Sohag ⑥

Sohag governorate, 115 km (71
miles) S of Asyut. 🏚 *210,000.*
🚉 🚌 ℹ️ *Governorate Bldg (093)
461 0093.*

An agricultural town and
commercial centre, Sohag
has a large Coptic Christian
community and, like many
other cities in Middle Egypt,
is a place of sporadic unrest.
A museum housing a wealth
of local archaeological finds,
including those from the
ongoing excavations of the
temple of Ramses II in
Akhmim, opened in 2011
and aims to increase tourism
in the town. Many visitors
usually prefer a brief visit to
Sohag as a daytrip from
Luxor. A large animal
market is held in the town
each Monday.

SECURITY IN THE REGION

This area has long been associated with religious extremists
who want to turn the country into an Islamic state. Asyut
University was a hotbed for Islamic fundamentalists in the
late 1970s, and the early 1990s saw several attacks on tourists
around Qena, Asyut and Dairut. The Egyptian government
has tightened security, especially since the 1997 massacre
at Luxor, but tension continues and police presence is high.
Although tour groups tend to avoid the region, officially it
is possible to travel freely in this area and visitors rarely
encounter trouble. The most common way to see sites such
as the Temple of Hathor at Dendara *(see pp178–9)* is on a
day trip from Luxor, usually with a police escort. The situation
is always changing, however, and visitors should contact local
tourist authorities and their embassy for the latest advice.

Environs

A short drive west of Sohag, the **White Monastery** (Deir al-Abyad) dates from the early 5th century AD. Named for the colour of its masonry, the monastery was built using chunks of white limestone taken from local Pharaonic temples. The monastery, founded by the Coptic saint Pjol, was once home to 2,000 monks. Today very little remains within its high fortress walls apart from a church, dedicated to Saint Shenouda. On 14th July every year thousands of pilgrims attend a moulid at the site.

Four kilometres (2.5 miles) north of the White Monastery lies the **Red Monastery** (Deir al-Ahmar). Built in the 6th century AD by Shenouda's disciple Bishoi – a repentant robber who became a saint – the monastery has two churches within its grounds. The main church is decorated with beautiful frescoes dating from the 10th century. These wall paintings are being restored, and the colours and designs that have been revealed are extraordinary.

On the eastern bank of the Nile, just across the river from Sohag, is **Akhmim**, which can be reached by microbus. The town is known for its hand-woven hangings and throws. The town's main attraction is an 11-m (36-ft) high statue of Queen Meret Amun – the fourth daughter of Ramses II.

Icon of Christ in the White Monastery

White Monastery
10 km (6 miles) W of Sohag.
🚗 🔵 daily. 🎆 14th July.

Red Monastery
14 km (9 miles) NW of Sohag.
🚗 🔵 daily.

The Red Monastery near Sohag, founded by the Coptic saint Bishoi

The chapel of Osiris in the Cenotaph Temple of Seti I in Abydos

Abydos ❼

Sohag governorate, 46 km (29 miles) SW of Sohag; 10 km (6 miles) W of Al-Balyana. 🚌 or day trip from Luxor, with convoy.

Abydos, the cult centre of Osiris, god of the dead, was regarded as the holiest of Egyptian towns in Pharaonic times. All ancient Egyptians tried to make the pilgrimage to the town during their lifetime or hoped to be buried here. Many tombs were painted with scenes of the deceased making the posthumous journey to Abydos. Tradition had it that Osiris – or at least his head – was laid to rest here after he was murdered by his brother Seth and his mutilated body strewn over the country.

Abydos was once a vast walled town with several ancient cemeteries, lakes and temples, including the important Temple of Osiris. Today, almost all that can be seen is the stunning 19th-Dynasty **Cenotaph Temple of Seti I**. Built during Seti I's reign between 1294–1279 BC, it is one of the most intact temples in Egypt. Constructed using white limestone, this secondary mortuary temple possesses some of the finest bas-reliefs of the New Kingdom; many have retained their original colour. After the death of his father, Ramses II (1279–1213 BC) built his own temple to the north of Seti's temple. Although only partially intact, it is noted for its interesting hieroglyphs.

Entrance to the temple is gained via the first hypostyle hall. The temple's highlights include the bas-relief scenes in the second hypostyle hall, which show Seti I with the gods Osiris and Horus. Just beyond, the seven chapels dedicated to a deified Seti I and the gods Ptah, Ra-Harakhty, Amun, Osiris, Isis and Horus are remarkable for their coloured reliefs and delicate decoration. Each chapel contained the statue and barque of the relevant god and would be served daily by the high priests. Behind the temple, Seti had built the Osirieon (the tomb of Osiris) from huge blocks of stone. Today it is partly underwater.

Cenotaph Temple of Seti I
🔵 8am–5pm daily. 📷

Dendara ⑧

Dendara, where Hathor supposedly gave birth to Horus's child, the god Ihy, was Hathor's cult centre from pre-Dynastic times. Buried under sand until the 19th century, the vast Temple of Hathor remains remarkably intact. The current temple is Graeco-Roman but its design imitates typical Pharaonic tem-

Bes, patron god of childbirth

ple architecture – a series of large hypostyle halls leading to a sanctuary, surrounded by store rooms, chapels and crypts. Other buildings include two *mammisi* (birth houses) and a Coptic basilica.

★ Astronomical Ceiling
In this detail from the ceiling, the sun-god Ra is shown sailing his sacred barque across the sky.

Temple Façade
The façade shows Tiberius and Claudius making offerings to Horus and Hathor.

TEMPLE OF HATHOR RECONSTRUCTION
The intricate carved reliefs that adorn the temple were originally painted in vivid colours.

Dendara Zodiac A copy of the famous zodiac ceiling is located in one of the roof-top sanctuaries. The original was removed in 1820 and is now in the Louvre, Paris.

Entrance to temple

★ Hathor-headed Columns
Hathor is shown in her human form with cow's ears at the head of the 18 columns in the hypostyle hall.

STAR FEATURES

★ Astronomical Ceiling

★ Hathor-headed Columns

CULT OF HATHOR
Hathor was the goddess of pleasure and love, and wet nurse and lover of Horus. Every year she was carried on a barque to Edfu *(see p204)* to be reunited with Horus. The Festival of Drunkenness, celebrating the divine union, followed. On New Year's Day, Hathor's statue was carried up the decorated west staircase of the temple to the open-air kiosk on the roof, where it was revitalized by the sun.

Hathor with the sun disk and cow horns

Cleopatra and Caesarion

A huge relief on the southern exterior wall shows Cleopatra making offerings to Hathor. Caesarion, her son by Julius Caesar, stands in front of her burning incense.

The east staircase led back down into the temple.

VISITORS' CHECKLIST

5 km (3 miles) SW of Qena, the provincial capital; 60 km (37 miles) N of Luxor. 🚌 or tour from Luxor. **Travel restrictions may apply in this area** *(see p332)*.
⬜ 7am–6pm daily in summer (to 5pm in winter). 📷

The open-air kiosk was the focus of the New Year celebrations. It may have had a light wooden cover that was removed to expose the statues to the sun.

The New Year Chapel is where rituals were performed before Hathor's statue was taken up to the roof. The ceiling shows Nut giving birth to the sun.

Elaborate bas-reliefs depicting offerings to Hathor

Roman Mammisi

This small temple celebrated the divine birth of Hathor's son. The southern wall has some exquisite reliefs on its exterior.

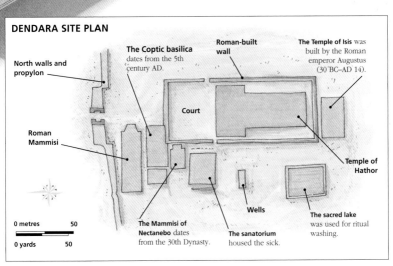

DENDARA SITE PLAN

North walls and propylon

The Coptic basilica dates from the 5th century AD.

Roman-built wall

The Temple of Isis was built by the Roman emperor Augustus (30 BC–AD 14).

Court

Roman Mammisi

Temple of Hathor

Wells

0 metres 50
0 yards 50

The Mammisi of Nectanebo dates from the 30th Dynasty.

The sanatorium housed the sick.

The sacred lake was used for ritual washing.

Luxor and Thebes ❾

Modern Luxor grew out of the ruins of Thebes, once the capital of ancient Egypt's New Kingdom (1550–1069 BC). The monumental temples at Luxor and Karnak were famed throughout the ancient world and have attracted tourists since Greek and Roman times. Across the Nile, on the West Bank, lies the Theban Necropolis, perhaps the world's richest archaeological site. To foil thieves, the Theban kings hid their tombs deep in the surrounding hills, away from their mortuary temples on the flood plain. Visiting the Luxor monuments is straightforward, but due to the number of sights and the distances involved, some planning is needed to get the most out of a visit to the West Bank.

Detail from the Colossi of Memnon

Medinet Habu ⑦
Second only to Karnak in size, the Mortuary Temple of Ramses III was modelled on the Ramesseum.

LUXOR AND THEBES

① Luxor Temple *(pp186–7)*
② Luxor Museum *(p187)*
③ Karnak Temple *(pp188–90)*
④ Valley of the Kings *(p192–4)*
⑤ Tombs of the Nobles *(p195)*
⑥ Hatshepsut Temple *(pp196–7)*
⑦ Medinet Habu *(pp198–9)*
⑧ Valley of the Queens *(p199)*
⑨ The Ramesseum *(pp200–1)*
⑩ Colossi of Memnon*(p202)*
⑪ Temple of Merneptah *(p202)*
⑫ Deir al-Medina *(pp202–3)*
⑬ Temple of Seti I *(p203)*
⑭ Howard Carter's house *(p203)*
⑮ New Gurna *(p203)*

KEY

🚉 Train station

▦ Town area

0 kilometres   1

0 miles   0.5

Valley of the Kings ④
Hatshepsut Temple ⑥
Tombs of the Nobles ⑤
Deir al-Medina ⑫
Valley of the Queens ⑧
The Ramesseum ⑨
⑪ Temple of Merneptah
⑩ Colossi of Memnon
General ticket kiosk
Medinet Habu ⑦
New Gurna ⑮

T H E B E S

G E

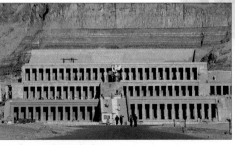

Hatshepsut Temple ⑥
Discovered only in the mid-19th century, and still being restored by the Polish Mission, the Mortuary Temple of Hatshepsut rises out of the desert in a series of terraces that merge with the sheer limestone cliffs behind.

◁ A flotilla of feluccas heading south up the Nile at Luxor

GETTING AROUND
Luxor Temple is in the centre of town and easily accessible on foot; Karnak Temple can be reached by minibus, bicycle, taxi or caleche. Most Luxor hotels offer tours to the West Bank including the services of a guide. Alternatively, you can cross by ferry from Luxor Temple and hire a taxi in Gezira village, on the other side of the river. Bicycles can be hired from Luxor for the day and taken across on the ferry.

The Ramesseum ⑨
Built to perpetuate the pharaoh's glory, the Mortuary Temple of Ramses II was part of a large complex that included a royal palace and a great many granaries and storerooms. Both pylons are decorated with scenes from the Battle of Qadesh.

TIPS FOR VISITORS

• Do not try and see everything at once. Limit yourself to two or three major sights per day.

• To avoid the post-midday heat, most people visit the area early in the day, although late afternoons can be less crowded.

• All ticket kiosks are open 6am–4pm (till 5pm summer). Tickets are valid only on the day of purchase.

• Tickets for the Valley of the Kings, the Queens and for Hatshepsut Temple can all be purchased on site.

• Holders of a valid ISIC card are entitled to a 50 per cent reduction in admission prices.

• Photography and guides are prohibited inside all tombs.

• Always carry plenty of water and maybe a snack as facilities are limited and expensive.

⑭ Howard Carter's house

⑬ Temple of Seti I

Plaza

RIVER NILE

Karnak ③ Temple

② Luxor Museum

R A

L U X O R

Local ferry

① Luxor Temple

Avenue of the Sphinxes (under excavation)

Karnak Temple ③
The Karnak complex was known as "Ipet-Isut" ("the most perfect of places") to the ancient Egyptians.

Luxor Temple ①
Founded by Amenhotep III, Luxor Temple was dedicated to the Theban triad of Amun, Mut and Khonsu, who are celebrated at the annual Festival of Opet (see p190).

Street-by-Street: Luxor

Built on the site of the New Kingdom
capital city of Thebes, Luxor has returned
to prominence as the tourist mecca of the
Nile Valley. The exciting excavations that were
led by European archaeologists in the 19th and
early 20th centuries, especially the discovery of
Tutankhamun's tomb, aroused international
interest in the town and visitors have been
coming to marvel at the amazing concentration
of ruins here ever since. Today the livelihood
of Luxor's resident population depends
almost entirely on tourism and visitors can
expect to be approached by salesmen and
touts at every turn. The bustling town is
centred around the magnificent Luxor Temple, an
enduring symbol of its glorious past.

**Stone Ramses
II at Luxor
Temple**

Sharia Souk
*Gated and paved, the market
may have lost some charm,
but good local products
are still available.*

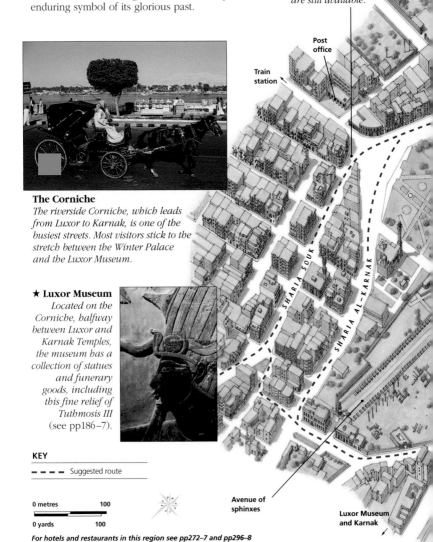

Post
office

Train
station

The Corniche
*The riverside Corniche, which leads
from Luxor to Karnak, is one of the
busiest streets. Most visitors stick to the
stretch between the Winter Palace
and the Luxor Museum.*

★ **Luxor Museum**
*Located on the
Corniche, halfway
between Luxor and
Karnak Temples,
the museum has a
collection of statues
and funerary
goods, including
this fine relief of
Tuthmosis III
(see pp186–7).*

SHARIA SOUK

SHARIA AL–KARNAK

KEY

– – – Suggested route

| 0 metres | 100 |
| 0 yards | 100 |

**Avenue of
sphinxes**

**Luxor Museum
and Karnak**

For hotels and restaurants in this region see pp272–7 and pp296–8

Winter Palace Hotel
Founded in 1887, the most famous of Luxor's hotels has played host to celebrities such as Agatha Christie and Noel Coward.

VISITORS' CHECKLIST

Luxor Governorate, 674 km (419 miles) S of Cairo.
🏨 360,000. ✈ 🚉 🚌 🛈
Opposite Luxor railway station (095) 2373 294. 🏪 daily. 🎭
Moulid of Abu al-Haggag, two weeks before Ramadan.

Felucca on the Nile at Luxor

Corniche

Public ferry

The Abu al-Haggag Mosque stands amid the ruins of Luxor Temple.

★ Luxor Temple
With its grand colonnades, Luxor Temple is one of the most impressive ancient monuments in Egypt. It is situated on the waterfront in the heart of modern Luxor and looks particularly beautiful when illuminated at night (see pp186–7).

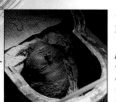

★ Mummification Museum
The ancient Egyptian practice of mummification is explained in detail in this fascinating museum close to the river (see pp186–7).

STAR SIGHTS

★ Luxor Temple

★ Mummification Museum

★ Luxor Museum

Exploring Luxor

Spread out along the east bank of the Nile, Luxor today is a bustling town of some 360,000 inhabitants. The main tourist attractions are concentrated in the heart of town between Sharia al-Karnak and the Corniche. Luxor Museum is a short distance away on the Corniche in the direction of Karnak. Walking around town is a great way to soak up the atmosphere though it can also be fun to ride through the streets in a *caleche* (carriage).

originally one of a pair; the other was removed in the early 19th century and re-erected in the Place de la Concorde in Paris, a gift from the Egyptian ruler Mohammed Ali to the people of France.

Beyond the first pylon lies the Court of Ramses II, with the Abu al-Haggag Mosque towering over the courtyard to the east. The height of the mosque above the stone floor demonstrates the depth of debris that once buried the entire temple. The western corner of the court incorporates an earlier barque shrine (to house the gods' sacred boats) dedicated to the Theban triad. A double row of papyrus-bud columns encircles the court, inter-spersed with huge standing colossi of Ramses II.

More giant black granite statues of Ramses guard the entrance to the original part of the temple, which begins with the majestic Colonnade of Amenhotep III, with its avenue of 14 columns. The walls here were embellished during the reign of Tutankhamun and depict the annual Opet festival, when the images of Amun, Mut and Khonsu were taken in procession from Karnak to Luxor (*see p190*). The western wall shows the outward journey to Luxor and the eastern wall the return journey to Karnak. The colonnade leads to the superb Court of Amenhotep III, which is noted for its double rows of towering papyrus columns, the

The first pylon, built by Ramses II, forming the façade of Luxor Temple

Luxor Temple

Corniche el-Nil. ◻ *winter: 6am–8:30pm daily; summer: 6am–9:30pm daily.* ▨

Dominating the banks of the Nile in the centre of town, Luxor Temple is an elegant example of Pharaonic temple architecture. Dedicated to the Theban triad of Amun, Mut and Khonsu, the temple was largely completed by the 18th-Dynasty pharaoh Amenhotep III and added to during the reign of Ramses II in the 19th Dynasty. Although the temple was further modified by later rulers, including Alexander the Great, its design remained strikingly coherent in contrast to the sprawling complex that developed at nearby Karnak. In the 3rd century AD the temple was occupied by a Roman camp and the site was subsequently abandoned. Over the centuries it was engulfed in sand and silt, and a village grew up within the temple walls. Then in 1881 archaeologist Gaston Maspero rediscovered the temple in remarkably good condition, but before excavation work could begin the village had to be removed. Only the **Abu al-Haggag Mosque**, built by the Arabs in the 13th century, was left intact, standing high on the layers of silt accumu-

lated over the years. An avenue of sphinxes, which stretched all the way from Luxor to Karnak, almost 2 km (1.2 miles) away, is being excavated, and will link the two temples once more. Fronting the entrance to the temple, the gigantic first pylon is decorated with scenes of Ramses II's victory over the Hittites in the battle of Qadesh. Two enormous seated colossi of Ramses and a huge 25-m (82-ft) high pink granite obelisk flank the gateway to the temple. The obelisk was

The Abu al-Haggag Mosque in Luxor Temple

The avenue of sphinxes leading to the entrance of Luxor Temple

Colonnade of Amenhotep III with its lofty papyrus columns

best preserved and most elegant in the temple. In 1989, work here on the foundations of the court led to the discovery of 22 New Kingdom statues, now on display in the Luxor Museum.

The hypostyle hall on the southern side of the court served as a vestibule to the main temple. It has 32 papyrus columns in four rows of eight, bearing the later cartouches of Ramses II, Ramses IV, Ramses VI and Seti I. The antechamber beyond was converted into a church by the Romans in the 4th century AD, its Pharaonic reliefs being plastered over and covered with Christian paintings. A second, smaller antechamber, the offerings chapel, leads on to another columned hall with the Sanctuary of the Sacred Barque in the centre. Rebuilt by Alexander the Great, this granite shrine was where Amun's barque ended its journey from Karnak in the Opet festival (see p190). It is decorated with scenes of Alexander making offerings to the Theban triad. The birth room to the east has reliefs depicting the divine birth of Amenhotep III, intended to validate his claim to be the son of Amun. Finally, behind the Sanctuary of the Sacred Barque, another hall leads to a small, damaged sanctuary that once housed a golden statue of Amun.

Pink granite obelisk

Mummification Museum

Corniche el-Nil, opposite Mena Palace Hotel. *Tel* (095) 2381 501. ⬭ *9am–2pm and 4–9pm daily (5–10pm summer); 9am–3pm Ramadan.*

This small museum on the banks of the Nile houses a fascinating display describing the process of mummification performed by the ancient Egyptians (see pp28–9). Instruments for removing internal organs, substances to treat the body and items needed by the mummy on its journey to the afterlife are all displayed here. The intact mummy of Maseharti, a 21st-Dynasty high priest and general, was found at Deir el-Bahri along with Maseharti's painted coffin. A mummified cat, the symbol of the goddess Bastet, and a mummified ram, the symbol of the god Khnum, are among the other exhibits. Among the informative items on display is a cross-section of a mummified skull, stuffed with material where the brain has been removed. There is also a piece of a mummified toe.

Sharia Souk

Sharia Souk, opposite Luxor train station. ⬭ *24 hours daily.*

Sharia Souk is a street market that has been cleaned up in an attempt to appeal to tourists. What was an authentic market street has been paved over but the stalls still sell the usual market wares, such as fabrics, pottery, spices and food. There are also cafés, restaurants and hotels alongside it. The market is kept swept and cleaned all night long, but tourists may prefer to shop at the stalls in the dusty, more characterful streets north of Sharia Souq.

Luxor Museum

Corniche el-Nil, Luxor. *Tel* (095) 2380 269. ⬭ *9am–2pm and 4–9pm daily (5–10pm summer); 9am–3pm Ramadan.*

Situated on the Corniche halfway between Luxor Temple and Karnak, this well-designed museum has an excellent collection of statues and artifacts found in temples and tombs in the Luxor area. Near the entrance is a stunning gilded head of Hathor, the cow-goddess, discovered in the tomb of Tutankhamun in the Valley of the Kings. Also on the ground floor look out for the large pink granite head of Amenhotep III and the beautiful carved figure of a youthful Tuthmosis III.

On the first floor further exhibits from Tutankhamun's tomb include a funerary bed and two model barques. Also exhibited here are three busts of Amenhotep IV (Akhenaten) and a reconstructed wall made up of 283 sandstone blocks from Akhenaten's temple at Karnak. The relief scenes depict daily life during Akhenaten's reign and show the heretical pharaoh and his wife Queen Nefertiti making offerings to the sun-god Aten.

Statue of Tuthmosis III in the Luxor Museum

The spectacular lower hall near the entrance on the ground floor is a highlight. It displays a collection of beautifully preserved New Kingdom statues, discovered at Luxor Temple in 1989. The pieces include a near-perfect 2.5-m (8-ft) high statue of Amenhotep III and a statue of the gods Mut and Amun.

Two mummies, Ahmes I and (possibly) Ramses I, are on display in the Thebes Glory wing.

Painted relief from Akhenaten's Karnak Temple in Luxor Museum

Karnak: Temple of Amun

Statue of a scarab beetle

At the heart of the immense Karnak complex lies the Temple of Amun, dedicated to the king of the gods. With its endless courts, halls and colossi and huge sacred lake, the scale and complexity of this sprawling temple is overwhelming. From its modest 11th-Dynasty beginnings, pharaoh after pharaoh added to and changed the existing buildings, seeking to make their mark on the country's most important temple. No expense was spared and during the 19th Dynasty some 80,000 men worked in the temple as labourers, guards, priests and servants. The temple lay buried under sand for more than 1,000 years before excavation work began in the mid-19th century. Today, the huge task of restoration continues.

★ Great Hypostyle Hall
The glorious highlight of Karnak, this cavernous hall was supported by 134 gigantic columns.

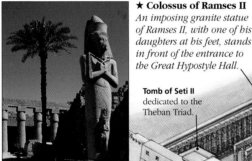

★ Colossus of Ramses II
An imposing granite statue of Ramses II, with one of his daughters at his feet, stands in front of the entrance to the Great Hypostyle Hall.

Tomb of Seti II
dedicated to the Theban Triad.

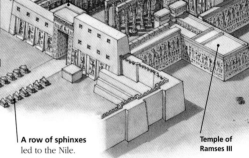

RECONSTRUCTION OF THE TEMPLE OF AMUN
The temple's brightly coloured exterior is visible in this reconstruction, which shows how the temple would have looked in around 1000 BC.

A row of sphinxes
led to the Nile.

Temple of Ramses III

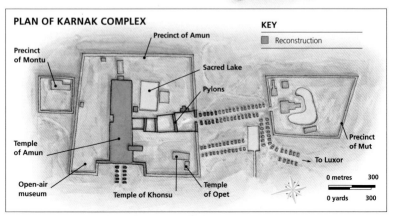

PLAN OF KARNAK COMPLEX

KEY

☐ Reconstruction

Precinct of Montu

Precinct of Amun

Sacred Lake

Pylons

Temple of Amun

Open-air museum

Temple of Khonsu

Temple of Opet

Precinct of Mut

To Luxor

0 metres   300
0 yards   300

Botanic Gardens
Part of the temple built by Tuthmosis III, this roofless enclosure lies behind the Great Festival Temple. It is decorated with reliefs of exotic flora and fauna, brought back to Egypt by the pharaoh during his campaign in Syria.

VISITORS' CHECKLIST

Sharia al-Karnak, 3 km (2 miles) NE of Luxor. 🚌 or microbus, bicycle, caleche. 🕐 summer: 6am–6pm daily; winter: 6am–5pm daily. **Sound and Light Show** *Three shows daily from 8pm (6:30pm in winter). Check for language and time details at www.soundand-light.com.eg.* 🖼

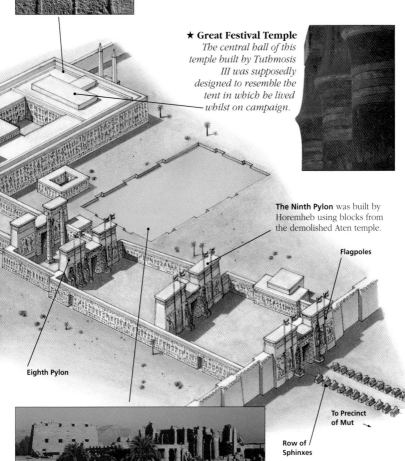

★ Great Festival Temple
The central hall of this temple built by Tuthmosis III was supposedly designed to resemble the tent in which he lived whilst on campaign.

The Ninth Pylon was built by Horemheb using blocks from the demolished Aten temple.

Flagpoles

Eighth Pylon

To Precinct of Mut

Row of Sphinxes

Sacred Lake
Priests purified themselves in the holy water of the Sacred Lake before performing rituals in the temple. North of the lake is a huge stone scarab of Khepri, built by Amenhotep III.

STAR FEATURES

★ Great Hypostyle Hall

★ Colossus of Ramses II

★ Great Festival Temple

Exploring Karnak

After the pyramids of Giza, Karnak is Egypt's most important Pharaonic site. Excavations over the years have gradually uncovered the original structure of the temple complex, which was built over a 1300-year period and covers a vast area just north of Luxor. As well as the colossal Temple of Amun, the 100-acre site comprises a fantastic array of temples, chapels, pylons and obelisks, all testifying to the importance of Thebes.

Statues of the lioness-goddess Sekhmet line up in the Precinct of Mut

SOUND AND LIGHT

The sheer size of the Karnak complex means that one visit is seldom enough to take it all in. A good way to revisit the site is to attend the spectacular Sound and Light Show, which helps to unravel the complex 1500-year history of the building of the Temple of Karnak. The shows are performed in various languages, and there are three shows each evening. Check with Luxor Tourist Office or at www. soundandlight.com.eg for details of times and prices.

⋔ Temples of Khonsu and Opet

Dedicated to the son of Amun and Mut, the well-preserved Temple of Khonsu was built largely during the reigns of Ramses III and IV. The main entrance is via a magnificent gateway, built by Ptolemy III, which is still virtually intact.

Close by is the smaller Temple of Opet (the goddess thought to be the mother of Osiris). It contains some finely decorated reliefs dating from Ptolemaic and Roman times, but is closed for excavation.

⛪ Open-air Museum

Located to the northwest of the Precinct of Amun, the open-air museum contains a fine collection of monuments that were discovered during an excavation of the Third Pylon. Among the museum's main attractions is the lovely, reconstructed, 12th-Dynasty White Chapel of Senusret I. This has delicate carvings of the king making offerings to Amun. The restored 18th-Dynasty Red Chapel of Hatshepsut can also be seen here; the chapel served as a shrine for the barque of Amun. Other attractions include the Alabaster Chapel of Amenhotep I and the Shrine of Tuthmosis III.

A separate ticket for the museum must be purchased before entering the complex.

⋔ Precinct of Mut

Built by Amenhotep III, the precinct contains the ruins of a temple dedicated to Amun's consort Mut. Huge, black granite statues of the lioness-goddess Sekhmet line the temple courts. To the west of the sacred lake surrounding the temple is the ruined 20th-Dynasty Temple of Ramses III. Relics of the Temple of Amenhotep III, dedicated to Amun, lie to the northeast.

⋔ Precinct of Montu

The Precinct of Montu is just north of the Temple of Amun. Montu, the warrior god, was the original deity of Thebes and was still worshipped after Amun rose to pre-eminence. The precinct contains Amenhotep III's Temple of Montu and the Temple of Amun, which was added during the 20th Dynasty. Both are closed to the public at present.

THE FESTIVAL OF OPET AT KARNAK

Amun was the principal god of Thebes who, along with his consort Mut and their son Khonsu, was worshipped as part of the Theban Triad. Once a year, during the flood season, the Festival of Opet celebrated the king's rebirth as the son of Amun. Accompanied by priests and revellers in a riotous festival, the images of Amun, Mut and Khonsu were carried on decorated barques to the Nile and then to Luxor Temple. Even today, elements of the Opet festival live on in the Islamic Moulid of Abu al-Haggag, a five-day event preceding Ramadan. Luxor occasionally stages a recreation of the festival for tourists on the 4th of November, the anniversary of the discovery of Tutankhamun's tomb.

Priests carrying the image of Amun in his barque during the Opet festival

Cruising the Nile

Along with the Grand Tour of Europe, a trip to Egypt was one of the most exciting journeys available to the 19th-century traveller. Having disembarked at Alexandria, wealthy European and American tourists were transported to Cairo – in the early days by boat, later by train. After several days visiting the sights of Cairo, often staying at the world-famous Shepheard's Hotel, passengers would board a *dahabiyya* (large sail boat) or steamer, and set off

Death on the Nile by Agatha Christie

for a trip up the Nile. The pace was languid: a steamer took three weeks to reach Aswan, while a sailing boat could take six to twelve weeks. Slow days on deck alternated with treks through the desert to marvel at the newly found secrets of ancient Egypt. It was not uncommon for tourists to come across or even fall into hitherto undiscovered tombs. Expeditions were led by local guides, while servants carried supplies of food and drink for picnics amid the ruins.

Thomas Cook, the founder of modern tourism, played a dominant role in the development of Egyptian travel. He once owned all the steamers plying the Nile.

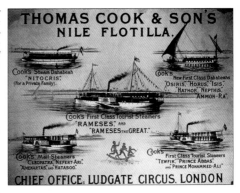

Florence Nightingale *described her 1848 trip up the Nile in a series of letters. Other writers inspired by the trip include Agatha Christie, who wrote* Death on the Nile.

Shepheard's Hotel *was the focus of European life in Egypt from its founding in 1841 until it was burned down in 1952.*

The highlight of a trip *to Egypt for 19th-century travellers was then, as now, a visit to the Great Pyramids and the Sphinx at Giza. As seen in this illustration, these sites had yet to be fully excavated.*

Exciting new *discoveries from Egypt's ancient past provided an added thrill for early visitors to the country. Each year new finds were made.*

Thebes: Valley of the Kings

TOMB OF TUT ANKH AMON NO. 62

The most famous tomb in Thebes

The remote, barren Valley of the Kings was the necropolis of the New Kingdom pharaohs. By digging their tombs deep into the Theban Hills, pharaohs from Tuthmosis I (c.1500 BC) on hoped to stop robbers stealing the priceless possessions buried with them. It was an unsuccessful strategy. Despite their hidden locations, every burial chamber was raided except for those of Yuya and Tuya *(see p77)*, and Tutankhamun, discovered by Howard Carter in 1922, its glorious treasures still intact *(see pp74–7)*. But for all that, the structures themselves remain, their dramatic corridors and burial chambers stunningly adorned with symbolic accounts of the journey through the underworld and ritual paintings to assist the pharaohs in the afterlife.

Tomb of Horemheb (No.57)
Horemheb was the final pharaoh of the 18th Dynasty. His tomb departs from the usual style of 18th-Dynasty tombs in that it consists of a single straight corridor with side-chambers. It is decorated with reliefs from the Book of Amduat.

Valley of the Kings, chosen as a burial ground because of its secluded location amid limestone hills

THE VALLEY TOMBS

Sixty-three tombs have been found in the Valley of the Kings and 62 are numbered on the map in the order of their discovery. The most significant tombs, some of which are described on *p194*, are marked with a red bullet. Of all the tombs, only about eleven are open at any one time.

Tomb of Tuthmosis III (No.34)
Dug 30 m (98 ft) above ground in a vain attempt to stop thieves, today the tomb is reached by a metal staircase. The walls are painted with rows of figures portraying the Book of Amduat (see p29), and a red granite sarcophagus is the sole remaining artifact.

For hotels and restaurants in this region see pp272–7 and pp296–8

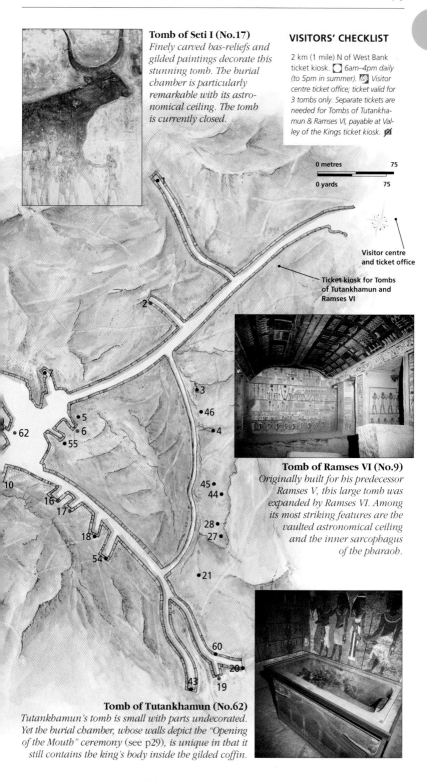

Tomb of Seti I (No.17)
Finely carved bas-reliefs and gilded paintings decorate this stunning tomb. The burial chamber is particularly remarkable with its astronomical ceiling. The tomb is currently closed.

VISITORS' CHECKLIST

2 km (1 mile) N of West Bank ticket kiosk. ⬭ 6am–4pm daily (to 5pm in summer). 🎫 *Visitor centre ticket office; ticket valid for 3 tombs only. Separate tickets are needed for Tombs of Tutankhamun & Ramses VI, payable at Valley of the Kings ticket kiosk.* 📷

0 metres		75
0 yards		75

Visitor centre and ticket office

Ticket kiosk for Tombs of Tutankhamun and Ramses VI

Tomb of Ramses VI (No.9)
Originally built for his predecessor Ramses V, this large tomb was expanded by Ramses VI. Among its most striking features are the vaulted astronomical ceiling and the inner sarcophagus of the pharaoh.

Tomb of Tutankhamun (No.62)
Tutankhamun's tomb is small with parts undecorated. Yet the burial chamber, whose walls depict the "Opening of the Mouth" ceremony (see p29), is unique in that it still contains the king's body inside the gilded coffin.

Tomb of Ramses IV (No.2)

Although Greek and Coptic graffiti mar the walls of this 20th-Dynasty tomb, there are some beautiful, vividly coloured scenes from the Book of the Dead. In the burial chamber, the goddess Nut stretches across the blue ceiling. The enormous pink granite sarcophagus is covered with magical texts and carvings of Isis and Nephthys, designed to protect Ramses's mummy from danger.

Tomb of Ramses IX (No.6)

This typical late Ramesside tomb is long and steep, with interesting scenes on the sloping corridor walls taken from the Litanies of Ra, a religious work celebrating the solar deity's nightly journey. A four-pillared room precedes the burial chamber, which has an impressive astronomical ceiling, featuring the goddess Nut surrounded by sacred barques full of stars. Gods and demons are painted on the dark walls. Only the mark of the sarcophagus remains on the floor.

Tomb of Merneptah (No.8)

The tomb of 19th-Dynasty pharaoh Merneptah, son of Ramses II, was excavated by Howard Carter in 1903. Reliefs of Isis and Nephthys worshipping the solar disc decorate the tomb's entrance. From here the corridor descends steeply to the burial chamber, where the sarcophagus still lies. A false burial chamber did not fool robbers, who escaped with treasures but dropped the heavy sarcophagus lid in one of the corridors.

Tomb of Ramses III (No.11)

Discovered by the Scottish traveller James Bruce in 1768, the tomb of Ramses III is known as the "Tomb of the Harpists" after the bas-relief of two blind musicians in one of the side chambers. It is beautifully preserved and, unusually for a royal tomb, its colourful reliefs include scenes taken from everyday Egyptian life.

Tomb of Queen Tawsert/ Sethnakht (No.14)

Originally built for the wife of Seti II, Queen Tawsert, this tomb was appropriated by 20th-Dynasty pharaoh Sethnakhte after he ran into difficulties building his own tomb. The well-preserved wall paintings include depictions of the "Opening of the Mouth" ceremony and, in the burial chamber, the gods greeting Sethnakhte.

Tomb of Ramses I (No.16)

The tomb of Ramses I, founder of the 19th Dynasty, is small but exquisitely decorated. Discovered in 1817 by the Italian explorer Giovanni Battista Belzoni, the walls are painted with scenes relating to the Book of Gates. A large granite sarcophagus remains in the burial chamber.

Tomb of Amenhotep II (No.35)

This is one of the deepest tombs in the valley, with 90 steps leading down to different levels. Although thieves made off with the treasure, Amenhotep's mummy was still in its decorative sarcophagus when the tomb was discovered by

Victor Loret in 1898. Nine other royal mummies, hidden in the tomb by priests, were also found. The pillared burial chamber is decorated with illustrations and texts from the Book of Amduat.

Colourful wall painting from the well-preserved Tomb of Siptah

Tomb of Siptah (No.47)

The Tomb of Siptah, who reigned briefly at the end of the 19th Dynasty, is one of the longest in the valley, stretching 106 m (350 ft) into the rock. Lightly coloured bas-reliefs decorate the walls and the ceiling is painted with a procession of vultures whose wings spread the width of the corridor.

KV5

In 1994 the American archaeologist Kent Weeks began excavating a tomb that had previously been considered unimportant by Egyptologists. What he found is the largest and most complex tomb in the Valley of the Kings. Known as KV5, the tomb is believed to be the burial site for Ramses II's sons. A 16-pillared entrance hall and more than 121 corridors and chambers have so far been discovered and although no treasure has been found, thousands of important artifacts have been recovered from the rubble. The tomb is currently still undergoing excavation.

Amenhotep II's burial chamber, containing the pharaoh's sarcophagus

Thebes: Tombs of the Nobles

Extending over a large area to the south of the Valley of the Kings, the Tombs of the Nobles is made up of more than 400 tombs of Theban nobles and high officials, mainly from the New Kingdom. The tombs lie close to the surface of the hills overlooking the Nile. Because of the poor quality of the limestone here, the tombs are painted and there are few carved reliefs. Vivid artworks cover the walls, providing an invaluable insight into daily life in the New Kingdom. The Sheikh Abd al-Gurna Tombs are clustered around the village of Old Gurna. Further east, tombs at the necropolises of Khokha, Assasif and Abu al-Naga are now open to the public. Of all the tombs, only a few open at any one time.

Richly detailed paintings of life in ancient Egypt in the Tomb of Sennefer

VISITORS' CHECKLIST

Thebes/Luxor, West Bank (follow signposts for Sheikh Abd al-Gurna Tombs). ◯ daily. 📷 payable at West Bank ticket kiosk; entrance to Assasif Tombs payable at Hatshepsut Temple ticket kiosk.

Khokha Tombs
Three tombs, discovered here in 1915, were opened for the first time in 1995. The **Tomb of Djehuty-Mes (No.295)** shows this 18th-Dynasty priest with his wife and family. The **Tomb of Neferronpet (No.178)**, a scribe during the reign of Ramses II, contains a painting of the scribe and his wife before Osiris. The **Tomb of Nefersekheru (No.296)**, another 19th-Dynasty scribe, shows a similar scene.

Assasif Tombs
The **Tomb of Kheruef (No.192)**, steward to Queen Tiy, contains scenes of the queen and 18th-Dynasty pharaoh Amenhotep III watching a dance in their honour. The nearby **Tomb of Anchhor (No.414)**, overseer of the priests of Amun, is an elaborate structure, but the decoration is not well preserved. The **Tomb of Pabasa (No.279)**, a 26th-Dynasty official, is noted for the pillared first court with its very detailed fishing, bee-keeping, wine-making and fruit-picking scenes.

Abu al-Naga Tombs
The first tombs in this area opened in 1999. The **Tomb of Roy**, a steward in the 18th Dynasty, and the **Tomb of Shuroy**, an 18th-Dynasty official, both have colourful tableaux of daily life.

Sheikh Abd al-Gurna Tombs
All the tombs here date from the 18th Dynasty. The **Tomb of Sennefer (No.96)**, mayor of Thebes and overseer of the gardens of Amun under Amenhotep II, is one of the best preserved. The ceiling is covered with brightly-coloured paintings of vines, and Sennefer is shown with his family and making offerings to the gods. The **Tomb of Rekhmire (No.100)**, a vizier during the reigns of Tuthmosis III and Amenhotep II, shows servants at work and Rekhmire collecting taxes and receiving gifts from foreign lands.

The **Tomb of Nakht (No.52)** is decorated with scenes of rural life, such as fishing, harvesting and hunting in the Nile delta. Nakht was the scribe and astronomer of Tuthmosis IV. The well-preserved **Tomb of Menna (No.69)**, an inspector of estates, shows Menna and his

Treading grapes – Tomb of Nakht

wife making offerings to the gods. It contains a detailed harvest scene and paintings of fishing and hunting.

The **Tomb of Ramose (No.55)**, governor of Thebes before and during Akhenaten's reign, has reliefs showing both the old style of worship and the worship of Aten imposed by the heretic pharaoh. The **Tomb of Userhat (No.56)** has detailed scenes of everyday life, including a trip to the barber's. Userhat was one of Amenhotep II's scribes.

The **Tomb of Khonsu (No.31)**, an adviser to Tuthmosis III, is painted with colourful scenes of the Festival of Montu, while the **Tomb of Benia (No.343)** has vignettes of daily life and statues of the deceased and both his parents.

Recording the harvest scene, Tomb of Menna

Thebes: Hatshepsut Temple

Head of Hatshepsut

Against its stark mountainous backdrop, the partly rock-hewn Mortuary Temple of Hatshepsut at Deir al-Bahri is a breath-taking sight. It was designed by Queen Hatshepsut's architect Senenmut in the 18th Dynasty and is an extraordinary monument which rises from the desert plain in a series of imposing terraces. The temple was damaged by Ramses II and his successors, and Christians later turned it into a monastery (hence the name Deir al-Bahri, which means "Northern Monastery"). However, the ongoing excavation of the site by the Polish mission continues to reveal much exquisite decoration. Adjacent to the main temple are the ruins of the much older Temple of Montuhotep II, the ruler of the 11th Dynasty who managed to unite Egypt, and the 18th-Dynasty Temple of Tuthmosis III.

Temple of Montuhotep II
The prototype for Hatshepsut's Temple, the older Temple of Montuhotep II now lies in ruins.

Temple of Tuthmosis III

The imposing Hatshepsut Temple, in its stunning setting at the foot of a sheer limestone cliff-face

RECONSTRUCTION OF THE TEMPLES AT DEIR AL-BAHRI

This reconstruction shows the Temples of Montuhotep II, Tuthmosis III and Hatshepsut as they would have looked during the reign of Tuthmosis III in the 18th Dynasty. Partly rock-cut and partly free-standing, the three temples are set into a natural amphitheatre and are given added majesty by the dramatic cliffs behind them.

STAR FEATURES

★ Reliefs of Punt Expedition

★ Chapel of Hathor

★ Statues of Hatshepsut

★ **Chapel of Hathor**
This chapel is noted for its Hathor-headed columns. The walls have retained much original colouring, including this relief of the ankh and djed pillar, symbols of life and stability.

★ **Statues of Hatshepsut**
The columns of the portico around the upper terrace were decorated with Osiride statues of Hatshepsut, characteristically represented as a male king with a beard. Although many statues were destroyed by later pharaohs, several have been reconstructed from their fragments.

The Shrine of Amun was dug into the cliff behind the temple.

VISITORS' CHECKLIST

2 km (1 mile) NE of West Bank ticket kiosk. 🚌 or on foot or bike from other sites. 🕐 6am–4pm daily (5pm in summer). 📷

Sanctuary of the Sun

Chapel of Anubis
This chapel contains brightly coloured murals, including a relief of Tuthmosis III making offerings to the sun god Ra-Harakhty.

Myrrh trees planted in the gardens yielded a gum that was burnt as incense.

Avenue of sphinxes led off in the direction of the temple complex at Karnak.

Birth Colonnade
Scenes along the Birth Colonnade portray the divine birth of Hatshepsut, designed to legitimize the queen's claim to the throne. On the right, the young queen is shown in the arms of the goddess Neith.

★ **Reliefs of Punt Expedition**
Faded reliefs relate Hatshepsut's journey to the Land of Punt (Somalia). The king of Punt is seen here with his wife Ati (left), who is depicted suffering from obesity.

Thebes: Medinet Habu

Detail from cartouches of Ramses III

Second only to Karnak in size and detail, the magnificent precinct of Medinet Habu is one of the less-visited sights in Thebes. The mortuary temple of the early 20th Dynasty pharaoh Ramses III was first excavated in 1859 and remains the focal point of the complex. However the area was a sacred sight prior to his reign and even today is considered magical among local farmers, the *fellaheen*. The enclosure walls provided refuge for the entire population of Thebes during invasions later in the 20th Dynasty. Later still, the temple was appropriated by the Coptic Church, ironically preserving some remarkable polychrome reliefs, which the Christians had covered in mud.

Libyans from his chariot and scribes tallying vanquished foes by the traditional counting of severed hands and genitals. Osirid statues of Ramses III line the First Court. The Window of Appearances on the left provided a view of the king in his adjacent palace.

Imposing osirid columns featuring Ramses III line the First Court

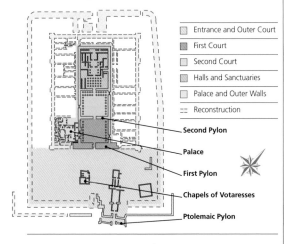

| Entrance and Outer Court |
| First Court |
| Second Court |
| Halls and Sanctuaries |
| Palace and Outer Walls |
| Reconstruction |

Second Pylon

Palace

First Pylon

Chapels of Votaresses

Ptolemaic Pylon

ENTRANCE AND OUTER COURT

The complex is still accessed, as Ramses intended, via the Migdol Gate, which lies adjacent to the 3rd century BC Ptolemaic Pylon. The three-storey gatehouse is modelled on a Syrian fortress. The second floor holds a suite where the pharaoh frolicked with his harem. It is decorated appropriately with reliefs of scantily clad women. As you enter the outer courtyard the small temple called Djeser Set, or "Holy of Place", is dedicated to Amun. It was built by Hatshepsut around 1490 BC and later added to by Tuthmosis III and successive pharaohs. The Chapels of the Votaresses (priestesses of Amun) were built during the Nubian-led

25th Dynasty. Excellent reliefs are found in the chapel forecourt and in the shrine of Amenirdis, sister of King Shabaqo. Sadly, access to the roof, where the views are excellent, is no longer permitted.

THE FIRST COURT

The temple itself is a slightly smaller replica of the nearby Ramesseum *(see pp200–1)* built by Ramses II but the pylons at Medinet Habu are the most imposing of any temple in Egypt. Massive reliefs on the first pylon, which reaches 27 m (89 ft), show Ramses defeating the Nubians on the left and the Syrians on the right, although he fought neither. The inner pylon reliefs depict actual events and show an oversized Ramses scattering

THE SECOND COURT

The second pylon, which is approached via a ramp, is etched with further scenes of Ramses' god-given victories over the Sea Peoples, including the Philistines, and over Asia Minor. The ceiling of the pylon gateway merits attention for its painted winged cobras and sun-disks. The citizens of the Coptic settlement of Djeme removed the Osirid columns to build a church within the Second Court. They have been returned but are still damaged, however, the beautifully coloured reliefs were preserved when Christians covered their sacrilegious content with mud.

THE HALLS AND SANCTUARIES

The Hypostyle Hall is similar in style and scope to that of Karnak. Archaeologists assume that the damage to this part of the temple was caused by the earthquake of 27 BC. The roof and the eight-columned central aisle are no more, and all that remains of the 24 pillars are their hieroglyphic-covered bases. To the right are locked rooms, presumed to have been treasuries, as their reliefs

Thebes: Valley of the Queens

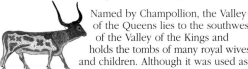

Celestial cow in Nefertari's tomb

Named by Champollion, the Valley of the Queens lies to the southwest of the Valley of the Kings and holds the tombs of many royal wives and children. Although it was used as a burial site in the 18th Dynasty, it was only from the reign of the 19th-Dynasty pharaoh Ramses I that royal wives were laid to rest here. Of the nearly 80 tombs populating the valley, the most famous is that of Queen Nefertari and only a few are open to the public at any one time.

depict the weighing of items such as myrrh, gold and lapis. Opposite is a series of chapels dedicated to Ramses, his namesake Ramses II and to the gods Ptah, Osiris and Sokar. Approaching the holy sanctuaries to the Theban Triad (Mut, Amun and Khonsu) are two pillared halls holding the funerary chamber of Ramses III to the left, and an altar to Re to the right.

Hieroglyphic-covered pillar bases in the Hypostyle Hall

THE PALACE AND OUTER WALLS

The now-ruined mud-brick Palace is too small to have been a long-term residence for the pharaoh, but he did grace his favourites with gifts from the Window of Appearances during visits. A rugged walk along the exterior of the outer walls provides the highlight of Medinet Habu: a series of detailed and unique reliefs. A royal hunt covers the first pylon, the dying bulls and antelope having been depicted with great empathy. As you continue, the reliefs show a Calendar of Festivals, on the short axis of the enclosure walls, the Nubian and Libyan Wars, followed by an assessment of the captives as you turn the corner. Further along Ramses charges the Libyans then battles the Sea Peoples (Sardinians, Philistines and Cretans); this is Egypt's sole relief of a naval battle. The fighting is broken up by another hunting scene to extol Ramses' courage.

Tomb of Amunherkhepshep (No.55)

The elegant, well-preserved tomb of Prince Amunherkhepshep (Amun), son of Ramses III, is the highlight of the Valley of the Queens, unless you can afford the VIP entrance to Nefertari's tomb *(see box, below)*. Amun would have succeeded his father as pharaoh but he died when he was a child and was buried in this royal tomb.

Steps lead down to the tomb hall, which contains beautiful, brightly-coloured wall paintings of Ramses accompanying his young son on a visit to pay homage to the gods of the underworld. Amun is easily recognizable because he is wearing the characteristic braided hairstyle of a prince. From here, a corridor decorated with the Keepers of the Gates leads to the burial chamber, where the skeleton of a five-month-old foetus is on display in a glass cabinet. Foetuses have been found in other burial chambers and may have been placed there as part of the ritual of rebirth.

Tomb of Queen Titi (No.52)

Queen Titi was married to one of the Ramesside pharaohs of the 20th Dynasty, although it is unclear which one. Her tomb is small and damaged in parts, but certain sections have particularly colourful paintings. Some of the best scenes are in the burial chamber, where Hathor appears in both bovine and human form.

Tomb of Prince Khaemweset (No.44)

This is the tomb of another of Ramses III's sons who died in infancy. Its intricate reliefs have preserved much of their colour. Ramses is shown introducing his son to the different deities and making offerings to them. The goddesses Isis, Nephthys, Neith and Selket are also depicted.

REPAIRING QUEEN NEFERTARI'S TOMB

Queen Nefertari wearing a white gown and jewels

Regarded as the most beautiful in Egypt, Queen Nefertari's tomb (No. 66) was first discovered in 1904. Carved from poor quality limestone, its reliefs have sustained damage over time and despite a restoration project that began in 1986 the tomb remains extremely fragile. Access can be gained only by applying to the Secretary General of the Supreme Council of Antiquities and payment of a LE 20,000 fee.

Thebes: The Ramesseum

Wall relief of Amun in the hypostyle hall

Pharaoh Ramses II, ruler of Egypt for 67 years in the 19th Dynasty, built his mortuary temple, the Ramesseum, as a statement of his eternal greatness and to impress his subjects. The huge complex, which took more than 20 years to complete, now lies largely in ruins. Dedicated to Amun, it once boasted an 18-m (60-ft) high, 1,000-tonne colossus of Ramses, parts of which lie scattered at the site. The complex also included a smaller temple dedicated to Ramses's mother Tuya and his wife Nefertari, as well as a royal palace and storehouses.

★ Osiride Columns
Statues of Ramses as Osiris, god of the underworld, face into the second court. These figures, arms crossed bearing the crook and flail, signal the funerary nature of the temple.

★ Head of the Colossus of Ramses
The shattered head and shoulders of the immense colossus of Ramses now lie in the second court. An image of this evocative sight inspired Percy Bysshe Shelley to write his famous poem "Ozymandias".

Royal palace

Landing stage provided mooring for boats from the Nile.

RECONSTRUCTION OF THE RAMESSEUM

This reconstruction shows how the Ramesseum would have looked when it was completed in around 1250 BC. The flooding of the Nile and earthquakes later took their toll, leaving today's atmospheric ruins.

STAR FEATURES

★ Osiride Columns

★ Head of the Colossus of Ramses

First Pylon
The imposing first pylon was decorated with scenes of Ramses in battle. Sadly, an earthquake badly damaged the pylon, and the gateway to the first court is now supported by concrete.

Hypostyle Hall Plant Capital
The hypostyle hall roof is supported by tall columns. The still colourful patterns of papyrus and lotus plants symbolize the union of Lower and Upper Egypt.

VISITORS' CHECKLIST

1 km (0.6 mile) NE of West Bank ticket kiosk. 🚌 or on foot or bike from other sites. ◯ 6am–4pm daily (5pm in summer). ♿

Vestibules led to the sanctuary.

Mudbrick Stores
Innumerable vaulted mudbrick magazines once surrounded the temple, used as store-rooms, workshops and living quarters.

Huge mudbrick walls protected the entire temple complex.

Foundations of the Temple of Tuya
A small temple dedicated to Ramses's mother Tuya and his wife Nefertari stood to the north of the hypostyle hall.

BATTLE OF QADESH

Ramses II portrayed himself as a warrior pharaoh of great bravery and military prowess. Around 1275 BC, he led the Egyptian army into battle against the Hittites at Qadesh, an important trading town in the Orontes Valley in Syria. Although the battle was really a draw, Ramses paraded it as a victory on the walls of several of his great temples, including the Ramesseum. Ramses is depicted firing arrows at the fleeing Hittites and, in tradi-tional pose, holding his enemy's head, about to inflict the fatal blow.

Wall relief on the inner face of the second pylon, depicting Hittites slain at the Battle of Qadesh

Exploring Other Sites in Thebes

Scattered amid the wadis and hills of the West Bank are several other sites well worth a visit. Often by-passed in favour of the more famous Theban attractions, these additional sites can be visited in relative peace, well away from the tourist hordes. Deir al-Medina provides a rare insight into the lives of ordinary people in ancient Egypt, as well as containing some exquisite tombs. The Temple of Merneptah hosts some outstanding reliefs and is complemented by a well laid out and informative museum.

The awesome Colossi of Memnon on the flat desert plain of the West Bank

∩ Colossi of Memnon
500 m (0.3 mile) E of West Bank ticket kiosk.

Soaring 18 m (60 ft) into the sky, the two enthroned statues of Amenhotep III are the first monuments most visitors see on arriving in the West Bank. They originally guarded Amenhotep's mortuary temple – thought to have been the largest ever built in Egypt – which was plundered for building material by later pharaohs and gradually destroyed by the annual floods. However, ongoing excavations are revealing a wealth of immense statues that have been buried in the silt for millennia. The area is out of bounds, but the finds can be viewed from the roadside.

During the Roman period the northernmost statue became a popular tourist attraction as it was heard to "sing" at sunrise. Prominent visitors to the site to hear this included the Emperor Hadrian, and the colossi are mentioned by classical authors such as Strabo and Pliny. The Greeks had attributed the sound to Memnon greeting his mother Eos, the goddess of dawn, with a sigh. In fact, the statue had been badly damaged in an earthquake in 27 BC and its musical talent probably had a purely physical cause related to the damage it had sustained. Whatever the reason, once the statue had been repaired in AD 199 by the Roman emperor Septimius Severus, the singing stopped.

∩ Temple of Merneptah
NE of West Bank ticket kiosk.
◻ *6am–4pm daily (5pm in summer).*

Merneptah was the 13th of Ramses II's 52 sons and became his successor in 1213 BC only because he outlived his 12 older brothers. He ascended to the throne at the age of 50, ruling for just 10 years. In design, Merneptah's temple is a smaller version of his father's Ramesseum (*see pp200–1*). Merneptah located his temple on the same flood-plain as the inundated temple of Amenhotep III, from where he plundered most of his building materials and statuary. Not surprisingly, it was similarly washed away. British archaeologist William Matthew Flinders Petrie examined the site in the 1890s but the temple was then forgotten until the 1970s.

There are no massive pylons here, but an excellent museum displays some small detailed works and fragments of a colossal limestone sphinx. A series of polychrome reliefs of Amenhotep III, discovered and displayed here, are probably the finest examples known in Egyptian art history.

∩ Deir al-Medina
1 km (0.6 mile) NW of West Bank ticket kiosk. ◻ *6am–4pm daily (5pm in summer).* separate ticket required for Tomb of Pashedu.

The craftsmen, servants and labourers who worked on the royal tombs lived in the village of Deir al-Medina, also known as the Workmen's Village, to the south of the

Painted relief from the Ptolemaic temple at Deir al-Medina

Sennedjem and his wife worshipping gods in his tomb at Deir al-Medina

Valley of the Queens. They were buried in the nearby necropolis, in tombs that were intricately decorated and surmounted by a small pyramid. One of the most beautiful is the **Tomb of Sennedjem (No.1)**, a 19th-Dynasty servant. Discovered in 1886, its yellow ochre walls are in perfect condition; they show Sennedjem and his wife, Iyneferti, worshipping different gods and working in the fields of the underworld. The adjacent **Tomb of Inherkhau (No.359)**, the "foreman of the mayor of the Two Lands", is equally beautifully decorated with memorable scenes, including the Cat of Heliopolis killing the serpent Apophis under the holy tree. The small size of these tombs means that only ten people are allowed in them at one time. The **Tomb of Pashedu (No.3)**, a servant during the Ramesside era, is renowned for its delicate paintings and for a famous scene of Pashedu crouching next to a stream under a palm tree.

To the north of the village is a small Ptolemaic temple, dedicated to the goddesses Hathor and Maat. During the Coptic period it was turned into a monastery, which led to the site being named Deir al-Medina or "City Monastery".

Temple of Seti I
3 km (2 miles) E of West Bank ticket kiosk. *6am–4pm daily (5pm in winter).*
Away from the popular tourist trail, the 19th-Dynasty mortuary Temple of Seti I, the northernmost of all the temples of Thebes, is dedicated to Amun and to the cult of Seti's father, Ramses I. After Seti's death, his son Ramses II completed the temple. Although the pylons and surrounding buildings are in ruins, the sanctuary, halls and antechambers of the main sandstone temple are well preserved and there are some interesting, high-quality reliefs, including those showing Seti and Ramses II making offerings to Amun. Part of the roof, featuring vultures and the winged sun disc, is still intact. The German Archaeological Institute is in the process of restoring the site.

Howard Carter's house
3 km (2 miles) E of West Bank ticket kiosk. *6am–4pm daily (5pm in summer).*
British archaeologist Howard Carter, best known for his discovery of the tomb of Tutankhamun in 1922 *(see pp20–1)*, lived for many years in this domed house north of the Temple of Seti I. In 2010, the house opened as a museum displaying pictures of Carter's discoveries, copies of letters to his patron Lord Carnarvon, and a short 3D film that brings his character to life.

The Villages of Gurna
Built on and around the Tombs of the Nobles *(see p195)*, Old Gurna, with its brightly painted mudbrick houses, was long considered a threat to the tombs. In the 1940s, New Gurna was built to rehouse residents. Designed by architect Hassan Fathy, it was inspired by traditional Nubian architecture, yet it failed to lure the Old Gurna residents who believed they should safeguard both the monuments and tourists. A Palace of Culture is being developed in New Gurna.

Today most of Old Gurna has been demolished and the government has moved residents to purpose built housing in Tarfa and Gabawy to the north-east. Only a few examples of the old villages remain, with their decorations of pilgrimages to Mecca, on the hillside near Medinat Habu, however the villages are now empty.

Part of a village near Old Gurna, in the foothills of the Theban hills

New Gurna
2 km (1 mile) SE of West Bank ticket kiosk.

Gurna
500 m (0.3 mile) N of West Bank ticket kiosk.

The domed house of British archaeologist Howard Carter

Detail of the Temple of Khnum's astronomical ceiling at Esna

Esna ⑩

Qena governorate, 54 km (33 miles) S of Luxor. 🏛 55,000. 🚉 🚌 🚤 🚢 *from Luxor or Aswan.*

The sleepy farming town of Esna lies on the western bank of the Nile, just south of a sandstone dam across the river, built in 1906. Known as Latopolis by the ancient Greeks because the Nile perch (*lates* in Greek) was worshipped here, Esna is today best known for the **Temple of Khnum**. This Graeco-Roman structure was designed to resemble a much earlier temple on the site, built by 18th-Dynasty pharaoh Tuthmosis III *(see p49).* Both temples were dedicated to the ram-headed god Khnum, who, according to one of the Egyptian creation myths, fashioned mankind out of Nile clay using a potter's wheel.

Gradually, repeated flooding by the Nile buried the Graeco-Roman structure under layers of silt and mud, and the modern town of Esna was built on top of it. Excavation work on the site began in the 1860s but this has only cleared one part of the temple, the Roman hypostyle hall, which was built

during the reign of the Roman emperor Claudius (AD 41–54). Today this well-preserved hall stands in a huge excavation ditch 10 m (33 ft) below street level in the centre of town. Its roof, which remarkably is still intact, is on the same level as the foundations of the surrounding houses. The façade of the hall is inscribed with the cartouches of Roman emperors Claudius, Vespasian (AD 69–79) and Titus (AD 79–81). Inside the hall the last emperor mentioned is Decius, who died as late as AD 249. The roof is supported by 24 columns inscribed with hieroglyphs and fascinating texts describing the sacred festivals of Esna and recording hymns to the god Khnum. The colours of the astronomical ceiling have been blackened by smoke but it is still possible to make out the zodiac register, remarkable for its subtlety and detail.

> 🎭 **Temple of Khnum**
> ⏰ *7am–4pm daily (to 5pm in summer).* 📷

Edfu ⑪

Aswan governorate, 115 km (71 miles) S of Luxor; 104 km (65 miles) N of Aswan. 🏛 56,000. 🚌 🚤 🚢 *from Luxor or Aswan.*

Edfu stands beside the Nile almost exactly half-way between Luxor and Aswan. It was an important sacred site to the Egyptians because, according to ancient myth,

this was where the falcon god Horus fought a fierce battle with his uncle Seth, who had cruelly murdered Horus's father Osiris *(see p26).*

The **Temple of Horus** at Edfu, which was buried under sand and silt for nearly two thousand years, is the largest and best preserved Ptolemaic temple in Egypt. Construction of the temple began under Ptolemy III Euergetes in 237 BC and the main temple complex took 25 years to complete. However, construction continued up to the time of Ptolemy XII Neos Dionysus (80–51 BC). Despite its relatively recent construction, the temple is of particular interest to Egyptologists because it closely imitates much older Pharaonic designs. The imposing 36-m (118-ft) high first pylon is typically decorated with Pharaonic scenes of Ptolemy XII defeating his enemies in front of Horus and Hathor. Two elegant black granite statues of Horus flank the entrance to the pylon, which leads to a large colonnaded court and the first hypostyle hall. Behind this lies a second, smaller hypostyle hall with chambers off to the side. Gifts for the gods were stored in these rooms before being taken into the hall of offerings beyond. Stairs lead from the hall of offerings to the roof, which is inaccessible; however the staircase walls are beautifully decorated with scenes from the New Year

Granite statue of the falcon god Horus

Pylon of the Temple of Horus in Edfu with reliefs showing pharaoh Ptolemy XII

festival, a ritual celebrated in temples all over Egypt. On the first day of the year, in each temple, a procession of priests carried the statue of the temple god up to the roof to be revitalized by the sun. Beyond the hall of offerings is the sanctuary of Horus with its black granite shrine which contains a model of Horus's sacred barque. Several chapels with excellent reliefs surround the sanctuary.

Southwest of the temple lie the remains of Horus's birth house. This was the focus of the annual Coronation Festival, a ritual celebrating the birth of Horus and his incarnation as the reigning pharaoh.

Temple of Horus
7am–6pm daily (to 8pm in summer).

Postcard of Bedouin and camels – both at home in the desert

SHIPS OF THE DESERT

The *Camelus dromedarius* or one-humped Arabian camel has been an essential part of life in Egypt for thousands of years. Used primarily for transporting goods, the camel also provides milk, wool and meat. Contrary to myth, the camel's hump is not filled with water; it contains fat which allows the camel to survive for up to a week without food. Camels are ideally suited to desert life with their third, transparent eyelid that allows them to see in sand storms, nostrils that close between breaths and their unique body thermostat that minimizes unnecessary water loss through sweating. When they walk, camels move both legs on one side and then both legs on the other. This creates a rolling motion, hence their nickname "ships of the desert".

Relief of Sobek, the crocodile god, in the temple of Kom Ombo

Temple of Kom Ombo ⓬

40 km (25 miles) N of Aswan. 🚌 🚌 🚌 *from Aswan or Luxor.* 🕐 *7am–7pm daily (8pm in summer).*

Surrounded by fields of sugar cane and corn, Kom Ombo is a pleasant agricultural town, home to many Nubians displaced by the creation of Lake Nasser *(see p210)*. The town's ruined yet imposing Graeco-Roman temple is in a particularly beautiful setting overlooking the Nile. The temple building is totally symmetrical with two entrances, two halls and

two sanctuaries. This unusual structure is the result of the temple's dedication to two gods – the left side to the falcon god Haroeris (Horus the Elder) and the right side to Sobek, the local crocodile god. The construction of the temple was begun by Ptolemy VI Philometer in the 2nd century BC and mostly completed by Ptolemy XII Neos Dionysus during the 1st century BC. Finally the Roman emperor Augustus added the entrance pylon in around 30 BC. From the largely ruined forecourt, two doors lead to the hypostyle hall, which contains scenes relating to Haroeris on the left wall and Sobek on the right. The many columns are carved with the lotus or lily of Upper Egypt and the papyrus of the Delta. A series of halls and vestibules leads through to the sanctuaries of Haroeris and Sobek.

A museum near the exit of the temple houses 40 crocodile mummies from the nearby crocodile necropolis.

Daraw ⓭

8 km (5 miles) S of Kom Ombo. 🚶 *31,000.* 🚌 *from Kom Ombo.* 🕐 *Tue.*

Travellers sometimes combine a trip to Kom Ombo with a visit to the nearby village of Daraw for the famous Tuesday camel market, when hundreds of camels are up for sale. Most of the camels have been brought from Sudan on a month-long journey along "The Forty Days Road", an ancient droving route and former slave trail. The market is chaotic, colourful and noisy. Traders travel from Cairo to haggle for camels to sell at the famous Birqash camel market *(see p168)*, while locals come in search of a bargain.

Camels for sale in the famous Daraw camel market, held every Tuesday

Aswan ⑭

Relief from the Temple of Khnum

Situated downriver from the First Nile Cataract, Aswan is Egypt's southernmost city. From Old Kingdom times, this strategically important garrison town guarded Egypt's southern frontier and was a base for military incursions into Nubia and Sudan. Located at the crossroads of ancient trade routes between Egypt, Africa and India, the town was also a prosperous marketplace, where exotic goods were traded. Aswan stands on the most enchanting part of the Nile, where the desert comes right down to the water's edge and the river is dotted with islands. It is home to a large Nubian community, and the town's laid-back atmosphere makes it one of the more relaxing places in Egypt to visit.

The imposing Sofitel Old Cataract Hotel overlooking the Nile at Aswan

🚲 Sofitel Old Cataract Hotel

Corniche el-Nil. *Tel (097) 2316 000.*
The English crime-writer Agatha Christie penned part of her best-selling novel "Death on the Nile" in this impressive Moorish-style hotel, which opened in 1899. Set in beautiful gardens, with superb views over the Nile and Elephantine Island, it is one of the most famous hotels in Egypt. Past guests include the German Field Marshal Rommel, Sir Winston Churchill and King Farouk. Soak up Aswan's romantic atmosphere while sipping afternoon tea on the verandah. Currently closed for renovation – due to re-open by 2012.

🏛 Nubian Museum

Off road to Aswan Dam, 1 km (0.6 mile) S of Aswan. *Tel (097) 2319 222.*
◯ 9am–9pm daily; 9am–5pm Ramadan. 🎫
This well laid-out museum traces life in Nubia – the area between Aswan in Egypt and Khartoum in Sudan – from the earliest settlements to the present day. Nubian crafts such as basket making and pottery are featured and there

is a fascinating display about the UNESCO-backed projects to save Nubian monuments from submergence under Lake Nasser *(see p210)*. The garden contains a reconstructed cave with prehistoric rock carvings, a Nubian house and a water feature showing the Nile's course and cataracts.

🔩 Unfinished Obelisk

1.5 km (1 mile) S of Aswan, next to Fatimid Cemetery. ◯ 7am–4pm daily (to 5pm in winter). 🎫
A gigantic obelisk, dating from the New Kingdom, lies semi-finished in an ancient granite quarry just south of Aswan. Had it been completed, it would have weighed a staggering 1.8 million kg (1,197 tons) and stood 41 m (134 ft) high. Three sides of the shaft were quarried before a flaw was discovered in the stone and the obelisk had to be abandoned, still partly attached to the parent rock. To the west of the quarry, the Fatimid cemetery contains several hundred mudbrick Islamic tombs, built between the 8th and 12th centuries.

🛒 Souq

Sharia as-Souq. ◯ daily.
From embroidered *galabiyyas* and coloured caps to aromatic spices, live chickens and fresh vegetables, there is a vast array of goods on sale in Aswan's lively and extensive market. Renovations have eroded some of the narrow alleyways and chaotic atmosphere but this is still a fascinating place to take in the exotic and colourful environment. The market runs parallel to the Nile and becomes noticeably less tourist-orientated further inland from the busy main street, Sharia as-Souq.

Spices on Sharia as-Souq, the main street through Aswan's famous market

◁ **Detail of a relief showing the journey to the land of Punt – Hatshepsut Temple, Deir al-Bahri**

A colourful Nubian village on the banks of Elephantine Island

⌂ Elephantine Island

Aswan. 🚢 🛶

Known as Yebu (meaning "elephant") during the Old Kingdom, Elephantine Island is the oldest inhabited part of Aswan. It is not known whether the island was named after the huge granite boulders at the southern end of the island, which resemble bathing elephants, or because it was a major ivory trading post.

In ancient times, the island was the cult centre of the ram-headed god Khnum, creator of humankind and god of the Nile flood. Among the ruins of the ancient fortress town that once stood on the southern end of the island are the ruins of the **Temple of Khnum**, built by

Nectanebo in 4th century BC. An impressive gateway, added in the 1st century BC, showing Ptolemy XI worshipping Khnum, can be seen on the west side of the temple. Immediately to the north is the Graeco-Roman **Necropolis of the Sacred Rams**, and to the east, the **Temples of Satet**, built by Queen Hatshepsut. This area is being excavated by German archaeologists and some areas are out of bounds.

In the middle of the island, two traditional Nubian villages are distinguished by their brightly coloured homes.

⌂ Nilometer

Elephantine Island.
🕐 8am–4pm daily (to 5pm in summer). 🚫

The steep Nilometer steps descend into the river. The walls were calibrated to record the height of the annual flood and so indicate the likely crop yield for the next year. Dating from Pharaonic times, the Nilometer was briefly put back into use after its discovery in 1822.

Calibration on walls of Nilometer

VISITORS' CHECKLIST

Aswan governorate, 215 km (133 miles) S of Luxor; 900 km (560 miles) S of Cairo. 🏠 220,000. ✈ 25 km (15 miles) SW of town. 🚉 🚌 ℹ Located outside railway station (097) 2312 811. 🚢 daily.

🏛 Aswan Museum

Elephantine Island. 🕐 8am–4pm daily (to 5pm in summer). 🚫

The Aswan Museum is set among pleasant, sub-tropical gardens near the southern end of Elephantine Island. It is home to a collection of artifacts found on digs in and around Aswan and Elephantine Island. Exhibits range from primitive prehistoric weapons to Graeco-Roman mummies and are labelled in chronological order. An annexe displays finds from the island, including jewellery discovered at the island's Temple of Satet and a marriage contract dating from 350 BC.

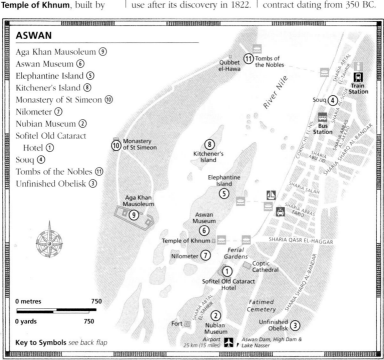

ASWAN

- Aga Khan Mausoleum ⑨
- Aswan Museum ⑥
- Elephantine Island ⑤
- Kitchener's Island ⑧
- Monastery of St Simeon ⑩
- Nilometer ⑦
- Nubian Museum ②
- Sofitel Old Cataract Hotel ①
- Souq ④
- Tombs of the Nobles ⑪
- Unfinished Obelisk ③

Qubbet el-Hawa
Tombs of the Nobles ⑪
River Nile
Souq ④
Train Station
Bus Station
Monastery of St Simeon ⑩
Kitchener's Island ⑧
Elephantine Island ⑤
Aga Khan Mausoleum ⑨
Aswan Museum ⑥
Temple of Khnum
Nilometer ⑦
Ferial Gardens
Coptic Cathedral
Sofitel Old Cataract Hotel ①
Fatimed Cemetery
Fort
Nubian Museum ②
Airport 25 km (15 miles)
Unfinished Obelisk ③
Aswan Dam, High Dam & Lake Nasser

SHARIA ABTAL ELTAHRIR
SHARIA AL MARKAZ
SHARIA ABBAS ALTAYAR
SHARIA ABU ZID
SHARIA SHARO AL-BANDAR
SHARIA SALAH
SHARIA ABBAS FARIQ
SHARIA QASR EL-HAGGAR
SHARIA SHARO AL-BANDAR
CORNICHE EL-NIL

0 metres 750
0 yards 750

Key to Symbols see back flap

Lush botanical gardens stocked with plants from all parts of the world on Kitchener's Island, Aswan

Kitchener's Island

Aswan. ⛴ 🚻 ☕ ◯ *daily.* 📷
Situated in the Nile, west
of Elephantine Island, the
smaller Kitchener's Island
(also known as the Island of
Plants) is one of the most
delightful places in Aswan.
The lush botanical gardens
that cover the island make it
an ideal place to go for a
peaceful stroll or simply relax
in the shade of the trees.

The British general Horatio
Kitchener was presented
with the island in the 1890s
as a reward for leading the
Egyptian army's successful
campaigns in Sudan. He
made the island his home
and indulged his passion for
beautiful flowers by covering
it with exotic plants imported
from all around the world.

The huge sycamore trees,
coconut palms and date palms
that tower into the sky are
filled with colourful birds

and egrets, and as the sun
begins to go down the entire
island rings out with the
sound of their calls.

Aga Khan Mausoleum

West bank, on the road to the
Monastery of St Simeon.
🚫 *to the public.*
Standing on a barren hillside
on the west bank of the Nile,
opposite Aswan, is the Aga
Khan Mausoleum. Aga Khan
III (1877–1957), the 48th
Imam, or leader, of the Ismaili
sect of Shi'ite Muslims, fell in
love with Aswan, where he
spent the winter every year.
After his death in 1957, his
widow, the Begum, erected a
mausoleum in his honour on
the hillside behind their villa.

The domed and turreted
sandstone construction is
outwardly modelled on
Cairo's Fatimid tombs (*see
p102*). Inside, there is a
marble shrine and the
Aga Khan's sarcophagus,
inscribed with texts
from the Quran.
Until her

death in 2000, the Begum
spent part of each year in the
villa and would visit the
mausoleum every day to
place a red rose on her
husband's sarcophagus.

Lake Nasser, an enormous blue
expanse in the desert

LAKE NASSER

Stretching south more
than 500 km (310 miles)
from the High Dam and
reaching depths of over
180 m (590 ft), Lake Nasser
is the world's largest artificial lake. It was created by
the construction of the High
Dam and holds Egypt's
only wild crocodiles. The
lake flooded a huge expanse
of land between Aswan and
Abu Simbel, homeland of
the Nubians since before
Pharaonic times. About
800,000 Nubians were dis-
placed, many settling in
Aswan, and dozens of
ancient temples had to be
carefully relocated (*see p21*).

Mausoleum of the Aga Khan on a barren hillside opposite Aswan

For hotels and restaurants in this region see pp272–7 and pp296–8

The imposing fortifications of the Monastery of St Simeon, Aswan

n Monastery of St Simeon

West bank. 🚤 🐫 *then by camel or on foot.* ⬜ *7am–4pm daily (to 5pm in summer).* 📷

The desert Monastery of St Simeon, on the west bank of the Nile, was built in the 7th century AD. Once home to a community of around 300 monks, it was abandoned in the late 12th century after an attack by the famous Arab leader Salah ad-Din.

The monastery was built as a fortress and, though the main buildings now lie largely in ruins, the imposing fortification walls remain. The lower levels of the complex, which comprised a church, living areas for the monks, stables and work quarters, are made of stone, while the upper levels are made of brick. In the roofless basilica, frescos of the Apostles are still visible, their faces scratched out by Muslims. In the evening, the monastery offers fantastic views of the sun setting over the desert.

HARNESSING THE POWER OF THE NILE

The Aswan Dam was built to regulate the flow of the Nile and so increase Egypt's cultivable land and provide hydro-electric power. However, it soon proved too small to control the river's unpredictable floods. President Nasser's solution was the construction of the High Dam and the creation of Lake Nasser. The resultant increases in agricultural production and hydroelectricity have arguably saved Egypt from famine, but there have been environmental consequences. The rising water table is destroying ancient monuments and silt, previously deposited in the Delta, is retained in Lake Nasser, forcing Egypt's farmers to use potentially harmful chemicals.

The Aswan Dam, built by the British to regulate the flow of the Nile

n Tombs of the Nobles

Qubbet al-Hawwa, West bank. 🚤 🐫 *then by camel or on foot.* ⬜ *7am–4pm daily (to 5pm in summer).* 📷

The hills on the west bank of the Nile, north of Kitchener's Island, are pock-marked with the rock-hewn Tombs of the Nobles. Dating from the Old and Middle Kingdoms, many of the tombs are decorated with scenes of everyday life. The largest and best preserved tomb is that of Prince Sarenput II (No. 31), governor of southern Egypt during the 12th Dynasty. The burial chamber is decorated with statues of the prince and paintings of him and his son hunting and fishing. The tombs of Mekhu (No. 25), a noble from the 6th Dynasty who was murdered while on a military expedition in Nubia, and his son Sabni (No. 26), are crudely decorated with funeral and family scenes. Only one tomb may be open at any one time however, probably

that of Sarenput II. The ancient necropolis is lit up by spotlights at night and looks particularly magical when viewed from across the river in Aswan.

⛩ Aswan Dam

11 km (7 miles) S of Aswan. 🚗

Stretching across the Nile, just beyond the First Cataract, the Aswan Dam was built by the British between 1898 and 1902. At the time of its construction it was the largest dam in the world, and its height was twice raised again in an effort to control the river. The roads to Abu Simbel and the airport cross the dam and the views over the river and islands are stunning.

⛩ High Dam

6 km (4 miles) S of Aswan Dam. 🚗 🅿 📷 🚫

Built between 1960 and 1971, the immense High Dam measures 3,830 m (12,562 ft) across, 111 m (364 ft) high and 980 m (3,214 ft) wide at its base. At the eastern end of the dam there is a visitors' pavilion detailing the construction of the dam and at the western end there is a lotus-shaped tower, built to commemorate the Soviet Union's support in the building of the dam.

The Tombs of the Nobles in the cliffs on the west bank of the Nile near Aswan

The Temple of Kalabsha, dominating the shores of Lake Nasser close to the High Dam

Temple of Philae ⓯

Agilika Island, S of Aswan Dam. 🚗
from Aswan to Shellal then 🚤.
🕐 *6am–4pm daily (5pm in summer).*
🎭 **Sound and Light Show** *Two or
three shows daily from 6:30pm (8pm
in summer). See www.soundandlight.
com.eg for language and time details.*

As the centre of the
cult of Isis, the island
of Philae was an
important place of
pilgrimage for worship-
pers until long into the
Christian era. From
Philae, Isis was said to
watch over the sacred
island of Biga, one
of the mythical
burial sites of her
husband Osiris.

**Lion in the Temple
of Isis, Philae**

After the building
of the Aswan Dam
(1898–1902), the island's
temples were partly sub-
merged in water and visitors
peered at the remains from
rowing boats. With the building of the High Dam (1960–
71), the monuments were
relocated to the nearby island
of Agilika. The UNESCO-led
project lasted until 1980, by
which time Agilika had been
landscaped to look like Philae.

Boats now drop visitors at
the southern end of Agilika,
near the oldest building on
the island, the **Kiosk of
Nectanebo II**, which dates
from the 4th century BC.
From here, a long courtyard,
flanked by colonnades, leads
to the magnificent **Temple of
Isis**, the main building in the
Philae temple complex. Built
in the late Ptolemaic and early
Roman periods, the huge
temple combines ancient
Egyptian and Graeco-Roman

architecture. Ptolemy XII Neos
Dionysos built the first pylon,
which has scenes of him mas-
sacring his enemies, watched
by Isis, Horus and Hathor. The
birth house, built by Ptolemy
VI and altered by later rulers,
is dedicated to Isis's son Horus.
To the west of the temple lies
the **Gate of Hadrian**, which
was inscribed, in 24th
August AD 394, with
Egypt's last hieroglyphics.
On the eastern side of
the island, the small
Temple of Hathor
contains reliefs of
musicians, among
them Bes, the god
of singing. Further
south, close to
the edge of the
water, is the 14-
columned **Kiosk
of Trajan**, which
has scenes of the Roman
emperor burning incense in
front of Osiris and Isis. At the
northern end of the island,
the **Temple of Augustus** and
Gate of Diocletian lie in ruins.

Temple of
Kalabsha ⓰

W of High Dam. 🚗 *from Aswan.*
🕐 *7am–4pm daily (to 5pm in
summer).* 🎭

The imposing temple of Kalabsha was built under Emperor
Augustus in the 1st century AD
on the site of earlier buildings
by Amenhotep II and Ptolemy
IX. Dedicated to the fertility
god Marul (known as Mandulis
by the Greeks), it was moved
50 km (31 miles) north of its
original location in 1970 in a
German-funded rescue operation following the flooding of
Nubia. The temple now
dominates a stretch of Lake
Nasser's shore, just west of the
High Dam. The land here often
forms an island due to the
changing water levels.

From the water's edge an
imposing causeway leads to
the temple's first pylon, beyond
which there is a colonnaded
court. The roofless hypostyle
hall is noted for its ornate

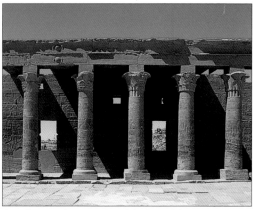

The well-preserved western colonnade leading to Philae's Temple of Isis

column capitals and its reliefs, which include Amenhotep offering wine to Marul.

Environs
Moved at the same time as Kalabsha Temple, the battered remains of the Roman **Kiosk of Qertassi** lie to the northwest. Two Hathor-headed columns mark the entrance to this small kiosk, which commands fine views of Lake Nasser. The nearby **Temple of Beit al-Wali**, also relocated from Nubia, was built during the reign of Ramses II. Its walls depict Ramses's great battles, notably against the Nubians.

Avenue of sphinxes leading to the Temple of Wadi as-Sebua

Temple of Wadi as-Sebua ⑰

140 km (87 miles) S of High Dam. 🚌 🚗 from Aswan. ◯ daily. 📷

Approached by the remains of an avenue of sphinxes, this temple was built by Ramses II and dedicated to the deified pharaoh, Amun-Ra and Ra-Harakhty. In the early 1960s the temple was moved a short distance west to its current site. Two colossi and statues of Ramses adorn the temple, which is partly carved directly into the rock. The inner sanctuary was converted into a Christian church and faint images of saints can be seen over the ancient reliefs.

Environs
Just to the north, the **Temple of Dakka** was begun by the Ethiopian king Arkamani in the 3rd century BC and added

to in the Ptolemaic and Roman eras. Dedicated to the god Thoth, it was originally 40 km (25 miles) further north. The huge pylon is still in good condition. Also relocated here, the **Temple of Maharraka** dates from Roman times. The best remains can be found in the hypostyle hall.

Temple of Amada ⑱

185 km (115 miles) S of High Dam. 🚌 🚗 from Aswan. ◯ daily. 📷

Dedicated to Amun-Ra and Ra-Harakhty, the Temple of Amada was constructed by Tuthmosis III and Amenhotep II, and added to by Tuthmosis IV. Moved just 3 km (2 miles) from its original site, it is the oldest surviving Nubian temple. It also has some of the best preserved Nubian reliefs, including those on the sanctuary's back wall, which depict Amenhotep killing his Syrian prisoners of war.

Environs
A short distance across the desert is the relocated **Temple of Derr**. Built under Ramses II, it was later converted into a church. Although badly damaged, some colourful reliefs remain, particularly in the second pillared hall, where the pharaoh is seen presenting flowers and offering wine to the gods. The nearby rock-cut **Tomb of Pennout**, viceroy of northern Nubia under Ramses VI, was previously 40 km (25 miles) south of Amada in a necropolis of Old and New Kingdom tombs at Aniba. The

Finely preserved relief from the tomb of the Nubian viceroy Pennout, near Amada

tomb is decorated with scenes of Pennout and his family, and the "weighing of the heart" ceremony (see p29).

Qasr Ibrim ⑲

60 km (37 miles) N of Abu Simbel. 🚌 ◯ daily. 📷

The ruined fortress of Qasr Ibrim is on its original site, although the flooding of the region means that whereas it once stood on a high plateau overlooking a valley it is now close to the water's edge. It is believed there was a fort here as far back as 1000 BC. By Roman times, seven temples stood within the fortified walls, including a temple dedicated to Isis and a 7th-century BC temple built by the Nubian king, Taharaqo. One of the last strongholds of paganism, Qasr Ibrim finally submitted to Christianity and a cathedral was built here in the 10th century AD. It resisted Islam until the 16th century, when Bosnians invaded the fort on orders from the Ottoman sultan and the cathedral was turned into a mosque. Still under excavation, the fort can only be visited by cruise boats on the lake.

The ruined fortress of Qasr Ibrim on the shores of Lake Nasser

Abu Simbel ⑳

Carved baboon at Abu Simbel

Hewn out of a solid cliff in the 13th century BC, the Great Temple of Abu Simbel and the smaller Temple of Hathor are a breathtaking sight. Although dedicated to the patron deities of Egypt's great cities – Amun of Thebes, Ptah of Memphis and Ra-Harakhty of Heliopolis – the Great Temple was built to honour Ramses II. Its 33-m (108-ft) high façade, with four colossal enthroned statues of Ramses II wearing the double crown of Upper and Lower Egypt, was intended to impress and frighten, while the interior revealed the union of god and king.

★ Temple Façade
Buried in sand for centuries, the façade was discovered in 1813 by Swiss explorer Jean-Louis Burckhardt.

Store rooms held offerings to the gods and ritual items.

Baboons greeting the rising sun

Statue of Ra-Harakhty

Relocated Temples at Abu Simbel
In the 1960s, as Lake Nasser threatened to engulf the temples, UNESCO cut them from the mountain and moved them to an artificial cliff 210 m (688 ft) back from and 65 m (213 ft) above their original position.

Ramses II Colossi
Accompanied by carved images of captives from the north and south, the four colossi on the temple façade boast of a unified Egypt. Ramses's names adorn the thrones in cartouche form.

The broken colossus lost its head in an earthquake in 27 BC.

STAR SIGHTS

★ Temple Façade

★ Hypostyle Hall

★ Inner Sanctuary

Entrance to temple

The vestibule is adorned with scenes of Ramses and Nefertari making offerings to Amun and Ra-Harakhty.

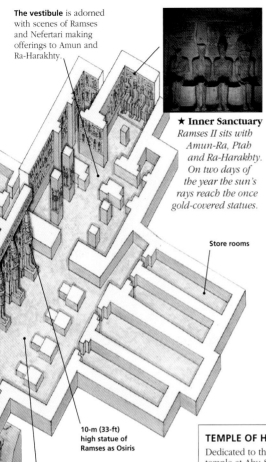

VISITORS' CHECKLIST

Aswan governorate, 280 km (174 miles) S of Aswan. 🚌 ✈
🚌 🚐 ○ 6am–5pm (later when there are evening flights).
Sound and Light Show 6pm, 7pm, 8pm in winter; 8pm, 9pm, 10pm in summer. 📷
www.soundandlight.com.eg

★ **Inner Sanctuary**
Ramses II sits with Amun-Ra, Ptah and Ra-Harakhty. On two days of the year the sun's rays reach the once gold-covered statues.

Store rooms

Battle of Qadesh
Reliefs inside the hypostyle hall show Ramses II defeating Egypt's enemies including, on the right hand wall, the defeat of the Hittites in the Battle of Qadesh c.1275 BC.

10-m (33-ft) high statue of Ramses as Osiris

TEMPLE OF HATHOR

Dedicated to the goddess Hathor, the smaller temple at Abu Simbel was built by Ramses II to honour his favourite wife, Nefertari. The hypostyle hall has Hathor-headed pillars and is decorated with scenes of Ramses slaying Egypt's enemies, watched by Nefertari. The vestibule shows the royal couple making offerings to the gods, and the inner sanctuary holds a statue of Hathor in the form of a cow.

Statues of Nefertari as goddess Hathor alternate with Ramses II on the façade of Queen Nefertari's Temple

★ **Hypostyle Hall**
In Osiride form – carrying crook and flail – the colossi on the southern pillars wear the Upper Egypt crown, while the northern ones wear the double crown of Upper and Lower Egypt. The walls show Ramses II making offerings to his deified self.

SINAI AND THE RED SEA COAST

Treasured in Pharaonic times for its turquoise, copper and gold quarries, the region today is a magnet for tourists, attracted by the white, sandy beaches and fantastic marine life. Sinai is a region of great religious significance; its rugged interior was the setting for many important events in the Bible and remains a holy place for Jews, Muslims and Christians alike.

Wedged between Africa and Asia, the Sinai peninsula is bordered by the Mediterranean Sea, the Gulfs of Aqaba and Suez, and Egypt's Suez Canal zone. The area has been plagued by conflict, most recently between 1967 and 1982 when it was occupied by Israel before being returned to Egypt in the Camp David peace treaty. However, since the late 1980s tourism has boomed along Sinai's eastern coast with resorts such as Sharm el-Sheikh becoming popular holiday destinations. Besides the dry, sunny climate, the main attraction of the region is the underwater world – the Red Sea coral reefs and teeming marine life make this area one of the world's richest dive sites. Yet despite the rapid growth of tourism, much of Sinai's stunning mountainous interior, inhabited by the nomadic, tribal Bedouin people, remains unexplored.

Egypt's Red Sea Coast stretches more than 1,250 km (777 miles) from the Suez Canal to the Sudanese border. Separated from the Nile Valley by the hills of the Eastern Desert, the coastline is famed for its brilliant turquoise waters. The area around the diving resort of Hurghada has developed massively as many more new resorts and hotels have been built here.

The Suez Canal, a phenomenal feat of engineering when it opened in 1869, separates Sinai from mainland Egypt. In the past it was a cause of conflict; today it is one of Egypt's most important sources of revenue.

Shopping for fruit and vegetables in the Red Sea diving resort of Hurghada

◁ Exquisitely coloured coral reef in the warm waters of the Red Sea

Exploring Sinai and the Red Sea Coast

With its combination of mountains and sea, the natural beauty of the Sinai peninsula is awe-inspiring. Most visitors head for the sea, where there is an ever-growing string of tourist resorts from Taba to Sharm el-Sheikh. St Catherine's Monastery in the interior can be visited as a day trip. On the western Red Sea coast, Hurghada is the main resort and from here the monasteries of St Anthony and St Paul make interesting excursions. The Suez Canal to the north is hardly picturesque, but the canal town of Ismailia is pretty and Port Said has good duty-free shopping.

Monastery of St Anthony, inland from the western Red Sea coast

KEY

═══	Motorway
───	Major road
⋯⋯	Minor road
───	Scenic route
▪▪▪▪	Main railway
───	Minor railway
_ _	Track
▪▪▪▪	International border
▪ ▪	Disputed border
△	Summit

0 kilometres   100

0 miles   50

Luxury resorts and diving centres around Naama Bay, to the north of Sharm el-Sheikh

SIGHTS AT A GLANCE

Ain Musa **4**
Al-Arish **14**
Al-Quseir **19**
Dahab **10**
Hurghada **17**
Ismailia **2**
Marsa Alam **20**
Monastery of St Anthony **15**

Monastery of St Paul **16**
Nuweiba **11**
Pharaoh's Island **12**
Port Safaga **18**
Port Said **3**
Ras Mohammed
    National Park **9**

St Catherine's Monastery
pp222–5 **7**
Serabit al-Khadim **5**
Sharm el-Sheikh **8**
Suez **1**
Taba **13**
Wadi Feiran **6**

Map labels:
PORT SAID
Bur Fu'ad **3**
Bur al-Abd
ISMAILIA **2**
Fayid
Cairo
SUEZ **1**
AIN MUS **4**
Gebel Kheiyala 591m
Beni Suef   Zafarana
MONASTERY OF ST ANTHONY **15**
MONASTERY OF ST PAUL **16**
Ab Zenim
South Galala Plateau   Ras Ghari
Gebel Gharib 1757m
Gebel el Kharaza 1359m
Arabian Desert
Gebel Zubeir 1397m
Eastern Desert
Qen

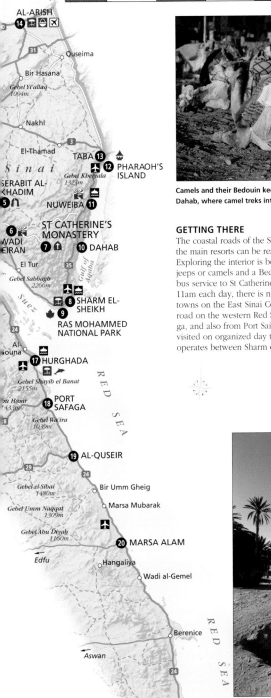

Gaza
AL-ARISH 14
31
Quseima
Bir Hasana
Gebel Yi'allaq
1094m
Nakhl
3
El-Thamad
3
Sinai TABA 13
PHARAOH'S
12 ISLAND
Gebel Khelyala
1323m
SERABIT AL-
KHADIM
5
NUWEIBA 11
ST CATHERINE'S
MONASTERY
6
*WADI
EIRAN*
7 10 DAHAB
El Tur
35
Gebel Sabbagh
2266m
Gulf of Aqaba
8 SHARM EL-
SHEIKH
9
RAS MOHAMMED
NATIONAL PARK
24
*Al-
Gouna*
17 HURGHADA
Gebel Shayib el Banat
2155m
*m Hamr
433m* 18 PORT
SAFAGA
Gebel Wa'ira
1039m
8
19 AL-QUSEIR
29
24
Gebel el-Sibai
1480m
Bir Umm Gheig
Gebel Umm Naqqat
1309m
Marsa Mubarak
Gebel Abu Diyah
1160m
20 MARSA ALAM
Edfu
Hangaliya
Wadi al-Gemel
*RED
SEA*
Berenice
Aswan
*RED
SEA*
24

Camels and their Bedouin keepers at Assalah, to the north of
Dahab, where camel treks into the interior can be arranged

GETTING THERE

The coastal roads of the Sinai peninsula are good and
the main resorts can be reached by bus, car or service taxi.
Exploring the interior is best done on organized trips with
jeeps or camels and a Bedouin guide. Although there is a
bus service to St Catherine's Monastery from Cairo at
11am each day, there is no bus service to here from
towns on the East Sinai Coast. There is a good coastal
road on the western Red Sea to Hurghada and Port Safaga, and also from Port Said to Suez. Inland sites are best
visited on organized day trips or by taxi. A ferry service
operates between Sharm el-Sheikh and Hurghada.

SEE ALSO

• **Where to Stay** pp277–80

• **Where to Eat** pp299–300

Ain Musa's springs, reputedly made drinkable
when Moses, guided by God, threw in a branch

A fishing boat dwarfed by a cruise ship in the Suez Canal

Suez ❶

134 km (83 miles) E of Cairo.
👤 490,000. ℹ️ Sharia Suez Canal (062) 3331 141. 🚌 🚉 🚗

Situated at the southern end of the canal, Suez was a prosperous port in medieval times. In the 18th century, it was used by the British as a staging post on the route to India. Following the opening of the Suez Canal in 1869, it expanded further, but was severely damaged during the 1967 and 1973 wars with Israel. Thanks to money from Gulf states, however, Suez has been rebuilt and it is one of Egypt's most important ports and a major industrial centre. Suez holds little of interest for the tourist but those travelling to or from Sinai use the Ahmed Hamdi Tunnel, 12 km (7 miles) to the north of town or the bridge at Al-Qantara.

Ismailia ❷

120 km (74 miles) NE of Cairo.
👤 600,000. 🚌 🚉 🚗

Named after its founder Ismail Pasha, who ruled Egypt from 1863 to 1879, Ismailia was developed for foreign engineers and labourers working on the Suez Canal in the 1860s.

Ismailia is the prettiest and most populous of the canal towns. South of the railway line, huge European-style villas with lush gardens and large terraces line the wide boulevards. On Mohammed Ali Quay, the house of Ferdinand de Lesseps, director of the Suez Canal Company and French

vice-consul to Egypt at the time of its construction, is an impressive example of these grand houses. It now serves as a hotel for guests of the Suez Canal Authority.

The **Ismailia Museum** nearby is home to a small collection of Pharaonic and Graeco-Roman artifacts, of which the highlight is a 4th century mosaic floor. To visit the nearby Garden of Stelae and its Pharaonic remains, permission is needed from the museum.

The Sweetwater Canal, built to bring fresh water from the Nile to the canal workers, leads to Lake Timsah (Crocodile Lake), which has some pleasant beaches. A ferry from Ismailia runs to the east bank of the canal, where Egypt launched its celebrated attack on Israeli forces in 1973.

🏛️ **Ismailia Museum**
Sharia Salah Salem. ⭕ daily. 📷

A sphinx outside the Ismailia Museum

Port Said ❸

225 km (139 miles) NE of Cairo.
👤 526,000. ℹ️ 8 Sharia Palestine (066) 3235 289. 🚌 🚉 🚗

On the coast where the Suez Canal meets the Mediterranean, Port Said was founded in 1859 by Khedive Said Pasha to house workers on the canal. For years, the city was associated with drugs and smuggling but it has now shaken off its seedy past and is today mostly renowned as a tax-free shopping zone and minor beach resort.

Port Said, which is largely built on land reclaimed from Lake Manzila, is surrounded by water. It was heavily bombed during the 1956 Suez crisis and during the conflicts with Israel in 1967 and 1973, but most of the damage has since been repaired. The distinctive green domes of the Suez Canal Building, built in 1869 on Sharia Palestine, are one of the city's important landmarks.

Nearby, **Port Said National Museum** covers Egyptian history from ancient times; exhibits include Coptic antiquities and Pharaonic mummies. It is currently closed for restoration.

The **Military Museum** on Sharia 23rd July presents a vivid account of the various conflicts that have chequered the history of the canal.

A 19th-century colonial-style villa in Ismailia

View across the Suez Canal from Port Said to Port Fuad

🏛 **Port Said National Museum**
Sharia Palestine. 🔵 *closed for restoration.* 🖾

🏛 **Military Museum**
Sharia 23rd July. ⏲ *8am–3pm Sat–Thu.* 🖾

Ain Musa ❹

25 km (15 miles) SE of Ahmed Hamdi Tunnel. 🚌 *from Cairo or Port Said.*

Also known as the Springs of Moses, Ain Musa lies to the southeast of the Ahmed Hamdi Tunnel, which runs under the Suez Canal near its junction with the Gulf of Suez. According to the Old Testament, it was here that Moses, after leading the Israelites across the Red Sea, turned a bitter spring into sweet drinking water by throwing a branch into it, as instructed by God.

Although Ain Musa was a main source of fresh water for the local town until the 1860s, only one of the 12 springs mentioned in the Book of Exodus remains today. It was used as a strategic stronghold by the Israeli army during their occupation of Sinai from 1967, but was recaptured by Egyptian forces in 1973.

Just over 3 km (2 miles) north of the springs is the Military Touristic Memorial of Ain Musa, a small museum dedicated to the achievements of the Egyptian army.

Serabit al-Khadim ❺

32 km (20 miles) E of Abu Zneima, Sinai.

Built during the 12th Dynasty, the rock temple of Serabit el-Khadim (Heights of the Slave) is perched on a 755-m (2,500-ft) summit to the east of the petroleum-industry town of Abu Zneima. In Pharaonic times the area was rich in copper and turquoise and thousands worked in the mines. The temple was dedicated to Hathor, goddess of love and "Mistress of the Turquoise". Some jeep safaris

from Naama Bay (near Sinai's southern tip) include Serabit al-Khadim in their tours of this beautiful part of Sinai's rugged interior. Hiring a four-wheel-drive vehicle is an alternative, as is a camel safari, accompanied by a local guide.

Wadi Feiran ❻

60 km (37 miles) W of St Catherine's Monastery, Sinai. 🏔 *650.*

Lying halfway between St Catherine's Monastery and the Red Sea coast, at the foot of the 2,000-m (6,560-ft) high Mount Serbal, Wadi Feiran is the largest oasis in south Sinai. A winding valley, thick with shady palms, tamarisks and orchards, the oasis is believed to be the *Rephidim* mentioned in Exodus – the last place of rest for the weary Israelites before they reached Mount Sinai.

An early Christian community flourished here and, in AD 451, it became the seat of a bishopric that governed St Catherine's Monastery *(see pp222–5)*. The bishop's palace and convent were destroyed in the 7th century, but a small convent was rebuilt on the site with stone from the original Byzantine buildings. Today, the oasis belongs to the Tawarah tribes.

Palms flourishing in the oasis of Wadi Feiran, south Sinai

St Catherine's Monastery ❼

Nestling at the foot of Mount Sinai, the Greek Orthodox monastery of St Catherine is thought to be the oldest continuously inhabited Christian monastery in the world. Founded in AD 527 by Emperor Justinian, it replaced a chapel built by the Empress Helena in AD 337 on the site where it is believed that Moses saw the Burning Bush. The monastery was renamed St Catherine in the 9th or 10th century after monks claimed to have found the intact body of the saint on a nearby mountain.

Library
The collection of priceless early Christian manuscripts is one of the most important in the world.

★ **Icon Collection**
The monastery holds 2,000 icons, including this of St Peter. A selection on view, along with treasures gifted over the years.

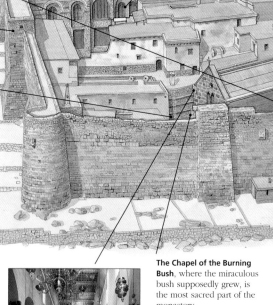

The Walls of Justinian, dating from the 6th century, are part of the complex's original structure.

The Burning Bush
This evergreen is said to be from the same stock as the bush from which God instructed Moses to lead his people out of Egypt to the Promised Land.

The Chapel of the Burning Bush, where the miraculous bush supposedly grew, is the most sacred part of the monastery.

★ **Basilica of the Transfiguration**
This richly decorated church owes its name to a rare 6th-century Mosaic of the Transfiguration in the apse. The mosaic is located behind the gilded 17th-century iconostasis.

STAR FEATURES

★ Basilica of the Transfiguration

★ Museum Icon Collection

Bell Tower
Built in 1871, the tower houses nine bells donated by Tsar Alexander II of Russia. They are only rung on religious festivals.

The Mosque was built in 1106 by converting a chapel originally dedicated to St Basil. Its creation was an attempt to placate local Muslim rulers.

Monks' quarters

St Stephen's Well

Dispensary

VISITORS' CHECKL

Sinai, 90 km (56 miles) W of Dahab and Nuweiba. **Tel** (069) 3470 343. ✈ 10 km (6 miles) NE of monastery. 🚌 one bus per day from Cairo to St Catherine's village (Al-Milga), then taxi 3 km (2 miles). Most visitors come with a tour. Petrol available at the monastery. ⏰ 9am–11:45am Mon–Thu and Sat, 11am–noon Fri. ⚫ Sun, Greek Orthodox holidays. 📷 (museum)

Monastery Gardens
A cemetery is located in the orchard from where monks' bones are periodically exhumed and taken to the Charnel House.

Charnel House & Guesthouse

The elevated entrance, reached by a pulley system, used to be the only access.

The underground cistern was dug to store fresh water from the monastery's springs.

Visitors' entrance

Well of Moses
Inside the outer wall lies the monastery's main water source where Moses is said to have met his future wife, Zipporah, Jethro's daughter.

ST CATHERINE OF ALEXANDRIA
St Catherine was one of the most popular early Christian saints. Supposedly born into a wealthy Alexandrian family in the early 4th century, she was tortured for her beliefs, first spun on a spiked wheel (hence Catherine wheel) and then beheaded by the pagan emperor. A marble sarcophagus in the monastery's Church of St Catherine contains two silver caskets said to hold part of her remains, found by monks 600 years after her death.

Detail of St Catherine from clerical vestments

Exploring St Catherine's Monastery

Completely isolated for many years, and surrounded by red granite mountains, the monastery is now on the main tourist trail and busloads of visitors arrive each day. Around 20 or so monks (mostly from Greece) still live in the monastery, and hence its opening times are strictly controlled. The surrounding mountains are incredibly beautiful and most visitors climb the well-worn path to the top of Mount Sinai – where Moses is said to have received the Ten Commandments – to enjoy the spectacular view over this setting of profound biblical significance.

Ornately carved wooden inner door to the 6th-century Basilica

Inside the monastery

Entry is through a small postern or gateway in the north-eastern wall. The elevated entrance above it contains a pulley and used to be the only way into the monastery after the main gate was blocked as a defence against raiders in the Middle Ages. Parts of the huge granite walls date from the 6th century although they have been substantially rebuilt over the years – firstly, after an earthquake in the 14th century and again in 1800 when Napoleon sent masons from Cairo to restore the stonework.

The monastery's main church, or Basilica, built by Emperor Justinian's architect Stephanos Ailisios in AD 527, is known as the Basilica of the Transfiguration. It is one of the few remaining churches in the region which survive from this period. Massive 11th-century wooden doors open onto the narthex (porch). Beyond is another door, carved with reliefs of animals,

birds and flowers, which is believed to be the original from Justinian's church. The central nave is flanked by six pillars bearing Byzantine icons of saints worshipped in each month of the year. The marble floor and coffered ceiling are 18th century. A gilded iconostasis, painted in the early 17th century, separates the nave from the altar. Behind this, the roof of the apse is decorated with a superb 6th-century mosaic of the Transfiguration. Beyond the altar lies the Chapel of the Burning Bush, the holiest place of the monastery, which is closed to the public. The thorny, evergreen bush, reputedly a descendant of the original Burning Bush from which Moses heard the Lord speak, is of a species found nowhere else in Sinai.

The monastery's library, with over 3,000 ancient manuscripts in Greek and other languages, is second in importance only

Monks' skulls inside the Charnel House

to that of the Vatican. One of the highlights is the *Codex Syriacus*, a 5th-century Syriac version of the New Testament. The priceless icons, dating from the early Byzantine period, are among the only survivors from the Iconoclast era (726–843) when such images were held to be heretical. They include a *St Peter* (5th–6th century), and the 7th-century *Christ in Majesty* and *Ladder of Paradise*. A selection of icons and manuscripts are on display in the excellent museum near the entrance to the monastery.

In the garden, dense with olive and apricot trees, is the monastery cemetery and the Chapel of St Triphonius. The latter's crypt holds the Charnel House, which contains the bones of monks who have died here over the centuries. The monastery guesthouse is set near the lovely orchards and gardens, and has a good courtyard café.

Environs

Rising to a height of 2,286 m (7,500 ft), **Mount Sinai** is held to be the Biblical Mount Horeb (Exodus 24) where Moses spent 40 days and nights before receiving the Ten Commandments. There are two paths to the top, both starting behind the monastery. The more gentle "Camel Path", created by Abbas Hilmi I, Pasha of Egypt from 1849–54, is the usual route up. Camels can be hired from the

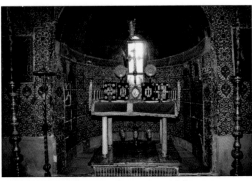

Chapel of the Burning Bush, viewable only by special dispensation

For hotels and restaurants in this region see pp277–80 and pp299–300

View of St Catherine's Monastery from path leading to Mount Sinai

foot of the mountain, though the last 700 steps have to be undertaken on foot. The 3,700 steps of the "Stairs of Repentance" is a steeper route. Along it are several votive sites, including Moses' Spring, which gushes from a small cave, and St Stephen's Gate. Most visitors climb at night to reach the summit in time for sunrise.

Around 700 steps below the summit is **Elijah's Basin**, a sandy plain dotted with cypress trees, one of which is estimated to be 1,000 years old. This is where those who accompanied Moses are said to have waited while he climbed to the summit alone. Camping here, rather than at the summit, is recommended for those wanting to spend the night on the mountain.

At the summit, where God is believed to have spoken to Moses from a fiery cloud, is a 12th-century mosque and the small **Chapel of the Holy Trinity**, built in 1934 on the site of a 6th-century church. Neither of these is currently open to the public.

To the southwest of Mount Sinai, **Mount Catherine**, Egypt's highest mountain at 2,642 m (8,666 ft), offers a steep but picturesque climb. At the summit there is a small chapel containing many icons, and a truly outstanding view, taking in the gulfs of Aqaba and Suez and the mountains of both Africa and Saudi Arabia.

St Catherine's Protectorate

Formally established in 1996, the Protectorate covers an area of 4,350 sq km (1,672 sq miles) around Mount Sinai. Its aim is to protect the area's plant and animal life and conserve historic and religious sites. A Trekkers' Code urges visitors to avoid leaving litter, removing rocks or plants and writing or carving graffiti.

A series of guides produced by the Protectorate details hikes in the area along **Wadi Arbaein** and **Wadi Shrayj**, taking in cultural sites and beauty spots. One describes the climb up **Abbas Pasha Mountain**, which leads to an incomplete 19th-century palace at 2,383 m (7,816 ft) – intended as a sanatorium for the sick Pasha. The books can be purchased and guides organized (walkers must be accompanied by a Bedouin guide) from the Visitors' Centre near the monastery and at the Protectorate Management Office in St Catherine's village.

THE BEDOUIN OF THE SINAI PENINSULA

The Bedouin of the Sinai, descendants of tribes from the Arabian peninsula, have lived a nomadic lifestyle in harsh arid regions for centuries, depending on sheep, goats and camels for a livelihood and sleeping in tents made of goatskin. Their name derives from the Arabic word *bedu*, meaning "desert dwellers". The Bedouin are distinctive in their traditional garb: the women don black garments with sequinned veils and the men wear long white robes. Their tightly wrapped figures invariably accompany images of bleak, sandswept landscapes. But life is rapidly changing for these denizens of the desert. With government resettlement programmes and tourism encroaching all over the Sinai, the old ways are under threat. TV aerials protrude from concrete houses and children are increasingly dressed in western-style clothes. While some Bedouin are still nomadic livestock breeders, many now work with jeeps not camels, and make a living from the tourist trade.

Bedouin woman in traditional dress

Naama Bay, a popular resort area in Sharm el-Sheikh

Sharm el-Sheikh ❽

300 km (187 miles) SE of Suez.
35,000. ✈ 🚌 ⛴ 🛈 *Ras Moham-med National Park (069) 3660 559.*

The popular resort of Sharm el-Sheikh, north of Ras Mohammed, stretches over 20 km (12 miles) along the coast and is a renowned diving and snorkelling destination.

Sharm, as it is known to visitors, is divided into two main parts – the town and port to the south and **Naama Bay**, the upmarket tourist enclave 7 km (4 miles) to the north. Om El Sid (El Hadaba) sits on the cliff between them.

After it was captured in the 1967 war, the port was developed by the Israelis, who began to build hotels along the coast. The development that began in the late 1980s is still booming.

With diving schools and hotels lining the Corniche, Naama is far removed from the traditional Bedouin way of life. Nevertheless the water here is beautiful and there are many accessible dive sites along the coast – both for beginners and more experienced wreck divers.

After a rare spate of shark attacks in 2010, beach controls have been put in place, such as designated swimming spots and lookout towers.

Environs
Around 10 km (6 miles) north of Naama is **Shark's Bay**, a quieter but expanding resort area. The coral gardens and tropical fish here are beautiful and despite its name, there

are no sharks. North of Shark's Bay, where the Red Sea meets the Gulf of Aqaba, lie the Tiran Straits. Diving trips to **Tiran** and **Sanafir Island** leave from Naama, Sharm and Shark's Bay. Further up the coast is the **Nabq National Park**, which has also been developed into a resort area. It remains popular, however, with birdwatchers as the most northerly mangrove forests in the world are home to many birds such as grey and white herons, ospreys and storks. Animals suited to the arid conditions, such as gazelles, rock hyraxes and desert foxes, live inland.

Turtle swimming in the Red Sea

🦋 Nabq National Park
29 km (18 miles) N of Sharm el-Sheikh. 🚌 🚍 ◯ *daily.* 🎫 🅿

Ras Mohammed National Park ❾

20 km (12 miles) S of Sharm el-Sheikh.
✈ 🚌 *to Sharm el-Sheikh, then taxi.*
🛈 *Visitors' Centre (069) 3660 559.*
◯ *daily.* 🎫 🅿

Covering the southernmost tip of the Sinai peninsula, Ras Mohammed became Egypt's first marine National Park in 1989. The wealth of underwater life and extensive reefs dotted with brilliant corals and sponges make it one of the best places for diving and snorkelling in the world. Over 1,000 species of colourful fish populate the clear waters and barracuda, reef sharks, turtles and manta rays are among the more unusual creatures to look out for. Above water, the park is home to ibexes, gazelles and a wide range of birdlife. The mangrove forests here grow in a shallow channel south of the peninsula and are an important breeding area for birds. A visitors' centre in the park shows videos about the area and also offers a map of the colour-coded tracks which lead to the different beaches. Although thousands of tourists visit the park each year, considerable effort is made to protect the area from serious damage by not allowing any hotels to be built and carefully restricting the number of dive boats.

One of Sharm el-Sheikh's many diving centres

Coral Reefs of the Red Sea

Coral reefs are one of the richest ecosystems on earth. Coral is made up of colonies of tiny animals called polyps that need precise environmental conditions to grow. There are two types of coral: hard corals, which form hard outer skeletons for themselves, and soft corals, that do not. Most reefs are built over thousands of years from the accumulated skeletons of dead hard corals. In places, the Red Sea reefs form sheer walls covered with exotically shaped corals of pastel pink,

Colourful racoon butterfly fish

yellow and red. Scuba diving in the Red Sea is the highlight of many visitors' holidays and the area is well served for dive centres *(see pp316–21)*. However, if using an aqualung does not appeal, the reefs create shallow lagoons, perfect for exploring with a snorkel. These beautiful, calm lagoons serve as nurseries for schools of smaller fish. A word of caution: although the reefs seem robust, they are an extremely fragile environment and swimmers should look but not touch.

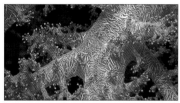

Soft corals *require salty, clear water and warm, gentle currents to bring them their food. At night the coral polyps use their fine tentacles to sting and capture plankton as it swims past.*

The jewel grouper *favours shady areas of the reef, for in the dim light this hunter's stunning colouring becomes surprisingly good camouflage as it waits for its smaller prey to swim past.*

Sea anemones *look like colourful plants but they are in fact animal predators. They use their stinging tentacles to stun their prey and feed it to their centrally located mouth.*

Blue-spotted rays *glide across the sea floor scooping up snails, worms and crabs before crushing them with special flattened teeth.*

Reef walls *plunge to depths of 80 m (260 ft) or more and provide a home for over 1,000 species of fishes and more than 150 types of coral.*

Camels and their Bedouin keepers near Dahab

Dahab ⑩

100 km (62 miles) N of Sharm el-Sheikh.

The word *dahab* means gold in Arabic, and the name of this popular resort derives from its tawny golden beaches. The resort grew up around the Bedouin village of Assalah, to the north of the town, where the beach huts, hotels, restaurants, dive centres and market stalls lining the waterfront cater mostly for independent young travellers on tight budgets.

To the south of the town, in Dahab "city", the scene is distinctly up market, with luxury holiday resorts attracting a very different clientele. For all tourists, however, the sea is the main attraction, and the coral reef, with its immensely rich marine life, is close to shore. A popular dive site is the Blue Hole, to the north of Dahab. This is almost entirely surrounded by coral reefs and drops to a depth of 80 m (260 ft) just a few metres from the shore. The Blue Hole and the nearby Canyon can be dangerous for inexperienced divers and lives have been lost here in the past. A safe alternative is to use snorkelling equipment to admire the reef.

Jeep and camel safaris into the mountains can be easily arranged from Dahab. These are a great way to explore Sinai's beautiful, rugged interior and to see something of the Bedouin way of life.

Nuweiba ⑪

85 km (53 miles) N of Dahab. from Aqaba (Jordan).

Located midway along the Gulf of Aqaba coast, Nuweiba is divided into three areas, spread over a 10-km (6-mile) stretch. To the north is the Bedouin settlement of Tarabeen, where campsites with bamboo and concrete huts are flanked by a couple of hotels. In the village are the restored ruins of a 16th-century fortress, which was built by the Mamluk sultan Ashraf al-Ghouri. About 1 km (0.6 mile) south of Tarabeen, reasonable but not particularly luxurious resort accommodation can be found in Nuweiba City. If you are planning to catch the ferry to Aqaba, there are a few hotels in the unattractive port of Nuweiba, 8 km (5 miles) further south.

All along the coast around Nuweiba, hotels and camp sites are being built, offering

Windsurfer on the Gulf of Aqaba, Dahab

a choice of 5-star and budget accommodation. The setting is particularly beautiful with the Sinai mountains providing a hazy backdrop and those of Saudi Arabia clearly visible across the water.

Nuweiba is a quiet resort offering magnificent beaches and a chance to unwind. Accessible snorkelling off the beaches provides an easy way to explore the magnificent coral reefs and marine life.

Also popular is a trip to the ancient city of Petra, taking the catamaran from Nuweiba port to Aqaba. This spectacular metropolis, 96 km (60 miles) north of Aqaba, was carved out of desert rock between the 3rd century BC and 1st century AD.

Environs
Nuweiba is a good base for exploring the interior, and jeep and camel trips are easily arranged. The **Coloured Canyon**, about 30 km (19 miles) inland from Nuweiba, is a popular destination. It is reached via the oasis of Ain al-Furtaga, usually by four-wheel-drive vehicle, though it is possible to get there (more slowly) by camel. The narrow gorge gets its name from the pink, brown, green and yellow layers caused by the oxidation of minerals.

South of Nuweiba is the **Abu Galum Nature Reserve**, a prime destination for dive safaris. Inland from its lovely deserted beaches is a maze of wadis teeming with plants and wildlife, including desert foxes, ibexes and hyraxes.

A resort near Nuweiba, with Saudi Arabia visible across the sea

◁ St Catherine's Monastery, founded in the 6th century AD in a valley at the foot of Mount Sinai

Crusader castle on Pharaoh's Island, south of Taba, in the Gulf of Aqaba

Pharaoh's Island ⑫

7 km (4 miles) S of Taba. 🚌 🚐 then ferry.

Surrounded by fabulous reefs, Pharaoh's Island (known as Coral Island by Israelis) is popular with divers. The island is just 250 m (820 ft) from the shore, close to the border with Israel, and boats leave from the Salah ad-Din Hotel on the coastal road opposite the island.

Worth exploring are the restored ruins of a 12th-century Crusader castle, strategically placed to ensure the safety of pilgrims to the Holy Land. The castle was captured by Salah ad-Din in 1170 and used as an Arab stronghold against the Crusaders until 1183, when it was eventually abandoned.

Taba ⑬

70 km (43 miles) N of Nuweiba. 🚐

On the border with Israel, Taba was only returned to Egypt in 1989 after international intervention. Egypt was determined to reclaim all its land from Israel and the dispute over this area lasted for seven years after the rest of Sinai had been recovered.

There are a few high-end hotels and local eateries at Taba, but most visitors are just crossing between the two countries. The 70-km (43-mile) stretch between Taba and Nuweiba has been dubbed "The Egyptian Riviera" by the government. It is a priority development area with many hotels and resorts under construction.

If you are leaving Egypt at Taba, note that an Israeli stamp in your passport means that entry into some Arab countries, notably Lebanon and Syria, will be denied. Ask to have a separate piece of paper stamped.

Al-Arish ⑭

48 km (30 miles) SW of Rafah. 🏃 40,000. 🛈 Sharia Fuad Zikry (068) 3363 743. 🚐 🚌 Thu.

Sinai's north coast is largely ignored by tourists, but there are some interesting places to visit, including the coastal town of Al-Arish. The palm-fringed white beaches and warm Mediterranean waters are the major attraction here, but Al-Arish is much more conservative than the laidback resorts along Sinai's Gulf of Aqaba coast.

On Thursdays there is a Bedouin market where women in traditional costume sell embroidered clothing and silver Bedouin jewellery. The **Al-Arish Museum** has exhibits ranging from Pharaonic statues and Coptic icons to Bedouin handicrafts and heritage.

Popular with birdwatchers, the Zerenike Protectorate extends along the coast from the salt lagoon of Lake Bardawil, about 25 km (15 miles) east of Al-Arish.

🏛 **Al-Arish Museum**
Outskirts of Al-Arish, on road to Rafah. **Tel** (068) 3324 105. ☐ 9am–2pm Sat–Thu. 🈂

Palm-lined promenade in the Mediterranean resort of Al-Arish

For hotels and restaurants in this region see pp277–80 and pp299–300

The distinctive façade of the Monastery of St Anthony with the Red Sea Mountains in the background

Monastery of St Anthony ⑮

47 km (29 miles) W of Zafarana. 🚌 from Cairo, Suez or Hurghada. ⭕ daily.

Isolated in the Red Sea Mountains, St Anthony's Monastery (AD 361–3), marked the beginning of the monastic tradition. It is the oldest Coptic monastery in Egypt. Legend has it that Anthony, orphaned at 18, retreated to the mountains to serve God. His disciples built the monastery on the site of his grave.

The monastery complex has retained much of its original appearance, despite attacks from Bedouin tribes in the 8th and 9th centuries, from Muslims in the 11th century and a murderous revolt by Bedouin servants in the 15th century. It is the largest in the country, with several churches and chapels and extensive living quarters, but only 25 resident monks. On the interior walls of the Church of St Anthony are some vivid 13th-century murals. Two kilometres (just over one mile) to the north-east of the monastery is the cave where St Anthony is said to have spent his last years.

Monastery of St Paul ⑯

80 km (50 miles) SE of St Anthony's Monastery. 🚌 from Cairo, Suez or Hurghada. ⭕ daily.

A winding road leads to the Monastery of St Paul, hidden behind lofty walls. St Paul (AD 228–348) was from a wealthy Alexandrian family but became the earliest known hermit when he retreated to the Eastern Desert at the age of 16. The monastery's turreted walls were built around the cave where he lived for decades. The main Church of St Paul is painted with murals representing the Virgin and Child, and the archangels. The chapels contain scores of icons while ostrich eggs, a symbol of the Resurrection, hang from the ceiling. A five-storey keep behind the church, supplied with water from a hidden canal, was used to protect the monks from Bedouin raids.

Two of the monks at the Monastery of St Paul

Hurghada ⑰

320 km (200 miles) S of Suez. 🚶 180,000. ✈ 🚌 🚗 🚢 daily catamaran and weekly ferry services from Sharm el-Sheikh. 🛈 Sharia Banque Misr (065) 3444 420.

Hurghada, on the Red Sea coast, has undergone a complete transformation since the early 1990s when it was little more than a fishing village. Now a sprawling tourist town with resorts stretching all along the coast, it is famous for its dive centres which offer scuba and snorkel trips to view the fantastic Red Sea marine life. There is a wide choice of accommodation with cheaper lodgings centred around

Windsurfer at Sindbad Beach in Hurghada on the Red Sea coast

For hotels and restaurants in this region see pp277–80 and pp299–300

Ad-Dahar, at the northern end of town, while Sigala to the south is more upmarket. Some hotels have good private beaches, and a variety of off-shore excursions are on offer, including day trips to **Giftun Island**. For those who wish to enjoy the wonders of the deep without getting wet, submarine tours are available from Sindbad Submarine or trips in a glass-bottomed boat can be arranged through most hotels. There is an **Aquarium** on the corniche and a **Marine Museum** north of town. In response to environmentalists' fears that the influx of tourists was damaging marine life, the Hurghada Environmental Protection and Conservation Association (HEPCA) was set up in 1992 to raise awareness and preserve the reef.

✗ Aquarium
Al-Corniche. ⬜ 9am–10pm daily.

✗ Marine Museum
7 km (4 miles) N of Hurghada.
⬜ daily. 🖼

Environs
Just 30 km (19 miles) north of Hurghada, **El-Gouna** is a luxurious resort and ever-expanding town. Set on a beautiful strip of coastline, the dome-roofed hotels and villas have a distinct Nubian theme.
Soma Bay, 45 km (28 miles) to the south of Hurghada, is another sprawling tourist development with an 18-hole golf course, a marina, and upmarket hotels and villas.
Remains of two Roman quarries in the Red Sea Mountains are accessible on day trips from Hurghada and the coast. **Mons Porphyrites**, 60 km (37 miles) north of town, was the site of ancient porphyry quarries. The pinky-purple stone was mined by the Romans for building and sent throughout the Empire. Parts of the Roman mining town are still in evidence. The mines at **Mons Claudianus**, around 50 km (31 miles) southeast of Hurghada, supplied the Romans with black granite columns – some of which still support the Pantheon in Rome today. Ruins of the fort and of the Roman town can also be visited.

Traditional ship-building at Port Safaga

Port Safaga ⑱

58 km (36 miles) S of Hurghada.
🏯 33,500. 🚌 🚐

Just to the south of several upmarket resorts, Port Safaga is within easy range of some stunning reefs. Local weather conditions are ideal for windsurfing and in 1993 the World Windsurfing Championships were held here. Apart from tourism, Port Safaga's principal activities are exporting locally mined phosphates and ferrying travellers to Saudi Arabia.

Colourful house in a street of the Red Sea port of Al-Quseir

Al-Quseir ⑲

80 km (50 miles) S of Port Safaga.
🏯 20,500. 🚌 🚐

The small town of Al-Quseir has a distinguished history. Queen Hatshepsut left from here on her famous expedition to the Land of Punt (see p197). Known in Ptolemaic times as

Leukos Limen (White Harbour), it was the largest Red Sea port until the 10th century, popular with pilgrims travelling to Mecca. After the opening of the Suez Canal in 1869, Al-Quseir declined and today is little more than a quiet fishing village. The 16th-century Ottoman fortress of Sultan Selim still overlooks the town.
As a relatively late starter, development has arrived with a little more environmental awareness. Regular dive trips are offered to the islands of Big Brother and Little Brother, 67 km (42 miles) northeast of Al-Quseir. For those who prefer to sample more of the local life, however, the town has a traditional *souk*, and a Bedouin community. An ancient caravan trail to Qift in the Nile valley leads from the town through the mountains, passing several Pharaonic and Roman sites on the way.

Marsa Alam ⑳

132 km (82 miles) S of Al-Quseir.
🏯 6,000. 🚌 🚐

With the completion of the airport north of Marsa Alam, this most southerly section of the Red Sea coast is being developed into large resorts as well as more rustic eco-lodges. The diving is excellent and secluded here, close to the Sudanese border. Head further south to Berenice and Elphinstone Reef. Berenice lies 250 km (155 miles) south of Marsa Alam and is similarly being developed. It is linked by road to Aswan.

THE DELTA AND THE NORTH COAST

Fanning out between the two main branches of the Nile, the Delta is a green triangle in a desert landscape. Several Pharaonic dynasties ruled from here but, apart from the ruins of Bubastis and Tanis, most sites have long disappeared. The resorts of the North Coast are popular with Egyptians seeking relief from the summer heat.

The Nile Delta, Egypt's most fertile and densely populated region, produces the bulk of the country's crops, helping to feed the huge and ever-increasing population. To the east of the Delta, beyond the Suez Canal, lies the Sinai peninsula; to the west is the legendary city of Alexandria and a sandy coastline that stretches for over 500 km (310 miles) to the Libyan border.

Although the north coast between Alexandria and Libya enjoys clear seas and beautiful beaches, many stretches are inaccessible because of landmines left over from World War II. However, there are dozens of holiday villages along the route to Marsa Matruh and more are planned.

Most visitors to Lower Egypt, as the north of the country is called, head straight for Alexandria, Egypt's cosmopolitan second city. Its rich history, links with Cleopatra's reign, moderate climate and pleasant beaches, make Alexandria the region's key attraction.

Although usually ignored by tourists, the Delta itself is worth exploring. This is the rural heart of the country: crisscrossed by irrigation canals, the flat land is rich with cotton, maize, sugar cane and vegetables. Buffalo plough the fields, donkeys pull carts, and mudbrick pigeon huts punctuate the picturesque landscape.

The lakes in the northeast attract an amazing variety of birdlife, especially during the annual winter migration south. Off the tourist trail, Rosetta's rich Ottoman architecture is one of the highlights of the area. Another is the cycle of lively *moulids* (religious festivals) that begin in October and transform the Nile Delta into a joyful place of celebration.

Colourful river taxis at Rosetta where a branch of the Nile flows into the Mediterranean

◁ Typical architectural motifs of stripes, porticos and balconies near Mosque of Abu al-Abbas Mursi, Alexandria

Exploring the Delta and the North Coast

Annual flooding and plundering over the centuries have ensured that little remains to testify to the role of the Delta in ancient Egyptian history. However, the ruins at Tanis and near Zagazig hint at the area's importance in ancient times. Damietta and Rosetta have fine examples of Ottoman architecture, while Alexandria retains the faded grandeur of 19th-century colonial architecture and offers glimpses of its greatness as the Graeco-Roman capital of Egypt. Along the Mediterranean coast are a growing number of resorts, while the cemeteries at El-Alamein serve as reminders of the World War II battles that were fought here.

One of three sphinxes from a tomb near Pompey's Pillar, Alexandria

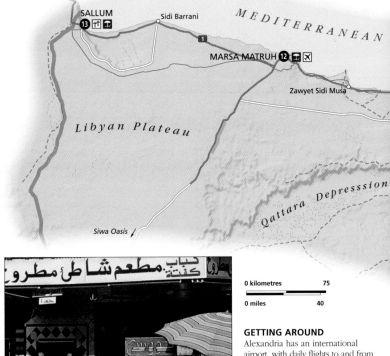

Street scene in Marsa Matruh, a resort to the west of Alexandria

0 kilometres   75

0 miles   40

GETTING AROUND

Alexandria has an international airport, with daily flights to and from Cairo. Trains run regularly between the two cities, and the desert road linking them makes car and bus travel easy. Other towns in the Delta are served by buses, minibuses, service taxis and trains. A frequent bus service runs along the north-coast road to the Libyan border, and a very slow train runs between Alexandria and Marsa Matruh in summertime. The latter is also served by a domestic airport.

SIGHTS AT A GLANCE

Fort Qaitbey, dating from the 1480s and occupying the site of the Pharos – Alexandria's legendary lighthouse

SEA

BALTIM
ROSETTA (RASHID) ❺ 🏛
Baira el Burullus
Nile Delta
Ras al-Bar
DAMIETTA (DUMYAT) ❶
Baira el Manzala
ABU QIR ❽
Idku
MONTAZAH PALACE ❼
ALEXANDRIA ❻ 🏛
Disuq
Kafr el Garayda
Shirbin
Port Said
El Matariya
AGAMI ❾
Abu Sir
Damanhur
El Maialla el Kubra
El Mansura
44
Hosh 'Isa
El Dilingat
San el-Hagar
TANIS ❹
⓫ 🏛
EL-ALAMEIN
ABU MINA ❿
TANTA ❸
Zifta
El Saliiya
11
Tala
Abu Kebir
Shibin el Kom
ZAGAZIG ❷ 🏛
Minuf
Benha
40
⓭
Bilbeis
41
Cairo

Bahariyya Oasis

SEE ALSO

• *Where to Stay* pp280–82

• *Where to Eat* pp300–1

KEY

═══ Motorway

─── Major road

▪ ▪ Road under construction

═══ Minor road

─── Scenic route

▪▬▪ Main railway

─── Minor railway

▪ ▪ Track

▬▬ International border

Sidi Abdel Rahman, near the El-Alamein battlefield memorials

Detail of building in Damietta old town, illustrating Delta-style architecture

Cat worship near Zagazig

Damietta ❶

210 km (131 miles) NE of Cairo.
👥 78,000. 🚌 🚗 🚉

Damietta (or Dumyat) is an industrial port known for its furniture, textiles, sweets and fishing, that lies on Egypt's north coast, next to the eastern branch of the Nile. A wealthy port in the Middle Ages, the town was attacked by the Byzantines, occupied twice by Christian forces then completely destroyed in 1250 by the Mamluks. Damietta was rebuilt by the Ottomans (though sadly few of their "Delta-style" villas can still be seen today) and its importance as a port was restored. The completion of the Suez Canal in 1869, and the subsequent growth of Port Said to the east, however, seriously undermined Damietta's prosperity, although the building of a new port in 1987 resulted in an economic revival.

There is not a great deal to do here, though the restoration of three of the city's ancient mosques is a potential draw. To the east of Damietta, the huge expanse of **Lake Manzila** – a saltwater lagoon separated from the sea by a narrow peninsula – is a popular destination for birdwatchers who come to observe the migrating flamingos, herons, pelicans and storks that stop here. Egypt is on one of the major migration routes for many species, and millions of birds pass through this region every autumn and spring.

To the north of Damietta is the small beach resort of **Ras al-Bar**, which has numerous restaurants, hotels and tea houses.

Zagazig ❷

80 km (50 miles) NE of Cairo.
👥 268,000. 🚌 🚗 🚉

Built in the 1830s to house workers on the Nile Barrages (see p169), Zagazig's main claim to fame is as the birthplace of Colonel Ahmed Orabi, the nationalist who led the 1882 revolt against British rule, and whose statue stands outside the railway station. The town has a small museum that displays archaeological finds from the region.

Just to the southeast of Zagazig are the sparse ruins of **Bubastis**, capital of ancient Egypt in the 22nd and 23rd Dynasties and cult centre of the cat-goddess Bastet. It is believed that huge festivals in her honour were held at Bubastis and attracted thousands of revellers. The events involved dancing, vast quantities of alcohol and sacrifices to the goddess. Work began on the Temple of Bastet at Bubastis during the 6th Dynasty and, for nearly 1500 years, it was regularly added to; now, all that remains to be seen are scattered stones. Nearby, in the underground galleries of a cat cemetery where mummified cats were buried, bronze statues of the sacred animal have been discovered. A museum opened on the site in 2011.

MOULIDS

Meaning "birth" in Arabic, a *moulid* commemorates the birthday of a local saint or holy person. Celebrated by Muslims and Christians alike, the moulid probably has its roots in the customs of ancient Egypt when, on festival days, a statue of the local god was paraded in a boat (see p178). Nowadays, big moulids in Cairo, Luxor and Tanta draw millions of people, allowing everyone a release from everyday concerns. After visiting the tomb or church, revellers might attend a *zikr*, a ritual chanting of Allah's name to induce a trance-like state. *Tartours* (cone-shaped hats) and *fawanees* (lanterns) are sold, while traditional entertainment such as puppet shows and stick dancing take place alongside more modern funfair attractions. Usually lasting a week, moulids climax on the Great Night or *Leila al-Kebira*.

Reeds of Lake Manzila (Damietta) providing cover for migrating birds

Tanta ❸

94 km (58 miles) N of Cairo.
🚶 *373,000.* 🚃 🚌

Tanta, Egypt's fifth largest city
and an important university
town, is best known for its
eight-day festival, or moulid,
which is held each year after
the October cotton harvest. Up
to two million people
take part in the event, which
honours Sayyid Ahmed al-
Badawi, the 13th-century
founder of one of the largest
Sufi brotherhoods in Egypt.
Groups of Sufis from throughout Egypt camp in makeshift
lodgings around the city and
hold *zikrs* – lengthy sessions of
chanting, singing and swaying,
intended to achieve unity with
Allah. A procession led by the
current sheikh closes the
moulid on the eighth morning,
but in recent years officials
have toned down this event.

Although fundamentally a
spiritual occasion, this annual
festival is also an important
social event, allowing young
Egyptians to let off steam in
the boisterous atmosphere.

**21st- and 22nd-Dynasty tombs at
the royal necropolis at Tanis**

Tanis ❹

70 km (43 miles) NE of Zagazig. 🚌

Near the modern village of
San el-Hagar, to the northeast
of Zagazig, lie the jumbled
ruins of the ancient Egyptian
city of Djanet, known by the
Greeks as Tanis. For several
centuries, Tanis was one of
the largest cities in the Delta
and became the capital of
Egypt during the 21st
Dynasty. Flooding led to its
decline, however, and by the
14th century the area was
practically deserted. San el-
Hagar grew up on reclaimed
land during the 1820s.

Panelled wall in the Ottoman House of Amasyali in Rosetta

Excavations at Tanis have
revealed ruins dating back
to the 6th Dynasty: huge
blocks and fragments of
statues from the Ramessid
Temple of Amun, as well as
the foundations of many
other temples, are among
the remains on site. Several
intact 21st- and 22nd-Dynasty
tombs, including those of
Psusennes I and Sheshonq III,
were discovered at the royal
necropolis, which lies to the
south of the temple. The
breathtaking treasures can
be seen at the Egyptian
Museum in Cairo *(see pp74–5).*

Rosetta (Rashid) ❺

65 km (40 miles) E of Alexandria.
🚶 *58,000.* 🚃 🚌

Founded in the 9th century by
Ibn Tulun, the Muslim governor of Egypt, Rosetta (which is
also known by the modern
name of Rashid) became one
of Egypt's most important
ports, reaching its heyday during the 17th and 18th centuries.
With Alexandria's revival in the
19th century, however, Rosetta
fell into decline and today it is
little more than an attractive
fishing village surrounded by
palm and orange groves.

Many beautiful Ottoman
houses and mosques – reminders of Rosetta's more glorious
past – can still be seen around
the town and a few are open
to visitors. Among the most
beautiful are the House of
Amasyali on Sharia Amasyali
and the Kili House on Midan al-

Gumhuriyya, which is now a
small museum. Next to the
House of Amasyali is the well-
preserved Abu Shahim Mill,
and to the south of town is the
ornate 18th-century Azouz
hamman (public baths).

Rosetta is best known for the
famous Rosetta stone *(see p22),*
which was discovered here by
French soldiers in 1799. Part of
a black basalt stele dating from
the 2nd century BC, the stone
was carved with a decree by
Ptolemy V, written in ancient
hieroglyphics, Greek and
demotic Egyptian. From these
inscriptions, French professor
Jean-François Champollion was
able, in 1822, to formulate a
system for deciphering
hieroglyphics – a feat that
was to unlock much of
ancient Egyptian history.

Conceded to the British in
1801, the Rosetta stone
remains on display at the
British Museum in London.

**Palm trees bordering the Rosetta
branch of the Nile Delta**

Alexandria 🟢

Stretching 20 km (12 miles) along the coast, Alexandria
is Egypt's second largest city. Founded in 332 BC by
Alexander the Great, the city grew to rival Rome before
falling into decline in the 4th century AD. In the 19th
century, the Pasha Mohammed Ali revived Alexandria's
fortunes as a port by linking it to the Nile. This prosperity
drew many Europeans, who fostered the decadent atmosphere chronicled by writers such as Lawrence Durrell and
Constantine Cavafy. This era ended in the 1950s as the
foreigners fled Nasser's revolution. Little remains of the
city's ancient magnificence, but it is hoped that excavations will reveal the tombs of Cleopatra and Mark Antony.

Colourful fishing boats in Alexandria Harbour

🏛 Midan Saad Zaghloul

Situated on the seafront, Midan
Saad Zaghloul is at the heart of
modern Alexandria. From this
square, a statue of Egyptian
nationalist leader Zaghloul
(1860–1927) *(see p62)* watches
over the eastern harbour and
the busy tram and bus stations
in the adjacent Midan Ramla.

Sadly, nothing remains of
the Caesareum, a magnificent
temple built on the site more
than 2,000 years ago. Begun by
Cleopatra VII for Mark Antony
and finished by Octavian after
their deaths in 30 BC *(see
pp54–5)*, only two obelisks
survived its destruction in 912.
Known as Cleopatra's Needles,
they were relocated to London
and New York in the 1800s.

Today the square consists of
shops, hotels and three 1920s
Art Deco cafés, Athineos,
Délices and
Trianon.
South is Sharia
Nabi Daniel,
believed to
be the ancient
Street of
Soma – a
marble road
lined with
columns. It is

**16th-century woodcut showing the
Library of Alexandria on fire**

now lined with street vendors,
and its glory has faded.

🏛 Bibliotheca Alexandrina

Shatbi. *Tel* (03) 483 9999. ☐
*11am–7pm Sat–Thu, 3–7pm Fri
(11am–3pm during Ramadan).*
Founded in the 3rd century
BC, the Bibliotheca Alexandrina was the greatest library
in the ancient world, attracting the best international
scholars. The library and
cultural centre was
re-inaugurated in October
2002, more than two millennia after the original building
was destroyed by fire.

The Bibliotheca Alexandrina
is striking in its architecture
and also contains a Planetari-
um and four interesting
museums. The main library is
encased in a giant cylindrical
building at the far northern
end of the
corniche.
The circular
outer wall
is made of
Aswan granite
engraved with
letters from
world alpha-
bets. The
partly-glazed

roof which tilts towards the
sea is designed to angle sunlight on to the desks of the
seven-tier 2,000-seat reading
rooms. Eventually, the library
will contain 8 million volumes.

🏛 Sofitel Cecil Hotel

16 Midan Saad Zaghloul.
Tel (03) 487 7173.
One of the more obvious
landmarks of Midan Saad
Zaghloul is the Moorish-style
Sofitel Cecil Hotel, which
featured in Lawrence Durrell's
Alexandria Quartet. Opened in
1929, it is reputed to be built
on the site where Cleopatra VII
committed suicide after her
Egyptian fleet was defeated by
Octavian in the Battle of
Actium in 31 BC.

During World War II the
hotel was used by the British
Secret Service and later
played host to politicians and
writers such as Winston
Churchill, Somerset Maugham
and Noel Coward. Though
restoration has not quite
captured its past grandeur, the
roof garden is a pleasant
place to enjoy a drink.

Façade of Sofitel Cecil Hotel

🏛 Cavafy Museum

4 Sharia Sharm el-Sheikh, off Sharia
Nabi Daniel. ☐ *Tue–Sun.*
The poet Constantine Cavafy
(1863–1933) was born to
Greek parents but spent most
of his life in Alexandria. This
small museum is housed in
the flat where he spent the
last 25 years of his life. Some
of the rooms are arranged as
they would have been when
he lived here – the display of
possessions includes his bed,

For hotels and restaurants in this region see pp280–82 and pp300–1

Marble benches capable of seating up to 800 Romans in the Amphitheatre at Kom al-Dikka

VISITORS' CHECKLIST

Alexandria governorate. 4 million. ✈ 5 km (3 miles) SE of the city. 🚉 Masr Station, Midan al-Gumhuriyya; Sidi Gaber Station. 🚌 Muharram Bey Bus Station. ℹ Midan Saad Zaghloul (03) 485 1556; Masr Station (03) 392 5985.

under what was known as Kom al-Dikka (Mound of Rubble) after the remains of a Napo-leonic fort were levelled for a housing project. The 13 tiered rows of marble seats, excavated by Polish archaeologists aided by the Graeco-Roman Museum, date from the 2nd century AD. Originally a small theatre, the building was altered over time and served as an assembly hall. A couple of sections of the original mosaic floor are on view in front of the theatre.

Other excavations are still under way. To the north lie the brick ruins of a Roman bath-ing complex. A series of basins and channels reveal how water would have passed through the

heating system to the marble covered baths. To the east lie the ruins of a residential area dating from the 1st century AD, where the Villa of the Birds, a beautifully colourful nine-panelled mosaic, has been uncovered.

Some items found at an underwater excavation near Fort Qaitbey, including part of an obelisk from the era of Seti I and a weather-beaten sphinx, are on show in the amphitheatre grounds.

Roman mosaic at Kom al-Dikka

desk, death mask, rare editions of his books as well as some of his letters. Cavafy is buried in the Greek Cemetery nearby.

Another room in the small museum is devoted to one of Cavafy's students, the Greek writer Stratis Tsirkas (1911–81).

🎭 Roman Amphitheatre at Kom al-Dikka

Sharia Yousef. ⬤ 9am–4:30pm daily. 🖼

In 1965, a semi-circular Roman amphitheatre was discovered

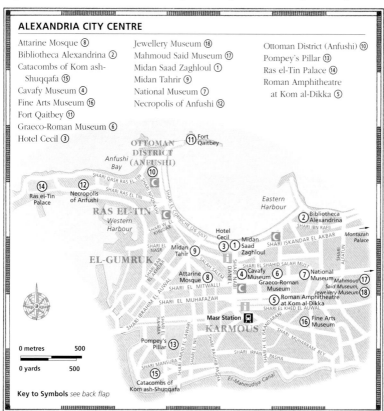

ALEXANDRIA CITY CENTRE

0 metres 500

0 yards 500

Key to Symbols see back flap

Alexandria: Graeco-Roman Museum

Situated in the heart of modern Alexandria, the Graeco-Roman Museum contains around 40,000 artifacts, mostly covering around 1,000 years of history from the founding of the city in 331 BC to the Arab conquest in AD 640. The museum was established in 1892 by Khedive Abbas II. Its 25 rooms and central gardens are crammed with items found in Alexandria and the sur-

Terracotta Pharos lantern

rounding areas, including a large mosaic from the 3rd century BC. The vast collection of artifacts from ancient Egyptian, Classical and Christian cultures testifies to the city's complex history. The museum is currently closed for major renovations.

Museum Gardens
In the museum's central gardens, amongst a wealth of tombs, statues and other artifacts, sits the head of a once huge statue of Mark Anthony.

Statue of Aphrodite (2nd century AD)

Tomb Painting
Two oxen driving a waterwheel (an invention of Alexandrian scientists) are depicted in this tomb fresco dating from the 2nd century AD.

White Marble Sarcophagus
A bas-relief from the 2nd century AD depicts Dionysus and his retinue as they find Ariadne asleep on the island of Naxos before she was abandoned by her lover, Theseus.

Sacred Crocodile
This mummified crocodile was carried in processions honouring Sobek, the crocodile-god.

Terracotta models of town monuments are displayed in Hall 18.

★ **Tanagra Figures**
This intriguing collection of Graeco-Roman terracotta figures, found in the city's many necropolises, provides an insight into social life and the costume of the era.

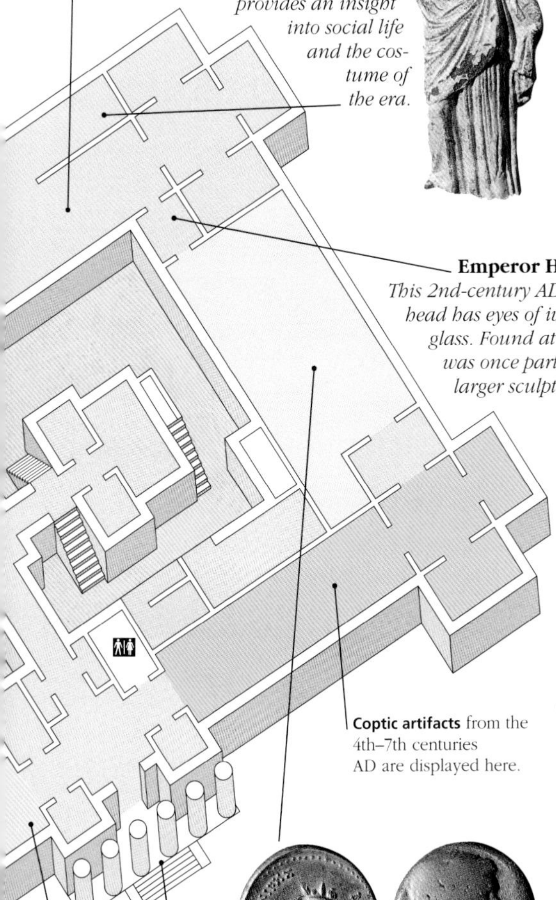

VISITORS' CHECKLIST

5 Sharia al-Mathaf. *Tel* (03) 486 5820. 🚌 🚐 🚕 ⬤ *Currently closed for major renovation; for more information about when museum will re-open contact local tourist office (03) 484 5820.*

Emperor Hadrian
This 2nd-century AD bronze head has eyes of ivory and glass. Found at Qena, it was once part of a larger sculpture.

GALLERY GUIDE
The museum is organized in chronological order running clockwise from the entrance. This order is interrupted only by two large themed areas: the first contains handicrafts from all eras and the other a vast collection of coins. Also worth visiting is the garden, with some fine statues and a reconstructed temple of the crocodile-god from Fayoum.

Coptic artifacts from the 4th–7th centuries AD are displayed here.

Entrance

KEY

▨	Coptic
▨	Ptolemaic
▨	Pharaonic
▨	Graeco-Roman
▨	Handicrafts (all periods)
▢	Coins
▨	Non-exhibition space

★ **Antique Coins**
The magnificent collection of coins includes some bearing Cleopatra's profile (above right).

Alexander the Great (356–323 BC)
Sculpted from marble, this head of Alexander the Great is one of several portraits of the leader in the museum. He became the object of a cult worship that spread throughout the ancient world.

STAR EXHIBITS

★ Antique Coins

★ Tanagra Figures

The Italianate National Museum of Alexandria

🏛 National Museum of Alexandria

110 Sharia Horreya. **Tel** *(03) 483 5519.* ⬜ *9am–5pm daily.* 📷

Over 1,800 artifacts, many in ingenious hanging diagonal glass showcases, are on display in this museum. It is located in a restored three-storey Italianate building, which dates from 1929 and is set in a large garden of rare trees and plants.

Most of the museum's treasures were excavated in and around the city itself. The basement spans pre-dynastic and ancient Egyptian artifacts, featuring a replica of a tomb similar to those found in the Valley of the Kings. The first floor has Graeco-Roman finds, including several beautifully painted terracotta Tanagra figurines.

A black basalt statue of a high priest of the goddess Isis, excavated from the seabed in 1998, is a star exhibit of the Coptic and Islamic collection.

🕌 Attarine Mosque

Sharia Attarine.

Topped by a pretty minaret, the Attarine Mosque lies just south of Midan Tahrir. It was

built on the site of the fabled Mosque of a Thousand Columns, which itself stood on the site of a church dedicated to St Athanasius in AD370.

Napoleon's men removed a seven-ton sarcophagus from the mosque, believing it to be Alexander's. Handed over to the British it was found to be the sarcophagus of Nectanebo II, the last Egyptian pharaoh.

Around the Attarine Mosque, the sprawling antiques district begins. Shops piled high with European furniture, and trinkets dating back to Napoleonic times, fill the backstreets. Here also, the intriguing belongings of many Europeans who fled the 1952 revolution are up for sale. However, the area is well known by international antiques dealers and genuine bargains can be hard to find.

🕌 Midan Tahrir

Originally known as Place des Consuls, the square was the centrepiece of Pasha Mohammed Ali's new Alexandria in the 1830s. In 1873 his equestrian statue was set in its place on a high plinth and the square was thereafter known as Midan Mohammed Ali. After the destruction brought about by the British bombardment in 1882 *(see p.59)*, the area was rebuilt as Midan Mansheiyya, before Nasser's revolution in 1952 renamed the square Midan Tahrir.

It was here that an assassination attempt was made on President

Nasser as he gave a speech in 1954. This gave him the opportunity to remove any opposition to his rule. Two years later, in 1956, it was from Midan Tahrir that Nasser shocked the Western world and announced the nationalization of the Suez Canal.

To the north is Midan Orabi, a major transport hub with tram, minibus and bus depots. The grand Neo-Classical Monument to the Unknown Soldier, designed by the Italian architect Verucci and erected in 1937, stands on the corniche, facing out to the sea.

Detail of Andalusian-styled Mosque of Abu al-Abbas Mursi in Anfushi

🕌 Ottoman District (Anfushi)

The peninsula leading to Fort Qaitbey was home to the inhabitants of Alexandria in Ottoman times (1517–1914). The atmosphere here differs from the rest of the city and it is best experienced on foot. To the south, lively souqs sell medicinal herbs and perfume while Turkish-style houses overhang the narrow streets.

Ottoman mosques are also dotted throughout the area, with the El-Shorbagi Mosque Complex at the heart of the district. Built in the mid-18th century it has a distinctive gallery on the first floor with shops below. The Terbana Mosque on Faransa Street was originally built in 1685 and two antique columns, taken from another site, support the minaret. Further north, in Midan El-Gawamaa is a mosque, dedicated to the

Midan Tahrir at the centre of Alexandria

PHAROS LIGHTHOUSE

Built in the 3rd century BC on an island in the eastern harbour, the Pharos Lighthouse stood up to 150 m (492 ft) high and was one of the Seven Wonders of the ancient world. Built mainly of limestone to the design of the Asiatic Greek architect Sostratus, the lighthouse had three differently-shaped storeys. The base was square and used as lodgings for mechanics and for storing fuel. The second storey was octagonal and the third, which contained the lantern mechanism, was circular and topped with a huge bronze statue of Poseidon, god of the sea. Used for nearly 1,000 years, the lighthouse was neglected during the Arab occupation. The lantern collapsed in AD 700 and the lighthouse was later destroyed by a series of earthquakes in the 12th and 14th centuries. Underwater excavation has discovered blocks of stone believed to be from the Pharos Lighthouse and a temple dedicated to Isis (*see pp26–7*) which stood nearby.

Reconstruction of the Pharos Lighthouse

13th-century Andalusian, Sidi Abu al-Abbas Mursi, the city's patron saint of fishermen. The current structure was designed in 1945 by Italian architect Mario Rossi. The octagonal-shaped building has a 73-m (240-ft) minaret.

Fort Qaitbey

Corniche. 15.
9am–4pm daily.
Although the turretted Fort Qaitbey situated on the tip of the Eastern Harbour looks like some kind of toy castle from the corniche, up close it is an imposing building. The fort was built in the 1480s by Sultan Qaitbey (1468–96) on the site of the Pharos Lighthouse, using stones from the dilapidated building. Within the keep there is a small mosque – the oldest in Alexandria – and a Naval Museum displaying relics from ships sunk nearby, the result of Roman and Napoleonic sea battles. These include bottles of wine and astronomical instruments retrieved from the French ship *L'Orient*. The fort was badly damaged by the British bombardment in 1882 when the mosque's minaret was blown clean off. From its elevated position, set back from the corniche, the fort has fantastic views of Alexandria and out to sea.

Necropolis of Anfushi

Sharia Ras el-Tin, Anfushi. daily.

The five rock tombs in the Necropolis of Anfushi date from around 250 BC and were discovered in 1901 and 1921. Cut into limestone, the tombs consist of a stairway leading down to a central courtyard with individual burial sites located off to the side. Tomb No. 2 is the most interesting and best preserved. The stairway walls are decorated with paintings of Osiris, Horus and Isis with the deceased as well as scenes of daily life and even an example of ancient Greek graffiti. The wall paintings and decoration are significant as they combine features of Greek and Egyptian art. There are also two vestibules with burial chambers; the one to the northeast is painted with black and white squares to resemble more expensive alabaster and marble tiling. The door to the burial chamber is flanked by two small stone sphinxes on stands, keeping watch over the tomb.

Fort Qaitbey from across the Eastern Harbour, built by recycling the stones from the Pharos Lighthouse

🪦 Ras el-Tin Palace

Sharia Ras el-Tin, Bahari. 🚌 🚗

Overlooking Alexandria's Western Harbour, Ras el-Tin Palace is surrounded by elegant, formal gardens. The palace was built originally by Ottoman Pasha Mohammed Ali (1805–48) so that he could keep watch on his new fleet. Under King Fuad I (1917–36), it was redesigned by Italian architects and served as the government's summer seat.

During the 1952 revolution, the palace was besieged by Nasser's men and King Farouk was forced to abdicate and flee to Italy with his family and retinue. The palace is now Admiralty headquarters and is reserved for state guests; however its pleasant gardens are open to the public.

⋔ Pompey's Pillar

Sharia Ahmoud al-Saweiri, Karmous. 🚌 16. ◯ 9am–4pm daily. 🎟

To the southwest of the city, in the impoverished district of Karmous, Pompey's Pillar is a striking sight. Made of red Aswan granite, the 27-m (89-ft) high pillar was erected around AD 297 in tribute to the Roman emperor Diocletian. On its base is written in Greek "To the most just of emperors, the divine protector of Alexandria, Diocletian the invincible: Postumus, prefect of Egypt."

The monument's popular name may have come from medieval travellers who thought that the Roman general Pompey, murdered in Egypt in 48 BC, was buried here; in fact, the pillar came from the Serapeum complex or Temple of Serapis, which was built in the mid-3rd century BC. (Serapis was an Egyptian deity, very popular in the Graeco-Roman period, who combined aspects of the gods Osiris and Apis). The pillar would have been freestanding and is all that remains of the temple which was once an important repository of religious texts and the "daughter library" of that of Alexandria.

Enlarged by the Emperor Hadrian in the 2nd century AD, when it was described as second only to the Capitol in Rome, the temple was destroyed by Christians in AD 391.

Pompey's Pillar, once part of the beautiful Temple of Serapis

Nearby there are some underground galleries, where the sacred Apis bulls *(see p164)* were buried, as well as several statues of the Sphinx that originally stood at Heliopolis.

⋔ Catacombs of Kom ash-Shuqqafa

Sharia al-Nasserieh. 🚌 16. ◯ 9am–4:30pm daily (Ramadan: 9am–3pm). 🎟

Dating from the 2nd century AD, the catacomb complex of Kom ash-Shuqqafa (Mound of Shards) just south of Pompey's Pillar is the largest Graeco-Roman necropolis in Egypt. Dug into the rock to a depth of about 35 m (115 ft), the complex has three levels. However, flooding has made the lowest level inaccessible.

The catacombs are reached via a spiral staircase encircling a shaft down which bodies of the deceased were lowered.

On the first level there is a central rotunda and a large banquet hall, the Triclinium, where friends and relatives of the deceased gathered to pay their last respects.

To the east of the rotunda is the Caracalla Hall, an older burial complex that became accessible from the main chamber when tomb robbers broke through the wall. This area is dedicated to Nemesis, the goddess of sport.

From the central rotunda, stairs lead down to a second storey with a vestibule and burial chamber. Here the decorated sarcophagi and wall reliefs display a mixture of Egyptian, Roman and Greek styles: by the doorway, Anubis, the god of the dead, is shown as a Roman legionary with a dragon's tail. On either side of the burial chamber, below heads of Medusa, are carved two giant serpents, wearing the double crown of Egypt.

From the burial chamber, eerie passages lead off in all directions to rooms containing more than 300 loculi – small chambers for bodies.

Back above the ground, the enclosure is strewn with sarcophagi and the broken remains of several sphinxes. The surrounding area of Karmouz is worth a visit to see the colourful markets and vibrant local life, where rare foreign tourists make rare visitors.

🏛 Fine Arts Museum

18 Sharia Menasce. ***Tel*** (03) 393 6616. ◯ 10am–1pm Tue–Sun. 🎟

A short distance to the southeast of Masr station, the Fine

Relief of Anubis presiding over a mummification at Kom ash-Shuqqafa

Arts Museum is housed in a beautiful villa that was donated in 1954 to the city of Alexandria by the wealthy Jewish Menasce family. The museum is used mainly for frequently changing exhibitions of contemporary foreign and Egyptian artists. The museum is also known for hosting the Alexandrian Biennial, a showcase for art from Mediterranean countries.

A statue by Mahmoud Mokhtar (1891–1934), who has been acclaimed as the first sculptor in the modern Egyptian art movement, stands in the gardens outside.

Montazah Palace, an eclectic mix of Turkish and Florentine architecture

🏛 Mahmoud Said Museum Centre

6 Sharia Said Pasha, Gianaclis.
Tel *(03) 582 1688.* 🚐 🚆 *2.*
⏱ *10am–6pm daily.* 📷

An Alexandrian aristocrat, Mahmoud Said (1897–1967) was one of Egypt's most important modern artists. The museum that bears his name is housed in what was the family villa.

Said trained originally as a lawyer and worked as a judge, but painting was his passion and in 1947 he gave up law to dedicate himself to art. His work combines western techniques with Egyptian and Pharaonic themes to produce stunning, sensuous paintings. His 1924 self-portrait echoes a haunting Fayoum mummy portrait *(see p169).*

The first floor of the museum contains works by the prolific Alexandrian painters, the Wanly brothers, Seif (1906–79) and Adham (1911–59). The eclectic choice of paintings includes portraits, landscapes, and even a few cartoons.

The lower floor of the museum is also worthy of a visit. Here a small modern art gallery displays the works of other Egyptian artists.

Elsewhere in the museum, portraits of the Royal Family adorn the walls alongside period light fittings, which are works of art in themselves. The gorgeous inlaid wooden floors, considered too beautiful to walk on, are protected by raised walkways in places.

🏛 Royal Jewellery Museum

27 Sharia Ahmed Yehia Pasha, Gleem. 🚐 🚆 *2.* ***Tel*** *(03) 582 8348.*
⏱ *9am–2:15pm and 5–6:15pm daily.* 📷

This building was originally constructed for Mohammed Ali's granddaughter, Princess Fatima el-Zaharaa (1903–83), and later used as a palace by King Farouk. The museum has an extensive collection of jewels dating from Pasha Mohammed Ali's rule in the early 19th century to the end of King Farouk's reign in 1952.

Key pieces include a gold snuff box with Mohammed Ali's name spelled out in diamonds, King Farouk's gold-and diamond-studded chess set, Prince Youssef Kamal's gold desk inlaid with 166 diamonds, and a fabulous platinum crown glittering with well over 2,000 diamonds.

The palace is lavishly, if not always tastefully, decorated with stained-glass vignettes of life in 18th-century France. The two bathrooms, the ladies' tiled with scenes of nymphs bathing in Alpine surrounds and the men's with pictures of French fishermen and seagulls, should not be missed. The museum has undergone an impressive renovation programme and is now a real highlight of Alexandria's numerous attractions. There is also a pleasant café in the garden which makes a good place to relax after a tour of the jewels.

Montazah Palace ➐

18 km (11 miles) E of Alexandria. 🚐
🚆 ***Tel*** *(03) 547 7153.* ⏱ *daily.* 🚗

Montazah Palace is set in extensive gardens and overlooks a truly beautiful stretch of coast. Built at the beginning of the 20th century by Khedive Abbas II, a relative of King Farouk, the palace mixes Turkish and Florentine architecture:the central tower was inspired by the Palazzo Vecchio in Florence. Although the palace itself is closed to the public, the lush park and the semi-private beach are popular places to relax.

To the east lies the private beach resort of **Mamoura**. It has a more relaxed dress code than public beaches and the sand is relatively clean.

🏖 Mamoura
Sharia Abu Qir. 📷

The elegant gardens and groves of Montazah Palace, Alexandria

Abu Qir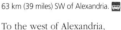

24 km (15 miles) E of Alexandria.
🚶 33,000. 🚐 🚌

The small fishing town of
Abu Qir, on the coast to
the east of Alexandria, is
renowned for two reasons:
historic battles and excellent
fish restaurants. It was at Abu
Qir Bay that Admiral Nelson
destroyed the French fleet in
the dramatic Battle of the Nile
in 1798. With the loss of his
ships and army, Napoleon's
plans for an eastern empire
were effectively ruined. A year
later the tables were turned
slightly when Napoleon's
troops repulsed a landing
attempt by a British contingent
of 15,000 Turkish soldiers and
many thousands drowned.

Since 1998, underwater
excavation work by teams
of French and Egyptian divers
has uncovered many artifacts
from the sunken warships
including gold coins, cannons,
and plenty of everyday items.
There are plans to build a new
museum to display these finds.

Although the beach at Abu
Qir is not suitable for bathing,
at the weekend the streets are
filled with Alexandrians who
come to savour the delights
of a small seaside town. These
include eating in one of the
many seafront restaurants that
serve delicious seafood.
Sitting right on the beach,
the Zaphyrion (see p300) – the
ancient Greek name for Abu
Qir – is reputed to be one of
the best restaurants in Egypt.

Brightly painted fishing boats at Abu Qir

Agami �ⓐ

20 km (12 miles) W of Alexandria. 🚌

Agami was traditionally the
summer resort of the Cairene
and Alexandrian elite during
the 1950s. Known as the
Egyptian St Tropez, it is far
less exclusive these days. The
semi-private beaches are less
conservative and less crowded
than in Alexandria, and the
nightlife is livelier. High-rise
apartment blocks have replaced
most of the original resort
architecture. Exceptions include
the **Beit al-Halawa**, designed in
1975 by Abd el-Wahid el-Wakil
and the extreme angular lines
of **Villa Lashin**, built in 1962
by the architect Ali Azzam.

Environs
Other popular resorts nearby
include the small village of
Hannoville, 1 km (0.6 mile)
to the west, notable for its
inexpensive accommodation,
and the private beach resort
of **Sidi Krear**, which lies 14
km (8.5 miles) further west
along the coast.

Abu Mina 🟓

63 km (39 miles) SW of Alexandria. 🚌

To the west of Alexandria,
15 km (9 miles) inland from
Abu Sir on the coast, lies the
Coptic Monastery of Abu
Mina (Deir Mari Mina). St
Mina was an Alexandrian-born
Roman legionary who was
tortured and killed in Phrygia
(Asia Minor) at the end of the
3rd century for his Christian
beliefs. His body is said to
have been buried here after a
camel carrying it home refused
to go any further. Legend has
it that a spring with miraculous
powers immediately started
flowing nearby and a church
and basilica were built around
the tomb. After the Emperor
of Byzantium's daughter was
cured by the waters in the 4th
century its fame spread. The
water was exported throughout
Christendom and Abu Mina
became a busy pilgrim town.
However, after repeated
sackings by the Bedouin,
the town fell into decay as
the water source dried up.

Today a modern monastery
dominates the site and there
are few impressive remains to
see, although there are plans
for a museum and archaeo-
logical park. The area is still
important to pilgrims who visit
the monastery, especially on
11th November, St Mina's day.

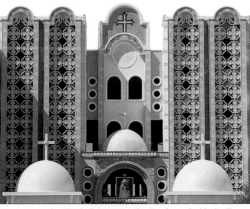

Monastery at Abu Mina built in 1959 on the site of a much older basilica

◁ Colourful fishing boats on the seafront at Abu Qir

El-Alamein ⓫

105 km (65 miles) W of Alexandria.
🏛 1,800. 🚌

El-Alamein, a small village on the coast to the west of Alexandria, was the site of a World War II battle which changed the course of the North Africa campaign in the Allies' favour. On 23rd October 1942, the British General Montgomery's Eighth Army attacked Field Marshal Rommel's German-Italian Afrika Korps at El-Alamein. After 11 days of fierce fighting, Rommel's troops retreated to Tunis to surrender six months later. More than 11,000 soldiers died and at least 70,000 were injured in the battle.

The **War Museum** to the west of town shows the stages of the North Africa campaign using electronic displays and many World War II mementoes. Tanks and artillery used during the battle are on display in the grounds. The **Commonwealth War Cemetery** to the east, where row upon row of Allied graves lie surrounded by the desert, is a chilling testimony to the war. A memorial here also lists the names of over 11,000 men whose bodies were never found. On the coast, 4 km (2.5 miles) west, lies the **German Cemetery**. This imposing fortress of a memorial overlooking the sea honours the 22,000 Germans who died in the North Africa campaign. The **Italian**

Gravestones at the Commonwealth War Cemetery at El-Alamein

Sherman tank outside the War Museum

Cemetery is just 3 km (2 miles) further west along the coast, with a marble tower in honour of the 22,000 Italian soldiers killed in the fighting.

Further west, a string of resort villages line the coast. One with a particularly stunning beach is the upmarket and unspoilt resort at **Sidi Abdel Rahman**, 23 km (14 miles) west of El-Alamein.

🏛 **El-Alamein War Museum**
🕐 9am–4pm daily. 🎫

Marsa Matruh ⓬

290 km (180 miles) W of Alexandria.
🏛 52,000. ℹ Governorate Building, Al-Corniche (046) 493 1841. 🚌 🚗

The coastal town of Marsa Matruh is a very popular summer resort for Egyptians.

However, although the coast is beautiful, the town itself and its beaches are pretty tatty and the resort lacks appeal for most tourists.

The town has a historical pedigree and was founded by Alexander on his way to the oracle at Siwa; later it served as a port for Anthony and Cleopatra's doomed fleet and this link is reflected in many of the place names.

West of town the sea is gorgeous. **Cleopatra Beach** is 7 km (4 miles) west, though rocks and a sudden drop in the sea bed make this a difficult place to swim. The royal queen herself is said to have bathed at Cleopatra's Bath nearby. The best place to swim is **Agibah Beach**, 28 km (17 miles) west on the coastal road. A steep path leads down to a cove where rock shelves make ideal platforms for diving into the sea.

Sallum ⓭

222 km (137 miles) W of Marsa Matruh. 🏛 6,000. 🚌

Sallum is the last Egyptian town before Libya and an important trading centre for the Bedouin. The town sits high up on a cliff looking out to sea, with a small harbour down below. This was the ancient Roman port of Baranis, and there are still some Roman wells in the area.

Sallum is not traditionally a tourist area, and although the beaches in town can be dirty, to the east there are stretches of golden sand and crystal waters that permit relatively secluded swimming. Visitors should check with the local Tourist Police first that bathing is allowed as some areas and beaches are out of bounds.

There is also a small **Allied War Cemetery** where soldiers killed fighting with Rommel's Afrika Korps lie buried.

A huge Palestinian refugee camp, 10 km (6 miles) east of town, houses those expelled from Libya in 1994.

Waves crashing into the rocks at Cleopatra's Beach, Marsa Matruh

For hotels and restaurants in this region see pp280–82 and pp300–1

THE WESTERN DESERT

E gypt's vast Western Desert stretches over nearly 3 million sq km (1.2 million sq miles), from the west bank of the Nile to Libya, and from Sudan towards the Mediterranean Sea. Despite covering over two-thirds of Egypt's total land area, the desert is virtually uninhabited, except for the fertile oases where communities and crops flourish amid barren desert surroundings.

There are five oases in the Western Desert: Siwa, Kharga, Dakhla, Farafra and Bahariyya. Except for Siwa, the oases have been under the control of the rulers of the Nile Valley since Pharaonic times, when they were crucial stopping points on the busy caravan trading routes from Africa. The Ptolemaic temples and Roman forts dotted around the oases bear witness to their past importance and ongoing archaeological work is continually uncovering new finds.

Each of the Western Desert oases has its own unique character. While the main settlements of Bahariyya and Farafra are little more than villages, those of Dakhla and Kharga are towns, surrounded by fascinating historical sites. In Siwa, isolated near the Libyan border, the inhabitants retain their own language and distinct culture.

In the late 1950s a plan was made to reclaim part of the desert and relocate thousands of people there from the crowded Nile delta and valley. The area, covering Bahariyya, Farafra, Dakhla and Kharga oases, was named the New Valley. Although some building began, very few people moved, and financial constraints together with the questionable sustainability of the water supply meant that the project was virtually abandoned.

The Western Desert today remains one of the few places in the world where travellers can experience a feeling of total isolation. Its sheer scale is overwhelming. From huge dunes to fantastical rock formations, the landscape varies dramatically and camping out overnight in such astonishing surroundings can be one of the highlights of a trip to Egypt.

Taking a break during the heat of the day in Dakhla, one of the Western Desert Oases

◁ The boundless expanse of the Great Sand Sea, close to Siwa Oasis

Exploring the Western Desert

The Western Desert offers visitors the chance to escape the crowded sites of Cairo and the Nile Valley and sample the peace and tranquillity of the empty desert and its green oases. In the northwest, the remote Siwa is the perfect place to relax. Further east, Bahariyya is a picturesque oasis within easy reach of Cairo. The road leading on to Farafra, the least developed of the oases, passes through the Black Desert and the incredible White Desert, with its mysterious, wind-eroded rock formations. Pockets of fertile land growing fruit, rice and peanuts are dotted among the sand dunes between Farafra and the beautiful Dakhla oasis. For lovers of ancient monuments, Dakhla and the more built-up Kharga have the most to offer.

Statue in the Oasis Heritage Museum, Bahariyya

Dakhla Oasis near Al-Qasr, showing the striking contrast between the fertile soil and the barren, inhospitable desert

GETTING AROUND

Travelling in the Western Desert is much easier than it used to be. Roads link the main oases and buses run fairly frequently. Siwa Oasis is best reached by bus from Marsa Matruh. Bahariyya and Farafra can be visited from Cairo, and Dakhla and Kharga can be reached quite easily from Asyut. There are airports at Dakhla and Kharga but flights are only once per week. Depending on time pressure and your sense of adventure, the 1,000-km (620-mile) Great Desert Circuit of Bahariyya, Farafra, Dakhla and Kharga is an option. Usually starting at Cairo and ending at Luxor or Asyut, the trip can be taken either with an organized tour, hired transport or by bus. It is also now possible to cross the desert track between Siwa and Bahariyya by 4-wheel drive. Your tour operator can organise permits.

Siwa Oasis, with the salt lake Birket Siwa visible in the distance, viewed from the Mountain of the Dead

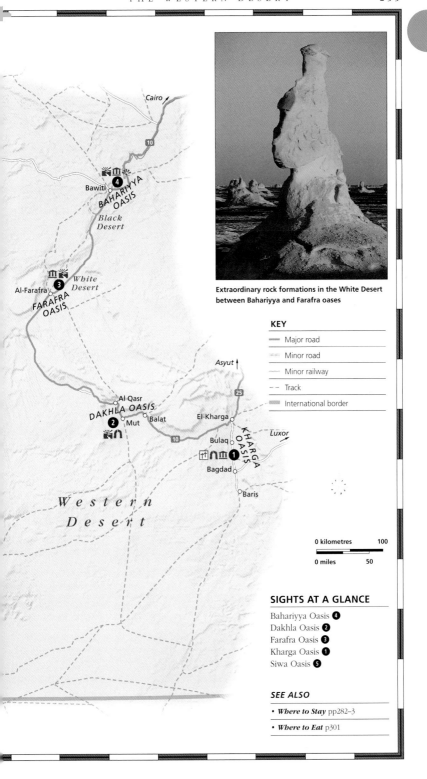

Extraordinary rock formations in the White Desert between Bahariyya and Farafra oases

KEY

— Major road

=== Minor road

— Minor railway

-- Track

▨ International border

SIGHTS AT A GLANCE

Bahariyya Oasis ④

Dakhla Oasis ②

Farafra Oasis ③

Kharga Oasis ①

Siwa Oasis ⑤

SEE ALSO

- *Where to Stay* pp282–3

- *Where to Eat* p301

Lush date groves surrounding the fertile fields of Dakhla, the prettiest of the Western Desert oases

Kharga Oasis ❶

233 km (144 miles) SW of Asyut.
🏠 65,000. ✈ 5 km (3 miles) N
of El-Kharga. 🚌 🛈 Government
building, Midan Nasser, El-Kharga
(092) 7921 206.

Kharga, the largest of the
oases, rose to prominence
as the penultimate stop on
"The Forty Days Road", the
infamous slave-trade route
between Sudan and Egypt.
Today the modern, sprawling
city of El-Kharga is capital of
the New Valley governorate,
which covers Kharga, Dakhla
and Farafra oases. The city
lacks charm, but its **Antiquities
Museum** displays impressive
archaeological finds from
Kharga and Dakhla.

Standing in palm groves just
north of the city, the **Temple of
Hibis**, built by Persian emperor
Darius I in the 6th century BC,
is the only sizeable Persian
temple left in Egypt. Also north
of the city is the **Necropolis of
al-Bagawat**. This Christian
cemetery contains

hundreds of domed, mudbrick
tombs decorated with Coptic
murals, dating from around the
4th to 6th centuries AD. The
best-preserved paintings are in
the Chapel of the Exodus and
portray Moses leading the Jews
out of Egypt, away from
Pharaoh's pursuing troops.

Environs
Perched on a hill on the road
south to Baris are the ruins
of the 25th-Dynasty **Qasr al-
Ghueita** hilltop fortress and
temple. Further south, Nasser
and Bulaq are known for their
thermal springs, reputed to
treat rheumatism.

🏛 **Antiquities Museum**
Sharia Gamal Abdel Nasser.
🕐 8am–5pm daily. 📷

⋔ **Temple of Hibis**
2 km (1 mile) N of El-Kharga.
🕐 daily. 📷

⋔ **Necropolis of al-Bagawat**
3 km (2 miles) N of El-Kharga.
🕐 8am–5pm daily. 📷

⋔ **Qasr al-Ghueita**
18 km (11 miles) S of El-Kharga.
🕐 8am–5pm daily. 📷

Dakhla Oasis ❷

190 km (118 miles) W of Kharga.
🏠 70,000. ✈ 10 km (6 miles) SW
of Mut. 🚌 🛈 Sharia as-Sawra al-
Khadra, Mut (092) 7821 686.

With many springs set in a lush
landscape, Dakhla is regarded
as the prettiest of the oases. A
long band of pinkish rock sits
along the northern horizon,
and olives, dates, wheat and
rice thrive on the fertile land.
The capital, Mut, has an
Ethnographic Museum displaying figures sculpted by a local
artist, Mabrouk.

Dakhla's ancient sites are
situated in the outlying parts
of the oasis. They can easily
be reached by hiring a pick-
up truck from Mut.

Environs
With its narrow, winding streets
and mudbrick houses, **Al-Qasr**,
27 km (17 miles) northwest of
Mut, retains a strong medieval
feel. The town has a museum,
a 12th-century mosque and a
10th-century *madrassa*
(school), with superb rooftop
views. Care is needed, however, as the roof is dilapidated.
The **Al-Muzawaka tombs** date
from Pharaonic times. The two
best are those of Petosiris and
Petubastis, which have vivid
coloured reliefs, but are
currently closed for restoration.
Just 10 km (6 miles) to the
west, the remnants of **Deir al-
Hagar** temple, built in the first
century AD, stand isolated in
the desert. **Balat**, a medieval
village on the site of an Old
Kingdom settlement, lies
35 km (22 miles) east of Mut.

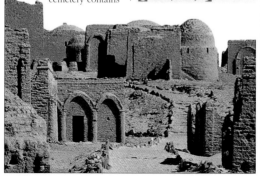

Mudbrick tombs in the Necropolis of al-Bagawat, Kharga Oasis

For hotels and restaurants in this region see pp282–3 and p301

🏛 **Ethnographic Museum**
Sharia as-Salem. ⬤ 8am–5pm. 📷

⋔ **Al-Muzawaka tombs**
5 km (3 miles) W of Al-Qasr. ⬤ for
restoration.

⋔ **Deir al-Hagar**
12 km (7 miles) W of Al-Qasr.
⬤ 8pm–5pm daily. 📷

Farafra Oasis ❸

310 km (192 miles) NW of Dakhla.
🏃 2,800. 🚌

The most isolated and least
populous of the New Valley
oases, Farafra is an extremely
peaceful place to visit. Its
mainly Bedouin inhabitants
are well known for their
strong traditions and religious
piety. The largest settlement,
Al-Farafra, is built like the
other oasis towns around a
ruined fortress, where villagers
would shelter from attacks.
Though the traditional mud-

Bizarre rock formations caused by wind erosion in the
White Desert, near Farafra Oasis

brick, painted houses remain,
concrete developments have
sprung up due to government
efforts to attract outsiders to the
area. The curious little **Badr's
Museum** displays sculptures by
well-known local artists.

Environs
Farafra is an ideal base for
exploring the **White Desert**,
41 km (25 miles) from
Al-Farafra on the road to
Bahariyya. Named after its
bright-white rock formations,
the White Desert resembles a
haunting lunar landscape.

Bahariyya Oasis ❹

185 km (115 miles) NE of Farafra.
🏃 33,000. 🚌 ℹ Town council
building, Bawiti (02) 3847 3035.

This oasis was a key agricultural centre in Pharaonic times,
exporting large quantities of
wine to the Nile Valley. Today
it is famed for its honey, dates
and olives. Bawiti, the main
village, has very picturesque
surroundings of palm groves.
The **Oasis Heritage Museum**
has clay figures by local artist
Mohammed Eed. Hot and

cold springs
surround the
oasis and just
west of Bawiti
a hot spring,
Ain Bishmu, is
used by the
villagers for
washing and
swimming.
Further afield,
a few ruins of
the **Temple of
Alexander the Great**, built in
332 BC, lie just north of the
discovery of the Golden
Mummies. The nearby 26th-
Dynasty **Temple of Ain al-
Muftela** is better preserved.
 Bahariyya is surrounded by
hills, and the **Black Mountain**,
7 km (4 miles) northeast of
Bawiti, is worth a visit. Also
called the "English Mountain",
it is crowned with an old
World War I British outpost.
Climbing to the top takes
about an hour, but the view
is very rewarding.

Environs
The **Black Desert**, created
by wind eroding the dark,
rocky outcrops, begins 20 km
(12 miles) south of Bahariyya.
Further south are the mainly
quartz rock formations of
Crystal Mountain.

🏛 **Oasis Heritage Museum**
1 km (0.6 mile) N of Bawiti. ⬤ daily.

⋔ **Temple of Alexander
the Great**
6 km (4 miles) SW of Bawiti.
⬤ ask at Tourist Office. 📷

⋔ **Temple of Ain al-Muftela**
5 km (3 miles) W of Bawiti.
⬤ ask at Tourist Office. 📷

GOLDEN MUMMIES

Since 1996, around 250
Graeco-Roman mummies
have been unearthed near
Bahariyya, about 3 km
(2 miles) south of the
Temple of Alexander the
Great. Most of the mum-
mies remain in situ in their
tombs within the "Valley
of the Golden Mummies",
but five gilded mummies
have been removed and
are currently on display
at the Antiquities
Inspectorate Museum in
Bawiti (open 8am–4pm
daily). One ticket pur-
chased here allows entry
to most of the cultural
treasures at Bawiti and
Bahariyya. Archaeologists
have ceased excavations
of the mummies for the
moment, but work is
continuing at an extensive
26th-Dynasty site known
as the Sheikh Subi Tombs.

Clay figures in the Oasis Heritage Museum, Bahariyya Oasis

A blue-painted mudbrick dwelling in Siwa Oasis

Siwa Oasis ⑤

550 km (341 miles) W of Cairo, 305 km (189 miles) SW of Marsa Matruh. 🚶 30,000. 🛈 Opposite Arous al-Waha, road to Marsa Matruh (046) 4601 338 or (010) 5461 992. 📧

Siwa Oasis seems to spring out of nowhere, its lush, green orchards glistening like a mirage in the surrounding barren and inhospitable desert. More than 300 fresh-water springs and streams sustain this remote desert oasis, feeding 300,000 date palms and 70,000 olive trees. Huge saltwater lakes add to the spectacular scenery. Isolated on the edge of the Great Sand Sea, Siwa remained unchanged and largely unvisited for centuries. In the 1980s, a road was built to Siwa from Marsa Matruh, bringing an influx of tourists to the area. Another rough road heading southeast to Bahariyya, is only passable by 4-wheel drive, but makes a memorable journey through the empty desert.

The ruins of the ancient mudbrick town of **Shali** tower above modern Siwa's main square. Built in 1203 to house the 40 survivors of a tribal attack on the nearby settle-ment of Aghurmi, this walled, hilltop town protected the entire Siwan population for centuries. Though the houses were abandoned in 1926 after heavy rain, the steep maze of streets can still be explored, and several buildings have been rebuilt and restored.

Close to Siwa's town centre, the **House of Siwa Museum** displays a collection of typical Siwan clothing, jewellery and handicrafts. The museum was the brainchild of a Canadian ambassador who feared the threat posed by tourism to Siwa's traditional way of life. A short distance north of the town, the limestone **Mountain of the Dead**, or Jebel al-Mawta, is riddled with tombs from the 26th Dynasty, Ptolemaic period and Roman era. When fighting spread to Siwa during World War II, the Siwans

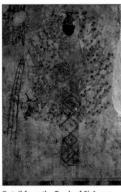

Detail from the Tomb of Si-Amun on the Mountain of the Dead, Siwa

sheltered in the tombs from bombing attacks. The 3rd-century BC **Tomb of Si-Amun** contains scenes depicting the deceased – a Siwan of Greek origins – with his family and the gods.

About 3 km (2 miles) east of Siwa, the **Temple of the Oracle**, built between 663 and 525 BC, stands on a rock that was once at the heart of the ancient settlement of Aghurmi. The Oracle's fame was widespread and Alexander the Great came here to consult it in 332 BC after liberating Egypt from Persian rule. The steep climb to the top is worthwhile for the stunning views it affords over the palm trees and lakes below.

A short distance away is **Cleopatra's Pool**. Despite the name, Cleopatra never bathed here, but many people do venture into the circular pool for a swim, undeterred by algae floating on the surface of the water and onlookers watching from the path.

A better place for swimming can be found on **Fatnis Island** (also known as Fantasy Island), on the salt lake Birket Siwa, 6 km (4 miles) west of the town. A narrow causeway leads to the island, which is covered in palm trees and has a freshwater pool in the centre.

A day trip can be organised to the remote oasis of Qara, 125 km (78 miles) northeast of Siwa.

🏛 **House of Siwa Museum**
Siwa. 🕙 9am–3pm Sun–Thu. 🎫
🏔 **Mountain of the Dead**
1 km (0.6 mile) N of Siwa.
🕙 9am–5pm daily.

SIWAN CULTURE

Far removed from the rest of Egypt, Siwans have their own distinct culture and way of life, although these are increasingly threatened by tourism. Siwi, a Berber language, is spoken alongside Arabic, and Siwan women, who are rarely seen in public, dress in costumes decorated with coins. The oasis is renowned for its silver jewellery and handwoven baskets. Siwans are very conservative and visitors should dress modestly.

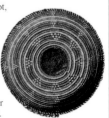

Traditional handwoven Siwan basket

◁ Mural on a Siwan house encouraging pilgrims to make the journey to Mecca

Oases in the Egyptian Deserts

A welcome sight for tired and weary travellers, oases have sufficient water to allow permanent plant growth and human settlement. The major depressions beneath Egypt's Western Desert give rise to a chain of oases west of the Nile, for here the water table is near the earth's surface. The oasis of Siwa, for example, lies 18 m (59 ft) below sea level. Oases vary considerably in size and can be anything from just a few palms around a spring to large expanses of

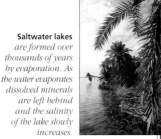

Little green bee-eater

water capable of sustaining cities. As well as supporting human population, they also offer ideal conditions for many species of wildlife, such as the striped hyena, the Egyptian mongoose and the little green bee-eater. However, the combination of a growing population and increasingly intensive farming is threatening the water supply. The oasis of Fayoum *(see p168)* now has to channel water from the Nile to supplement its inadequate natural resources.

Saltwater lakes *are formed over thousands of years by evaporation. As the water evaporates dissolved minerals are left behind and the salinity of the lake slowly increases.*

Human settlements *have developed around many oases. These isolated, self-sufficient communities are typically surrounded by green patches of cultivation and separated from each other by areas of dry desert.*

Agriculture *thrives on the fertile land of the oases. Rice, wheat, olives, dates, figs, mangoes and apricots are some of the crops grown.*

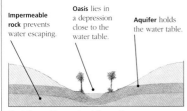

Date palms *have always been a multi-purpose crop, providing food, timber and leaves for thatching.*

THE FORMATION OF OASES

Rain falling a long way from the oasis seeps into porous rocks, known as aquifers, through which it slowly flows. This water emerges at an oasis, either where the water table is at or near the surface, or where pressure created by the flow of water in the aquifer forces it up through a fault in the rock.

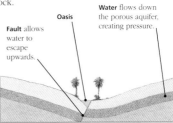

Impermeable rock prevents water escaping.

Oasis lies in a depression close to the water table.

Aquifer holds the water table.

Fault allows water to escape upwards.

Oasis

Water flows down the porous aquifer, creating pressure.

Oasis formed by a natural depression

Oasis resulting from a fault in the rock layers

For hotels and restaurants in this region see pp282–3 and p301

TRAVELLERS' NEEDS

WHERE TO STAY

In colloquial Egyptian, the word for hotel *(funduq)* derives from a verb meaning "to leave wide open" – as in leaving a door ajar – and this phrase reflects the traditional Egyptian sense of hospitality. Visitors will find "open doors" throughout the country, with hotels offering accommodation at a wide range of prices and an even wider range of quality. At the top end are grand old colonial hotels, along with a growing array of modern, four- and five-star high-rises and resort complexes. Even at such expensive places,

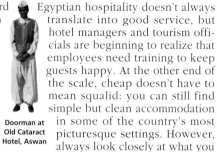

Doorman at Old Cataract Hotel, Aswan

Egyptian hospitality doesn't always translate into good service, but hotel managers and tourism officials are beginning to realize that employees need training to keep guests happy. At the other end of the scale, cheap doesn't have to mean squalid: you can still find simple but clean accommodation in some of the country's most picturesque settings. However, always look closely at what you are getting before handing over your money: demanding customers are more likely to end up as satisfied customers.

WHERE TO LOOK

Tourism has long been a major industry in Egypt and, as a result, you will find hotels just about everywhere. In Cairo, the luxury hotels are clustered in three main areas, catering to the different purposes and needs of visitors to the city. Several are situated to the northeast of the city, around the airport and the suburb of Heliopolis, making them convenient for air travel but rather far away from the city's major tourist attractions. Then there are the downtown luxury hotels, which are found mainly along the banks of the Nile. These offer great views and are a more convenient base for getting around the city sights, but they leave the traveller right in the thick of downtown Cairo, which can be a daunting prospect. Finally, there are hotels around the pyramids in Giza. For many visitors, staying right next to what they consider to be Egypt's biggest tourist attraction may outweigh the disadvantage of being further away from other sights in central and Islamic Cairo, such as the Egyptian Museum and Khan al-Khalili. Alternatively, you can find smaller and cheaper hotels throughout the city. Many low-budget, backpacker hotels are located in the downtown area near Midan Talaat Harb and Midan Tahrir. The leafy island of Zamalek has a few pleasant mid-range hotels and, though the area has few sights of its own, it is good for nightlife and is handy for accessing the rest of the city.

The same general pattern can be found in most towns in Egypt, with large five-star hotels in the town centre, low-budget places clustered around the train station, and mid-range options

Marble-floored foyer of the Sofitel Winter Palace, Luxor *(see p276)*

scattered throughout the rest of the town. Except for the most important tourist destinations, most towns in Upper Egypt and the Delta do not have any five-star hotels at all.

HOTEL TOUTS

The newly arrived traveller in Cairo may fall prey to hotel touts who attach themselves to the unwary, using every trick in the book to get them to the hotel for which they are hustling. Some taxi-drivers are part of the scam, earning a commission from the hotels to which they take their fares. To avoid being taken in by these tricksters, be alert to their strategies and be very firm about your plans. If possible, book a room in advance and don't be diverted from going there, whatever claims are made. If a taxi-driver says he hasn't heard of your hotel, don't get in his cab. Never let anyone go into the hotel with you.

The Sofitel Hotel on Gezira island, Cairo

◁ Restaurant in Sofitel Old Cataract Hotel, Aswan

BOOKING A ROOM

Higher-category hotels follow standard international procedures for reservations, with customers often being asked to give their credit card number as confirmation of a booking. Hotels lower down the scale may do the same, but with slightly less reliable results. The more popular inexpensive hotels sometimes operate on a first-come, first-served basis but most now accept reservations by phone or email.

Siwa Safari Paradise Hotel, set in palm groves near the Temple of Amun

HOTEL GRADING AND FACILITIES

Egyptian hotels are graded on a star-rating system with up to five stars, which are allocated by the government. Large, internationally run chain hotels generally get into the four- and five-star class, while locally owned premises fill out the middle and lower ranges.

Hotel gradings can appear a little arbitrary at times and, in many cases, seem to owe more to influence than to actual quality and service. Sometimes the only tangible difference between two stars and no stars is price – and five-star hotels are certainly not all equal in the facilities or service offered. A five-star hotel will, however, always include several restaurants, a bar, and some form of nightclub or disco. There will also always be a swimming pool and health-club facilities. Five-star hotels at resorts are likely to include facilities such as riding stables, diving centres, tennis courts and similar amenities.

A four-star hotel will usually have a coffee shop, restaurant, a bar of sorts, and usually a smaller swimming pool that is good enough for a cooling-off dip.

Hotels at the lower end also usually have some kind of eating establishment, but alcohol will rarely be served in such premises. It is rare to find telephones in the rooms of smaller establishments, but most will have a telephone at the front desk and Internet or wireless facilities.

HIDDEN EXTRAS

Apart from some of the Red Sea resorts, which are all-inclusive, normal practice is to pay for extras as you use them. Up to 23 per cent tax may be added to your hotel bill, along with charges for phone calls and other services. In smaller, two- and three-star hotels, check exactly what is included: you may be charged extra for breakfast and for having a fridge, air conditioning and TV in your room. Tipping (*baksheesh*) is a way of life in Egypt: many hotel workers survive on the tips they get for carrying out minor tasks for guests, such as carrying bags or flagging taxis. A couple of Egyptian pounds is sufficient.

DISCOUNTS

Discounts on hotel rooms are rarely offered and are available only through travel companies. In low season (July–September) in Upper Egypt, however, it may be possible to bargain down room prices, especially in hotels in the lower price categories. Egyptians and foreigners with residence permits, however, qualify for vastly cheaper rates.

CHAIN HOTELS

The familiar international chain hotel names can all be found in Egypt: Hilton, Sheraton, Marriott, Sofitel, Meridien, Mövenpick, Swissôtel, Four Seasons, Sonesta and Hyatt are all present. The big chain hotels are the most luxurious and the most expensive in the market and they generally offer a dependable level of service, despite the occasional variation from international standards.

There is no established chain of cheap or budget hotels in Egypt: the vast number of mid-level and inexpensive hotels in the country are usually family-owned and independently run.

The spectacular entrance hall of a luxury hotel in Alexandria

The Sofitel, Four Seasons and Grand Hyatt hotels in Cairo *(see p270)*

SMALLER HOTELS

The choice of mid-range hotels and amenities for the independent traveller in Egypt is continuously expanding across all destinations. Previously, most tourism in Egypt had been of the five-star or budget backpacker variety, with a great deal of choice at either end of the scale but little in the middle.

Every major destination in Egypt has a wide selection of small, cheap hotels catering for the young traveller. For those willing to forsake private bathrooms and air conditioning, the price can be amazingly low. Many small hotels offer a variety of rooms, including those with or without bathrooms and air conditioning. All have the option of more than one bed in the room. In Cairo and Alexandria, most small hotels are located on the upper floors of old apartment buildings, which can provide an intimate setting that is full of character. At most places, the price includes a simple continental breakfast.

Two- and three-star hotels are more likely to take up a whole building. Such establishments often include a coffee-shop and a small restaurant, and their rooms always have bathrooms and air conditioning; they also increasingly have a small swimming pool. Quality var-

ies widely and, while some mid-range hotels are excellent and quite charming, others are not even remotely worth the price. When negotiating for a room in a one- or two-star hotel, check the room to see whether facilities such as hot water and clean bed linen are provided, and confirm with the proprietor whether breakfast is included in the price.

BUSINESS TRAVELLERS

Cairo is rapidly turning into a major business centre and its hotels are adapting to the new market. New, ultra-luxury, five-star hotels are springing up with the

Hotel Metropole, Alexandria

requirements of the travelling business executive in mind, distinguishing themselves by the extra services and facilities that such clients expect. Well-trained concierges and an efficient, well-equipped 24-hour business service are becoming standard in Cairo's resort hotels, from the Four Seasons hotels, one on each bank of the Nile, to the Conrad on the Corniche. These have rooms furnished with computers, fax, voice mail, and internet connections. Well-equipped meeting rooms and conference facilities are available, as are chauffeur-driven limousines to ferry guests to and from Cairo's international airport.

DISABLED TRAVELLERS

Egypt is not the easiest destination for the disabled visitor. With many cheaper hotels located on the fairly inaccessible upper storeys of tall buildings, wheelchair-bound travellers are usually restricted to the modern five-star hotels. Even many of those still have stairs instead of ramps at vital places, though that is starting to change. What Egypt does have in its favour, however, is friendly people for whom disability carries no stigma and who will be more than ready to assist travellers with extra needs with a minimum of fuss.

CHILDREN

Egyptians love children and consider them a blessing, so bringing them should not present any particular problems. This is not to say that Egyptian hotels make any special provisions in terms of extra activities – the exception being some of the luxury resort hotels, which organize daily programmes for children. Even if you are not staying at a four- or five-star hotel, either in Cairo or at a resort, many of the bigger hotels have swimming pools that they allow non-residents to use, often without charge for children, and this can provide an excellent way of soothing frazzled youngsters when the heat and bustle get too much.

BUDGET OPTIONS

Egypt can be a paradise for travellers on low budgets, as witnessed by the generations of young backpackers who visit the country, whether seeking Pharaonic ruins, exotic culture, or a bit of sun and surf in the Sinai peninsula.

No matter where you are in Egypt, there will always be hotels offering fairly

The luxury As-Salamlek Hotel in Montazah Palace grounds, Alexandria

decent accommodation at fairly low prices. Youth hostels exist, but comparing their poor quality with the other available options, they are best avoided: why settle for a three-tier bunk bed when a clean room can be found closer to the city centre for only a few pounds more?

In any case, most of Egypt's cheaper hotels, which are not by any means frequented only by young backpackers, offer the camaraderie familiar in youth hostels worldwide.

Camping in Egypt is a little more problematic and is not particularly recommended in most towns. Campsites can be

YHA sign at youth hostel in Aswan

found in Luxor and some of the other southern cities, but the facilities are rudimentary at best.

Rather better opportunities exist for camping elsewhere in the country, however. There are some beautiful places in the Sinai, including the Ras Mohammed National Park *(see p226)*, near Sharm el-Sheikh, and a night under the stars in the Western Desert is an experience not to be missed.

Safaris, consisting of a guide with a large four-wheel-drive, can be organized out of any of the oasis towns. It should be borne in mind that camping in the Western Desert is mainly a winter activity, and that the nights can be cold. Desert camping is not recommended during high summer and, in fact, very few guides will be interested in venturing out during that time. Wherever you camp, follow common-sense rules and keep all your valuables with you. Litter is a problem in Egypt so be sure to remove yours when leaving a camp.

DIRECTORY

Choosing a Hotel

The hotels in this guide have been selected across a wide range of price categories for the excellence of their facilities, location or character. This chart first lists hotels in Cairo, followed by a selection of places to stay in the rest of Egypt. For a listing of recommended restaurants, see pages 290–301.

PRICE CATEGORIES (IN EGYPTIAN POUNDS – EGP)
For a standard double room per night, with breakfast, tax and service charge included.
£ Under 200 EGP
££ 200–350 EGP
£££ 350–700 EGP
££££ 700–1,200 EGP
£££££ Over 1,200 EGP

CAIRO

CAIRO Al-Hussein Hotel
£
Midan Hussein, Hussein, Cairo **Tel** *02 2591 8664* **Fax** *02 2591 8479* **Rooms** *48*   **Map** *2 F5*

Located in the Islamic area of Cairo, close to the bustling Khan al-Khalili, this hotel offers basic accommodation. Not all the rooms have air conditioning or private bathrooms, so it's best to state any specific requirements in advance. Views of the fascinating medieval part of Cairo can be enjoyed from balconies and the rooftop restaurant.

CAIRO Berlin Hotel
£
2 Sharia el-Shawarby, Downtown, Cairo **Tel** *02 2395 7502* **Rooms** *12*   **Map** *1 C5, 5 C3*

The Berlin Hotel is housed in an unassuming building in one of Cairo's busy thoroughfares, but step inside and the reception area and rooms retain a traditional character. The host is helpful and will assist with organizing excursions and airport pick-ups. **berlinhotelcairo@hotmail.com**

CAIRO Garden City House Hotel
£
23 Sharia Kamal al-Din Salah, Garden City, Cairo **Tel** *02 2794 8400* **Rooms** *40*   **Map** *5 B4*

Old-fashioned, large, clean rooms and friendly staff make this one of Cairo's best budget options. The restaurant is sociable and the shared balconies are a pleasant place to relax. The location is also excellent; just two minutes' walk from either the Corniche or Midan Tahrir. **www.gardencityhouse.com**

CAIRO Hotel Osiris
£
49 Sharia Nubar, Bab al-Louq, Downtown, Cairo **Tel** *02 2794 5728* **Fax** *02 2794 2981* **Rooms** *16*   **Map** *3 C1*

The Osiris offers excellent value for money and the helpful, friendly owners will arrange any kind of excursion. Rooms are modern, quiet and comfortable, and also have wireless Internet. The hotel is decorated in a Oriental-inspired style and there's a rooftop terrace with panoramic views of Cairo. The restaurant serves delicious Egyptian food.

CAIRO Ismailia House
£
Midan Tahrir, Downtown, Cairo **Tel** *02 2796 3122* **Rooms** *40*   **Map** *1 C5, 5 B4*

Ismailia House is cheap and cheerful. Some rooms have air conditioning, fridge and satellite television. There are also cheaper rooms with shared bathrooms. Its location is good for local attractions, shops and restaurants, and there are amazing views out over Midan Tahir. **www.ismailiahotel.com**

CAIRO Lotus Hotel
£
12 Sharia Talaat Harb, Downtown, Cairo **Tel** *02 2575 0966* **Rooms** *50*   **Map** *1 C5, 5 B3*

With an authentic Art Deco interior decor that has certainly seen better days, the Lotus is nevertheless a pleasing base in one of Cairo's main downtown thoroughfares. It is popular with both business and leisure travellers, and staying here is like taking a step back in time. **www.lotushotel.com**

CAIRO Mayfair Hotel
£
9 Sharia Aziz Osman, Zamalek, Cairo **Tel** *02 2735 7315 or 02 2735 9594* **Fax** *02 2735 0424* **Rooms** *45*   **Map** *1 A3*

If luxurious surroundings are a must, then this hotel will not entirely fit the bill, but it is clean and attractive and some rooms have air conditioning. Older rooms still share bathrooms. It is also located in one of the upmarket areas of Cairo, Zamalek, with good nightlife, restaurants and shopping. **www.mayfaircairo.com**

CAIRO Carlton Hotel
££
21 Sharia 26th July, Downtown, Cairo **Tel** *02 2575 5022* **Fax** *02 2575 5323* **Rooms** *60*   **Map** *1 C4, 5 C2*

Housed in a building constructed in 1935 but renovated to a modern standard that includes air conditioning and wireless Internet, this hotel retains many original features, which add to its charm. The rooms are attractive, and the restaurant and rooftop bar are full of atmosphere. **www.carltonhotelcairo.com**

CAIRO Odeon Palace Hotel
££
6 Abdel Hamid Said, Downtown, Cairo **Tel** *02 2577 6637* **Fax** *02 2576 7971* **Rooms** *30*   **Map** *1 C4, 5 C2*

Probably best known for its 24-hour rooftop bar, where guests and locals alike socialize, the Odeon Palace is a well-kept secret. It is located in a quiet side street in downtown Cairo and could be easily missed. Its rooms are of a mid-range standard, though a little worn, and its restaurant serves Egyptian fare. **www.hodeon.com**

Key to Symbols *see back cover flap*

CAIRO Pension Roma

169 Sharia Mohammed Farid, Downtown, Cairo **Tel** *02 2391 1088* **Fax** *02 2579 6243* **Rooms** *39*   **Map** *2 D4, 6 D2*

This pension is cheap and simple, but it has earned a reputation for being clean and safe. Some rooms have showers, others share bathrooms, and seven have air conditioning. The atmosphere is great, with antique furniture, traditional decor and helpful staff. Booking ahead is essential. **www.pensionroma.com.eg**

CAIRO Windsor Hotel

19 Sharia Alfi Bei, Downtown, Cairo **Tel** *02 2591 5810* **Fax** *02 2592 1621* **Rooms** *55*   **Map** *2 D4, 6 D2*

Built around 1900 as the baths for the Egyptian royal family and used as a British officers' club, the Windsor is one of Cairo's landmark buildings. It retains its atmosphere and has appeared in numerous films. Rooms are spartan, however, although the Barrel Lounge bar is a colonial dream. **www.windsorcairo.com**

CAIRO Atlas Zamalek Hotel

20 Gamiat ad-Dowal al-Arabiyya, Mohandiseen, Cairo **Tel** *02 3346 5782* **Fax** *02 3347 6958* **Rooms** *77*

A traditional hotel built to a high-rise design, the Atlas Zamalek is located on the West Bank in a modern neighbourhood – right on one of Cairo's main thoroughfares, in Mohandiseen. Rooms are nicely presented, and the hotel also boasts a characterful restaurant and a pool. **atlas_zamalek_hotel@hotmail.com**

CAIRO CairoTel Hotel

19 Misr-Helwan Agricultural Road, Maadi, Cairo **Tel** *& Fax 02 2358 8131 or 02 2358 6819* **Rooms** *162*

A modern hotel with a lavish feel, the CairoTel offers rooms with many facilities, including private bathrooms and televisions. The hotel is located within an easy walk of the Nile riverside, and a short drive into downtown Cairo – a combination that makes it popular with both businesspeople and leisure travellers.

CAIRO Caroline Crillon

49 Sharia Syria, Mohandiseen, Cairo **Tel** *02 3346 5101* **Rooms** *34*

Located in the residential area of Mohandiseen, the Caroline Crillon prides itself on offering five-star service in a three-star hotel. This air-conditioned hotel provides good Egyptian hospitality and food (Italian too), not to mention comfortable rooms with a range of high-quality amenities. **www.atchotels.com**

CAIRO Cosmopolitan Hotel

1 Sharia Ibn Tahlab, Downtown, Cairo **Tel** *02 2392 3956* **Fax** *02 2393 3531* **Rooms** *100*   **Map** *1 C3, 5 C3*

The downtown Cosmopolitan Hotel oozes Old World colonial charm and is full of character. Dotted throughout the communal areas are dark lacquered pieces of antique furniture. The rooms are not so inspiring, however, but rates are competitive. There's free wireless Internet in the lobby.

CAIRO Horus House Hotel

21 Sharia Ismail Mohammed, Zamalek, Cairo **Tel** *02 2735 3634* **Fax** *02 2735 3182* **Rooms** *35*   **Map** *1 A3*

The Horus is a warm, welcoming place, full of guests who come back time and again. It may not have many facilities (just a bar and a small restaurant), but it is clean and well presented, especially the rooms, which have wireless Internet. It is located in a smarter area of Cairo, close to many tourist attractions. **hotel_horus@yahoo.com**

CAIRO Hotel Longchamps

21 Sharia Ismail Mohammed, Zamalek, Cairo **Tel** *02 2735 2311* **Fax** *02 2734 9644* **Rooms** *31*   **Map** *1 A3*

A very welcoming hotel that is often full with return guests – a source of pride to the owner Heba. With two balconies in the public areas and a quiet setting in the leafy residential suburb of Zamalek, this hotel makes a peaceful retreat after a day of sightseeing. Rooms have wireless Internet access. **www.hotellongchamps.com**

CAIRO Kempinski Nile Hotel

12 Sharia Ahmed Ragheb, Corniche et-Nil, Garden City, Cairo **Tel** *02 2789 0000* **Rooms** *650*   **Map** *5 A5*

As this hotel, previously the Sheraton Cairo, is in a renovated old building, rooms and bathrooms are on the small side. They are lavishly appointed, however, with stylish decor, comfortable beds and fluffy towels. Some rooms have views of the Nile. The restaurants are excellent and wireless Internet is available throughout. **www.kempinski.com**

CAIRO The President Hotel

22 Sharia Taha Hussein, Zamalek, Cairo **Tel** *02 2735 0718* **Fax** *02 2736 1752* **Rooms** *117*   **Map** *1 A2*

The President Hotel offers a comfortable, pleasant and convenient place to stay. It is one of the most popular hotels for businesspeople and visitors in this upmarket area, occupying an unassuming high-rise building. The views are amazing and the Cellar Bar is a Cairo institution. **www.presidenthotelcairo.com**

CAIRO Talisman Hotel

39 Sharia Talaat Harb, Downtown, Cairo **Tel** *02 2393 9431* **Rooms** *22*   **Map** *2, D4*

The Talisman can be tricky to find as it's located down a side street, but it's worth the effort: There's a gorgeous, authentic 1930s lift, with mirrors, panels and wrought-iron gates, and each room is individually decorated and painted in rich colours. The staff is warm and friendly and the breakfasts excellent. **www.talisman-hotel.com**

CAIRO Victoria Hotel

66 Sharia Al-Gomhuriyya, Downtown, Cairo **Tel** *02 2589 2290* **Fax** *02 2591 3008* **Rooms** *92*   **Map** *2 D5, 6 D1*

A great-value hotel built in the early 1900s, within walking distance of many of Cairo's major tourist attractions. It has a small terrace coffee shop and an appealing period bar, while its rooms are nicely presented and have amenities such as satellite television and air conditioning. **www.victoria.com.eg**

CAIRO Flamenco Hotel
£ £ £ £ Map 1 A2

2 Sharia Gezirat al-Wosta, Zamalek, Cairo **Tel** *02 2735 0815.* **Fax** *02 2735 0819* **Rooms** *182*

This traditionally styled mid-range hotel is popular with businesspeople and tourists alike, thanks to its homely, welcoming feel. Part of the Golden Tulip chain of hotels, the Flamenco sits alongside the Nile and has a lovely bakery and a decent bar. **www.goldentulipflamenco.com**

CAIRO Cairo Marriott Hotel
£ £ £ £ £ Map 1 B3

Zamalek, Cairo **Tel** *02 2728 3000* **Fax** *02 2728 3001* **Rooms** *1,124*

Renowned for its lavish Oriental-inspired decor and architecture, this 19th-century hotel was originally built for the opening of the Suez Canal in 1869. It is as popular today as it was then, when visitors first began arriving in Cairo. Facilities include gardens and terraces, as well as spacious rooms full of refinement. **www.marriott.com**

CAIRO Conrad International Hotel
£ £ £ £ £ Map 1 B1

1191 Corniche el-Nil, Bulaq, Cairo **Tel** *02 2580 8000* **Fax** *02 2580 8080* **Rooms** *617*

Egypt is awash with luxury five-star hotels, and this is certainly among the best, although the staff can be aloof. The reception area is designed to capture the essence of Cairo, while the rooms are presented with lavish soft furnishings and every amenity. Most have views of the Nile. **www.conradhotels.com**

CAIRO Four Seasons Nile Plaza Hotel
£ £ £ £ £ Map 5 A5

1089 Corniche el-Nil, Garden City, Cairo **Tel** *02 2791 7000* **Fax** *02 2791 6900* **Rooms** *366*

The Four Seasons offers a panoramic view of the Nile and a supremely convenient location. Each room or suite is lavish and comes complete with truly luxurious amenities. Another Four Seasons, the First Residence, is located in Giza, by the zoo. **www.fourseasons.com**

CAIRO Grand Hyatt Cairo
£ £ £ £ £ Map 3 B1, 5 A5

Corniche el-Nil, Rhoda, Cairo **Tel** *02 2365 1234* **Fax** *02 2362 1927* **Rooms** *714*

One of the largest of the purpose-designed hotels in Cairo, the Grand Hyatt is located on the northernmost tip of Rhoda Island. It is far enough out to be relaxing, and yet the city centre is within easy reach. Rooms and facilities are as one would expect of a five-star hotel, and the Nile views are breathtaking. **www.cairo.grand.hyatt.com**

CAIRO Hilton Cairo World Trade Centre Residence
£ £ £ £ £ Map 1 B1

1191 Corniche el-Nil, Bulaq, Cairo **Tel** *02 2580 2000* **Fax** *02 2579 0577* **Rooms** *225*

Part of the World Trade Centre complex on the banks of the Nile, this all-suites hotel attracts both businesspeople and discerning travellers. Its restaurants serve top-quality Mediterranean cuisine, while its rooms have every luxury expected of a top-end hotel, including Internet connection. **www.hilton.com**

CAIRO Mercure Cairo Le Sphinx
£ £ £ £ £ Map

1 Alexandria Desert Road, Giza, Cairo **Tel** *02 3377 6444* **Fax** *02 3377 4930* **Rooms** *280*

If visiting the Pyramids, you couldn't find a hotel that is more conveniently located than the Mercure Le Sphinx. It stands in an outstanding park at the very foot of the Pyramids of Giza and the Sphinx. Nearby, you will find many cultural and tourist attractions, superb shopping outlets and a wealth of recreational facilities. **www.accorhotels.com**

CAIRO Pyramisa Hotel
£ £ £ £ £ Map 3 A2

60 Sharia Giza, Doqqi, Cairo **Tel** *02 3336 7000* **Fax** *02 3360 5347* **Rooms** *377*

This sprawling hotel overlooks the Nile, and is situated a few minutes' walk from the Cairo Opera House on the west bank. Rooms are equipped with a wide range of amenities. Inward-facing rooms with views of the pool are much quieter. The hotel offers fine restaurants, a spa, pools and sports facilities. **www.pyramisaegypt.com**

CAIRO Ramses Hilton Hotel
£ £ £ £ £ Map 5 A1

1115 Corniche el-Nil, Maspiro, Cairo **Tel** *02 2577 7444* **Fax** *02 2575 2942* **Rooms** *771*

A landmark building renowned for the outstanding views of the Nile and the Pyramids from its 36th-floor rooftop restaurant, the Ramses Hilton Hotel is popular with both business and leisure travellers. Standard rooms are looking outdated, however, and the pool is rather noisy. The Indian restaurant is excellent. **www.hilton.com**

CAIRO Semiramis Intercontinental
£ £ £ £ £ Map 1 B5, 5 A4

Corniche el-Nil, Garden City, Cairo **Tel** *02 2795 7171* **Fax** *02 2796 3020* **Rooms** *730*

If money is no object, then a stay at the Semiramis Intercontinental will make a trip to Cairo an even more memorable experience. Most of this hotel's rooms, including its collection of luxury suites, which attract the world's wealthiest, look straight out over the Nile. A seemingly endless list of amenities is on offer. **www.intercontinental.com**

CAIRO Sofitel Cairo Maadi Towers
£ £ £ £ £ Map

29 Corniche el-Nil, Maadi, Cairo **Tel** *02 2526 0601* **Fax** *02 2526 1133* **Rooms** *173*

Combining luxury with a characterful decor that aims to capture Egyptian architecture and style, this hotel offers attractive, fully equipped rooms, as well as pools, a fitness centre, a casino and facilities for children. It also prides itself on providing for guests with mobility restrictions. Situated 12 km (7.5 miles) from the city centre. **www.sofitel.com**

CAIRO Sofitel El-Gezirah
£ £ £ £ £ Map 3 A1

3 Sharia al-Majlis al-Thawra, Gezirah, Cairo **Tel** *02 2737 3737* **Fax** *02 2736 3640* **Rooms** *433*

The 27-storey round Sofitel El-Gezirah enjoys stunning views of the city's landmarks, not to mention top-class facilities and exceptionally tasteful luxury rooms. The hotel stands on the southern tip of Gezirah on the banks of the Nile. The restaurants and bars in the hotel are some of the city's best. **www.sofitel.com**

Key to Price Guide *see p268* **Key to Symbols** *see back cover flap*

GIZA AND HELIOPOLIS Baron Hotel Heliopolis

8 Sharia Maahad El Saharaa, Heliopolis, Cairo **Tel** *02 2291 5757* **Fax** *02 2270 7077* **Rooms** *126*

A landmark building, the Baron Hotel is located in the Heliopolis district of Cairo. It overlooks the 19th-century Baron Empain's Palace. The hotel has a range of amenities that include a health suite, a pub and shops. The rooms are attractively presented, and most boast stunning panoramic views.

GIZA AND HELIOPOLIS Concorde El Salam Hotel

65 Sharia Abdel Hamid Badawi, Heliopolis, Cairo **Tel** *02 2622 6000* **Fax** *02 2622 6037* **Rooms** *256*

Conveniently close to the airport, the Concorde El Salam is popular with businesspeople as well as leisure travellers. It has four fine restaurants serving Indian, Chinese, Italian and Oriental cuisine, along with many amenities and two swimming pools. The attractive rooms are of a high standard. **http://cairo.concorde-hotels.com**

GIZA AND HELIOPOLIS Hotel Beirut

56 Sharia Beirut, Heliopolis, Cairo **Tel** *02 2291 1092* **Fax** *02 2290 4065* **Rooms** *90*   **Map** *1 A2*

A modern mid-priced hotel, located in an upmarket suburb northeast of Cairo, that has old world charm. With air conditioning throughout, well-presented rooms with good facilities and restaurants offering a mix of international and Egyptian cuisine, the hotel offers excellent value for money. **www.beiruthotelseg.com**

GIZA AND HELIOPOLIS Le Meridien Heliopolis

Sharia Al Orouba, Al Horreya, Heliopolis, Cairo **Tel** *02 2290 5055* **Fax** *02 2291 8591* **Rooms** *283*

Whether relaxing at the bar, around the pool or in any one of its elegant restaurants or simply taking it easy in the privacy of your own room, Le Meridien offers a truly chic atmosphere. It is just 15 minutes or so from Cairo's airport, but longer from the city centre. **www.lemeridien.com/heliopolis**

GIZA AND HELIOPOLIS Novotel Cairo Airport Hotel

Cairo Airport, Heliopolis, Cairo **Tel** *02 2291 8520* **Fax** *02 2291 4794* **Rooms** *207*

At first glance, this establishment seems above all a practical solution for an overnight stay, but in reality it is a surprisingly comfortable hotel with good amenities that include a sauna, tennis courts and restaurants. As its name suggests, it is close to the airport, and as such it is popular with businesspeople. **www.novotel.com**

GIZA AND HELIOPOLIS Mena House Oberoi

Sharia al-Ahram, Giza, Cairo **Tel** *02 3377 3222* **Fax** *02 3376 7777* **Rooms** *420*

Situated right in front of the Pyramids, with a wonderful garden pool, Mena House Oberoi is always popular with tourists. Golfers, too, are drawn to play its course. The hotel's rooms are beautifully presented, while its reception is reminiscent of the 19th-century hunting lodge it once was. **www.menahouse.com**

GIZA AND HELIOPOLIS Mövenpick Pyramids Resort

Cairo-Alexandria Desert Road, Giza, Cairo **Tel** *02 3377 2555* **Fax** *02 3377 5006* **Rooms** *240*

Location is one of the keys to the success of this exceptionally comfortable hotel. It is ideally situated for the Pyramids. The hotel offers beautifully presented rooms with many facilities, as well as a large swimming pool and sports amenities. **www.moevenpick-hotels.com**

GIZA AND HELIOPOLIS Oasis Hotel

Cairo–Alexandria desert road, Giza, Cairo **Tel** *02 3838 7333* **Fax** *02 3838 7916* **Rooms** *300*

With all rooms in bungalows set in 9 acres of lush gardens this is truly an oasis. The setting, pool, sports facilities and children's playground make this more of a resort than a hotel. Its location, 7 km (4 miles) from the Pyramids, the free shuttle into Cairo and polite staff make for a relaxing stay. **www.oasis.com.eg**

MAADI Villa Belle Epoque

Near Road 9, Maddi, Cairo **Tel** *02 2516 9656* **Rooms** *13*

This 1920s villa, with its beautiful period-style rooms, each with balcony or conservatory, is one of Cairo's best boutique hotels. The gardens and pools are delightful and the restaurant has an excellent chef. It is located in the leafy residential suburb of Maadi, 8 km (5 miles) south of downtown Cairo. **www.eugenie.com.eg**

6TH OF OCTOBER CITY Sheraton Dreamland Hotel

Sharia Wahat, 6th of October City, Cairo **Tel** *02 3859 5000* **Rooms** *358*

In the self-contained Dreamland suburb, the Sheraton Dreamland Hotel is popular with tourists and businesspeople alike. Offering five-star facilities such as a spa, valet service and restaurants serving fine cuisine, it is a good choice in the high-end bracket. With a theme park attached, it attracts families too. **www.starwoodhotels.com**

AROUND CAIRO

FAYOUM Zad Al Mosafer

Tunis Village, Fayoum **Tel** *084 6820 180* or *010 6395 590* **Fax** *084 6820 180* **Rooms** *29*

This eco-lodge in Tunis Village began as a writers' retreat and is now expanding to accommodate its growing number of fans, while Tunis itself is becoming a literary enclave. It is the perfect place for a relaxing, rustic stay, with access to the local flora and fauna, scenic desert trips and art. Some rooms share bathrooms. **abdogbair48@maktoob.com**

FAYOUM Helnan Auberge   🍴 ♨ 🛏 💿   ©©©©
Lake Qarun, Fayoum **Tel** *084 6981 200* **Fax** *084 6981 300* **Rooms** *100*

The faded glory of King Farouk's hunting lodge has been restored with the renovations undertaken by Helnan. In a wonderful location, perched on the edge of Lake Qaran at the Fayoum Oasis, the auberge combines superb rooms with rural gardens. Winston Churchill visited in 1945. Very kind and helpful staff. **www.helnan.com**

SAQQARA Saqqara Country Club & Hotel   💳 🍴 ♨ 🛏 💿   ©©©
Saqqara Rd, Abu El-Nomros, Saqqara **Tel** *02 3381 1307* **Rooms** *20*

Located in a picturesque village setting outside of Cairo, surrounded by date palms and near to the Saqqara pyramids, this country club is a charming place to stay. The hotel is well-managed, but don't expect luxury as the rooms are a little dated. The food is decent, however, and there are good horse-riding facilities.

THE NILE VALLEY

ABU SIMBEL Nefertari Hotel   🍴 ♨ 🛏 💿   ©©©©
Abu Simbel **Tel** *097 3400 508* **Fax** *097 3400 510* **Rooms** *122*

A sizable establishment that stands in its own gardens, the Nefertari is close to the Temple of Ramses II. Its pool is attractive and offers a great view out over Lake Nasser, while its restaurant and rooms are well presented, if a little on the basic side. Its location is convenient, but the hotel is in need of updating.

ABU SIMBEL Seti Abu Simbel Hotel   🛜 🍴 ♨ 🛏 💿   ©©©©©
Abu Simbel **Tel** *097 3400 720* **Fax** *097 3400 829* **Rooms** *138*

A short walk from the Grand Temple of Ramses, the Seti Abu Simbel enjoys splendid views across the waters of Lake Nasser. The public areas feature striking Nubian-style domes, and there are three pools with waterfalls and a large garden. Live entertainment is arranged most nights. **www.setifirst.com**

ASWAN El Salam Hotel   💳 🛜 ♨ 📶   ©
101 Corniche el-Nil, Aswan **Tel & Fax** *097 2302 651* **Rooms** *70*

The front rooms at this hotel on the Corniche offer excellent Nile views but can be noisy. Those at the back are quieter but lack the views. The El Salam is jaded and old-fashioned, but the large rooms, high level of cleanliness and central location make it a great budget option. **elsalamhotelaswan@yahoo.com**

ASWAN Hathor Hotel   💳 🛜 ♨ 🛏   ©
99 Corniche el-Nil, Aswan **Tel** *097 2314 580* **Fax** *097 2303 462* **Rooms** *60*

A slightly older-style hotel that holds a few surprises. On the roof, the area centred around the hotel pool has been attractively decorated with pots and shrubs. The views of the Nile are outstanding from here. Most of the rooms have views of the river, too, although these tend to book up quickly. **www.hathorhotel.com**

ASWAN Keylany Hotel   💳 🍴 🛏   ©
Sharia Keylany, Aswan **Tel** *097 2323 134* **Rooms** *30*

This is an attractive and beautifully clean hotel, and the owners clearly take great pride in it. Continuing expansion now includes wireless Internet access and a lovely rooftop restaurant. Rooms have bathrooms, air conditioning and televisions, all for cheap rates. The hotel's central location to Aswan's attractions is another bonus. **www.keylanyhotel.com**

ASWAN Memnon Hotel   💳 🛜 🍴 ♨ 🛏 📶   ©
Corniche el-Nil (above National Bank), Aswan **Tel & Fax** *097 2300 483* **Rooms** *50*

Situated on two floors above the National Bank in the middle of the Corniche, central Aswan, the Memnon has friendly staff and makes a good budget choice for such a central location. The pool is very small but there are fantastic Nile views from some rooms, although these can be noisy. **www.memnonhotel-aswan.com**

ASWAN New Abu Simbel Hotel   💳 🛜   ©
Sharia Abtal el-Tahir, Aswan **Tel** *097 2306 096* **Rooms** *38*

The New Abu Simbel is an unassuming building inside and out, but it is a welcoming establishment, its staff friendly and helpful. Rooms are simply decorated but immaculately clean. Location-wise, the hotel is close to the banks of the Nile on the northern side of Aswan.

ASWAN Nourhan Hotel   🛏   ©
Off Sharia Souq, Aswan **Tel & Fax** *097 2326 069* **Rooms** *36*

Set over four floors, the two-star Nourhan offers clean accommodation at very competitive prices. All rooms have air conditioning or fans. The hotel also incorporates an excellent coffee shop, featuring mostly typical Egyptian and Arabic drinks. It is a great place to meet fellow backpackers.

ASWAN Nuba Nile Hotel   💳 🛜 🍴 ♨ 🛏 💿   ©
Sharia Abtal al-Tahrir, Aswan **Tel** *097 2313 267* **Rooms** *52*

Located just off the main square in front of the railway station, this hotel is a decent budget option. It has friendly staff and comfortable rooms with fridges and satellite TV. The tiny rooftop pool is more for cooling off than swimming, but is still a welcome feature.

Key to Price Guide *see p268* **Key to Symbols** *see back cover flap*

ASWAN Nubian Oasis Hotel

234 Sharia Saad Zaghlou, Aswan **Tel** *097 2312 123* **Fax** *097 2312 124* **Rooms** *32*

The Nubian is a cheaper-end hotel. It offers no frills but is well located in downtown Aswan, and guests can enjoy the many attractions the city has to offer on the doorstep. Rooms are basic but clean, some with private bathrooms, and some offer views of Aswan. Close by are enough shops and restaurants to suit all tastes.

ASWAN Ramses Hotel

Sharia Abtel al-Tahrir, Aswan **Tel** *097 2304 000* **Fax** *097 2315 701* **Rooms** *112*

The staff at the Ramses are friendly and helpful, and always willing to help guests organize their stay, booking trips and excursions on their behalf. Location-wise, the hotel overlooks the river and is within walking distance of bustling Nile Street. Its facilities are good for a budget hotel and include air conditioned rooms with private bathrooms.

ASWAN Orchida St George Hotel

9 Sharia Mohammed Khalid, off Corniche el-Nil, Aswan **Tel** *097 2315 997* **Fax** *097 2332 919* **Rooms** *40*

The decor might be dated and the pool very small, but this hotel is very centrally located, just off the Corniche. Sharia Souk is close by and there's a café-bar on the roof. Newer rooms are boxy but bigger and better equipped than the older ones. There is a large restaurant. **www.orchida-sg-hotel.com**

ASWAN Oscar Hotel

Sharia El Barka, Aswan **Tel & Fax** *097 2310 742* **Rooms** *42*

Despite being a mid- to low-end hotel, the Oscar is a pleasant little place to stay. Its rooms are nicely presented, and some have air conditioning and private bathroom facilities, while the hotel itself has a brightly coloured restaurant where delicious home-made Egyptian cuisine is served. There's also a subterranean bar.

ASWAN Philae Hotel

79 Corniche el-Nil, Aswan **Tel** *097 2312 090* **Fax** *097 2310 572* **Rooms** *66*

The Philae Hotel must be one of the best bargains in town. Pleasingly presented, it is competitively priced and yet stands right in the centre of Aswan, on the Corniche. Second floor rooms enjoy river views and guests can relax in the hotel's restaurant and bar area.

ASWAN Basma

Sharia El Fanadek, Aswan **Tel** *097 2310 901* **Fax** *097 2310 907* **Rooms** *189*

Perched on Aswan's highest hill, the Basma has one of the most panoramic views imaginable, encompassing both the city and the Nile. Its richly planted gardens revolve around a floodlit pool, while inside, the decor is classic. Rooms are well equipped, if a little dated, and prices can be negotiated. **www.basmahotel.com**

ASWAN Isis Corniche Hotel

Corniche el-Nil, Aswan **Tel** *097 2315 200* **Fax** *097 2315 500* **Rooms** *100*

One of the best things about staying at the Isis is that you can step outside and literally be beside the Nile. The hotel is right on the river and it's a great base for exploring local sights. Chalet-style rooms are pleasant, although not luxurious, with good private bathrooms and air conditioning. There's a good pool.

ASWAN Nile Hotel

15 Corniche el-Nil, Aswan **Tel & Fax** *097 2314 222* **Rooms** *30*

The bright but plainly decorated rooms at the Nile Hotel are comfortable and spacious, with air conditioning and heating. Located on the Corniche, the hotel offers wonderful views over Elephantine and Kitchener Islands and is next to the beautiful Ferial Gardens. There is free wireless Internet. **www.nilehotel-aswan.com**

ASWAN Sara Hotel

Sharia El Fanadek, Nasser City, Aswan **Tel** *097 2327 234* **Fax** *097 2327 236* **Rooms** *60*

A location right above a cliff top, on the edge of a coral island and opposite Salouga Island, ensures that the views from rooms are breathtaking. The hotel has an international flavour, with restaurants serving cuisine from abroad, alongside Egyptian fare. Rooms are equipped above their three-star rating. Prices are negotiable. **www.sarahotel-aswan.com**

ASWAN Hotel New Cataract Aswan

Sharia Abtal el Tahir, Aswan **Tel** *097 2316 001* **Fax** *097 2316 011* **Rooms** *144*

Located on the banks of the Nile opposite Elephantine Island and just metres from the Nubian Museum, this hotel is ideal for sightseeing enthusiasts. The hotel itself sits in attractive landscaped gardens and rooms have balconies with wonderful views of the Nile. It's located adjacent to the Old Cataract hotel *(see p274)*. **www.sofitel.com**

ASWAN Marhaba Hotel

Corniche el-Nil, Aswan **Tel** *097 2330 102* **Fax** *097 2330 105* **Rooms** *78*

Set back off the Corniche behind a small garden, the modern Marhaba is brightening up the area around the railway station. There is a decent pool and the rooms are well proportioned. The Marhaba is efficiently run though some bathrooms are poorly maintained. **www.marhaba-aswan.com**

ASWAN Mövenpick Resort Aswan

Aswan **Tel** *097 2303 455* **Fax** *097 2303 485* **Rooms** *230*

This modern waterfront hotel offers the variety of restaurants and sports amenities, such as tennis courts and pools, one would expect of a five-star establishment. Its air conditioned rooms and suites have a luxury feel, and many have stunning views of the Nile. **www.moevenpick-hotels.com**

ASWAN Pyramisa Isis Island Resort and Spa

Isis Island, Aswan **Tel** *097 2317 400* **Fax** *097 2317 405* **Rooms** *447*

The Pyramisa Isis Resort stands in what can only be described as an oasis – an island in the middle of the Nile. Its rooms are well presented, most with a view of the river from a private balcony or terrace. The hotel itself features many amenities, including a health centre, sporting activities and a spa. **www.pyramisaegypt.com**

ASWAN Sofitel Old Cataract Hotel

Sharia Abdal El Tahrir, Aswan **Tel** *097 2316 000* **Fax** *097 2316 011* **Rooms** *131*

A stay at this establishment will feel like taking a step back in time. Providing a backdrop for Agatha Christie's novel *Death on the Nile*, the hotel was built in the late 19th century and retains much of its historic character, albeit with a modern twist. Reopened in 2011 following extensive refurbishment. **www.sofitel.com**

ASYUT YMCA

Sharia Salah ad-Din al-Ayyubi, Asyut **Tel** *088 2313 118* **Rooms** *30*

When checking into a YMCA establishment, one wouldn't generally expect lots of frills, but this air conditioned youth-style hotel in the very heart of Asyut is surprisingly comfortable and welcoming. Most of its rooms are carpeted and come complete with a private bathroom and television.

ASYUT Assiutel Hotel

146 Sharia el-Nil, Asyut **Tel** *088 2312 121* **Fax** *088 2312 122* **Rooms** *30*

Located right in the centre of Asyut, on the Corniche, this hotel offers excellent views from most of its rooms. The mid-range Assiutel is also a great base from which to explore the surrounding areas. There's a choice between standard and luxury rooms, and all rooms have wireless Internet. The breakfast is decent.

LUXOR Boomerang Hotel

Sharia Mohamed Farid, East Bank, Luxor **Tel** *019 136 1544* **Rooms** *24*

The family-run Boomerang is one of the best budget hostels on the East Bank. Rooms are spotless, almost all have both a balcony and air conditioning, and each has satellite TV and an en suite bathroom. It's a ten minute walk from the railway station and less than ten minutes from the Luxor Temple and Corniche. **www.boomerangluxor.com**

LUXOR El-Fayrouz Hotel

Bayrat al-Gezira, West Bank, Luxor **Tel** *095 2312 709* **Rooms** *22*

The German- and Egyptian-run El Fayrouz has been a stalwart of the West Bank hotel scene for many years. Guests return year after year to enjoy comfortable, simply furnished rooms and excellent service. The sociable garden restaurant is perfect for a drink or high quality meal. **www.elfayrouz.com**

LUXOR El-Gezira Hotel

Bayrat al-Gezira, West Bank, Luxor **Tel &** **Fax** *095 2310 034* **Rooms** *11*

This traditional two-storey hotel may look unassuming from the outside, but it is very popular, so you should book ahead. Rooms are comfortable, with private bathrooms and air conditioning; some even have Nile views. The rooftop bar and restaurant (serving excellent Egyptian food) is a welcoming venue.

LUXOR Nefertiti Hotel

Sharia El-Sahaby, in the souq, Luxor **Tel &** **Fax** *095 2372 386* **Rooms** *30*

The Nefertiti is one of Luxor's best budget options. There's modern plumbing and electrics, as well as attractive Arabesque touches in the rooms and public areas. The breakfast buffet on the roof affords excellent views, and the tours and services provided by the hotel are reliable and hassle free. **www.nefertitihotel.com**

LUXOR Venus Hotel

Sharia Yussef Hassan, Luxor **Tel** *095 2372 625 or 095 2361 327* **Rooms** *21*

The Venus is a hotel with few frills but one that impresses money-conscious travellers with its location, close to the city centre. Its rooms are surprisingly comfortable for a budget hotel, and some have their own private bathroom and air conditioning. The hotel also offers a rooftop bar and restaurant with a great atmosphere.

LUXOR Al-Nakhil Hotel

Bayrat al-Gezira, West Bank, Luxor **Tel** *095 2313 922* **Rooms** *17*

On the edge of Gezira village, a few minutes' walk from the ferry landing, Al-Nakhil is excellent value, with attractive and well-equipped rooms. The rooftop restaurant has great views, and adaptations have been put in place for disabled guests. Altogether, it's quite a chic little hotel. **www.el-nakhil.com**

LUXOR Amon Hotel

Bayrat Al-Gezira, West Bank, Luxor **Tel** *095 2310 912* **Fax** *095 2311 205* **Rooms** *17*

This homely hotel may not be inspiring, but it is known as a friendly haven. Family-run, it is welcoming and clean, and many of the rooms have private bathrooms. It is situated close to the ferry landing in the centre of the village, in its own luxuriant gardens. A roof terrace is ideal for relaxing between sightseeing trips. **www.amonhotel.com**

LUXOR El-Gezira Gardens

Bayrat al-Gezira, West Bank, Luxor **Tel** *095 2312 505* **Fax** *095 2312 506* **Rooms** *30*

This is the sister hotel to the El-Gezira, which was the first hotel in this area. It offers peaceful rooms and apartments with a lovely pool, gardens and a rooftop restaurant with Nile views and an excellent breakfast that will keep you going through all the sights on the West Bank. **www.el-gezira.com**

Key to Price Guide *see p268* **Key to Symbols** *see back cover flap*

LUXOR Emilio Hotel   £££

Sharia Youssef Hassan, Luxor **Tel** *095 2376 666* **Fax** *095 2370 000* **Rooms** *101*

Popular with tour groups, which is often a good sign, this hotel is central, modern and clean and offers a range of good amenities, including a rooftop swimming pool with great views, European-style restaurants, a bar and a disco. Rooms are pleasantly decorated and comfortable.

LUXOR Flobater Hotel   £££

Sharia Khaled Edn El Walid, Luxor **Tel** *095 2270 418* **Fax** *095 2270 618* **Rooms** *40*

The three-star Flobater, located south of the city centre, has many rooms with views to the side of the Nile. Amenities are good for the price, although rooms are in need of a renovation. There's a small rooftop bar and an excellent value restaurant and the staff is unfailingly pleasant and helpful.

LUXOR Gaddis Hotel   £££

Sharia Khaled Ibn El Walid, Luxor **Tel** *095 2382 838* **Fax** *095 2382 837* **Rooms** *55*

An international service combined with warm Egyptian hospitality and style is what is promised by this centrally located Luxor hotel. Offering good amenities at a competitive rate, the Gaddis has attractively presented rooms, a small pool and free wireless Internet. **www.gaddishotel.com**

LUXOR New Phillippe Hotel   £££

Sharia Dr Labib Habashy, Luxor **Tel** *095 2372 284* **Fax** *095 2380 050* **Rooms** *68*

The renovated New Phillippe boasts standard, superior and Nile-view rooms, as well as a bar and a restaurant which provides 24-hour room service. The friendly staff, central location and passable pool make this a great Luxor option. The sister establishment, the Susanna, is also centrally located.

LUXOR Nour el-Gourna   £££

Gourna Antiquities Inspectorate, Luxor **Tel** *095 2311 430* **Rooms** *7*

An amazing Egyptian mudbrick house is the setting for this cute hotel in the heart of the West Bank's sights. The upper terrace has views of the Colossi of Memnon. There's a lovely garden and an excellent restaurant, although no alcohol is served. **www.nourelgourna.com**

LUXOR Pharaoh's Hotel   £££

Bayrat al-Gezira, West Bank, Luxor **Tel** *095 2310 702* **Rooms** *24*

This hotel's unassuming façade belies the fact that it has a classic interior and feels utterly welcoming. Rooms are clean and air conditioned and there's free wireless Internet in the lobby. The West Bank hills can be seen from most viewpoints. **www.hotelpharohs.com**

LUXOR St Joseph Hotel   £££

Sharia Khaled Ibn El Walid, Luxor **Tel** *095 2381 707* **Fax** *095 2381 727* **Rooms** *75*

Externally, the St Joseph is less than inspiring, but it is a popular and well-priced choice. It is situated in one of the newer parts of Luxor, but within easy reach of the city centre and plentiful nightlife. Rooms are well equipped and include private bathrooms, televisions and fridges.

LUXOR Beit Sabee   £££££

Medinet Habu, West Bank, Luxor **Tel** *010 5705 341* **Rooms** *8*

An Egyptian- and French-run hotel in a sundried mudbrick house situated in the fields around Medinet Habu offers a rural alternative. The brightly coloured rooms afford views over the ruins and there's a small courtyard and roof terrace. Traditional meals can be prepared on request for lunch and dinner. **www.nourelnil.com**

LUXOR Desert Paradise   £££££

Gabawy Village, West Bank, Luxor **Tel** *095 231 3036 or 016 997 7720* **Rooms** *10*

Constructed in the traditional style, Desert Paradise consists of domed rooms surrounded by a charming garden, with a secluded pool and outdoor restaurant in the grounds. The lodge is located in Gabawy village, far away from the tourist scene and 10% of every booking is donated to the Animal Care Egypt charity.

LUXOR Marsam Hotel   £££££

Gurna, West Bank, Luxor **Tel** *010 3426 471* **Rooms** *30*

Located amongst ancient monuments, the Marsam was built for American archaeologists in the 1920s and remains a popular haunt during the digging season. Mud-brick rooms are austere yet charming and the garden captivates any visitor. Delicious meals are served at the restaurant.

LUXOR Sofitel Karnak Hotel   £££££

Sharia El Zinia Gebly, Luxor **Tel** *095 2378 020* **Fax** *095 2378 021* **Rooms** *351*

Located beside the River Nile on the north side of Luxor city centre, the Sofitel Karnak is close to the Karnak Temple complex. Extensive amenities include tennis courts, a gymnasium and a swimming pool. Sunsets, viewed from the elegant gardens, are spectacular. **www.sofitel.com**

LUXOR Winter Pavilion Hotel   £££££

Corniche el-Nil, Luxor **Rooms** *237*

With luxuriant gardens and poolside areas lavishly planted with tropical plants, this hotel feels like an oasis in the centre of Luxor. It offers elegant rooms and a touch of luxury at affordable prices. Amenities include restaurants, pools and a beauty salon. The hotel adjoins the historic Old Winter Palace *(see p276)*.

LUXOR El-Luxor Hotel

Corniche el-Nil, Luxor **Tel** *095 2380 944* **Fax** *095 2374 912* **Rooms** *306*

Everything you would expect from a four-star hotel with the added bonus of rooms with Nile-view balconies and a crescent shaped pool. In an excellent location for all Luxor's sights, the El-Luxor also has enough facilities and services to keep everyone happy on a day away from the tourist attractions. **www.el-luxor-hotel.com**

LUXOR Iberotel Luxor Hotel

Sharia Khaled Ibn El Walid, Luxor **Tel** *095 2380 925* **Fax** *095 2380 972* **Rooms** *185*

Views of the Theban Hills, the West Bank and the Nile can be enjoyed from this hotel's themed restaurants, bars and poolside area, not to mention from some of its contemporary rooms. A pretty hotel centred around its fabulous Nile-side pool, the Iberotel Luxor is within walking distance from the Luxor Temple. **www.iberotel.com**

LUXOR Maritim Jolie Ville Island Resort

Kings Island, Luxor **Tel** *095 2374 855* **Fax** *095 2374 936* **Rooms** *327*

Surrounded by tropical fauna and flora, not to mention the River Nile, this attractive, elegant five star hotel has simply beautiful pools. Luxor city centre is a ten minute drive away, and the hotel's own free shuttle bus and boat ferry visitors the short hop to the mainland. Rooms are beautifully furnished. **www.jolieville-hotels.com**

LUXOR Pyramisa Isis Luxor

Sharia Khaled Ibn El Walid, Luxor **Tel** *095 2370 100* **Fax** *095 2372 923* **Rooms** *480*

Located on the banks of the River Nile in around eight acres of landscaped gardens, this hotel is just within walking distance of the Luxor Temple and the city centre. Rooms are beautifully presented, with most affording superb West Bank views. Amenities include good Italian and Chinese restaurants. **www.pyramisaegypt.com**

LUXOR Sonesta St George Hotel

Corniche el-Nil, Luxor **Tel** *095 2382 575* **Fax** *095 2382 571* **Rooms** *224*

A contemporary seven-storey building located in the centre of Luxor's shopping district. Indeed, the shopaholic will be spoilt for choice, since even the hotel features a lobby shopping arcade specializing in jewellery and local crafts. The hotel and its rooms are all beautifully presented, with top-quality facilities. **www.sonesta.com/luxor**

LUXOR Al-Moudira

Haggar Dabaiyya, West Bank, Luxor **Tel** *012 325 1307* **Fax** *012 322 0528* **Rooms** *54*

Set in a remote location surrounded by sugarcane fields, Al-Moudira is a tranquil oasis and a welcome respite from the hustle and bustle of Luxor. The hotel is set in lush gardens and incorporates traditional architecture. Each room is different, spacious and decorated with antiques, and the swimming pool is beautiful. **www.moudira.com**

LUXOR Hilton Luxor Resort & Spa

Sharia Karnak, Luxor **Tel** *095 2374 933* **Fax** *095 2376 571* **Rooms** *261*

Deep pockets may be required to stay at the Luxor Hilton, but its fabulous amenities and superb location close to the Temple of Karnak justifies the extravagant expense. Luxurious rooms, shops and restaurants are just some of the facilities on offer. There's also a gorgeous spa and kids' club. **www.hilton.com**

LUXOR M/S Iberotel Crown Emperor

M/S Iberotel Crown Emperor Pier, Luxor **Tel** *02 3854 3222* **Fax** *02 3854 3259* **Rooms** *118*

Sister to the Empress, the M/S Iberotel Crown Emperor takes passengers on a cruise along the Nile. On board, guests will find top-quality restaurants, bars and sleeping quarters. Cabins and suites come complete with a panoramic window to maximize on the river views and private bathroom facilities. **www.travcotels.com**

LUXOR M/S Iberotel Crown Empress

M/S Iberotel Crown Empress Pier, Luxor **Tel** *02 3854 3222* **Fax** *02 3854 3259* **Rooms** *128*

A floating hotel with a difference, the M/S Iberotel Crown Empress offers doubles, singles and suites equipped to the highest standard and complete with individually controlled air conditioning. The cruise ship offers the chance to see the Temple of Luxor and Valley of the Kings from the Nile. **www.travcotels.com**

LUXOR Sheraton Luxor

Sharia Khalid Ibn al-Walid, Luxor **Tel** *&* **Fax** *095 2274 544* **Rooms** *290*

Situated in one of Luxor's main thoroughfares and close to the city's major tourist attractions, the Sheraton offers a good location and high-quality amenities. Among them are sports facilities and a range of restaurants serving traditional European fare. Only the upper floors have Nile views. **www.sheraton.com**

LUXOR Sofitel Old Winter Palace

Corniche el-Nil, Luxor **Tel** *095 2380 425* **Fax** *095 2374 087* **Rooms** *92*

Staying at the Winter Palace, a famous and historic 19th-century Victorian building, is an elegant and nostalgic affair. Its rooms, restaurants and facilities are decorated to the high standard expected of a five-star hotel, and they ooze character and refinement, while the pool and gardens are simply divine. **www.sofitel.com**

MINYA King Akhenaten Hotel

Sharia el-Horreya, Minya **Tel** *&* **Fax** *086 2365 917* **Rooms** *48*

The Akhenaten is set on the Corniche in the attractive town of Minya and is a good place to stay to absorb the local atmosphere or venture further afield to see the sights. It is a little old, but offers comfortable rooms, mostly with views of the Nile, and there is a good, old-fashioned restaurant (no alcohol served). **www.kingakhenaten.com**

Key to Price Guide *see p268* **Key to Symbols** *see back cover flap*

MINYA Lotus Hotel

1 Sharia Port Said, Minya **Tel** *086 2364 500* **Fax** *086 2324 576* **Rooms** *175*

A traditional hotel with simply furnished rooms that have two big advantages: air conditioning and television. The hotel's restaurant is situated on the top floor of this high-rise building, and although its cuisine offers few frills, the views of Minya are outstanding. It is also a relaxing spot for a beer.

MINYA Horus Resort

Corniche el-Nil, Minya **Tel** *086 2316 660/1* **Fax** *086 2316 662* **Rooms** *80*

Chalet-style rooms on the bank of the Nile are tastefully decorated and very comfortable, although there's no room service. The huge pool is inviting and there's a children's play area, plus lots of outdoor space to relax with a drink. Ask for a room towards the end of the hotel as they are quieter. **www.horusresortmenia.com**

MINYA Nefertiti Hotel

Corniche el-Nil, Minya **Tel** *086 2331 515* **Fax** *086 2326 467* **Rooms** *54*

Located on the West Bank of the Nile, 2 km (1.2 miles) north of the town centre, this hotel provides a good sightseeing base in a town without many accommodation options. It offers a range of facilities, including a small swimming pool and international restaurants.

SOHAG Al Safa Hotel

Sharia el-Gomhoriya, Sohag **Tel** *& **Fax** 093 2307 701* **Rooms** *20*

Situated in a central location, this hotel prides itself on the personal touch that includes friendly, helpful staff. The rooms may be dull in decor, but they are clean and come with complimentary toiletries. Some rooms have balconies affording views of the Nile and there is a popular terrace coffee shop and free wireless Internet.

SINAI AND THE RED SEA COAST

DAHAB Alaska Camp & Hotel

Masbat, Dahab **Tel** *069 3641 004* **Rooms** *30*

The staff at Alaska is very professional and sets a high standard for budget hotels in Dahab, with a range of spotless rooms arranged on two levels around a garden. Basic rooms have a fan, while more expensive ones have air conditioning and balconies with sea views. All have en suite bathrooms and are bright and cheerful. **www.dahabescape.com**

DAHAB Bishbishi Camp

Mashraba, Dahab **Tel** *069 3640 727* **Rooms** *40*

Ideal for young travellers keen for the experience of living close to nature, Bishbishi Camp comprises of chalets equipped with only the bare essentials; though some have private bathrooms, and there is an attractive communal courtyard. More upmarket accommodation is available at their partner, the Sphinx Hotel. **www.bish-bishi.com**

DAHAB Jasmine Pension

Mashraba, Dahab **Tel** *069 3640 852* **Fax** *069 3640 885* **Rooms** *17*

The Jasmine Pension is an attractive alternative to the many camps that can be found in Dahab, and yet it is as affordable. The rooms are basic but comfortable, and equipped with their own bathrooms and air conditioning. The complex's own restaurant may not be luxurious, but it serves good, hearty food. **www.jasminepension.com**

DAHAB Nesima Hotel

Mashraba, Dahab **Tel** *069 3640 320* **Fax** *069 3640 321* **Rooms** *51*

The Nesima has one of the most popular diving centres in Dahab, and it is also known for its good restaurant. Its rooms are well presented, with many featuring domed ceilings and sea views. Its pool overlooks the sea. The hotel is well equipped to accommodate people with disabilities. **www.nesima-resort.com**

DAHAB Blue Beach Club

Lighthouse, Dahab **Tel** *069 3640 411* **Fax** *069 3640 413* **Rooms** *22*

The attractive rooms that form the Blue Beach Club are in two buildings, with older rooms nearer the sea and new rooms with mountain views. Facilities and decor are excellent in both, and it is ideal for couples looking for a relaxing base from which to explore the area. **www.bluebeachclub.com**

DAHAB Hilton Resort

Dahab Bay, Dahab **Tel** *069 3640 310* **Fax** *069 3640 424* **Rooms** *163*

The Hilton Resort is a landmark building in Dahab Bay. It is beautifully presented, with lush gardens and white-washed rooms that surround a lagoon-style swimming pool. The resort is situated right on the beachside, and offers some superb leisure amenities, including diving and windsurfing centres. **www.hilton.com/worldwideresorts**

EL-GOUNA Captain's Inn

Abu Tig Marina, El-Gouna **Tel** *& Fax 065 3580 170* **Rooms** *50*

The Captain's Inn is one of the lower budget choices in El-Gouna as it is not on the lagoon but in the marina. Shuttle buses ferry guests to all of El-Gouna's amenities and guests have free use of the pool in the hotel next door. The resort is friendly and rooms are cosy and appealing. **www.elgouna.com**

EL-GOUNA Dawar el-Umda

Kafr El-Gouna, El-Gouna **Tel** *065 3580 064* **Rooms** *66*

If you are after an intimate, chic hotel, then the Dawar el-Umda could fit the bill. Boutique in style, with attractive Arabic-inspired interior design and architecture, it has an elegant feel. In addition to an attractive central pool, the hotel benefits from a pleasant patio bar among flowery trees. **www.dawarelomda-elgouna.com**

EL-GOUNA Sultan Bey Hotel

Kafr el-Gouna, El-Gouna **Tel** *065 3545 600* **Fax** *065 3545 061* **Rooms** *115*

Set in the heart of an extensive resort and benefitting from its leisure amenities, which include swimming pools, watersports and a nearby golf course, this hotel is popular with families. It has an unusual Oriental theme, both inside and out, and the vaulted and domed rooms are attractively decorated. **www.optima-hotels.com**

EL-GOUNA Sheraton Miramar

El-Gouna Resort **Tel** *065 3545 606* **Rooms** *338*

The award-winning El-Gouna Resort, where this hotel is located, is a sprawling collection of villas and hotel apartments, including a few with private butler service. The Sheraton Miramar's leisure amenities are plentiful and include a marina, restaurants, pools, diving and scuba facilities, spas and a golf course. **www.sheraton.com**

HURGHADA 4 Seasons Hotel

Ad-Dahar, Hurghada **Tel** *065 3545 456* **Rooms** *14*

A small hotel, very much for budget backpackers, the 4 Seasons is within easy walking distance of the beach in the centre of the busy Ad-Dahar area of Hurghada. The pool of a neighbouring resort is available for guests' use. All of the rooms have balconies, some with beach views, although not all have air conditioning.

HURGHADA Triton Empire Hotel

Sharia Sayed Korayem, Hurghada **Tel** *065 3549 200* **Fax** *065 3549 212* **Rooms** *419*

A large hotel built to a traditional style and conveniently located for the centre of Ad-Dahar. The Empire boasts many facilities, including its own swimming pool and gardens, and it is a relatively short walking distance from the beach. Ideal for families, but also for those who are keen to experience local life. **www.threecorners.com**

HURGHADA Jasmine Village Hotel

Hurghada **Tel** & **Fax** *065 3460 460* **Rooms** *490*

The Jasmine Village Hotel is more of a resort than a hotel. Its accommodation is provided in bungalows that are nicely presented and surrounded by leisure amenities. These include a pool, playground and even a mini zoo. A dive centre and windsurfing facilities are within the complex. **www.jasminevillage.com**

HURGHADA Arabella Azur Resort

Al-Sakala, Hurghada **Tel** *065 3545 087* **Fax** *065 3545 090* **Rooms** *296*

A lively hotel with bars, a restaurant and one of Hurghada's most popular nightclubs, the Arabella is ideal for anyone looking for an activity-packed stay. All rooms are Nubian style domes with balconies and views. The town centre is about 3 km (1.8 miles) away. **www.azurhotels.com**

HURGHADA Sheraton Soma Bay Hotel

Soma Bay, Red Sea, Hurghada **Tel** *065 3562 585* **Fax** *065 3562 580* **Rooms** *310*

A beautifully presented hotel right on the beachside south of Hurghada, the Sheraton Soma Bay looks like an Egyptian temple, and indeed its design was inspired by Luxor's Karnak Temple. Extensive leisure facilities include a championship-standard golf course, a dive centre, spa and children's playground. **www.sheraton-somabay.com**

HURGHADA Tia Heights

Safaga Road, Makadi Bay, Hurghada **Tel** *065 3590 590* **Fax** *065 3590 595* **Rooms** *1048*

Located on a long stretch of sandy beach beside the Red Sea, this massive hotel offers five-star luxury. Rooms are extravagant, while the resort caters for guests of all ages, with facilities that include what is widely believed to be the largest swimming pool in the Middle East. **www.tiaheights.com**

HURGHADA Hilton Hurghada Plaza

Gabal El Hareem, Main Street, Hurghada **Tel** *065 3549 745* **Fax** *065 3547 597* **Rooms** *212*

The Hilton Hurghada Plaza will appeal to those who are after an active experience. Renowned for its scuba diving and watersports, the hotel offers a seemingly endless array of leisure amenities. An on-site restaurant offers international and Egyptian cuisine. **www.hilton.com**

HURGHADA InterContinental Abu Soma

Safaga Highway, Hurghada **Tel** *065 3260 700* **Fax** *065 3260 701* **Rooms** *445*

A large and luxurious resort, the InterContinental is set in extensive landscaped gardens that meander to the beach and the Red Sea. Its amenities include an excellent fitness centre, shops, a disco, tennis courts, a diving centre and other sporting facilities. **www.intercontinental.com**

ISMAILIA Mercure Forsan Island

Gezirat al-Forsan, Ismailia **Tel** *064 3916 316* **Fax** *064 3918 043* **Rooms** *129*

It would be hard to find a hotel that is quite so convenient as the Mercure Forsan Island. Situated on the edge of the city centre, close to attractions and yet enjoying the tranquillity of a private beach, it offers something for everyone. There is a swimming pool, restaurant, tennis court, watersports and garden lakeside walks. **www.mercure.com**

Key to Price Guide *see p268* **Key to Symbols** *see back cover flap*

MARSA ALAM Red Sea Diving Safari

Shagra Village, Marsa Alam **Tel** *065 3380 021* **Rooms** *50*

This environmental village is made up of huts and tents with shared bathrooms, and chalets with private bathrooms. It offers an outstanding diving programme and a range of leisure amenities. The complex is situated alongside the beach and opposite the famous Elphinstone Reef, a magnet for divers. **www.redseadivingsafari.com**

MARSA ALAM Shams Alam

Marsa Alam **Tel** *02 2417 0046* **Fax** *02 2417 0158* **Rooms** *160*

Shams Alam offers the chance to get away from it all, literally. This coastal resort is surrounded by open countryside, with little commercialism to be seen. On-site facilities include squash courts and table tennis, along with a swimming pool and restaurants. Rooms are housed in traditional vaulted buildings. **www.shams-dive.com**

NUWEIBA Basata Eco-lodge

Ras al-Burqa, Nuweiba **Tel** *069 3500 481* **Rooms** *26*

An extremely popular hotel and camp site, Basata lies around 22 km (14 miles) north of Nuweiba. Guests reside in mud and bamboo huts, an essential part of the owner's policy on eco-friendliness. The huts are located on the beach, a few steps from the sea. The hotel features its own kitchen and bakery. There are also a few chalets.

NUWEIBA La Sirene

Beach Road, Nuweiba **Tel** *069 3500 701* **Fax** *069 3500 702* **Rooms** *45*

La Sirene is set right on the beach at Nuweiba, halfway between the port and the city. It is a compact hotel that is pleasingly presented and well located for local amenities. It is getting a bit shabby and its facilities are few and far between, but they do include diving in season. **www.lasirene-hotel.de**

NUWEIBA Hilton Coral Resort

Nuweiba City **Tel** *069 3520 320* **Fax** *069 3520 327* **Rooms** *200*

This resort is located amid quiet beachside gardens and is famed for its tranquillity and beauty. It has lots of amenities, including diving, and tennis and squash courts. Other activities – such as kayaking, windsurfing and snorkelling – are all within walking distance. **www.hilton.com/worldwideresorts**

PORT SAFAGA Holiday Inn Resort Safaga Palace

Safaga, Red Sea **Tel** *065 3260 100* **Rooms** *327*

Situated on a long stretch of beach in a bay known for its excellent windsurfing, and with various water- and ball sports on site, this hotel is an activity enthusiast's delight. In addition, it offers good value for money, has well-presented rooms, live entertainment, restaurants and a fitness suite. **www.holidayinnresort.com/safagapalace**

PORT SAID Hotel de la Poste

Sharia al-Gumhuriyya, Port Said **Tel** *066 3224 048* **Fax** *066 3221 473* **Rooms** *51*

Entering the Hotel de la Poste is a little like stepping back in time. Although renovated, the hotel retains some of its 1940s architecture. All rooms have private bathrooms, fridge, air conditioning and TV. Apart from a small bar and a pâtisserie, it has few amenities, but its location in the heart of the city more than makes up for this.

PORT SAID Resta Port Said

Sultan Hussein Street, Port Said **Tel** *066 3325 511* **Fax** *066 3324 825* **Rooms** *110*

The Resta is popular with businesspeople and provides a good range of leisure amenities, such as a pool that over-looks the Suez Canal, a nearby fitness centre, shopping arcade, bar and choice of international restaurants. Rooms are modern and colourfully decorated. **www.restahotels.com**

QUSEIR Rocky Valley Beach Camp

North of El-Quseir, Quseir **Tel** *065 3335 247 or 010 6532 964* **Rooms** *10*

This is an unexpected gem of a camp, located a few kilometres north of El-Quseir town, with a lovely beach and good snorkelling. Quality huts, some with private bathrooms, run up the rocky hillside and the atmosphere is warm and welcoming. **www.rockyvalleydiverscamp.com**

QUSEIR Quseir-Sirena Beach Mövenpick

El Quadim Bay, Quseir **Tel** *065 3332 100* **Fax** *065 3332 129* **Rooms** *250*

This elegant hotel provides the perfect base for travelling the short distance into Quseir or the 125 km (78 miles) to Hurghada, and yet offers the chance of a relaxing break in a quiet resort beside the Red Sea. The rooms are beautifully presented. There are good leisure amenities and delightful gardens. **www.moevenpick-hotels.com**

RAS SUDR Moon Beach Resort

Ras Sudr, South Sinai **Tel** *062 4015 001* **Rooms** *50*

If a quiet, "get away from it all" break is required, then the Moon Beach Resort is perfect. Some 20 km (12 miles) from the nearest town, surrounded only by sand dunes and the clear blue Red Sea waters, it is renowned for its world-class kite surfing and windsurfing. The rooms are located inside domed huts.

SHARM EL-SHEIKH Shark's Bay Umbi Dive Village

Shark's Bay, Sharm el-Sheikh **Tel** *069 3600 942* **Fax** *069 3600 944* **Rooms** *96*

One of the most frequently visited camps in Sharm el-Sheikh and popular with families. Shark's Bay Camp sits on the beach in an isolated location, and has its own reef and diving centre, as well as a programme of safari and desert activities. Rooms are either bamboo huts or chalets, only the latter with air conditioning. **www.sharksbay.com**

SHARM EL-SHEIKH Amar Sina

Ras Um Sid, Sharm el-Sheikh **Tel** *069 3662 222* **Fax** *062 3662 233* **Rooms** *91*

The Amar Sina complex is designed and built to resemble a traditional white-washed Egyptian village, with architectural features like domes and arches. It has facilities such as a bar, shops, its own fitness centre and restaurants radiating from a central area. Rooms are pleasant, comfortable and air conditioned.

SHARM EL-SHEIKH Camel Dive Club and Hotel

Naama Bay, Sharm el-Sheikh **Tel** *069 3600 700* **Fax** *069 3600 601* **Rooms** *38*

Pretty and compact, the Camel has gained a reputation for providing not only top-class diving facilities, but also great cuisine in its award-winning restaurants. The hotel, which is located in Naama Bay, right in the centre of things, is renowned for its extensive facilities for disabled guests. **www.cameldive.com**

SHARM EL-SHEIKH Ritz-Carlton Resort

Om El Sid Peninsula, Sharm el-Sheikh **Tel** *069 3661 919* **Fax** *069 3661 920* **Rooms** *321*

Oozing luxury, this five-star hotel sits in beautifully landscaped gardens where cascading waterfalls combine with subtly lit pools and shrubbery. Its rooms are equally well presented, while on-site facilities include everything from fine international dining to superb golf, watersports and family activities. **www.ritzcarlton.com**

SHARM EL-SHEIKH Sofitel Sharm el-Sheikh

Naama Bay, Sharm el-Sheikh **Tel** *069 3600 081* **Fax** *069 3600 085* **Rooms** *302*

Perched high on the coastline next to the beach, this hotel offers what has to be the best panoramic view of Naama Bay. Amenities are in abundance and include a Turkish bathhouse complex, archery facilities, an ice-cream parlour and numerous restaurants. Guest rooms are attractive and most have sea views. **www.sofitel.com**

ST CATHERINE Al-Karm Eco Lodge

Wadi Gharbah, St Catherine **Tel** *069 3470 032/3* **Rooms** *50*

Located in a silent wadi, half an hour's drive from the village of El Tarfa, on the road between St Catherine's and Wadi Feiran, this bedouin-run lodge is a perfect getaway. There is great trekking in the vicinity. Staff speak little English, so it is probably best to arrange trips from St Catherine's with local help. **www.ecolodges.saharasafaris.org/alkarm**

ST CATHERINE Monastery Guest House

St Catherine's Monastery, St Catherine City **Tel** *069 3470 353* **Fax** *069 3470 343* **Rooms** *40*

Although a little lacking in luxuries, the Monastery Guest House more than makes up for it in atmosphere. Set against a stunning backdrop at the foot of Mount Sinai and right next to St Catherine's Monastery, it remains a firm favourite with travellers looking for a relaxing, "away from it all" establishment. The courtyard café serves alcohol.

SUEZ Red Sea Hotel

13 Sharia Riad, Port Tswfik, Suez **Tel & Fax** *062 3190 190* **Rooms** *75*

To some extent, the Red Sea Hotel has cornered the market in the Suez area – it is certainly one of the best hotels in which to stay. It is also known for its sixth-floor restaurant, which not only serves some fine international and Egyptian dishes and wine, but offers a truly great view over the Suez Canal. **www.redseahotel.com**

TABA Tobya Boutique Hotel

Km 2, Taba International Road, Taba **Tel** *069 3530 274 or 069 3530 275* **Fax** *069 3530 269* **Rooms** *100*

Though not exactly boutique, Tobya features outstanding architecture in a prime location, and it offers a highly personalized service, distinctive decor and good value. With its superb collection of attractive lamps, rugs and furniture, the hotel evokes a strong, almost museum-like atmosphere. **www.tobyaboutiquehotel.com**

TABA Marriott Taba Heights Beach Resort

Taba and Nuweiba Highway, Taba **Tel** *069 3580 100* **Fax** *069 3580 109* **Rooms** *394*

This is one of many luxury hotels on the extensive Taba Heights development. The Marriott's amenities are complemented by the resort's marina, an 18-hole golf course, a casino, a safari programme and top-class spas. The hotel restaurants cater for every taste from Japanese sushi and Indian dishes to European. **www.marriott.com**

ZAAFARANA Royal Zaafarana Resort

Coast Road, Zaafarana **Tel** *02 2417 2305* **Rooms** *221*

This popular resort is suitable for both active travellers, who will enjoy the range of watersports available at the beach (in particular windsurfing), and for those who like sightseeing, with the ancient monasteries of St Anthony and St Paul located nearby. As well as deluxe rooms, there are 45 villas which face onto the beach. **www.royalzaafarana.com**

THE DELTA AND THE NORTH COAST

ALEXANDRIA Acropole Hotel

27 Rue Chambre de Commerce, Midan Saad Zaghloul, Alexandria **Tel** *03 4805 980* **Rooms** *25*

The modest Acropole has few amenities, but it is housed in a fabulous Art Deco-style building with high ceilings and a touch of elegance – and all within easy reach of the beach and the bustling centre of Alexandria. Some of its rooms have balconies with either sea views or views of Midan Saad Zaghloul.

Key to Price Guide *see p268* **Key to Symbols** *see back cover flap*

ALEXANDRIA Union Hotel

164 Sharia 26th, Alexandria **Tel** *03 4807 312* **Fax** *03 4807 350* **Rooms** *40*

A mere ten-minute walk from Midan Saad Zaghloul, a must on the sightseeing agenda, this popular budget hotel is a good base to explore the city of Alexandria. The Art Deco-style building is full of character, while the rooms are comfortable and clean; most have private bathrooms and a balcony.

ALEXANDRIA Le Crillon Hotel

5 Sharia Adib Ishaq, Alexandria **Tel** *03 4800 330* **Rooms** *36*

Housed in a grand period building, Le Crillon Hotel doesn't pretend to be luxurious, but it is well presented and spotless. As such, it is hugely popular, and booking in advance is recommended. Many of the rooms have private bathroom facilities, and some have French doors and balconies with views out over the harbour.

ALEXANDRIA San Giovanni Hotel

205 Sharia Al Gueish, Stanley, Alexandria **Tel** *03 5467 775* **Fax** *03 5464 408* **Rooms** *32*

The mid-range San Giovanni is unfortunately located on a main road, busy with traffic, however rooms are pleasing and the price is fair. Some rooms have excellent sea views of Stanley Bay. Amenities include a pleasant bar and popular restaurants. **www.sangiovanni.com**

ALEXANDRIA Mercure Alexandria Romance

303 Sharla Al-Gueish, Saba Pasha, Alexandria **Tel** *03 5880 911* **Fax** *03 5880 526* **Rooms** *81*

In a modern and tastefully decorated high-rise building, this hotel stands proudly on the ridge of the upmarket Saba Pasha district, between Alexandria city centre and the Montazah Palace. Rooms are air conditioned and equipped with satellite television, and have a slight nautical theme. **www.accorhotels.com**

ALEXANDRIA Metropole Alexandria Hotel

52 Sharia Saad Zaghloul, Alexandria **Tel** *03 4861 467* **Fax** *03 4862 040* **Rooms** *66*

Clumsy makeovers have obscured some of the period detail, but rooms are large and many have good views. The hotel is situated on a busy thoroughfare that is great for absorbing the local atmosphere. The poet Constantine Cavafy is said to have stayed and worked here. **www.paradiseinnegypt.com**

ALEXANDRIA Sheraton Montazah Hotel

Corniche, Montazah, Alexandria **Tel** *03 5480 550* **Fax** *03 5401 331* **Rooms** *285*

The Sheraton Montazah stands at the end of a long stretch of beach and has a nice terrace, a disco and a bar. In addition to the bright, white wood decor, guests will also enjoy the location: less than 1 km from the Montazah Palace and gardens; around 10 km (4 miles) from the centre of town. **www.starwoodhotels.com**

ALEXANDRIA El-Salamlek Hotel

Montazah Palace, Alexandria **Tel** *03 5477 999* **Fax** *03 5473 585* **Rooms** *20*

Staying at the El-Salamlek will be a memorable experience, not least because the hotel is housed in a former palace. Built by HH Khedive Abbas Helmi II in 1892 as a hunting lodge, and later remodelled to become a refined hotel, it stands in gardens overlooking Montazah Bay and the sea. Luxury is guaranteed. **www.sangiovanni.com**

ALEXANDRIA Four Seasons

399 Sharia El Geish, San Stefano, Alexandria **Tel** *03 5818 000* **Fax** *03 5818 080* **Rooms** *118*

With stunning sea views of the Mediterranean and chic rooms designed by Pierre Yves Rocher, the Four Seasons is a glamorous addition to Alexandria's accommodation options. The hotel includes a spa and terraced restaurants with sea views. The San Stefano shopping complex and beach are nearby. **www.fourseasons.com/alexandria**

ALEXANDRIA Helnan Palentine Hotel

Montazah Palace, Alexandria **Tel** *03 5473 500* **Fax** *03 5473 378* **Rooms** *231*

This hotel has royal connections – not only does it overlook Montazah Royal Beach, it is surrounded by the gardens of the Montazah Palace, the summer home of the late King Farouk. A host of sports and leisure facilities is offered, along with decent rooms and relaxation areas. **www.helnan.com**

ALEXANDRIA Maritim Jolie Ville Alexandria

544 El Geish Avenue, Sidi Bishr, Alexandria **Tel** *03 5490 935* **Fax** *03 5497 690* **Rooms** *158*

Popular with business people, the Jolie Ville has above-average and well-presented amenities. These include good restaurants, a gym and valet service. The hotel is located in the Corniche at Sidi Bishr, overlooking the Mediterranean, a ten minute taxi ride from the city centre.

ALEXANDRIA Meditteranean Azur Hotel

Sharia Al-Gueish, Rushdi, Alexandria **Tel** *03 522 6001* **Fax** *03 522 6003* **Rooms** *160*

Unusually for Alexandria, this hotel is located directly on the beach, with chalets on two levels curved around gardens and pools. Quality furnishings make the modern rooms very comfortable, while public areas sparkle with marble and chandeliers. **www.azur.travel**

ALEXANDRIA Sofitel Cecil Hotel

16 Midan Saad Zaghloul, Alexandria **Tel** *03 4877 173* **Fax** *03 4855 655* **Rooms** *86*

Popular with corporate guests and tourists alike, this hotel is housed in a colonial-style building that gained its fame in the 1930s and 1940s when it hosted a myriad of famous guests. On-site facilities include a gym, sauna and a rooftop Chinese restaurant. **www.sofitel.com**

BAHARIYYA Desert Rose Eco Lodge 🍴 ⦿ ££

Bir Al-Matar, Bahariyya **Tel** *02 3984 0861* **Rooms** *11*

About 10 km (6 miles) north of the town centre, this charming guesthouse has mudbrick chalets with stone floors and palm trunk ceilings. The lodge feels rustic without sacrificing comfort and style. Organic produce is used in the restaurant and the desert safaris are excellent. Rooms are all triples. **www.desertrose-ecolodge.com**

MARSA MATROUH Reem Hotel 🍴 ££

Sharia El Corniche, Marsa Matrouh **Tel** *046 4933 605* **Fax** *046 4933 608* **Rooms** *59*

This hotel may not have many frills, but it is welcoming and the staff friendly. It is also situated right on the waterfront and close to the centre of Marsa Matrouh, making it a good base for sightseeing, coastal walks or visiting nearby resorts. Its compact restaurant offers a good choice of local and European fare.

MARSA MATROUH Rommel House Hotel £££

Sharia El Galaa, Marsa Matrouh **Tel** *046 4935 466* **Fax** *046 4932 485* **Rooms** *60*

The Rommel House is a small mid-range hotel in the centre of town. It offers pleasingly presented rooms with private bathroom facilities, televisions and fridges. While there is no restaurant as such, the hotel includes breakfast in the price. Staff can office advice on touring the area.

MARSA MATROUH Beau Site Hotel 📶🍴🏖🎬📺⦿🏊 ££££

Sharia El Shatee, Marsa Matrouh **Tel** *046 4932 066* **Fax** *046 4933 319* **Rooms** *170*

One of the most popular resort-style hotels in Marsa Matrouh, this modern, purpose-designed establishment nestles around its own private beach. It is a favourite of Egyptian families as well as foreign visitors. Air conditioned, it has pleasingly presented rooms with private bathrooms. **www.beausitehotel.com**

TANTA New Arafa Hotel 📶🍴🏖🎬📺⦿🏊 £££

Midan El Mahata, Tanta **Tel** *040 3405 040* **Fax** *040 3357 080* **Rooms** *62*

A mid-range, pink-painted establishment that tends to dominate Station Square, the New Arafa Hotel is well known locally and hugely popular. During the great Moulid of Sayed Ahmed al-Badawi festival in October it gets booked up quickly. Air conditioned and fairly modern, it has a delightful restaurant where alcohol is available.

THE WESTERN DESERT

BAHARIYYA Ahmed Safari Camp 🛏🍴 £

Bahariyya Oasis, Bawiti **Tel** *02 3847 2770* **Rooms** *20*

The Safari Camp comes as a bit of a surprise. Many of its rooms are beautifully presented, with domes adding to the character, while others have great views around their oasis setting. Most have private bathrooms. The camp, a favourite with travellers, has its own restaurant serving traditional dishes. **www.ahmedsafaricamp.com**

BAHARIYYA Alpenblick Hotel 🛏🍴📺 £

Bahariyya Oasis, Bawiti **Tel** *02 3847 2184* **Rooms** *23*

The oasis location of this hotel is like a magnet to budget travellers. The Alpenblick promotes a leisurely way of life, full of long evenings spent enjoying its traditional and hearty food and engaging in conversation with fellow backpackers. Rooms are simple and some have good private bathrooms, the luxury of hot water and air conditioning.

BAHARIYYA El-Beshmo Lodge 🛏🍴📺 £

Bahariyya Oasis, Bawiti **Tel** *02 3847 3500* **Rooms** *23*

To really get away from it all, you might want to book a stay at the El-Beshmo Lodge. It is beautifully located beside the palm-fringed El-Beshmo Springs at the Bahariyya Oasis, and offers an atmosphere of complete relaxation. Its rooms are comfortable and clean, with most featuring en-suite bathrooms and air conditioning. **www.elbeshmolodge.com**

BAHARIYYA Nature Lodge 🛏🍴 £££

Bir Al-Ghaba, Bahariyya **Tel** *012 1653 037* **Rooms** *14*

This is a peaceful retreat on the edge of the oasis, about 15 km (9 miles) north of Bawiti town, with gorgeous desert and mountain views all around. The reed huts have no electricity and share clean bathrooms. This is a great place to start a tour of the desert. **www.khaset-xp.com**

DAKHLA Bedouin Camp 🛏🍴 £

Sharia al-Qasr, Dakhla **Tel** *092 7850 480* **Rooms** *40*

Be prepared to relax and unwind in simple but delightful surroundings if staying at the Bedouin Camp. Its rooms are basic but comfortable, while its restaurant is housed in a tent, and diners sit on carpets and cushions on the floor. Hearty food is served. The Bedouin Camp is in an isolated location 7 km (4 miles) west of Mut. **www.dakhlabedouins.com**

DAKHLA El Negoum Hotel 🛏🏖📺⦿ £

Taril Elhendaw, Mut, Dakhla **Tel** *092 782 0114* **Fax** *092 787 3084* **Rooms** *56*

Located in a quiet street behind the tourist office in Mut, El Negoum offers clean, simply furnished rooms with private bathrooms, some with balconies overlooking the shaded garden. The price includes a basic breakfast. Larger groups can be catered for with buffet meals and there is a swimming pool.

Key to Price Guide *see p268* **Key to Symbols** *see back cover flap*

DAKHLA Mebarez Hotel

Sharia El-Tharwa, Mut, Dakhla **Tel & Fax** *092 7821 524* **Rooms** *33*

The Mebarez Hotel is popular with tour groups and individual travellers. It is situated on the main road to Al-Qasr and ideal for exploring the area. Rooms are comfortable, if drab, and have air conditioning and private bathrooms. A restaurant serving Egyptian cuisine adds to its charm.

DAKHLA Badawiya

Sharia Al-Qasr, Dakhla Oasis, Dakhla **Tel** *02 2526 0994* **Fax** *02 2528 7273* **Rooms** *50*

The Badawiya's traditional domed rooms line up along a small plateau with views to Al-Qasr. As part of the Badawiya Expedition Travel group, the hotel offers desert trips on camels, horses and bikes, as well as to the nearby hot springs. The restaurant serves simple but delicious Bedouin and international dishes. **www.badawiya.com**

DAKHLA Desert Lodge

Al-Qasr Village, Dakhla **Tel** *092 7877 062* **Fax** *02 2690 5250* **Rooms** *32*

Perched on top of a plateau behind the old village of Al-Qasr sits the Desert Lodge. The lodge's traditional domed rooms have ceiling fans rather than air conditioning. There is a pool in a private hot spring, a restaurant serving delicious local cuisine, a spa and a library. Desert trips can be arranged. **www.desertlodge.net**

EL KHARGA El Kharga Hotel

El Kharga Oasis, El Wadi El Guedid, El Kharga **Tel** *092 7924 940* **Fax** *092 7921 500* **Rooms** *30*

The El Kharga Oasis is a landmark building rising from the sand dune-surrounded oasis in which it stands. The staff are friendly and pride themselves on the lavishness of the well-kept tropical gardens filled with palm trees and native flowers. Rooms are simple and air conditioned in the main building, or there are chalets in the garden.

EL KHARGA Sol y Mar Pioneers Hotel

El Kharga Oasis, El Wadi El Guedid, El Kharga **Tel** *092 7929 751-3* **Fax** *092 7927 983* **Rooms** *102*

A stay at the Pioneers Hotel will feel a little like being on a film set – it is traditionally decorated in pure Egyptian style and stands surrounded by palm trees amid the sand dunes of the desert. The hotel lies minutes from the Hibis Temple and the Al-Bagawat Necropolis, both of which are must-visit sights on the tourist agenda. **www.solymar.com**

FARAFRA Badawiya Safari and Hotel

Qasr Al-Farafra **Tel** *092 7510 060* **Rooms** *33*

The Al-Badawiyya Safari and Hotel sounds grand. It is, in fact, a traditional mud-brick-constructed hotel – although you wouldn't guess it from its tasteful interior. Rooms are spacious and comfortable, and some have private bathrooms, while its restaurant is one of the best in this small village. There is an excellent pool area. **www.badawiya.com**

SIWA Alexander Hotel

Main Street, Siwa **Tel** *046 4600 512* **Rooms** *17*

A compact and modern hotel, the Alexander has a growing base of returning guests. It offers clean rooms with fans, some with private bathroom facilities. The hotel staff is especially proud of the Alexander the Great restaurant and delight in showing off the roof terrace.

SIWA Palm Trees Hotel

Siwa Oasis, Siwa **Tel** *046 4601 703* **Rooms** *26*

Situated just off the main street in the Siwa Oasis, this attractive little budget hotel stands in beautifully landscaped and tropical gardens. Its staff are friendly and always on hand to help organize excursions into the desert or further afield, but its amenities are few and some rooms are in need of an update.

SIWA Albabensha

Shali, Siwa **Tel** *046 4601 499 or 010 3614 140* **Rooms** *11*

This small hotel, created from the remains of the ancient gateway to Shali, combines tasteful luxury with simple rustic chic. The food is just wonderful, served on the rooftop terrace with views over the main square. Rooms are spacious and have large beds with white duvets and camel wool blankets.

SIWA Shali Lodge

Siwa Oasis, Siwa **Tel** *046 4601 299* **Fax** *046 4601 799* **Rooms** *16*

One of Siwa's hidden treasures. If you are planning a stay, be aware that booking is essential due to the hotel's small size and popularity. All the rooms are beautifully presented and set around a palm-fringed water feature, and are just seconds away from the hotel's outdoor restaurant, where the chef delights in banter.

SIWA Siwa Safari Paradise Hotel

Sharia Ein El Arais, Siwa **Tel** *046 4601 290* **Fax** *046 4601 592* **Rooms** *74*

Set in a delightful garden environment and close to the centre of Siwa and its amenities, the Siwa Safari Paradise is popular with travellers, tour groups and families alike. It resembles a small resort in style, and its pretty bungalows all feature air conditioning, televisions and en-suite bathrooms.

SIWA Adrere Amellal

Sidi Jaafar, Maraki Village, Siwa **Tel & Fax** *02 2736 7879* **Rooms** *35*

One of Egypt's first eco projects, the Adrere Amellal is built in the traditional Siwan style and amenities include its own spring-water supply. Its swimming pool is created out of the natural rocks that surround the spring. Its restaurant uses organically grown produce and dinner is a five star experience lit by starlight.

WHERE TO EAT

According to an Egyptian proverb, "the best food is that which fills the belly". Traditional Egyptian cooking combines Arabic and Turkish with European and African influences. The result is sometimes described as bland, but this is unjust. Hearty main dishes are usu-ally accompanied by a selection of pickles and dips, so you can spice up or cool down your meal as you wish. The cuisine is dominated by *semna* (clarified butter), which ensures a rich taste and a heavy impact on the arteries. Egyptians often say no

Aish bread filled with *taamiyya*

meal is complete without meat, yet *fuul* (mashed fava beans), *taamiyya* (deep-fried patties filled with fava bean paste and green herbs, otherwise known as *falafel*) and *koshari* (a mixture of noodles, rice, lentils and onions) – the meatless staples of the poor – are consumed by all classes. Most large Egyptian towns have a few old-fashioned European restaurants, along with growing numbers of fast-food outlets and restaurants serving a wide range of ethnic cuisines. Even better, restaurants are increasingly serving a variety of traditional local dishes.

RESTAURANTS AND BARS

In much of Egypt, the idea of dining out is quite new. As a result, the wide range of dishes that Egyptians eat at home is simply not available in restaurants. Their delicious meat and vegetable stews, for example, are hard to find in a restaurant, except during the month of Ramadan. There is, however, a distinct Egyptian cuisine that adapts remarkably well to modern demands for fast food. *Fuul* sandwiches or roasted chicken (*firakh*), for example, are likely to be sold in any settlement bigger than a hamlet. Most towns have at least one *kebabgi*, offering a selection of kebabs and a choice of several salads. These are often accompanied by dips such as *tahina* (made from sesame paste) and *babaghanoush* (grilled aubergine and *tahina*). Quality varies, but eating out at a good kebab place is an experience not to be missed. Pigeon is another popular

dish in Egypt. It is stuffed with rice and spices and roasted, or cooked in a stew (*tagine*) with onions and tomatoes.

The culture of dining out is most deeply rooted in the cosmopolitan Mediterranean city of Alexandria, where a number of Greek, Italian and French restaurants and cafés still thrive. Alexandria is also rightly famous for its seafood, which can be eaten at an open-air grill or in one of the town's restaurants. Either way it will be fresh and delicious.

In Cairo, the foreign embassy community alone is enough to keep several old European-style restaurants in business.

Younger expatriates and upper-class Egyptians tend to frequent Cairo's trendier restaurant-bars, with flashy décor, loud music and varia-tions on *nouvelle* Mediterra-nean fare. More and more ethnic restaurants are opening, and now it is possible to get a full range of Asian food, from Korean and Chinese to Thai and Indonesian.

Many fashionable restaurants double as bars, so going for an evening meal can easily turn into a full-scale night out. Cairo has the remnants of a colonial café scene and some of these places, such as Café Riche, are enjoying a revival. Cairo also has a few traditional-style pubs, which often provide some form of food. Bars usually display signs stating a minimum drinking age of 21, but this guideline is not applied very strictly.

Lively night-time café culture in Cairo

Modern Mediterranean dining at Maison Thomas, Cairo

OPENING HOURS

Street stalls selling snacks of *fuul* and *taamiyya* open at the crack of dawn for a basic breakfast. Juice bars are usually open from 8am–10pm, serving freshly squeezed juice. *Koshari* restaurants and shops selling *baladi* sandwiches (*baladi* is a flat, round, country bread) open around 10am. Most other restaurants, unless specifically serving breakfast, open at midday. Very few establishments open before 1pm on Fridays, except those that cater specifically for foreign visitors.

Egyptians tend to eat their main meal in the afternoon, and most restaurants close around 11pm to 1am.

PRICES AND PAYING

In Egyptian restaurants, dishes are usually ordered individually rather than as fixed combinations. In many establishments, *mezzes (see pp288–9)* will be brought to your table, whether or not you order them. These will be charged for, so send them back if you do not want them and make sure that they are not included on your bill.

A service charge of 12 per cent is added automatically to every restaurant bill, but customers are expected to pay a small tip as well – usually an additional 10 per cent, but not more than LE 10. So once the sales tax of 5 per cent is added on, diners are paying more than 20 per cent over the price of their food.

BOOKING

Reservations are required only at the most upmarket restaurants. Such places will have a telephone, and most of them will have at least some staff who speak English. Attempts to book a table at less upmarket establishments can prove frustrating, however, and it is likely that there will be no record of your call when you arrive at the restaurant. Nevertheless, the staff will probably be most accommodating and make every effort to find you a table.

ETIQUETTE

As is the case generally in Egypt, shorts and short skirts are not appropriate attire for restaurants. Other than that, however, most places are quite relaxed as far as dress code is concerned.

Traditional Egyptian dishes and formal dining at Alfi Bey restaurant, Cairo

Egyptians like to dress smartly when going out – including visits to fast-food outlets, which are considered trendy by young Egyptians. Foreign visitors can usually get away with wearing fairly casual clothing, but in more upmarket establishments a shirt with a collar, and shoes rather than sandals, would be advisable. On the other hand, it is not unusual to see women dressed in cocktail dresses, especially late in the evenings.

In Egypt, smoking is inescapable in bars and pervasive in restaurants. Some of the more expensive restaurants in Cairo have established no-smoking sections, but these areas tend to be small and are often tucked away in a corner, surrounded by smoking tables. Fast-food establishments are now smoke-free, thanks to a campaign by the environment ministry.

CHILDREN

Children are welcome in most restaurants and cafés before about 11pm, though it would not be appropriate to bring them along to places that are primarily drinking establishments. Some restaurants have gardens with play equipment. The Felfela and Andrea chains, for example, have several child-friendly branches, including those on the Corniche and in the Pyramids area.

A Cairo juice bar, offering a variety of freshly squeezed fruit juices

Stall in Aswan selling deep-fried fava bean and herb patties, known as *taamiyya*

DISABLED CUSTOMERS

Few Egyptian establishments have facilities for disabled customers, such as wheelchair access, though staff will be willing to help customers overcome any obstacles. Public toilets with wheelchair access are unheard of, but at least the traditional hole-in-the-floor type is almost extinct.

FAST-FOOD OUTLETS

While there has been some form of international fast-food in Egypt since the 1970s, the last few years have seen a proliferation of international brand names. All the big American chains (except for Burger King) are here, as well as some less well-known South African outlets. As in the rest of the world, these places have become favourite haunts of the young.

Apart from these international chains, Egypt has its own indigenous fast-food tradition. As well as the ubiquitous street stalls selling snacks of bread *(aish)* stuffed with *fuul* and *taamiyya*, there are stalls that specialize in other traditional snacks. *Koshari*, a mixture of rice, noodles and crispy fried onions in a spicy tomato sauce, is sold at stand-up stalls and sit-down restaurants, while more expensive, café-like establishments known as *fatatri* specialize in *fatir*. A cross between pancakes and pizzas, these are made from filo pastry and come with sweet or savoury fillings.

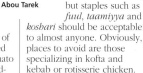

Koshari served at Abou Tarek

VEGETARIAN FOOD

Vegetarianism is extremely rare in Egypt and, as a result, vegetarian restaurants are almost unheard of – L'Aubergine in Zamalek *(p 293)* is one of the few exceptions. However, many Egyptian dishes contain no meat, and restaurants in the cheaper range frequently serve only meatless dishes. More expensive restaurants will usually have a few vegetarian dishes on the menu. Strict vegans could have a harder time, but staples such as *fuul*, *taamiyya* and *koshari* should be acceptable to almost anyone. Obviously, places to avoid are those specializing in kofta and kebab or rotisserie chicken.

HYGIENE

Suffering some degree of gastric ailment in Egypt seems to be fairly inevitable for anyone spending more than a few days there, but experienced travellers have come up with a few rules of thumb. Some suggest you avoid raw vegetables and salads, particularly lettuce, because these are often not properly washed. (Pickled vegetables that come as an appetizer should be safe,

Cairo's Café Riche – a reminder of Egypt's colonial café scene

however). Others believe that the real problem is with the meat. Although it might seem that eating only at the more expensive restaurants would minimize the risk, there are stories of people getting sick everywhere. Fast food is usually safer but, once again, there are exceptions and people have got just as sick from the big chains' burgers as from kofta sandwiches.

In major towns and cities, tap water is safe to drink though heavy chlorination does little for the taste. New arrivals should stick to mineral water *(mayya maadaniyya)*, which is readily available. When buying bottles of mineral water, always check that the seal is intact. *(see also Health Precautions, pp334–5)*.

RAMADAN

Ramadan is an interesting (though also potentially frustrating) time to be in Egypt. The ninth month of the Islamic calendar, Ramadan is a period akin to Lent in the Christian church, with a fast that involves abstention from food, drink and smoking during daylight hours. The fast is strictly observed and days revolve around waiting for sunset. Then the sunset call to prayer is made, lamps are lit on the minarets and everyone gets down to eating the first meal of the day and enjoying the night-time celebrations. During Ramadan, restaurants

Mint tea

may be open during the day, but only tourists will be eating and fewer options will be available. Travellers may prefer to postpone their meal until after sunset, especially since the cooks making the food and the waiters serving it will not have eaten all day. At sunset, most restaurants are packed, and many set up huge tents so they can fit in as many customers as possible. These feasts provide a good opportunity to get to meet a cross-section of Egyptian society. Everyone sits together at long tables and will probably be quite friendly – once they've eaten.

A wider, more interesting range of traditional dishes will be available during Ramadan, and restaurants will be open throughout the night, in order to serve *sohour*, the last meal before sunrise. In addition, certain drinks, such as apricot juice *(amar el din)*, and foods are specific to this time of the Islamic calendar.

ENTERTAINMENT

If you are keen to combine dining out with some form of entertainment, then your best bet is to book a table at one of Cairo's five-star hotels. Most of these have nightclubs where a flat charge covers an excellent four-course meal and a floor show featuring some of Egypt's most popular dancers and traditional musicians. Smart dress and reservations are required at these venues.

For a variation on this idea, you might like to try one of Cairo's floating restaurants. Many of these offer cruises on the Nile, during which lunch or dinner is served to the accompaniment of live Egyptian music or a floor show complete with belly dancers and band. In Zamalek and Giza there are also luxury Nile Cruisers from a bygone era that remain moored, serving food in opulent surroundings. These restaurants often also have live entertainment.

If five-star hotels are beyond your means, there are less expensive nightclubs, where dinner is served and entertainment is provided – though both food and performances are likely to be of variable standard. Several of these clubs are located on the Pyramids Road and Downtown.

Remember that nightlife in Cairo doesn't really begin until after midnight, with the floor shows going on as late as 3 or 4 in the morning.

Felfela restaurant in Cairo offers dishes with a European flavour

The Flavours of Egypt

Egypt shares many dishes with its Mediterranean and Middle Eastern neighbours. The cuisine leans heavily towards earthy pulses, brightly coloured vegetables, gamey meats and hearty stews, with the use of spices and simmering cooking methods infusing dishes with warmth. Cooking techniques from the time of the Pharaohs are still in existence today and the food in this part of North Africa excels in both freshness and flavour. If you are invited to an Egyptian home then you could expect to enjoy soup, some meat and a vegetable-based stew with bread and salad. Desserts are not as rich as those of many other Arab countries.

Fresh figs

Spices sit alongside coloured dyes on a market stall

MEAT, POULTRY & GAME

Egyptian families view meat as a luxury and it is often served in small amounts or combined with rice and vegetables, such as in stuffed vine leaves, to make it go further. As a result, whenever meat is to be served as a main dish it is prepared with a great deal of care and attention. Poultry is usually roasted, and lamb, mutton and veal are also popular, although beef isn't typically eaten. Meat and poultry may be stuffed with fruit, nuts and rice. Try the traditional delicacy that is pigeon *(hamaam)*. These birds are raised throughout the country and are stuffed with seasoned rice before being grilled. But be warned – some chefs serve the head of the bird, buried in the stuffing.

FISH & SEAFOOD

Ever since ancient times, Egyptians have enjoyed fish fresh from the Nile, salted or dried by being hung out in the strong sun to bake. Today Egyptians serve both freshwater and sea fish under the general term of *samak*. The best sea fish come from shallow coastal waters and the best fresh-water ones are found at Aswan, where they are

Hummus   *Babaghanoush*   Egyptian salad   Falafel   *Aish*
Olives   *Sabanikhiyat*
Fuul
Stuffed vine leaves

Some of the many dishes that make up typical Egyptian *mezzes*

EGYPTIAN DISHES AND SPECIALITIES

Koshari is the rich, hearty dish of pasta, pulses and vegetables that has long been considered part of the Egyptian identity, eaten both at home and at market. Another classic dish is *molokiya* – the best versions of this herby green soup are found in Aswan and Luxor, although variations are found throughout the land. The waters of the Red Sea teem with some of the country's finest perch and tuna, and *sayyaddia* (fish with rice) features on many an Egyptian menu. A *mezze* is an easy way to enjoy a whole range of bite-sized Egyptian delicacies such as *sabanikhiyat* (spinach turn-overs), *kofta* (meatballs), *babaghanoush* (a smoky aubergine/eggplant purée), hummus and *fuul* (a lemony broad/fava bean dip). Bread *(aish)*, in particular the flat *baladi* bread, accompanies dips.

Chickpeas (garbanzos)

Molokiya *soup is named for the muculaginous green mallow leaves that flavour it. It may be served without meat.*

Goods piled high in palm-leaf baskets at a village grocer's shop

caught from Lake Nasser. Common bass and sole feature frequently but so do shrimps, squid, scallops and eel. Eel can be sampled, deep-fried, at markets.

VEGETABLES & FRUIT

Robust root vegetables such as garlic and onion are vital to much of Egypt's cooking and are also cherished for their health benefits. Peas and beans are sometimes eaten on their own with a plain oil and vinegar dressing. Potatoes *(bataatis)* are often fried but can also be boiled or stuffed. Dried vegetables are also used a great deal. Egyptian salads *(salata)* feature lettuce, tomatoes, cucumber, potatoes, olives or eggs and sometimes even beans and yogurt. Fruit is eaten after a meal, with juicy

plums and pomegranates joining dates for a rich choice in sweetness. Figs have been hugely popular since ancient times. Fresh, dried or as a syrup, they appear in savoury dishes and breads as well as in sweets.

Waiter bringing a tray of mint teas at a Cairo café

DAIRY PRODUCE

Egyptian cheese, known as *gibna*, comes in two varieties. White, fresh *Gibna beida* has a salty, clean taste similar to Greek feta, while *gibna rumy* is a sharper-tasting cheese with a pale yellow colour. They are most often found in salads and sandwiches. *Bhouzat haleeb*, or ice cream, shares little in common with its rich Western namesake. It has a fresh, light texture that even stretches a little as you scoop it. Egyptian yoghurt *(laban zabadi)* is fresh and unflavoured but is usually served sweetened with such things as honey, jam, preserves, nuts, figs or dates.

WHAT TO DRINK

Despite Egypt being a Muslim country, alcohol is widely available in restaurants and bars. The local Stella and Sakkara lagers are good and the quality of Egyptian wines has improved greatly in recent years. Hot drinks include *chai* (mint tea) and *ahwa* (Arabic coffee) which is strong and either *ziyada* (sweet), *mazboota* (medium) or *saada* (bitter). *Karkade*, an infusion made from hibiscus leaves, is served hot or cold. Freshly squeezed fruit juices, including delicious and unusual ones such as apricot, are widely available and are very refreshing, as is *asab*, a sweet, light-green drink with a foamy head, made from pressed sugarcane.

Koshari *combines pasta, rice, lentils and pulses with a spicy tomato sauce and crispy onions.*

Sayyaddia *is simply a whole fresh fried fish such as sole, flounder, trout or bass, served with rice and lemon.*

Mahallabiyaa *is a delicately rosewater-flavoured ground rice dessert, topped with toasted nuts and cinnamon.*

Choosing a Restaurant

The restaurants in this guide have been selected across a wide range of price categories for their good value, good food, atmosphere and interesting location. This chart lists the restaurants by region. Within each town or city, entries are listed by price category, from the least expensive to the most expensive.

PRICE CATEGORIES (IN EGYPTIAN POUNDS – EGP)
For a three-course meal for one, including coffee, tax and service.
€ Under 30 EGP
€€ 30–50 EGP
€€€ 50–100 EGP
€€€€ 100–150 EGP
€€€€€ Over 150 EGP

CAIRO

CAIRO Abou Tarek
€

16 Sharia Marouf, Downtown **Tel** *02 2577 5935*　　　**Map** *5 C2*

Serving Egypt's universal staple dish *koshari*, a mix of pasta, rice, lentils and a tomato sauce with crispy onions, Abou Tarek is a renowned and well-liked eaterie. Order a medium or large bowl then finish your meal with *roz bi leban* (rice pudding).

CAIRO Koshari Embrator
€

Sharia 26th July, Downtown　　　**Map** *1 C4*

There are several Koshari Embrator branches in the city, but this one is conveniently located next to Nasser Metro, right in the centre. The *koshari* (a popular traditional Egyptian vegetarian dish, with rice, lentils and tomato) is excellent, and they also serve a variety of meat tagines (a slow cooked stew).

CAIRO Akher Sa'a
€€

8 Sharia Alfy Bey, Downtown　　　**Map** *2 D4*

This is the perfect place to introduce yourself to Egyptian staples such as *tamaiya* (a version of falafel that uses fava beans instead of chickpeas), *fuul* (a breakfast dish made out of fava beans), *shakshouka* (a kind of frittata) and salads, plus they do a perfect lentil soup. Food is served in a canteen-style environment that is purely functional, and it's open 24 hours.

CAIRO Ar-Rifai
€€

Sharia al-Barrani (opposite Sayyida Zeinab Mosque), Midan Sayyida Zeinab　　　**Map** *4 D2*

Dining on tasty traditional Egyptian dishes, including what many would say are the city's best kebabs, and watching the world go by is what makes Ar-Rifai a special kind of eaterie. Diners don't sit indoors – rather, a series of tables is laid out in the street outside. Closed for lunch.

CAIRO Didos Al-Dente
€€

Sharia Bahgat Ali, Zamalek **Tel** *02 2735 9117*　　　**Map** *1 A2*

This modern and bright restaurant offers an extensive and varied menu of international dishes. Didos Al-Dente is especially renowned for its pasta creations, which wouldn't be out of place in a top Italian eaterie. It is situated in one of the main thoroughfares of this upmarket Cairo district, close to tourist attractions and a market.

CAIRO Egyptian Pancake House
€€

Midan Hussein, Khan al Khalili　　　**Map** *2 F5*

If you are after pancakes – or *fateers*, the Egyptian equivalent made of pastry and served with chicken, fish or other meats, or fruit and honey as a filling – then the Egyptian Pancake House will satisfy your appetite. Located just off Midan Hussein, this place is easy to find and well worth seeking out.

CAIRO Fatari Pizza Tahir
€€

Sharia at-Tahrir, Downtown **Tel** *02 2795 3596*　　　**Map** *1 C5, 5 B4*

Visitors to this 24-hour downtown eaterie could be forgiven for thinking that it serves Italian pizzas. In fact, Fatari Pizza Tahir serves *fateers*, which are more like pancakes and thoroughly enjoyable. Toppings include various cheeses, meats and fish. Sweet versions with honey and fruit are also available.

CAIRO Pottery Café
€€

35 Sharia Mohammed Mahmoud, Downtown **Tel** *02 2796 0260*　　　**Map** *5 C4*

This cosy little café opposite the American University in Cairo Downtown campus will have more room now that the university has moved out of town. Pop in for refreshing juices, coffee, sandwiches, snacks and creative pasta dishes. There's also another branch in Zamalek. Both have an impressive range of *Sheeshas*.

CAIRO Abu Bassem Grill
€€€

2 Zuqqaq Al-Gahini, Midan Hussein, Khan al Khalili **Tel** *02 2593 7935*　　　**Map** *2 F5*

One of Cairo's best-kept secrets and a popular haunt of locals, Abu Bassem Grill serves some of the best kebabs and mezzes in the Midan Hussein area. Weather permitting, it is possible to eat alfresco. Diners who decide to stay inside, however, can gaze at the restaurant's medieval surroundings, which are outstanding.

Key to Symbols *see back cover flap*

CAIRO Abu Shakra

££££

69 Sharia Qasr El-Aini, Downtown **Tel** *02 2531 6111*

Open for over 60 years and still one of the oldest and best-loved grills in Cairo, Abu Shakra is a real institution. The restaurant is traditional and inviting, with leg of lamb, kofta and grilled chicken all key elements of the menu. Vegetarians can enjoy the selection of delicious salads and soups available.

CAIRO Alfy Bey

££££

3 Sharia Al-Alfy, Sharia Mohammed Alfy, Downtown **Tel** *02 2577 1888*   **Map** *6 D2*

Alfi Bey is well located for Cairo city centre and a great place to stop for a light lunch in between sightseeing excursions. It serves Egyptian food cooked to traditional recipes, along with salads and starters; your meal comes complete with a moderately priced bill. No alcohol is served, but there is a good choice of other beverages.

CAIRO Aly Hasan Al-Haty & Aly Abdou

££££

Sharia Halim Pasha, Downtown **Tel** *02 2591 6055*   **Map** *6 D2*

Housed in an elegant, high-ceilinged colonial-style property in a busy area of the city, this restaurant has a long history of being the natural choice for Cairo's elite – in its heyday, it was the haunt of movie stars and politicians. Nowadays, it is frequented by business people and tourists keen to sample its selection of meat and kebab dishes.

CAIRO Arabesque

££££

8 Sharia Qasr el-Nil, Zamalek, Downtown **Tel** *02 2574 8677*   **Map** *1 C5*

Conveniently located just off Midan Tahrir, three minutes' walk from the Egyptian Museum, Arabesque is appealingly decorated and dimly lit. Cuisine is chiefly Egyptian and the restaurant provides an opportunity to sample less commonly served recipes, such as *besara*, a thick bean paste.

CAIRO Arabica

££££

20 Sharia Mohammed Marashly, Zamalek **Tel** *02 2735 7982*   **Map** *1 A2*

A small but perfectly formed café with fresh juices and a delicious selection of salads and pastas. The signature dish is Egyptian pizza – the *fateer* in traditional sweet and savoury guises with some international twists. A good spot to hang out, read the huge selection of English language magazines, use the free wireless Internet access and people watch.

CAIRO Ataturk

££££

20 Sharia al-Riyadh, Mohandiseen **Tel** *02 3305 5832*

A restaurant serving an extensive menu of traditional dishes from Turkey, Ataturk is usually buzzing with diners. Its *mezzes* are especially popular; as a seemingly never-ending succession of dishes arrives at your table, you begin to wonder how long the meal will go on for. *Mezzes* can comprise up to 20 dishes. No alcohol is served. Open late.

CAIRO Bull's Eye

££££

32 Sharia Geddah, Mohandiseen **Tel** *02 3761 6888*

Cairo's closest thing to a pub, Bull's Eye hits the mark with excellent meals as well as a convivial atmosphere from the mix of locals and tourists. Come early for steak and pub meals then stay on for a game of darts (they have weekly tournaments) or, on Wednesday nights, some karaoke singing.

CAIRO Café Riche

££££

17 Sharia Talaat Harb, Downtown **Tel** *02 2391 8873*   **Map** *1 C5, 5 C3*

A lively downtown restaurant and bar serving traditional Egyptian and international cuisine, Café Riche is popular with both locals and tourists. With lots of atmosphere, this historic eaterie has portraits of some of its best customers, including a few Egyptian film and stage stars, adorning its richly coloured walls.

CAIRO Cellar Door

££££

9 Sharia 151 (off Midan El Horreya), Maadi **Tel** *02 2359 8328*

This popular bistro is one of the reasons Downtowners will make the journey out to Maadi. The experimental chef twists Italian cuisine and draws upon other European influences. Roast shoulder of lamb is a speciality, while pork also makes it onto the menu. Be sure to check the specials list. The wine list includes local and sometimes French wines. Closed Sunday.

CAIRO Chopsticks

££££

23b Sharia Syria, Mohandiseen **Tel** *02 3304 8568*

Chopsticks, as its name implies, is a lively, colourful restaurant serving some of the finest Chinese and Malaysian dishes in Cairo. Authentic specialities from Singapore are also on the menu. With prices that are competitive and a good wine list, the restaurant is popular with local residents, businesspeople and tourists alike.

CAIRO Citadel Studio Misr

££££

Al-Azhar Park, Sharia Salah Salem **Tel** *02 2510 9150*   **Map** *4 F1*

Located in a grand faux-Mamluk building, with commanding views over Islamic Cairo and the Al-Azhar Park, this restaurant serves grilled meats and *mezze*. You can choose from either a buffet or the a la carte menu, and there is a terrace for *al fresco* dining. This is also the perfect spot to watch the sunset.

CAIRO El-Nil Fish Restaurant

££££

21 Sharia Al-Bustan, Midan Falaki, Bab al-luq   **Map** *5 C3*

This is a reasonably priced and enduringly popular fish restaurant with a constant turnover of happy customers. Choose fresh fish from a selection on ice, to be grilled, baked or fried, and try not to fill up on all the *mezze* which is served beforehand. Eating here is a clean, simple, no frills experience.

CAIRO El-Tekkia

12 Midan Ibn al-Walid, Dokki **Tel** *02 3749 6673*

Conveniently located in the centre of Dokki, near the Shooting Club, and specializing in good, home-cooked Egyptian food, this air-conditioned restaurant is a good bet to experience local cuisine. The dishes are well presented, the atmosphere is welcoming, and the staff are helpful and friendly.

CAIRO Estoril

Sharia Talaat Harb, Downtown **Tel** *02 2574 3102*

Map *1 C5, 5 B3*

Located in downtown Cairo, away from the hustle and bustle of the city centre, this much-frequented Franco-Levantine restaurant renowned for its good food is a great place to dine at a relaxed pace. The menu features a good range of vegetarian dishes and mezes, including numerous local delicacies.

CAIRO Farahat

126a Sharia Al-Azhar, Khan al Khalili **Tel** *02 2592 6595*

Map *2 F5*

A café by day, Farahat becomes a restaurant after the dusk call to prayer. It is "the" place in Cairo for pigeon, which comes grilled or stuffed (with flavoured rice and heart or liver) and is delicious either way. If pigeon doesn't appeal, there are kebabs and *kofta* too. Join locals here until dawn, then watch the markets wake up.

CAIRO The Greek Club

Sharia Qasr el-Nil, Downtown **Tel** *02 2575 0759*

Map *5 C3*

The Greek Club, or Le Club Hellenique, is a great place to dine on traditional European dishes, especially in the summer months, when everyone moves outside on to the large balcony to eat alfresco. Colder evenings are spent in the colonial-style dining hall, which also oozes charm. This eaterie has its own bar and a wine list.

CAIRO Jo Sushi

47 Sharia Mohammed Mazhar, Zamalek **Tel** *02 2735 7746*

Map *1 A2*

One of the favourite haunts for the local community. This busy, successful restaurant is a great little place serving authentic Japanese and Chinese dishes at outstandingly good prices. The decor is a little plain, but the atmosphere and free starters more than make up for it. They also have a branch in Doqqi.

CAIRO Le Cairo 1940

17 Sharia Hassan Sabry, Zamalek **Tel** *02 2735 2906*

Map *1 A3*

In dining rooms with decor, furniture and memorabilia that takes guests back to the 1940s, this restaurant serves up delicious Egyptian specialities, including *tahina* and *hummus* with chunks of fresh bread, followed by *melokiyah* or another soup usually served at Ramadan but available any time here. No alcohol is served, but *sheesha* is available.

CAIRO Maison Thomas

157 Sharia 26th July, Zamalek **Tel** *02 2735 7057*

Map *1 A2*

Maison Thomas is widely regarded as the place to go for European-style sandwiches, light snacks, takeaways and Italian pizzas. Being located in the heart of the Zamalek district, close to many of Cairo's major tourist attractions, it makes a good stopping-off point for a quick bite between sightseeing tours. It is open round the clock.

CAIRO The Windsor

19 Sharia Alfy Bey, Downtown **Tel** *02 2591 5810*

Map *6 D2*

The historical Windsor Hotel is an institution in Cairo and whatever corners may be cut in the kitchen are more than made up for by the atmospheric restaurant and adjacent Barrel Lounge bar. Enjoy some Egyptian *mezzes* with a couple of local Stella beers for a truly Cairene experience.

CAIRO Bua Khao

9 Sharia 151, Maadi **Tel** *02 2358 0126*

A delicious and authentic family-run Thai restaurant in the leafy, up-river Maadi area, a 20 minutes' taxi ride from the city centre. Ingredients are flown fresh from Thailand and used to make such dishes as spicy red curry and light *pad Thai*. There are excellent Thai coffees too. Although the restaurant is spacious, reservations are recommended.

CAIRO The Cairo Jazz Club

197 Sharia 26th July, Agouza **Tel** *02 3459 939*

The Cairo Jazz Club, near Midan Sphinx, has earned a name for being "the" place to hear good, live music. This well-deserved reputation means the place is always buzzing with locals, as well as with tourists looking for a good evening's entertainment. The menu is Egyptian with a modern twist, and there is a good wine selection, too.

CAIRO Charwood's

53 Sharia Gamat al-Dowal el-Arabia, Mohandiseen **Tel** *02 3749 0893*

Map *2 D4, 5 C2*

Excellent service and a cosy environment has ensured a loyal following among locals and expats. Charwood's specialises in steaks served with a mixed salad and freshly baked bread made on the premises. There is also seafood on offer, although vegetarians may be limited to pizza. Desserts are varied but excellent. Alcohol is served.

CAIRO Felfela

15 Sharia Hoda Shaarawi, Downtown **Tel** *02 2404 8707 or 02 2392 2833 (take-away)*

Map *1 C5, 5 C3*

A cosy restaurant in downtown Cairo, Felfela has a true European flavour. Its staff speak good English, and its menu of chicken, meat, fish and vegetarian dishes is clearly designed to attract the tourists. However, the place is renowned for serving good-quality food at good prices. Don't miss one of the delicious, if extravagant, desserts.

Key to Price Guide *see p290* **Key to Symbols** *see back cover flap*

CAIRO Five Bells

13 Sharia Ismail Mohammed, Zamalek **Tel** *02 2735 8980*
Map *1 A2*

The menu at Five Bells has a tempting selection of classic French and Mediterranean dishes; none disappoints. Diners can choose to eat in the classic dining area inside or, on warmer days and evenings, outside in the restaurant's own garden. A fine wine list completes the superior experience.

CAIRO Harry's Pub

Cairo Marriott Hotel, Sharia Saray al-Gezira, Zamalek **Tel** *02 2735 8888*
Map *1 A2*

Harry's Pub is a popular restaurant-bar attracting both locals and tourists. Its extensive menu offers roasts, cottage pie, and steak and kidney puddings, all served with lashings of gravy; there's also a wine list to complete the meal. Sports fans can enjoy matches on the big-screen televisions and there's karaoke at the weekend.

CAIRO Kandahar

Sharia Gamaat al-Dawal al-Arabiyya, Mohandiseen **Tel** *02 3303 0615*

One of the best-established restaurants in Cairo, located just off the Midan Sphinx, Kandahar has a cosy, traditional ambience, which makes it a popular place. It serves a good selection of Far Eastern food, especially Indian dishes, which can be hot or moderate on request. Adjacent is Raousha, a good Lebanese from the same management.

CAIRO Khan Al-Khalili

5 Al-Badistan, Khan al Khalili **Tel** *02 2590 3788*
Map *2 F5*

Managed by the Oberoi Hotel group, the über-slick Khan Al-Khalili offers traditional Egyptian dishes in dramatic surroundings that have been created to resemble an Eastern salon – *sheeshas* add to the authenticity. It is popular with tour groups and tourists who have been tipped off by their holiday companies and locals too.

CAIRO Kowloon

Cleopatra Palace Hotel, 1 Sharia Bustan, Midan Tahir, Downtown **Tel** *02 2575 9831*
Map *5 B3*

Dining at Kowloon, the restaurant within the Cleopatra Palace Hotel, is a memorable experience, not least because of the fish tank and retro Asian decor. The food is also wonderful though, and inspired by the best Chinese and Korean standards of cuisine. A well-selected wine list complements the food perfectly.

CAIRO La Bodega

157 Sharia 26th July, Zamalek **Tel** *02 2735 0543*
Map *1 A2*

La Bodega is located in one of Zamalek's landmark buildings, the fabulously historic Art Deco-styled Baehler Mansions. Lively, fun and considered trendy among Cairo's younger, wealthy residents, it also offers a great romantic experience for visiting couples. The menu has an Asian and Italian flavour, and there is a lengthy wine list.

CAIRO L'Aubergine

5 Sharia Sayed al-Bakry, off Sharia Hassan Sabry, Zamalek **Tel** *02 2738 0080*
Map *1 A2*

Serving an extensive range of vegetarian dishes, along with international cuisine (some of it aimed at meat-eaters), L'Aubergine is frequented by discerning locals, arty types, businesspeople and tourists. The food is creatively presented, and its location close to the city centre makes it popular. There's a cool bar upstairs.

CAIRO Le Grillon

8 Sharia Qasr el-Nil, Downtown **Tel** *02 2574 3114*
Map *5 B3*

A delightful Arabic-inspired enclosed garden with shrubs and vines surrounds the dining area, making a meal here a special experience. The restaurant serves classic French and European cuisine, along with traditional Egyptian fare. The emphasis is on refined, freshly prepared dishes, which makes it popular with diners in the know. *Sheesha* is available.

CAIRO Le Tabasco

8 Midan Amman, Mohandiseen **Tel** *02 3336 5583*

Ask anyone where Le Tabasco is, and chances are they will have been there themselves – if they are of a certain age. Widely regarded as the coolest nightspot in town, it is frequented by Cairo's young and trendy, along with visitors to the city. The menu includes well-prepared Mediterranean dishes such as crêpes and pasta.

CAIRO Maharaja Restaurant

1115 Corniche el-Nil, Maspiro **Tel** *02 5744 400*

Located within the Hilton Hotel Ramses, in the centre of Cairo, and open to non-residents, the Maharaja serves exquisite Indian dishes straight from the kitchen's tandoori oven. Known for its curries and tandoori banquets, the restaurant is decorated with brightly coloured fabrics and silks.

CAIRO Makani

9 Sharia Amr (off Sharia Wadi el-Nil), Mohandiseen **Tel** *02 3338 6008*

Regarded by locals as one of the best sushi restaurants in town, Makani is also a great place for healthy sandwiches and salads, as well as tasty early bird breakfasts. With wireless Internet access and excellent service too, Makani is always hopping. There are also branches in Maadi and Heliopolis.

CAIRO Paprika

1129 Corniche el-Nil, Maspero **Tel** *02 2578 9447*
Map *1 B4, 5 A2*

Egyptian and international fare – such as top-quality mezes, *koshari* and stuffed vegetables, good steaks, French classics and Italian pasta dishes – is served at this popular restaurant with a classic atmosphere, along with a fine wine list. Paprika is located close to the Arab Television Building and is therefore easy to find.

CAIRO Roy's Country Kitchen

Sharia Saray al-Gezira, Zamalek **Tel** *02 2728 3000*

Map 1 A2

With no pretence to being luxurious, this fun and lively US-style eaterie serves abundant and hearty portions of Tex-Mex and southwestern American food. Its seemingly endless buffet breakfast will set you up for the day, although lunch and dinner menus are offered, too. Roy's Country Kitchen is located inside the Cairo Marriott Hotel.

CAIRO Sequoia

Sharia Abu al-Fida, Zamalek **Tel** *02 2735 0014*

Map 1 A1

Situated on the northern tip of Zamalek with panoramic views, Sequoia is "the" place to be seen. It has a very stylish outdoor lounge that's all white linen and wood. Dishes include pizza from a wood-fired oven, a range of Oriental specialities, plus sushi prepared by a dedicated sushi chef. There's a minimum charge and booking is necessary.

CAIRO Taboula

1 Sharia Amerika al-Latineya, Garden City **Tel** *02 2624 5722*

Map 5 B4

Some creative spelling on the menu (arty shouk and pommen grate) is all forgiven when the array of hot and cold *mezze* arrives with the freshest bread in town. Try the walnut, pomegranate and chilli hummus and the okra *fattah* – or any *fattah* for that matter. The decor is authentically Lebanese.

CAIRO Abou El Sid

157 Sharia 26th July, Zamalek **Tel** *02 2735 9640*

Map 1 A3

One of the few places in Cairo where you can eat traditional Egyptian dishes such as *koshari* and stuffed pigeon while drinking a beer and smoking *sheesha*. From its fabulous, if a little uncomfortable, interior design to the beautiful people lining the booths, Abou el Sid is a must during a trip to Cairo.

CAIRO Aqua

Four Seasons Nile Plaza, Garden City **Tel** *02 2791 7000*

Map 5 A5

A superb seafood restaurant with splendid views of the Nile and an excellent sushi bar serving incredibly fresh sushi and sashimi. Also on offer are fusion dishes such as sea eel and foie gras or lobster served four ways. At the entrance there is an impressive aquarium with exotic, brightly coloured fish.

CAIRO Asia Bar

Blue Nile Boat, 9 Saraya al-Gezira, Zamalek **Tel** *02 2735 1140*

Map 1 B4

With breathtaking river views from the swanky Blue Nile boat, Asia Bar is renowned for serving some of Cairo's best sushi. The menu boasts a variety of dishes inspired by the cuisine of India, Japan, Thailand and India. Dress up, as you could find yourself dining alongside Egyptian celebrities.

CAIRO The Bird Cage

Semiramis InterContinental, Garden City **Tel** *02 2795 7171*

Map 5 A4

Often touted as the best dining experience in Cairo, the Bird Cage is superb, from its delectable Thai dishes to the superior service and subtle decor. Sample a wide range of dishes on the degustation menu or choose your favourite Thai dish. Short of Bangkok, you won't find a more authentic Thai meal anywhere.

CAIRO El Kababgy

Sofitel El-Gezira, 3 Sharia El Thawra, Zamalek **Tel** *02 2737 3737*

Map 2 A3

The Sofitel El-Gezirah's Nile-side restaurant serves some of the best grilled meat in the city; other dishes and service can vary widely and it can get very busy if there's a tour group visiting. Panoramic Nile views and the sound of water lapping on the rocks make this a very relaxing spot.

CAIRO Le Steak

Le Pacha, moored off Sharia Saray al-Gezira, Zamalek **Tel** *02 2735 6730*

Map 1 A2

This floating restaurant moored in an upmarket area of Cairo allows you to experience the delights of sitting on a boat on the Nile, enjoying outstanding panoramic views of the area, fine wines and a menu of steaks and Middle Eastern specialities. Le Steak is always popular, and a smart dress code is in place.

CAIRO Promenade Café

Marriott Hotel, Sharia Saray al-Gezira, Zamalek **Tel** *02 2728 3000*

Map 1 B3

See and be seen in the sublime palace garden café at the Cairo Marriott Hotel. It's expensive, but the garden setting offers an oasis within the noisy, dusty city. Absorb the atmosphere and sample some excellent Egyptian cuisine served with fresh *baladi* bread, which is baked in a clay oven on the premises.

CAIRO Sangria

Corniche el-Nil (opposite the World Trade Centre), Bulaq **Tel** *02 2579 6511*

Map 1 B2

Elegant dining in an intimate atmosphere is available at Sangria, a restaurant that is perfect for special celebrations and romantic evenings. In addition to stunning views of the Nile, Sangria offers diners a wide range of cuisines: Japanese, Chinese, Lebanese, Italian, French and many more. Make sure you leave room for the divine desserts.

CAIRO Windows on the World Restaurant

1115 Corniche el-Nil, Maspiro **Tel** *02 2577 7444*

Ask anyone where the Windows on the World Restaurant is, and they will tell you it is on the 36th floor of the Hilton Hotel Ramses on Corniche el-Nil – it is that well known. Affording a great view of the Pyramids and the city, it serves top-quality Mediterranean cuisine accompanied by fine wines – all in an elegant environment.

Key to Price Guide *see p290* **Key to Symbols** *see back cover flap*

GIZA AND HELIOPOLIS Abu Haidar

15 Sharia Ibrahim al-Laqqani, Heliopolis

If you adore freshly squeezed mango juice and meat burgers straight off the grill, then a lunchtime stop at Abu Haidar could be the order of the day. Located on a busy thoroughfare in the Roxy area of historic Heliopolis, this streetside grill specializes in all manner of steaks, fish and traditional grilled Egyptian cuisine.

GIZA AND HELIOPOLIS Koshari Hind

Sharia Thawra, Heliopolis

Located near the Midan Korba and a few minutes' walk from the Baron's Palace, one of Heliopolis's major landmarks, Koshari Hind is well known for its excellent *koshari* – a mix of pasta, rice, lentils and tomato sauce, all topped off with crispy fried onions and served with *aish* bread. It is open late.

GIZA AND HELIOPOLIS Al-Kods

52 Sharia Haroun al-Rashid, Heliopolis, Cairo **Tel** *02 2632 3467*

This small and characterful eaterie is something of an institution in the Heliopolis area, especially since it has been run in the same manner for well over 40 years. Local residents and tourists alike visit it time and again. Much of the food is homemade, and its hummus, *fuul*, *aish* bread and falafel, along with its desserts, are really tasty and filling.

GIZA AND HELIOPOLIS Andrea

59 Sharia Al-Maryutiya, Giza **Tel** *02 3383 1333*

The best of a small chain of restaurants that is well respected locally, Andrea serves good Egyptian and European dishes, including a varied range of vegetarian specialities. Its wine list is carefully selected to complement the menu. Diners may eat inside or in the shadows of its garden dining area – the perfect spot after a day at the Pyramids.

GIZA AND HELIOPOLIS Deals 3

40a Sharia Baghdad, Heliopolis **Tel** *02 2291 0406*

One of the first pubs to open in Cairo, Deals now has three locations and makes an excellent place for a late dinner. A cheerful mix of locals and expats come here to eat, drink and be merry. Meal choices include both Asian dishes and British pub food. Try the Oriental *mezzes* or the fish and chips.

GIZA AND HELIOPOLIS Jaitta

120 Sharia al-Thawra, Heliopolis **Tel** *02 2415 2326*

Jaitta is one of the best Lebanese restaurants in Heliopolis, its speciality being a delicious version of *kofta*, a traditional dish of minced meat fashioned into balls and cooked in juices with herbs and spices. Be sure to try a water pipe, too. The restaurant has traditional decor and is a good place to meet and eat well.

GIZA AND HELIOPOLIS Fish Market Americana Boat

26 Sharia El-Nil, Giza **Tel** *02 3570 9693*

Ideally located for a lunch or evening meal following a sightseeing trip around the Pyramids, the Fish Market is lively, has a colourful decor and serves a vast array of fish and seafood cooked to traditional Egyptian and international recipes. Prices won't break the bank, and the restaurant is open until late.

GIZA AND HELIOPOLIS Le Chantilly

11 Sharia Baghdad, Heliopolis **Tel** *02 2415 5620*

Interior decor reminiscent of a Swiss chalet makes Le Chantilly the ideal setting in which to enjoy *fondue*. This Swiss restaurant also serves dishes from all around Europe, but is heavily influenced by Parisian brasserie style. Breakfasts are continental, with fresh breads and croissants made in its adjoining bakery. Alcohol is served.

GIZA AND HELIOPOLIS Romeo and Juliet

1 Alexandria Road, Giza **Tel** *02 3376 7555*

Informal yet elegant, Romeo and Juliet is every inch a Mediterranean eaterie, its decor and menu beautifully capturing the essence of southern Europe. The restaurant, located within the Sofitel Le Sphinx Cairo hotel, beside the Pyramids, serves various pasta dishes, buffet-style salads and pizzas, along with a wide selection of desserts.

GIZA AND HELIOPOLIS Wagamama

Citystars Mall, Heliopolis **Tel** *02 2480 2533*

Located inside the vast Citystars shopping mall, Wagamama makes a great place to refuel during a shopping trip. Modelled on the style of noodle bar popular in Japan, it serves up steaming bowls of delicious ramen noodles with a wide range of accompaniments, as well as *teriyaki* dishes and plenty of vegetarian options.

GIZA AND HELIOPOLIS Alexandria Restaurant

1 Alexandria Road, Giza **Tel** *02 3376 7555*

Located within the Sofitel Le Sphinx Cairo hotel, the elegant Alexandria is situated in parklands at the foot of the Pyramids of Giza and the Sphinx, providing excellent views of these sights. It serves buffet and à la carte international dishes, along with a selection of Egyptian specialities. The cellar holds a large range of wines from all over the world.

GIZA AND HELIOPOLIS La Gourmandise

First Mall, Sharia El Giza, Giza **Tel** *02 3776 5955*

Authentic French cuisine is difficult to come by in Cairo but the mall at the Four Seasons First Residence offers the best, cooked by a French chef. Take a table under the huge skylight and sample truly delectable salads, main courses and wines. Being French, the dessert trolley is to die for, offering exquisite patisserie and puddings.

GIZA AND HELIOPOLIS La Maison Blanche

Four Seasons First Mall, 35 Sharia Giza, Giza **Tel** *02 3571 7806*

The eclectic decor here, a mix of 1930s, art deco and ultra modern, makes you forget that you are in a mall. The French cuisine is about the best in Cairo. All the fish served is imported from France, and although portions are not large, they are adequate. Service is impeccable. Closed on Sundays.

GIZA AND HELIOPOLIS Le Château

El Nasr Building, Sharia el-Nil, Giza **Tel** *02 3748 6270*

This Swiss Restaurant is one of three similar eateries in and around Cairo, each offering a wonderful choice of breakfast, lunch and evening dishes that might have delighted generations of Swiss residents. There's also a vegetarian menu, along with a good wine list. The pretty decor is Swiss-inspired and there are Nile views.

GIZA AND HELIOPOLIS Moghul Room

Sharia al-Ahram, Giza **Tel** *02 3377 3222*

Located within the 19th-century former hunting lodge that is now the Mena House Oberoi, this ornately decorated restaurant has been designed to resemble a Moghul house. Its menu comprises good Indian food served in generous portions. Live music adds to the atmosphere and helps to make Moghul Room one of Cairo's most popular places.

AROUND CAIRO

FAYOUM Zad Al Mosafer

Tunis Village, Fayoum **Tel** *084 6820 180*

This eco-lodge began as a writers' retreat, but has expanded to offer more rooms and also to serve breakfast, lunch and dinner to non-residents. Homegrown produce is turned into delicious meals. These can be enjoyed in the first-floor dining room which offers panoramic views of Lake Qarun and is cooled by its gentle breeze.

FAYOUM Helnan Auberge Fayoum

Lake Qarun, Fayoum **Tel** *084 6981 200*

Set right on the edge of Lake Qarun and featuring a relaxing atmosphere, this is an elegant, sophisticated restaurant serving top-notch food. It is housed in a building that was once King Farouk's hunting lodge, and you can admire the wildfowl species that frequent Fayoum's salt lakes as you enjoy your lunch.

THE NILE VALLEY

ASWAN El-Medina

Sharia al-Souq, Aswan

A trip to the marketplace is a must during a visit to Aswan, but the hustle and bustle can become tiring in the heat, and the need for refreshment inevitable. Madena, a cosy little restaurant just opposite the landmark Cleopatra Hotel, has a good selection of juices and beverages, along with mainly meat-based Egyptian meals.

ASWAN Emy

Corniche el-Nil, Aswan

Emy is where the locals head when they have a celebration in the family or just want a special meal. A floating restaurant moored conveniently for the centre of town, it has wonderful views of Lake Nasser and Elephantine Island. Grilled fish is one of its most popular offerings, and the menu boasts a good selection of quality Egyptian cuisine.

ASWAN Hamam

Corniche el-Nil, Aswan

Hamam has no pretences of grandeur, but it does serve some exceptionally good and wholesome meals round the clock. Located in the very heart of Aswan and open 24 hours a day, it's one of those places that always seem to be buzzing with activity. It specializes in roasted meats, and every dish is served with rice.

ASWAN Sayida Nafisa

Sharia al-Souq, Aswan **Tel** *097 2317 152*

Amid the hustle and bustle of the marketplace off the Sharia al-Souq, in the centre of town, is this tiny, unassuming restaurant. The fact that this place is always bursting at the seams with locals as well as tourists speaks volumes about its authenticity. Sayida Nafisa serves a menu of pure Egyptian fare and mouth-watering fruit juices.

ASWAN Al-Masry

Sharia al-Matar, Aswan **Tel** *097 2302 576*

This air-conditioned restaurant is a veritable breath of fresh air when the sun is at its hottest, offering a welcoming place to linger over a light lunch or an evening meal. Al-Masry serves a wide and varied selection of Egyptian and European cuisine, including grilled chicken, fish, pigeon and kebabs. Its dessert trolley is utterly tempting.

Key to Price Guide *see p290* **Key to Symbols** *see back cover flap*

ASWAN Aswan Moon

Felucca Quay, Aswan

Located right on the waterfront in a lively area of Aswan that is an easy walk from the centre of town, Aswan Moon provides a glorious setting for a truly memorable meal. Top-quality Egyptian and European cuisine is served here, including a good choice of vegetarian dishes.

ASWAN Chef Khalil

Sharia Souq, Aswan

Bang in the middle of the souq, Chef Khalil's is nothing too fancy and really rather small, but the seafood here is excellent. Choose your fish from the cold counter by weight, or try the excellent fish soup, with squid, clams and crab in a saffron-flavoured broth. Alcohol is not served.

ASWAN Makka

Sharia Abtal al-Tahrir, Aswan **Tel** *097 2303 232*

Popular with tour groups, which is a good sign in Aswan, this is a spotless and pleasant restaurant that serves traditional Egyptian fare. Kebabs are the main delicacy, but a good selection of salads and starters should keep non-meat eaters happy.

ASWAN Nubian Restaurant

Essa Island, Aswan **Tel** *097 2300 307*

Hop on the free ferry from the dock opposite the Egypt Air office and take a memorable trip across the water to Essa Island to eat at the Nubian Duka – it will be worth the effort! Serving good international and Egyptian food, and offering live entertainment most nights, Nubian is a popular eaterie that attracts tourists.

ASWAN Trattoria

Corniche el-Nil, Aswan **Tel** *097 2315 100*

Located within the Isis Hotel, Trattoria is a cosy Italian restaurant with friendly waiters and a very accommodating chef who will serve up dishes that aren't even on the menu. It's a good location for a family meal of pasta and salad. Try to get the almost private table in the small garden.

ASWAN Orangerie

Elephantine Island, Aswan **Tel** *097 2303 455*

The Mövenpick Resort in Aswan hosts this beautifully renovated, open all hours restaurant that serves an impressive buffet three times a day. Alternatively, choose from their à la carte menu of local and international dishes or enjoy a snack by the pool.

EDFU New Egypt Restaurant

Midan Maabad, Edfu

Edfu, a small farming town on the West Bank of the Nile, has few eateries, and New Egypt Restaurant is probably the best option for lunch or dinner. Its menu is not necessarily adventurous, with grilled meats, chicken, rice dishes, stews and vegetables being the staples, but the food is cooked well and is remarkably tasty.

KOM OMBO Venus Cafeteria & Restaurant

Close to the Temple of Kom Ombo

The picturesque setting of this restaurant – alongside the Nile, on the main route to the great Temple of Kom Ombo – makes it a popular choice for visitors to this small agricultural town, but then, there are few alternatives. Venus's selection is fairly basic and not dissimilar to fast food, but eveything is home-cooked and plentiful.

LUXOR Kabab Abou Haggar

Sharia Abdel Moneim al-Adasi, Luxor **Tel** *095 2376 306*

This popular air conditioned restaurant in the centre of Luxor offers a wide range of simply prepared Egyptian and international dishes. Kebabs are among the favourites on the menu, unsurprisingly, so vegetarians will be left wanting. Kabab Abou Haggar is especially busy in the evenings and into the night.

LUXOR Qased Qear Restaurant

Sharia al-Mahatta, Luxor

If you are after authentic, freshly cooked beef and lamb kebabs, then Qased Qear is the place for you. This eaterie may be small, but the divine smells emanating from the grill make it easier to bear the cramped conditions. Close to the railway station, it is a good stopping-off point if you have just arrived or are about to depart from the city.

LUXOR Al-Gezira

Bayrate al-Gezira, Luxor **Tel** *095 2310 034*

A restaurant located on the rooftop of one of Luxor's most popular small hotels, Al-Gezira offers the chance to enjoy a fine meal while gazing across the waters of the Nile to the heady skyscape of Luxor lit up at night, making it a perfect addition to any holiday in Egypt. The menu is essentially Egyptian, with a few European flavours thrown in.

LUXOR Al-Ramesseum Resthouse

Next to the Ramesseum, West Bank, Luxor

Perfectly placed next to the Mortuary Temple of Ramses the Great, this shady terrace beckons for a cold beer after a day on the West Bank. The food is hearty and delicious. The grandfather of the present owner was part of Howard Carter's team when he discovered the tomb of Tutankhamun and photos adorn the walls.

LUXOR Memnon
Opposite Colossi of Memnon, West Bank, Luxor

The creative, experimental chef at Memnon is from Qurna and serves up Bedouin dishes with an international twist. All meals are freshly prepared using whatever looks good at the market. So place your order, relax and wait while looking at the colossal statues. They can source a beer for you, on request.

LUXOR Abou El-Hassan El-Shazly
Shana Al-Adasi (corner of Mohamed Farid), Luxor **Tel** *016 3429 164*

This is a simple, unfussy local eatery that attracts a few travellers due to its fixed price menu and clean and sanitary interior, although many people prefer to people-watch from the outside tables. The meat options are plentiful and tasty, but vegetarians should enquire after the daily specials; with luck it's *fusulia*, a delicious white bean dish.

LUXOR Côte Jardin
Sharia Khalid Ibn al-Walid, Luxor **Tel** *095 2380 925*

This elegant French-inspired restaurant serves good-quality buffet-style pan-European dishes. Côte Jardin is the main restaurant of the Iberotel Luxor Hotel. It has an amazing view out over the Theban Hills and the Nile to the West Bank from both the dining hall and its terrace.

LUXOR Kebabgy
Corniche el-Nil, Luxor **Tel** *095 2369 995*

Kebabgy's promenade location means excellent Nile views but a meal or drink can be interrupted by felucca captains asking if you want a ride. There's a range of Egyptian and international dishes on offer, as well as cold beers and ice creams. It is a popular hangout for tourists.

LUXOR King's Head Pub
Sharia Khalid Ibn al-Walid, Luxor **Tel** *095 2380 489*

English tourists keen to catch up on the latest news from home tend to head for the King's Head Pub. Here they can also top up their intake of traditional British dishes like roast with all the trimmings and steak and kidney pie, along with sandwiches, soups and snacks. It even has its own billiards table and dartboards.

LUXOR Oasis Café & Gallery
Sharia St Joseph, Luxor **Tel** *017 5954 667*

This tastefully decorated café, fitted with eclectic furniture, makes a restful location after a day's sightseeing. Relax and enjoy tasty pancakes, sandwiches or other freshly baked items as you gaze at the artwork on the walls and people watch. No alcohol is served but there are fresh juices and teas.

LUXOR A Taste of India
Sharia St Joseph, Luxor **Tel** *095 228 0892*

Surprisingly good Indian meals are served in this cosy and welcoming restaurant, located on a street that is fast becoming Luxor's dining out district. Meals are typically British-Indian, plus there are some international dishes on the menu. The staff is very accommodating.

LUXOR Genesis Pub
187 Sharia Hilton, Al-Karnak, Luxor **Tel** *095 2373 032*

This is a British-style pub designed by Egyptians and located at Karnak. It offers a menu of typical British dishes such as roast dinners and what is probably the only real bacon butty in Egypt. Quiz nights, karaoke and theme nights vie with sports on the television so it's only for those who can't do without a British pub while on holiday.

LUXOR Jamboree
Sharia el-Souq, Luxor **Tel** *012 7813 149*

Jamboree is located in the heart of the souq and is a very popular restaurant. A pleasant outdoor terrace overlooks the market square, while the air-conditioned interior is very welcome in the heat of the day. The menu mixes Oriental and international cuisine, and you can even pre-book a Sunday roast dinner.

LUXOR Sofra
90 Sharia Mohammed Farid, Luxor **Tel** *095 2359 752*

In a beautifully tiled 1930s building with a terrace, Sofra is an excellent Egyptian restaurant that serves classic cuisine and has an ambience to match. The menu offers all the best Egyptian dishes – *mezzes, fattahs* and *shakshouka* – all superb and with English explanations. It is the nicest dining experience on the East Bank.

LUXOR 1886
Corniche el-Nil, Luxor **Tel** *095 2380 425*

Don your dinner suit or cocktail dress for a candlelit dinner in this excellent French restaurant within the historical Sofitel Winter Palace Hotel. Take a delicious trip down memory lane with a drink in the Victoria Lounge bar first, followed by faultless food and service in the restaurant. Open for dinner only.

MINYA Akhenaton Restaurant
Akhenaton Hotel, Minya **Tel** *086 2365 917*

A varied menu of international dishes (pizzas, steaks and chicken, salads) with prices that won't break the bank is on offer at Akhenaton. Located within the eponymous hotel, this is a popular restaurant, especially in the evenings. Centrally located, it is frequented by travellers en route from the Western Desert across the Sahara.

Key to Price Guide *see p290* **Key to Symbols** *see back cover flap*

SINAI AND THE RED SEA COAST

AL-ARISH Maxim 🗔 🖬 €€€
Beachside, Sharia Fouad Zakry, Al-Arish

This restaurant is open only in the summer months, where it can usually be found thronging with discerning diners. It is located right on the beach and serves a wide range of top-class international and Egyptian dishes, including a selection of vegetarian delicacies. Maxim promises a memorable experience of dining amid palm trees.

DAHAB Lazy Camel Café 🗔 🖬 €€
In front of Sheikh Salem House, Assalah, Dahab **Tel** *069 3641 820*

The laidback lifestyle of Dahab extends to the beach here at the Lazy Camel. Located in the Bedouin section of Dahab, just in front of the Eel Garden, you can pop in for a snorkel as you wait for your fish to be cooked to your specifications. Eat well while relaxing on cushions at the low tables. Wireless Internet access is available here.

DAHAB Funny Mummy 🗔 🖬 €€€
In front of Sphinx Hotel, Mashraba, Dahab

One of the more established seafront restaurants in Dahab, Funny Mummy is a relaxed restaurant that serves up the usual mix of burgers and pizza along with Red Sea fish and Egyptian *mezzes* such as *tahini* and *babaghanoush*. Relax, play backgammon and watch the world go by. Funny Mummy stays open until you go home.

DAHAB Nesima Restaurant 🖒 🖬 🗏 €€€
Mashraba, Dahab **Tel** *069 3640 320*

Nesima is a cosy and intimate restaurant within the Nesima Hotel, which is renowned for its excellent diving centre. The à la carte menu features a range of international dishes, along with Egyptian specialities such as *koshari*, followed by traditional desserts. A rooftop bar completes the dining experience.

HURGHADA Felfela 🗔 🖬 🗏 €€
Sharia Sheraton, Sekala, Hurghada **Tel** *065 3442 410*

The Felfela chain is a great taste of Egypt, but the Hurghada location has the added bonus of clinging to a cliff and providing diners with stunning views of Griffin Island. It offers a wide range of Egyptian *mezzes*, as well as grilled fish and meats, including their speciality – stuffed pigeon. Save some room for the mouthwatering *om ali* dessert.

HURGHADA Summer Land 🗔 🖬 €€
Sharia el Menaa Sekala, Hurghada **Tel** *065 3446 186*

Join the locals at this traditional Egyptian restaurant that serves breakfast staples such as *taamiyya* and *fuul medames* all day long. Their speciality is *maashi* – vegetables stuffed with spiced meat. The usual hot and cold *mezzes* are delicious. Help them down with a freshly squeezed lemon juice.

HURGHADA El Joker 🗔 🖬 🗏 €€€
Midan Sekala, Sekala, Hurghada **Tel** *065 3152 921*

El Joker is a Hurghada institution, expanding annually from the small stall it once was to the terrace and inside tables it now offers. Fish and other delectable seafood is cooked in both local and international styles and served with fresh *baladi* bread. Plates of delicious hot and cold *mezzes* are equally delicious.

HURGHADA Portofino Restaurant 🖬 €€€€
Sharia Mostafa el-Aam, El Dahar, Hurghada **Tel** *065 3546 250*

An award-winning restaurant recommended by the Egyptian Ministry of Tourism and local businesses, Portofino is a slick operation. Its staff, and especially its owner, speak around nine languages and cater for an international clientele. Cuisine is predominantly classic Italian and seafood.

HURGHADA Oriental Restaurant 🗏 €€€€€
Sofitel Hurghada Red Sea Hotel, Sharia Safaga, Hurghada **Tel** *065 3464 646*

The Oriental is one of two smart restaurants located within the luxurious Sofitel Hotel. The main restaurant serves a buffet menu. This one is open for dinner only and has a Middle Eastern atmosphere. It offers an à la carte menu and focuses on serving local cuisine. The Oriental sometimes hosts theme nights.

NUWEIBA Blue Blue 🖒 🖬 🎵 🗏 🥢 €€€
Hilton Coral Resort, Nuweiba City **Tel** *062 3520 320*

Blue Blue is a bright, modern restaurant that overlooks the extensive beachside gardens of the Hilton Coral Resort. It is an ideal dining destination, both during the day and in the evening, when lighting shines on the pools and the luxuriant shrubs and palm trees. Cuisine is largely international and served buffet-style.

NUWEIBA Nakhil Inn 🗏 €€€
Tarabeen, Nuweiba City **Tel** *069 3500 879*

Located in the quiet village of Tarabeen, a few kilometres north of Nuweiba, this is a delightful beachside setting for a relaxed wining and dining experience. Italian and Oriental dishes are served and the only lighting is provided by stars and candles, unless you wish to eat in the little indoor restaurant.

PORT SAID Al Borg

Sharia Tahr al-Bahr, Al-Arab, Port Said **Tel** *066 3223 442*

Al Borg is a simple family restaurant next to the beach, but it's considered to be the best place in town. It is fitted out in a modern Egyptian style, and only the freshest seafood is prepared here, including a great local variation on *bouillabaisse*. The portions are huge and prices are reasonable. Be prepared to queue for a table on Friday afternoons.

SAFAGA Al-Fayrouz

Holiday Inn Safaga Palace, Safaga **Tel** *065 3620 100*

Al-Fayrouz may come as a culture shock if most of your holiday has been spent at dive camps or in small traditional Egyptian eateries. Catering for as many as 600 people, this vast restaurant serves a seemingly endless array of international foods buffet-style. Massive displays of fruit are a speciality.

SHARM EL-SHEIKH Kokai

Ghazala Hotel, Naama Bay, Sharm el-Sheikh **Tel** *069 3600 150*

This elegant grill room offers superbly flavoured renditions of the finest dishes in Polynesian and Chinese cuisine. Try the duck, the spring rolls and any of the variations on the rice. If you arrive early (around 6.30pm), you can also enjoy the experience of the teppan-yaki grill at your table.

SHARM EL-SHEIKH Little Buddha

Naama Bay Hotel, Naama Bay, Sharm el-Sheikh **Tel** *069 3601 030*

A sunny offshoot of the original Paris Buddha Bar in Hurghada, there isn't anything "little" about this Buddha, from the French-inspired Asian fusion menu to the Buddha overlooking it all, or the price tag. After a succulent dinner, hop upstairs for DJs, chillout tunes and drinks in the lounge.

SHARM EL-SHEIKH Silk Road

Grand Rotana Resort & Spa, Shark's Bay, Sharm el-Sheikh **Tel** *069 3602 700*

The perfect spot for dinner after a sundowner at the stunning Sky Bar. Leave Egypt behind and sample some of Sinai's best Asian cuisine from one of Silk Road's three open kitchens. Thai, Chinese and Indian aromas will entice to an extent that makes it difficult to choose between them.

SUEZ Fish Restaurant

Sharia as-Salaam, Suez

The Fish Restaurant is one of the Suez's worst-kept secrets – anyone who is anybody has eaten here. The restaurant has gained a remarkable reputation for serving the freshest of fish, which is charged by the weight and cooked so that it melts in the mouth. It is located right near the White House Hotel, in the centre of town.

THE DELTA AND THE NORTH COAST

ABU QIR Zaphyrion Restaurant

41 Sharia Khalid Ibn al-Walid, Abu Qir **Tel** *03 5621 319*

The place to visit for a refreshing change from the meat-heavy cuisine that appears on so many menus in Egypt. Although it doesn't shy away from meat dishes, Zaphyrion is mostly renowned for its delicious fish and seafood mezes. It is located right on the shores of the bay where Nelson fought the Battle of the Nile.

ALEXANDRIA Fuul Mohammed Ahmed

17 Sharia Shakour, Alexandria **Tel** *03 4873 576*

This traditional little restaurant has earned itself a reputation for serving excellent *fuul*, the Egyptian staple of fava beans mashed with lemon juice, a selection of herbs and oil. In fact, Fuul Mohammed Ahmed has even created a few variants on the theme, adding new flavours for *fuul* lovers, including a spicy version.

ALEXANDRIA Elite

43 Sharia Safia, Zaghloud, Alexandria **Tel** *03 4863 592*

A popular and lively restaurant, Elite is decorated with art posters, and it benefits from massive windows that open out on to the street, flooding the place with light. It is a great place for watching the world go by with a beer in hand. The menu offers a rich mix of Greek, French and Egyptian specialities.

ALEXANDRIA China House

Midan Saad Zaghloul, Alexandria **Tel** *03 4877 173*

China House is found on the rooftop of the colonial-style Sofitel Alex Cecil Hotel, in one of Alexandria's busiest commercial areas. As such, it is frequented by businesspeople, as well as tourists and locals. As the name suggests, the restaurant offers Chinese cuisine – indeed, some of the best to be found in the city.

ALEXANDRIA Trianon Restaurant

Sharia Saad Zaghloul, Alexandria **Tel** *03 4860 985*

The decor alone justifies a visit to the Trianon Restaurant. Recently restored, it is pure Art Deco and a symbol of the city's pre-revolution café scene. The menu is varied, with international and Egyptian dishes, not to mention a good dessert selection that includes Trianon's speciality *Umm Ali*, a pastry with nuts and fruit.

Key to Price Guide *see p290* **Key to Symbols** *see back cover flap*

ALEXANDRIA White and Blue

Greek Club, Sharia Bahary, near Qaitbey Fort, Alexandria **Tel** *03 4802 690*

Alexandria is famed for its many fish restaurants, but what makes this one particularly special is the location, elevated above a small beach and overlooking the fishing fleet gathered in a bay. The food is simply prepared, with fish chosen fresh from the ice. Alcohol is served, and the outside terrace attracts plenty of local characters. Book ahead on Fridays.

ALEXANDRIA Abu El-Sid

39 Sharia al-Huriya, Alexandria **Tel** *03 3929 609*

Situated in the old building which previously housed the historic Pastroudis restaurant, Abu El-Sid is an Orientalist's fantasy, with wooden window shutters, patterned floor tiles, copper lamps and contemporary artworks adorning the walls. Like its counterparts in Cairo, it's known for its authentic Egyptian home cooking, and serves alcohol.

ALEXANDRIA Al-Farouk Restaurant

As-Salamiek Palace Hotel, Montazah Gardens, Alexandria **Tel** *03 5477 999*

Housed within one of King Farouk's former hunting lodges that has recently been renovated, the Al-Farouk Restaurant forms part of a complex of elegant dining halls and bars. Its air of opulence is compounded by the top-quality international cuisine on offer and a cellar stocked with the finest wines from around the world.

THE WESTERN DESERT

BAHARIYYA Popular Restaurant

Bawiti, al-Bahariyya Oasis

Bahariyya Oasis offers little in the way of eating establishments other than those located in the hotels, but this is the exception. The Popular Restaurant is cosy and intimate, serving a good selection of typical Egyptian and European cuisine, such as grilled meats and vegetables. Beer is available.

DAKHLA Ahmed Hamdy's Restaurant

Mut, Dakhla Oasis **Tel** *092 7820 767*

A traditionally styled restaurant in the centre of Mut, Ahmed Hamdy's is well known for offering a good choice of dishes at competitive prices. Chicken, kebabs, mezes and stuffed vegetables all feature heavily on the menu. It is close to the Mebarez Hotel and popular with tourists and tour groups.

DAKHLA Badawiya Hotel

Sharia al-Qasr, al-Qasr, Dakhla **Tel** *092 7727 451*

The restaurant at Badawiya Dakhla Hotel, built in a modern Moorish style, is an attractive place to dine and serves reliable and honest oasis fare. There is a breezy outdoor terrace which enjoys spectacular desert views, and they don't mind if you bring your own alcohol along. It's best to phone ahead to warn them you are coming.

FARAFRA Hussein Restaurant

Qasr al-Farafra, Farafra

There are few places to find a good meal in Farafra Oasis, one of the most isolated areas in the Western Desert, but the Hussein Restaurant is certainly among the forerunners. The restaurant doesn't score high for decor, nor for a wide-ranging menu, but it does offer wholesome Egyptian meals all day at competitive prices.

FARAFRA Badawiya Safari and Hotel

Qasr al-Farafra, Farafra **Tel** *092 7510 060*

The Badawiya Safari and Hotel offers good food, the recipes for which have been handed down through generations of Egyptian families. Enjoying a cold beer here, in the unique setting of a small desert oasis town, is sure to be a magical highlight of a holiday spent in Egypt.

KHARGA Pioneers Hotel

El Kharga Oasis, El Wadi El Guedid, El Kharga **Tel** *092 7927 982*

Surrounded by palm trees and sand dunes, and decorated to an authentic Egyptian style, this restaurant within the Pioneers Hotel makes for a memorable experience. Its air-conditioned dining room also provides a welcome respite from the desert heat. The menu is varied and inspired by international cuisine.

SIWA Alexander the Great

Siwa Oasis, Siwa **Tel** *046 4600 512*

This modern little eaterie is housed within the recently opened Alexander Hotel, and offers good, traditional Egyptian food with an international twist. Its oasis setting and friendly staff make it a favourite for locals and, especially, travellers exploring this part of the country.

SIWA Shali Lodge

Sharia Ein El Arais, Siwa **Tel** *046 4601 299*

This delightful restaurant within Shali Lodge is probably the best place to eat in Siwa town. The inventive cuisine features local dishes alongside international fare, such as as chicken curry. Guests can enjoy meeting like-minded travellers at this lively terrace location.

SHOPPING IN EGYPT

When it comes to shopping, the souqs and bazaars are undoubtedly Egypt's main attraction. The biggest and most famous is Cairo's Khan al-Khalili (*see pp88–90*), a 500-year-old maze of commerce at the heart of the old Islamic city. While on first encounter it can seem to cater excessively to tourism, explore deeper and the narrow alleys become a bustling hive of small workshops turning out attractive jewellery, glass-, copper and brassware. Here you can buy direct

Souq trader in Luxor smoking a water pipe

from the artisans and cut out the middleman. Most other towns and cities throughout the country also have souqs, with particularly good ones in Alexandria, Aswan and Port Said. For visitors intending to shop in these places it is essential to become acquainted with the art of bargaining. In contrast to the traditional nature of the souq, larger cities, such as Cairo and Alexandria, also possess modern shopping precincts, as well as shopping centres filled with globally recognized brand names.

OPENING HOURS

There are no strictly defined opening hours in Egypt – it depends on each individual proprietor. Generally, however, except for local grocery stores, which open early, business activity begins at around 9 or 10am. Businesses tend to close for a siesta from around 2 to 5pm, except in Cairo, where shops remain open all day. They then typically stay open until 9pm or later. In summer, in busy commercial areas, and especially Khan al-Khalili, the shutters often do not come down until 10 or 11pm, as people prefer to shop when it is cooler. Other souqs keep shorter hours, with stalls and businesses packing up around sunset. Friday is the official day off, although in Cairo many shops are open seven days a week. Those open on Friday may still close for a couple of hours in the middle of the day for noon prayers. Businesses owned by Christians may close on Sunday. During Ramadan shops close 30 minutes before sunset but reopen a couple of hours later. The whole country shuts down on major feasts, which include Moulid an-Nabi, Eid al-Fitr and Eid al-Adha (*see p39*).

HOW TO PAY

Although their use as a form of payment is increasing, credit cards are typically still only accepted at larger or tourist-oriented shops, such as those found in hotel complexes or shopping malls. Likewise, traveller's cheques are hardly accepted anywhere. In most places, it is necessary to pay in cash. Egyptian pounds are the country's only legal currency and purchases cannot usually be made in dollars.

SOUQS AND MARKETS

Besides Khan al-Khalili there are numerous other souqs and markets in Cairo, many worth a visit irrespective of whether you intend buying anything. Fruit and vegetables are sold at the many street markets scattered throughout the city. Every neighbourhood has one. In central Cairo there is the Tawfiqiyya market, one block north of Sharia 26th July, open so late that many stall-holders don't bother going home; they simply sleep beside their carts. On the east bank of the Nile, opposite Zamalek, again just north of Sharia 26th July, is Bulaq market selling textiles, second-hand clothing, car parts and military surplus.

Cairo's Downtown bookshops are excellent for books on Egypt

An even stranger mix is presented at the weekly Souq al-Gomaa, or Friday market, held just south of the Citadel, where the trade is in bric-à-brac and animals. It must be one of the few markets where you can buy both a set of 1930s crockery and a squawking cockatoo. Next to Ataba metro station, just north of Midan Opera, is Al-Azbakiyya Gardens. Here, second-hand books and magazines, many of them in English, are sold from a collection of cabins.

In Alexandria, Attarine is not so much a market as a maze of narrow alleyways lined with antique shops that spill their goods out on to the street. Al-Arish in northern Sinai also has a colourful Thursday-morning market frequented by local Bedouin who sell embroidered dresses and distinctive, hand-crafted jewellery.

Stacked merchandise in one of Cairo's markets

Examining the brass- and copperware in Khan al-Khalili

SHOPPING CENTRES

Cairo – and Alexandria to a lesser extent – has a rapidly growing number of large shopping centres or malls. These are filled with standard arcade-type outlets that sell everything from greetings cards to electrical goods, most of which are US and European imports. They also usually incorporate fast-food outlets and multi-screen cinemas. **Nile City Towers**, on the Corniche in Rhod al-Farag, is a modern mall with inter-national brands and excellent dining options. Just south, in Bulaq, **Arkadia Mall** houses more than 500 stores, includ-ing many international outlets and plenty of snack bars. For a chic shopping destination, head to the **First Residence Mall** in Giza, which overlooks the zoo and forms part of an accommodation complex for the rich. The **Ramses Hilton Mall**, adjacent to the Ramses Hilton hotel in the city centre, is more family friendly and offers value-for-money shoes and clothing. On the top floor is a cinema and a snooker hall. Out in Nasr City, the vast **Citystars Centre** has shops galore, an excellent food court and a cinema, making it a popular hangout for local kids.

BUYING ANTIQUES

Most antiquities offered to visitors are anything but antique. "Old" papyrus may well have been painted just last week and probably not on papyrus (which has all but vanished) but on dried banana leaves. Similarly, so-called ancient scarabs are often made by carving them from old bone and then feeding them to turkeys – the birds' gastric juices create a realistic ageing effect. However, in some respects this is all just as well because genuine antiquities (in general, anything over 100 years old) can only be exported with a licence from the Department of Antiquities.

HOW TO BARGAIN

Buying and selling in Egypt is traditionally a highly ritualized affair, in which bargaining is far more than just haggling for a cheap price. The aim of the exercise is to establish a fair price that both vendor and buyer are happy with. As part of the process, a shop-owner may well invite you to have a cup of tea or coffee and may literally turn the place upside down to show something. You should not feel obliged to buy because of this, as it is a common sales practice and all part of the ritual.

Bargaining even happens in city-centre shops over goods which appear to have a fixed price. It is in the souq, however, that it becomes a necessity if you want to avoid paying greatly over the odds.

Once you have identified an article that interests you, especially if it is an expensive one, be brave enough to offer half the price quoted by the shop-owner. Don't be put off by feigned indignation or mockery on the shop-keeper's part, and only raise your next offer by a small amount. Through a process of offer and counter-offer you should eventually arrive at a mutually agreeable price. If you don't reach a price you think is fair then simply say thank you and leave. Making to walk away can often have the effect of bringing the price tumbling down.

In theory, although you may feel uncomfortable, no one gets cheated. You, the buyer, have set the price yourself, so it follows that you are happy with what you have agreed to pay. The shop-keeper, for his part, will never sell at a loss, so he will certainly have made a profit on the deal.

The brightly lit Citystars Centre in Nasr City, Cairo

Where to Shop in Egypt

Cairo's Khan al-Khalili *(see pp88–90)* is the first place to look for Egyptian souvenirs, while city-centre shopping focuses on the triangle of Sharia Talaat Harb, 26th July and Qasr el-Nil. The island suburb of Zamalek is a great hunting ground for boutiques specializing in ethnic crafts, designer wear and antiques. Elsewhere in Egypt, only the most determined shopaholics will find much to buy – perhaps colourful textiles and spices in Aswan and pottery and jewellery in the oases.

SOUVENIRS

Khan al-Khalili in Cairo and other tourist bazaars in Upper Egypt are crammed with incredibly kitsch items, such as Nefertiti reading lamps, alabaster pyramids, stuffed leather camels and Tutankhamun baseball caps.

There are more worthwhile items to be found, however: attractive backgammon boards, like those used in Egyptian coffeehouses, at least have a practical purpose. Or you could buy your own *sheesha* (waterpipe), though you will also need to stock up on the special tobacco and the small clay pots that the tobacco is stuffed into. Small boxes inlaid with mother-of-pearl are pretty and very inexpensive. Inlaid chessboards are also popular buys.

Almost everyone visiting Egypt picks up some papyrus – often cheap and poor quality, shoddily painted with scenes copied from pharaonic wall paintings. For better quality work, visit the **Dr Ragab Papyrus Institute**, a museum with a shop where you can get the genuine article, which will not crack or have the paint flake off when it is rolled.

Souvenir figure of Anubis

BRASS- AND COPPERWARE

Plates, coffeepots and trays of brass and copper are made in the workshops around Khan al-Khalili. For good examples, have a look at the Coppersmiths Market (Souq an-Nahassin) in Sharia al-Muizz li-Din Allah, south of the great mosques on Bein al-Qasreen.

Stallholder selling leather belts in Midan Ataba

HANDICRAFTS

Different parts of Egypt are associated with their own particular crafts, but much of the best of this work makes its way to Cairo. For example, **Al-Khatoun**, which is based in a restored Ottoman house behind the Mosque of al-Azhar, sells wrought-iron furniture that is made in a village just outside Cairo, as well as soft wall hangings, glassware and locally-made leather goods.

Their sister store, **Al-Qahira**, is in Zamalek and is housed in an attractive apartment building. Opposite the entrance to the Mosque of Ibn Tulun, also in Islamic Cairo, **Khan Misr Touloun** is a beautiful gallery selling local handicrafts from the villages and oases of Egypt. These include wooden chests, bowls and plates, blown glass, clay figurines, scarves and woven clothing. Based in Zamalek, **Egypt Crafts Centre** has Bedouin rugs and embroidery from Sinai and the northern Western Desert, hand-made paper from Muqattam and shawls from Upper Egypt. Also in Zamalek, **Nomad** specializes in jewellery and traditional Bedouin craft and costumes. Meanwhile, for crafts, lights and other home furnishings there is the shop **Caravanserai**.

CARPETS AND RUGS

Unlike Morocco, Turkey or Iran, Egypt is not a big carpet producer. What you will find, however, are hardwearing, brown and beige striped, camel-hair rugs of Bedouin origin. The biggest selection is to be found in the Haret al-Fahhamin, a tight maze of alleys behind the Mosque of Al-Ghouri, across the road from Khan al-Khalili in Islamic Cairo. Many of the places mentioned in the Handicrafts section also stock Bedouin rugs. Connoisseurs might want to visit the weekly markets at Al-Arish, in northern Sinai, and in Dahab. In the area of the Pyramids,

Coppersmith's workshop in Sharia al-Muizz li-Din Allah

Locals gather at one of Cairo's colourful carpet bazaars

just off the road to Saqqara, the **Wissa Wassef Art Centre** specializes in very distinctive woollen rugs and wall hangings depicting rural and folkloric scenes. These can also be bought at **Senouhi**, a fascinating little shop on the fifth floor of an apartment block in Downtown Cairo. Senouhi also sells good quality jewellery, antiques, Bedouin rugs and art.

CLOTH AND TEXTILES

Cotton is Egypt's biggest cash crop, and department and clothing stores in central Cairo and Alexandria carry excellent quality, plain cotton shirts, T-shirts and underwear. Look out, in particular, for branches of **Safari**, found in all the big malls and in some hotel shopping complexes. Down in Middle Egypt, just across the Nile from Sohag, the village of Akhmim is the centre of an ancient weaving tradition. Legend has it that pharaohs were buried in shrouds of Akhmim silk. Still in production, but now in factories rather than the local workshops, the cloth comes in deep, rich colours, with elaborate floral and paisley-style patterns. It is extremely beautiful, but hard to find. The best bet is to go direct to the factories; otherwise some of the hotel shops in Luxor carry a small selection.

BELLYDANCING COSTUMES

Sequinned bras, beaded hip-bands, veils and flimsy skirts are sold in a couple of specialist shops in Khan al-Khalili. One is in the small passageway leading from Muski to Fishawi's coffee house. Serious practitioners should pay a visit to the studio of **Amira al-Khattan** in Mohandiseen, who tailors costumes to order.

JEWELLERY

Egypt's gold and silver shops are concentrated in the centre of Khan al-Khalili. Jewellery is sold by weight, with a little extra added for workmanship. The current gold prices are listed each day in the *Egyptian Gazette*. The most popular souvenirs are gold or silver cartouches with a given name engraved in hieroglyphics. Most of the shops in Khan al-Khalili can arrange to have this done.

SPICES AND HERBS

Khan al-Khalili in Cairo and the souk in Aswan are both excellent for spices. Generally these are fresher and of better quality than any of the packaged variety sold in the West. They are also much cheaper, especially saffron. The stalls that sell spices often also have heaps of purplish, dried hibiscus leaves. When boiled up, strained and sugared, these make *karkade*, the excellent deep red, iced drink served in coffee houses. Some of the shop owners in the Spice Bazaar are also herbalists, who prepare traditional remedies for a variety of ailments.

A colourful display of aromatic spices in the Spice Bazaar

DIRECTORY

SHOPPING MALLS

Arkadia Mall
Corniche el-Nil, Bulaq, Cairo.
Map 1 B2.

Citystars Mall
Stars Centre, Nasr City, Heliopolis.

First Residence Mall
Sharia al-Giza, Giza, Cairo.

Nile City Towers
Corniche el-Nil, Rhod al-Farag.
Map 1 B2.

Ramses Hilton Mall
Midan Abdel Moniem Riad, Cairo.
Map 1 B4, 5 B2.

HANDICRAFTS

Al-Khatoun
3 Sharia Mohammed Abdu, Cairo.
Map 2 F5. **Tel** *(02) 2510 0448.*

Al-Qahira
6 Sharia Bahgat Ali, Zamalek,
Cairo. **Map** 1 A3. **Tel** *(011) 3133
932.*

Caravanserai
16 Sharia Mohammed Marashly,
Zamalek, Cairo. **Map** 1 A2.
Tel *(02) 2735 0517.*

Dr Ragab Papyrus Institute
Houseboat on Corniche el-Nil,
Cairo. **Map** 3 A2. **Tel** *(02) 3571
8675.*

Egypt Crafts Centre
27 Yehia Ibrahim, Zamalek, Cairo.
Map 1 A3. **Tel** *(02) 2736 5123.*
www.fairtradeegypt.com

Khan Misr Touloun
Sharia Tulun, Cairo. **Tel** *(02) 2265
3337.* **Map** 4 D2.

Nomad
14 Sharia Saray al-Gezira,
Zamalek, Cairo. **Map** 1 B4.
Tel *(02) 2736 1917.*

CARPETS AND RUGS

Senouhi
54 Sharia Abd al-Khaliq Sarwat,
Cairo. **Map** 5 C2.
Tel *(02) 2391 0955.*

Wissa Wassef Art Centre
Next to the Motel Salma, on the
road to Saqqara, Harranniya.
Tel *(02) 3385 0403.*

CLOTH AND TEXTILES

Safari
10 Sharia Lotfalla, Zamalek, Cairo.
Map 1 A3. **Tel** *(02) 2735 1909.*

BELLYDANCING COSTUMES

Amira al-Khattan
27 Sharia Basra, Cairo.
Tel *(02) 3749 0322.*

What to Buy in Egypt

Box inlaid with mother-of-pearl

Egypt's magical souqs and bazaars offer the visitor an eclectic mix of trinkets and souvenirs. The quality can vary greatly so always inspect the items closely and be prepared to haggle over the price *(see p303)*. Sheesha (waterpipes), backgammon boards, decorative boxes and an array of kitsch paraphernalia fill the market stalls alongside traditional handicrafts often made by local artisans. Egyptian copperware and Muski glass are produced in Cairo's Khan al-Khalili *(see pp88–9)*, while Bedouin jewellery traditionally comes from Sinai. The best hand-woven silk and cotton is made in Akhmim in Middle Egypt, famous for the quality of its weaving.

Sheesha
A fixture in every coffee house, a waterpipe makes an excellent gift. Decorated with stainless steel or brass fittings, the pipes use a special fragrant tobacco loosely packed into a clay pot.

Backgammon Board
Backgammon and chess are popular pastimes in Egypt. Sets of varying quality are readily available with the cheaper boards being crudely made and with little inlay. The better sets are made out of hard woods and inlaid with intricate designs of mother-of-pearl, bone or ivory.

Sandals
Reasonably priced leather items such as bags, wallets and hand-crafted sandals are sold in most bazaars.

Glass and Pottery
Hand-blown, blue Muski glass is uniquely Egyptian and fashioned into plates, vases, glasses and candle-holders. Good hand-made pots, like this sculpted alabaster vase, are also easily found.

Perfume Bottles
These delicate glass perfume bottles are fashioned into intricate shapes. They come in various sizes and make wonderful gifts.

Bedouin Jewellery
Bedouin jewellery traditionally comes from Sinai and Siwa Oasis, and often features coins in its designs. While truly authentic Bedouin jewellery is hard to find, its styles have been widely imitated. Other popular designs include those based on Pharaonic, Islamic and Nubian motifs.

Copperware
A wide range of copper and brass goods is sold through-out Egypt but the Cairo souqs and workshops offer the widest selection. Typical buys include Arabic coffeepots, trays and hanging lamps as well as decorative pieces such as plates embossed with classic arabesques.

Clothes and Textiles

Cotton is one of Egypt's major crops and cotton clothes are popular. Plain and embroidered cotton shirts, trousers and galabiyyas (loose, all-in-one robes) are usually of high quality and good value. The brightly coloured fabrics are excellent as scarves, cushion covers, wall hangings and throws. Garish belly-dancing outfits are also popular purchases.

Embroidered cotton shirts   Brightly coloured woven scarf   Sequined belly-dancing costume

Tourist souvenirs

A myriad of kitsch reproductions of Pharaonic art, alabaster pyramids, stuffed leather camels, busts of Nefertiti and sheets of papyrus painted with scenes from temples or tombs are sold in all tourist areas. These items, along with trinket boxes, ashtrays, chessboards and sheesha make popular and inexpensive gifts.

Stuffed leather camel

Papyrus with Pharaonic scenes

Carved figurines of
ancient gods

Bust of Nefertiti   Alabaster ashtray

Egyptian Music

The easiest way to recreate the Egyptian experience is to buy some Egyptian CDs or tapes. The choice ranges from traditional folk music and the mournful sounds of Umm Kolthum (see p125) to modern, bouncy Egyptian pop.

Spices and Flavourings

Colourful and fragrant, Egyptian spices can be located easily in the bazaars. Spices are sold loose by weight and are often far cheaper, fresher and of better quality than the pre-packaged ones sold in the west. One word of caution, however, Egyptian saffron is very cheap but it may not be top quality.

Carob   Cinnamon

Cloves   Chillies   Turmeric

Cayenne
Pepper   Cardamon
pods   Saffron
threads

ENTERTAINMENT IN EGYPT

ost people find that the range of entertainment options in Egypt, especially outside Cairo, is surprisingly limited. Locals tend to fill their free time with visits to friends or family, or, in the case of the menfolk, whiling away the hours in a coffeehouse. A few major, well-attended cultural events punctuate the calendar, notably the Cairo International Book Fair in spring and the Cairo International Film Festival in November and December *(see p41)*.

Passing time at a street-side coffeehouse in Cairo

Otherwise the annual high spots are tied into religion – the feast days of Eid al-Adha and Eid al-Fitr *(see p33),* and the holy month of Ramadan. On these occasions, temporary fairgrounds are often set up in main squares, and there are plenty of performances of traditional music and folk dancing. Old Ottoman houses in Islamic Cairo are often the venue for free concerts, so look out for posters in the area which advertise events.

Cairo by night, its bright lights reflected in the calm waters of the Nile

INFORMATION

There is no shortage of entertainment guides in Egypt. Each month a glossy magazine called *Egypt Today* is published and includes extensive coverage of artistic and cultural events taking place throughout the country. It is available from bookstands and newsagents everywhere. The weekly English-language newspapers *Al-Ahram Weekly* and *The Middle East Times* also carry good listings information on what is showing at cinemas, galleries and the theatre, although their coverage is limited solely to Cairo. *The Croc*, a free, quarterly, pocket-sized magazine covering the city's nightlife and entertainment scene, is very useful although hard to find – check out the website at www.icroc.com.

There is no central booking office for shows and concerts, and it is generally necessary to buy tickets from the

relevant theatre or concert hall box office. It is also a sensible precaution to book tickets several days in advance if possible.

ARABIC MUSIC

Much of the programming at the **Cairo Opera House** and Alexandria's **Sayed Darwish Theatre** involves live performances of Arabic classical music. In Islamic Cairo, particularly

during Ramadan, music evenings and theatre productions are held at the **Beit Zeinab Khatoun** and the **Al-Ghouri Palace for Traditional Culture**, part of the historic Al-Ghouri Complex *(see pp91–2)*. It is worthwhile trying to attend one or more of the performances at the Al-Ghouri Complex even if it is only to savour the atmosphere, as the stories are told in Arabic.

WHIRLING DERVISHES

The Wikala of al-Ghouri in Islamic Cairo stages whirling dervish performances on Mondays, Wednesdays and Saturdays, from 8pm. The shows are free. There is fairly limited seating, so go at 6:30pm to collect an advance ticket. It is permitted to take photos but not to film on video. More dance and musical events are held at the **Al-Sawy Culture Wheel** (see www.culturewheel.com).

Whirling dervish putting on a spectacular performance in Cairo

Belly Dancing

Despite a heritage that dates back to Pharaonic times, modern-day belly dancing owes more to the European experience of Egypt in the 18th and 19th centuries. The sensual movements of the Egyptian dancers, who blended folk, gypsy and Ottoman dances, fired the imaginations of repressed Europeans. It is largely due to their descriptions that the dancing was associated with prostitution. Even

A belly dancer's backing musician

dedicated, professional belly dancers, who prefer the term "oriental dancer", get tarred with this brush. The advent of cinema put belly dancing on the big screen, increasing its popularity and making stars of the performers.

Today, despite its popularity, belly dancing still carries a social stigma which discourages Egyptian women from entering the profession, and the gap is increasingly being filled by foreign dancers.

Dancers *played an important part in ancient Egyptian ritual and celebration. Their poses, as shown here, clapping or using castanets are very similar to modern Egyptian dancing.*

Salome, *in the Bible, asked Herod for the head of John the Baptist as reward for her dancing. Late 19th-century writers added eroticism to the story, resulting in a series of scantily-clad cabaret acts as depicted in this 1909 music sheet cover.*

Superstar Amira *dances at the Giza Pyramids. Although belly dancing's popularity has been hit by the rise of Islamic fundamentalism, its top stars are among Egypt's highest earners.*

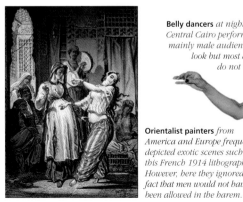

Belly dancers *at nightclubs in Central Cairo perform before mainly male audiences, who look but most definitely do not touch.*

Orientalist painters *from America and Europe frequently depicted exotic scenes such as this French 1914 lithograph. However, here they ignored the fact that men would not have been allowed in the harem.*

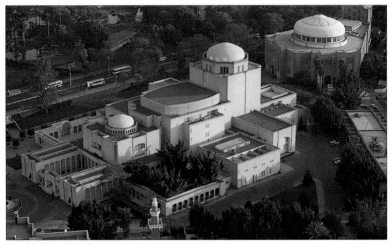

View of the Cairo Opera House from the top of the 185-m (606-ft) Cairo Tower *(see p84)*

BELLY DANCING AND FOLKLORIC DANCE

While the best dancers perform at the nightclubs attached to Cairo's five-star hotels, such as the **Haroun al-Rashid Club** in the Semiramis Hotel, where a seat costs about US $70 a head (buffet included), for pure entertainment visit the much cheaper **Sherherazade** on Sharia Alfy Bey, Downtown. The main act generally does not appear until at least 1am and the band will not call it a night until the sun is rising. Dancers can be seen at most hotels and tourist restaurants in the country. Venues in Luxor and Aswan, such as the **Aswan Cultural Palace**, often feature Egyptian folkloric dance troupes.

Billboards advertising forthcoming cultural events in Cairo

SOUND AND LIGHT SHOWS

Every major site in Egypt feels compelled to present a sound and light show. These begin once the sun goes down, and involve the monument being illuminated by coloured floodlights while a recorded voice narrates snippets of history and mythology. The narration often leaves a lot to be desired, but it is worth going just to revisit some of Egypt's sights by moonlight. The Pyramids at Giza, Luxor, Karnak, Philae and Abu Simbel all offer several shows a night in various languages.

WESTERN CLASSICAL MUSIC

Egypt's main classical music venue is the **Cairo Opera House** *(see p313)*, on the island of Gezira. Its main hall hosts regular performances from a variety of visiting international artists. On such occasions a jacket and tie is compulsory for men. The small hall has nightly recitals by quartets, soloists and ensembles and is also used by the Cairo Symphony Orchestra, which gives concerts here every Saturday from September to mid-June. The Cairo classical music scene is well covered in *Al-Ahram Weekly*. In Alexandria, both the **Alexandria Conference Hall** and **Sayed Darwish Theatre** host classical concerts organized by the French, Italian or German consulates. Details of what's on are posted in the window of the Elite restaurant *(see p300)*. Otherwise, you are unlikely to hear much Western classical music in Egypt.

OPERA AND BALLET

The premises of the **Cairo Opera House** are shared by both the Cairo Ballet Company and the Cairo Opera Company. The season is limited, and productions are few, although they are sometimes supplemented by visiting companies. There are also occasional dance performances at Cairo's **Gumhuriyya Theatre** *(see p313)*. Almost every year, the Ministry of Culture also mounts a grand production of *Aida*, the opera written in honour of the opening of the Suez Canal *(see pp60–61)*. Previous performances have been held at the temples of Hatshepsut and Karnak in Luxor, but most recently the venue has been the Pyramids. It is a very high-profile occasion, drawing opera-lovers from all over the world. Egypt's overseas tourist offices will be able to provide full details on when the next grand event takes place.

Inside a young and fashionable bar in upmarket Mohandiseen, Cairo

BARS AND DISCOS

Despite being predominantly Islamic, there are plenty of bars in Egypt beyond those in the hotels – look for signs for "cafeterias". Some of the best are to be found in Alexandria, notably the **Cap d'Or**, a beautiful old place that feels like a real blast from the past. In Cairo, nightlife centres on the upmarket neighbourhoods of Zamalek and Mohandiseen. Bars such as **Deals** and **L'Aubergine** cater mainly for young wealthy Egyptians, as well as the city's large expatriate community. Later on, those with the energy move on to the busy Downtown discos which play hiphop and dance music. These include **Purple**, the ultra-cool hotspot on the Nile.

Red Sea and Sinai resorts such as Sharm el-Sheikh, Naama Bay and Hurghada are also packed full of bars and discos. **Little Buddha** and **Pacha** are the current favourites in Sharm el-Sheikh, while Hurghada now has the very fashionable **Hed Kandi Beach Bar**.

A hotel disco at Agami, on the North Coast, west of Alexandria

The resorts along the north coast have few good bars or discos and typically those available are attached to hotels.

ROCK, JAZZ AND POP

Rock, jazz and pop concerts are virtually unheard of. A handful of artists, such as The Grateful Dead and Shirley Bassey have played the Pyramids but such events happen very rarely. Egyptian pop stars don't do concerts either. Practically the only place to hear live contemporary music is in hotel lounges and bars like the **Camel Bar** at the Camel Hotel in Sharm el-Sheikh. Each Thursday evening this lively bar puts on live bands who play varied styles of music, all good for dancing to. Every major five-star establishment has a resident cabaret singer or jazz quartet, but don't expect to recognize any names. About the only dedicated live venue in the country is the **Cairo Jazz Club**, a small, suitably smoky joint, with a band every night, usually drawn from the tiny but enthusiastic local scene.

DIRECTORY

The Cosmos cinema, one of many local movie houses in Cairo

CINEMA

In recent years, cinema in
Egypt has had an overhaul.
Large, modern multiplexes
have been opened in Cairo
and Alexandria and old movie
houses have been refurbished.
Programming is usually split
between Arabic films and the
latest Hollywood releases, with
foreign films screened in their
original languages and subtitled
in Arabic. All of the films
shown suffer
censorship except
those screened
during the Cairo
International Film
Festival *(see p41),*
where the
possibility of
seeing exposed
flesh on the big
screen ensures
packed houses.

Colourful advertising for
the Diana Palace cinema

A trip to the
cinema is an experience in
itself. Audiences are always
extremely animated, greeting
screen events with cheers,
boos or applause. In
Downtown Cairo, particularly
around the Sharia Talaat Harb
area, there are many old,
single-screen cinemas, several
of which, including the
Miami, **Cosmos** and **Odeon**,
show English-language films.
Better equipped cinemas
include the **Galaxy** and those
located in shopping malls,
such as **Stars** in Heliopolis,
the **Ramses Hilton** and the

Renaissance. In Alexandria,
the **Amir** is an outstandingly
beautiful period cinema,
worth a visit for the architecture alone. But by far the
most luxurious cinema in
Alexandria is the **Renaissance**,
attached to the Smouha Mall,
to the east of the city centre.

Up-to-date details of all the
films currently being screened
are published in *The Egyptian
Gazette, Al-Ahram Weekly*
and on www.icroc.com.

THEATRE

The numerous
local theatres
in Cairo are
testimony to a
strong dramatic
tradition in Egypt.
Productions are
performed in
Arabic and are
of local fare, typically slapstick
comedy with a bit of belly-
dancing thrown in. Cairo's
Downtown area, particularly

along Sharia Emad al-Din, is
home to several small theatres
including the **Gumhuriyya
Theatre**. Al-Azhar Park hosts
the new **Al-Genina Theatre**.
Non-Arabic speakers may wish
to visit the **Wallace Theatre**.
This venue stages a number
of plays throughout the year
which are performed in
English by students of the
neighbouring American
University in Cairo *(see p72).*
Occasionally, a high-profile
theatrical event takes place
at the **Cairo Opera House**. In
the past, it has received visits
from the likes of Britain's
Royal Shakespeare Company.

Once a year, the Interna-
tional Experimental Theatre
Festival *(see p41)* brings in
a variety of acting troupes
from all around the world to
perform at venues throughout
Cairo. The *Al-Ahram Weekly*
newspaper is an excellent
source of information on all
such events. The newspaper
also lists details of all the
regular theatre performances
taking place in Cairo.

CASINOS

Many of Egypt's five-star
hotels have casinos, open to
non-Egyptians only (passports
must be shown at the door).
All games are conducted in US
dollars or other major foreign
currencies, with a minimum
stake of US $1. The dress
code is smart casual. Hotels
with casinos include the
Semiramis Intercontinental,
the **Marriott Cairo** and the
Pyramisa in Cairo and the
As-Salamlek Palace in Alexandria. Note that in Egypt the
word "casino" is sometimes
used to denote a bar – this is
usually the case when it is
encountered outside a hotel.

Billboard advertising an Arabic theatre production

SPECTATOR SPORTS

Football rules in Egypt. A big match is one of the few times when the country is silent – at least until the final whistle, when the streets fill with flag-waving, horn-honking fans. Footballing life is dominated by Cairo, home to the country's two biggest clubs, Ahly and Zamalek. These clubs, along with Alexandria's Ittihad team, boast players of international standard. Games between Cairo's big clubs are the highlight of the sporting calendar and take place at the **Cairo Stadium** in Medinat Nasr. Tickets for all major games are in high demand and can be difficult to obtain.

Media sports coverage focuses almost entirely on football, even in summer when there are no matches. Of other sports, the most prominent is squash. The annual August Al-Ahram International Squash Tournament draws competitors from all over the world to play in glass-enclosed courts

Football fans cheering on the Egyptian national soccer team in Cairo

set up next to the Pyramids. The Pyramids also feature as the start and finishing point in the annual Pharaoh's Rally, a four-wheel-drive and trail-bike desert race in October. Other spectator sports include rowing races on the Nile every Friday between November and April, and horse racing at the **Gezira Sporting Club** and the **Alexandria Sporting Club** from October to May. Since the

year 2000, there has also been an annual showjumping competition held in the second two weeks of February at the Alexandria Sporting Club. For something more unusual, watch local Bedouin participate in inter-tribe camel racing as part of the annual Sharm el-Sheikh festival *(see p38)*.

Details of all sporting fixtures are in *The Egyptian Gazette* and *Al-Ahram Weekly*.

DIRECTORY

CINEMA

Amir
41 Sharia Horreyya, Alexandria.
Tel (03) 3927 693.

Cosmos
12 Sharia Emad el-Din, Cairo. **Map** 2 D3.
Tel (02) 2574 2177.

Galaxy
67 Sharia Abd al-Aziz al-Saud, Al-Manial, Cairo.
Tel (02) 2532 5745.

Miami
38 Talaat Harb, Downtown, Cairo. **Map** 5 C2.
Tel (02) 2574 5656.

Odeon
4 Sharia Dr Abdel-Hamid Sayed, Downtown, Cairo. **Map** 5 C2.
Tel (02) 2576 5642.

Ramses Hilton
Ramses Hilton Annex, Sharia al-Galaa, Downtown, Cairo.
Map 5 B2.
Tel (02) 2574 7436.

Renaissance
Nile City, Corniche el-Nil, Bulaq, Cairo.
Map 1 B2.
Tel (02) 2461 9102.

Renaissance
Zahran Mall, Semouha, Alexandria.
Tel (03) 4240 5897.

Stars
Citystars Center, Heliopolis, Cairo.
Tel (02) 480 2013/14.

THEATRE

Al-Genina Theatre
Al-Azhar Park, Cairo.
Map 2 F5.
Tel (02) 2362 5057.

Cairo Opera House
Sharia at-Tahrir, Gezira, Cairo. **Map** 1 A5.
Tel (02) 2739 8144 (info)
(02) 2739 0144 (info)
(02) 2739 8114 (box office)
www.cairoopera.org

Gumhuriyya Theatre
12 Sharia al-Gumhuriyya, Cairo. **Map** 6 D3.
Tel (02) 2390 7707.

Wallace Theatre
Sharia Mohammed Mahmoud, Downtown, Cairo.
Map 5 B4.
Tel (02) 2797 6935.

CASINOS

As-Salamlek Palace Hotel
Montazah Palace, Alexandria.
Tel (03) 547 7999.

Cairo Marriott Hotel
Saray al-Gezira, Zamalek.
Map 1 A4.
Tel (02) 2728 3000.

Pyramisa Hotel
60 Sharia el-Giza, Giza, Cairo. **Map** 3 A2
Tel (02) 3336 7000.

Semiramis Intercontinental
Corniche el-Nil, Cairo.
Map 1 B5.
Tel (02) 2795 7171.

SPECTATOR SPORTS

Alexandria Sporting Club
Mahatet al-Riada, Alexandria.
Tel (03) 542 0435.

Cairo Stadium
Medinat Nasr, Cairo.
Tel (02) 2260 7863.

Gezira Sporting Club
Zamalek, Cairo. **Map** 1 A4.
Tel (02) 2735 2272.

Coffee House Culture

Found on almost every street corner, the ubiquitous coffee house *(ahwa)* plays an important role in the everyday life of Egyptians. Like the cafés of continental Europe, *ahwas* are social places where Egyptians can meet to talk with friends, idle away an hour reading a newspaper, or watch football on TV. Frequented predominantly by men, coffee houses are busy at all hours of the day and many

Card players with *sheeshas* concentrate on their game

remain open around the clock. As well as tea *(shai)* and coffee *(ahwa)*, most serve fresh lemon juice *(lamoon)*, iced *karkade*, a refreshing crimson drink made from boiled hibiscus leaves, *zabaady*, a yoghurt drink and *sahleb*, a warm drink made with semolina powder, milk and chopped nuts. No coffee house would be complete without the *sheesha* (waterpipe) through which tobacco is smoked.

A typical coffee house, *such as Fishawi's in Khan al-Khalili, is often little more than a collection of old tables and chairs placed in a narrow alleyway.*

Chess *is not particularly common in Egypt but a few coffee houses are venues for fans of the game, including the popular Horreyya situated in Downtown Cairo.*

Backgammon *and dominoes are the most popular of the coffee house games with animated players slamming down their pieces.*

Sheeshas *(waterpipes) are offered in coffee houses as an accompaniment to drinks. The tobacco is soaked in molasses or sometimes apple juice.*

Coffee houses *are often all-male environments but foreign women are usually welcomed.*

CHILDREN'S ENTERTAINMENT

When the heat of Cairo becomes too much, **Dr Ragab's Pharaonic Village** can provide a welcome break and keep children thoroughly entertained. The village is an ancient Egypt theme park situated on the southern tip of Al-Qorsaiah Island which lies on the west bank of the Nile, 10 km (6 miles) south of the city centre. Visitors take small boats through the reed beds viewing scenes of Pharaonic daily life recreated by costumed actors. The park also boasts a replica temple.

The **Cairo Puppet Theatre**, just north of Midan Opera, gives performances of traditional tales like Sindbad and Ali Baba. The plays take place most mornings from October to May and although in Arabic, they are highly visual and easy to follow. Another alternative is the **Cairo Zoo** in Giza. The zoo is set in pleasant grounds on the west bank of the Nile opposite Rhoda Island. Although promises have been made regarding improving conditions, some may find the animal enclosures distressing.

On the outskirts of Cairo are several amusement parks. **Dream Park**, northwest of Cairo, has Disney-type rides, go-karts and games arcades, as well as golf and tennis courts. **Aquapark**, 32 km (20 miles) east of Cairo, offers waterchutes, a wave pool and a playground area. The nearby theme park **Gero Land** also has rollercoasters, go-karts and other thrill rides. Else-

Children enjoying themselves at the fairground of a local festival

where in Egypt there are few concessions made to children's entertainment. However, activities are often laid on for children during *moulids* (saints' days) and other festivals. At the coast, many of the bigger resort hotels now run activity centres designed to keep younger guests amused.

COFFEE HOUSES

There is an abundance of coffee houses *(ahwas)* in Egypt, each one filling its own niche and frequented by its own particular clientele. Several of the more interesting coffee houses are tucked away down tight alleys and include the Downtown **Ash-Shams**, notable for its garishly painted walls. One of the oldest and most famous of all the coffee houses is **Fishawi's** *(see p90)*. Buried in the narrow lanes of Khan al-Khalili, it is open 24 hours and is as much a

must-see sight for visiting out-of-town Egyptians as it is for foreigners. In Alexandria, coffee houses line the Corniche, while in Aswan and Luxor there are several dotted around the busy souq areas.

WEDDINGS

Thursday night is the end of the Muslim week and the traditional night for weddings in Egypt. Throughout the country celebrations are heralded with drums, tambourines, honking cars and women wailing. Weddings are very public affairs, where musicians, dancing processions and showers of rose petals fill the streets, and foreign spectators are often invited to join the celebrations.

DIRECTORY

CHILDREN'S ENTERTAINMENT

Aquapark
Sharia Ismailia.
Tel *(02) 4477 0099, 4477 0088.*

Cairo Puppet Theatre
Al-Azbakiyya Gardens, Cairo.
Map 6 D2. **Tel** *(02) 2591 0954.*

Cairo Zoo
Sharia al-Giza, Giza, Cairo.
Tel *(02) 3570 1552.*

Dr Ragab's Pharaonic Village
3 Sharia al-Bahr al-Azam,
Corniche el-Nil, Giza, Cairo.
Tel *(02) 3568 8601.*
www.pharaonicvillage.com

Dream Park
Sharia el-Wahat, 6th October City.
Tel *(02) 3855 3191 or 19355.*
www.dreamparkegypt.com

Gero Land
El-Obour City, Sharia Ismailia.
Tel *(02) 4610 3602.*

COFFEE HOUSES

Ash-Shams
Souq al-Tawfiqiyya, Cairo.
Map 1 C5, 5 C3.

Fishawi's
Khan al-Khalili, Cairo.
Map 2 F5.

Horreyya
Midan al-Falaki,
Sharia at-Tahrir, Cairo.
Map 5 C3.

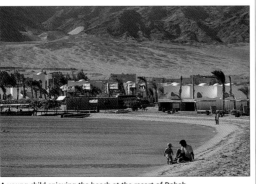

A young child enjoying the beach at the resort of Dahab

OUTDOOR ACTIVITIES AND SPECIALIST HOLIDAYS

E gypt's varied terrain – from the expansive plains and oases of the Western Desert to the rugged hills of the Sinai, and from the clear waters and colourful coral reefs of the Red Sea to the unique wetlands of the Nile Delta – offers an exciting range of activities for outdoor enthusiasts.

Year-round clement weather makes Egypt the ideal destination for all outdoor sports, and many five-star resorts around Hurghada and Sharm el-Sheikh, as well as several luxury hotels in Cairo, offer world-class golf and tennis facilities. Elsewhere, the choice of activities ranges from scuba-diving and water-skiing to hot-air ballooning; from horse and camel riding to four-wheel-drive safaris across the desert.

Starfish

Hot-air ballooning over the Valley of the Queens, Thebes

ADVENTURE PACKAGES

Specialist holidays can be booked directly with UK tour operators such as **Abercrombie & Kent Travel**, **Explore Worldwide** and **Guerba Intrepid**, or in the USA, **Overseas Adventure Travel**. Most adventure holidays can also be arranged on arrival through travel-agency desks at most large hotels, or through local tour operators, such as the Cairo-based **Egypt Exploration Society**.

Holidays off the beaten track can be arranged to suit all budgets and comfort zones: from desert safaris sleeping in tents, to air-conditioned four-wheel-drive journeys with luxury accommodation.

The rugged interior of the Sinai Peninsula is popular for climbing and hiking tours, while the extreme environment of the Western Desert offers a different type of adventure. An organized safari is the only way to experience the thrill of desert driving and camping, with experienced English-speaking guides and drivers, as well as a cook to prepare most meals. Trips into the desert from oases such as Kharga or Bahariyya are offered by many hotels and guesthouses in these areas.

The best season for a holiday off the beaten track is winter (Nov–Mar), when temperatures during the day are tolerable and nights are cool, even chilly.

Visitors intending to take an adventure holiday should ensure that their travel insurance offers adequate cover, including emergency medical evacuation.

BALLOONING

Hot-air balloon flights over the Valley of the Kings are run by several companies, such as **Balloons Over Egypt**, **Hod Hod** and **Magic Horizon**. Flights generally lift off early in the morning and take in the ancient sites, the surrounding mountains and the Nile. They often end with a champagne picnic at the landing site.

DIVING AND SNORKELLING

Renowned for the clarity of its waters and the variety of its spectacular corals and fish, the Red Sea offers a wide range of submarine habitats – from remote seamounts that attract large open-water species such as sharks and barracuda, to inshore, shallow-water reefs.

All the larger resorts on the southern tip of the Sinai Peninsula, the Gulf of Aqaba and the coast near Hurghada have dive clubs. As well as short trips to nearby dive sites, specialist dive operators offer live-aboard cruises that allow divers to spend up to two weeks at sea.

An underwater encounter with a lion fish in the Red Sea

Many dive clubs also offer a variety of courses. Before signing up for these, make sure that the dive centre is certified by a reputable international organization such as **PADI** or the **British Sub Aqua Club (BSAC)**. Recommended dive centres can be found on the websites of either of these organizations. Information, availability and reservations for numerous dive centres at all Red Sea resorts can also be found at www.goredsea.com.

The prestigious El Gouna resort complex has nine diving centres offering courses at all levels, including junior open-water diving courses for children.

Feluccas gliding lazily on the Nile

Windsurfing lesson at a beach on the Sinai Peninsula

For non-divers, snorkelling over shallow reefs is a great alternative. Most dive centres rent masks, fins and snorkels, but the masks are often old or leaky; bring your own, or buy a new one on arrival. For more on diving, see pp320–21.

WATERSPORTS

Both the Mediterranean and the Red Sea coasts offer excellent powered watersports. Water-skiing, jet-skiing and parascending are available at most beaches. All the major resort hotels have their own watersports centres. These may be a little more expensive than independent operations nearby, but they usually offer better-quality, more reliable equipment and trained English-speaking staff.

Wind and water conditions are reliably excellent for windsurfing at the Sinai resorts of Sharm el-Sheikh, Dahab, Taba and Nuweiba, with consistent cross-shore winds, shallow waters for novices, and larger swells further offshore that allow experts to use their jumping skills. Kite-boarding is also increasingly popular. Equipment for both sports can be rented at all resorts.

FELUCCA SAILING

The journey down the Nile from Aswan to Edfu by felucca takes two to three days. Boats with crew can be chartered at Aswan, where hundreds of feluccas are based and boat owners eagerly approach visitors to offer their services. In theory, prices are set by the government and the tourist office in Aswan can provide clear guidance as to the cost. In practice, however, many extra charges must also be negotiated.

Felucca travellers must bring necessities such as toilet paper, a torch and batteries, mosquito repellent and/or a mosquito net and alcoholic beverages if required. Boat owners provide food, water and soft drinks for an extra charge, which must also be negotiated. Felucca travellers can sleep on board under the stars or arrange hotel or guesthouse accommodation for each night along the way.

FISHING

The huge expanse of Lake Nasser, the world's largest artificial lake, offers anglers some of the best fishing in the world. The catch here is likely to be tiger fish and the giant Nile perch. Fly-fishing can also be practised, as can bait fishing for catfish, including the giant vundu, one of the world's largest freshwater fish. Boats with crew may be hired in Aswan through **The African Angler**. Equipment can also be hired.

GOLF AND TENNIS

Many five-star resorts around Cairo and on the Red Sea boast superb golf courses, often flanked by floodlit tennis courts. One of the country's newest developments is the 18-hole Karl Litten-designed **Dreamland Golf Course**, at the Dreamland City leisure development on the outskirts of Cairo. It also has floodlit tennis courts for night play. Other golf and tennis resorts around Cairo include **Katameya Heights**, with a 27-hole course and ten clay courts, and **Mirage City**, part of the JW Marriott, near the airport. Elsewhere, near Naama Bay, the **Maritim Jolie Ville Golf Resort** has a good international course.

The golfing green at Katameya Heights, not far from Cairo

BIRDWATCHING

Egypt is a rich environment for birdwatchers. There are around 150 resident bird species, but these are outnumbered by the 280 or more species that use one of the world's greatest migration corridors, between Eurasia and southern Africa. Millions of migratory birds traverse the Egyptian skies each year, with waves of storks, raptors and other migrants heading north from mid-February until April, and returning southward from August until early November. Organized birding package tours are available through **Sarus Bird Tours** and **Travel Egypt**.

HORSE AND CAMEL RIDING

Visitors to the Pyramids are usually approached by touts offering rides on mangy camels or flea-bitten nags. These are best avoided. Instead, rent a mount and guide in advance from a reputable livery stable, such as **Sheikh Tarek's AA** or **Recoub Al Sorat**, both in Giza. The latter offers countryside trail rides as well as rides around the Pyramids of Giza and Saqqara. At Sharm el-Sheikh, the Hotel Sofitel *(see p280)* has an excellent stable offering desert rides.

SPAS

Thanks to a boom in luxury resort developments, Egypt now has hotels with deluxe spa, health and beauty facilities to match any in the world. The prime spots for such hotels are Sharm el-Sheikh, which has the **Four Seasons**, the **Ritz-Carlton** and the **Hyatt Regency**; the purpose-built luxury resort of **El Gouna**, with its cluster of world-class hotels; and the international brand hotels of Cairo and its suburbs, such as **Le Meridien Heliopolis** and the **Oberoi Sahl Hasheesh**. The five-star **Angsana Spa** at the Mövenpick Resort & Spa El Gouna, is the first of its kind on the Red Sea. Managed by the award-winning Banyan Tree group, it offers an array of holistic and contemporary spa treatments. El Gouna's lavish golf clubhouse at the El Gouna resort complex *(see Directory, Golf and Tennis)* also houses a chic spa that offers Thai, Swedish and shiatsu massages, traditional Egyptian body-scrub treatments, a gym, sauna and Turkish baths. Hotels at all Egyptian destinations offer inclusive spa packages, and guests can also book spa, health and beauty treatments on an ad hoc basis on arrival.

Scarlet ibis stork

A yacht moored at the small harbour of Giftun Island

YACHTING AND MOTOR CRUISING

There are large marinas at ports such as Hurghada and El Gouna, where the Abu Tig Marina and Abydos Marina are rated the finest in the Red Sea. Sailing yachts – either crewed or on a bare-boat basis – can be chartered at both Hurghada and El Gouna.

OASIS AND DESERT SAFARIS

The Western Desert is an exciting destination for four-wheel-drive safaris using specially equipped desert vehicles with long-range fuel tanks, global satellite positioning (GPS), satellite communications equipment and trained drivers. The **Badawiya Safari Company** offers four-wheel-drive safaris through the White Desert. Oases easily accessible from the Nile corridor include Bahariyya, Farafra, Dakhla and Kharga, while longer-range desert safaris travel into the Great Sand Sea, and as far west as Siwa, or head for lesser-known oases such as Areg, Bahrein and Ain Della.

WALKING

Egypt offers walkers several spectacular walking routes. The St Catherine Protectorate region of southern Sinai peninsula is a hiker's paradise of jagged mountains, natural springs and forgotten ruins. Hikers must be accompanied by a local guide.

   Sheik Mousa organizes trekking tours led by Bedouins in the mountains of the Sinai. Treks include the well-trodden Mt Sinai, the summit of Jebel Abbas Pasha

Horse riding around the Pyramids at Giza

and gentler walks along dry river beds. Treks can also be arranged at St Catherine's village; for information, visit the Visitors' Centre at St Catherine's Monastery *(see pp222–5)*. A number of specialist tour operators in the UK, mainland Europe and North America also offer escorted walking packages.

Another focus for walking holidays is the Bahariyya Oasis in the Western Desert. Several specialist operators such as the Badawiya Safari Company *(see Oasis and Desert Safaris)* offer treks with Bedouin guides and accommodation in tents or village guesthouses.

DIRECTORY

ADVENTURE PACKAGES

Abercrombie & Kent Travel
Sloane Square House,
Holbein Place, London
SW1W 8NS, UK. **Tel** *800 554 7016.*
www.abercrombiekent. com

Egypt Exploration Society
c/o British Council,
192 Sharia el-Nil,
Agouza, Cairo, Egypt.
Tel *(02) 3300 1886.*
www.ees.ac.uk

Explore Worldwide
Tel *(0845) 013 1537.*
www.explore.co.uk

Guerba Intrepid
Wessex House,
40 Station Road,
Westbury, Wiltshire BA13 3JN, UK.
Tel *(0203) 147 7777.*
www.guerba.com

Overseas Adventure Travel
1 Mifflin Place, Suite 400,
Cambridge, MA 02138,
USA. **Tel** *1-800 493 6824.*
www.oattravel.com

BALLOONING

Balloons Over Egypt
Luxor.
Tel *(095) 370 368.*

Hod Hod
Luxor.
Tel *(095) 370 116.*

Magic Horizon
Luxor.
Tel *(095) 2365 060.*

DIVING AND SNORKELLING

BSAC
www.bsac.com

Colona Dive Centre and Live-Aboards
www.colona.com

Deep Blue Divers
www.divedahab.com

The Dive Connection
www.diveconnection.com

Emperor Divers
www.emperordivers.com

Euro Divers
www.euro-divers.com

PADI
www.padi.com

Oonas Dive Club
www.oonasdiveclub.com

Sinai Divers
www.sinaidivers.com

FISHING

The African Angler
PO Box 191, Aswan.
Tel *(097) 230 9748.*
www.african-angler.co.uk

GOLF AND TENNIS

Dreamland Golf Course
Dreamland City,
Alwahat Rd, Cairo.
Tel *(02) 3855 3164.*
www.dreamlandgolf.com

Katameya Heights Golf and Tennis Resort
New Cairo City, Cairo.
Tel *(02) 2758 0512.*
www.katameyaheights.com

Maritim Jolie Ville Golf Resort
Um Marikha Bay,
Sharm el-Sheikh.
Tel *(069) 360 3200.*
www.maritim.com

Mirage City
JW Marriott Hotel,
Ring Road, Cairo.
Tel *(02) 411 5588.*
www.marriott.com

BIRDWATCHING

Sarus Bird Tours
12 Walton Drive,
Walmersley,
Bury BL9 5JU, UK.
Tel *+44 (0) 161 761 7279.*
www.sarusbirdtours. co.uk

Travel Egypt (World Explorer Tours and Travel)
Suite 150,
4015 Nine McFarland
Drive, Alpharetta,
GA 30004, USA.
Tel *877 778 3497.*
www.travelegypt.com

HORSE AND CAMEL RIDING

Recoub Al Sorat
Mamouneya Road, Giza.
www.alsorat.com

Sheikh Tarek's AA
Tarek Abu Aziza, Giza.
Tel *(012) 296 0749.*

SPAS

Angsana Spa
Mövenpick Resort El
Gouna, El Gouna.
Tel *(065) 354 4501.*
www.moevenpick-hotels.com

El Gouna Resorts
www.elgouna.com

Four Seasons Sharm el-Sheikh
1 Four Seasons Boulevard,
Sharm el-Sheikh.
Tel *(069) 360 3555.*
www.fourseasons.com

Hyatt Regency Sharm el-Sheikh Resort
Gardens Bay,
Sharm el-Sheikh.
Tel *(069) 360 1234.*
www.sharmelsheikh. regency.hyatt.com

Le Meridien Heliopolis
51 El Orouba Street,
Heliopolis, Cairo.
Tel *(02) 2290 5055.*
www.starwoodhotels. com

Oberoi Sahl Hasheesh
Safaga, Red Sea.
Tel *(065) 3440 777.*
www.oberoihotels.com

Ritz-Carlton Sharm el-Sheikh
Om el-Seed,
Sharm el-Sheikh.
Tel *(069) 366 1919.*
www.ritzcarlton.com

OASIS AND DESERT SAFARIS

Badawiya Expedition Travel
42 Sharia 104,
Maadi, Cairo.
Tel *(02) 2526 0994.*
www.badawiya.com

WALKING

Sheik Mousa
St Catherine's, Sinai.
Tel *(069) 3470 457.*
www.sheikmousa.com

Scuba Diving and Snorkelling

Clear waters and abundant sea life make the Gulf of
Sinai one of the world's finest dive destinations, with
something for every skill level: from inshore reefs and
submarine canyons to shipwrecks and blue holes. The
major resorts – Hurghada, Sharm el-Sheikh, El-Gouna
and Dahab – have numerous dive centres where you
can rent equipment. Dive centres all offer internationally recognized learn-to-dive courses. Do a little
research and ensure that your dive centre of choice
is approved by a reputable organization such as
PADI or the British Sub Aqua Club (BSAC). Shallow
reefs close to the shore, often in only a few metres
of water, offer ideal conditions for snorkelling.

The impressive colours of the Red Sea

**The Thistlegorm wreck at Sha'ab
Ali ①,** probably the Red Sea's most
famous wreck site, lies in 20–30 m
(65–100 ft) of water, on the bed
of the Straits of Gubal. Legendary
diver Jacques Cousteau discovered
this wartime wreck in the 1950s
but kept its location secret, and
it was not until 1992 that it was
rediscovered.

Shaab Umm Qamar ⑥, a sloping
reef wall close to a tiny rocky islet
not far offshore from Hurghada, is
a magnet for marine life, especially
schools of pelagic and reef species,
all of which are accustomed to
divers and very approachable.
The wreck of a fishing boat at
25 m (80 ft) is an attractive focus
for divers, and there is plentiful
coral. Sharks are sometimes seen.

S I N A

Gulf of Suez

①

Hurghada ●
Port
Safag●

0 kilometres   140

0 miles   60

DIVE-SITE RATINGS

Dive sites here range from
novice-friendly shallow
reefs to deep-water dives
that should be attempted
only by experienced divers
with qualified guides.

	SNORKELLING	NOVICE DIVING	ADVANCED DIVING	EXPERT DIVING
THISTLEGORM ①			•	•
THE BELLS ②			•	•
THE ISLANDS ③	•	•	•	•
BLUE HOLE ④	•	•	•	•
SHARK BAY ⑤	•	•	•	•
SHAAB UMM QAMAR ⑥	•	•	•	•
THE BROTHERS ⑦	•		•	•
SAFAGA ⑧	•	•	•	•

Safaga (Kilo 32 North) ⑧ is a shore-entry dive
site south of Port Safaga, where bottlenose
dolphins, turtles and a wide variety of reef fish
may be seen in depths of 20–35 m (65–115 ft).
Reef walls pierced by crannies and caves
surround a shallow bay and are covered by
large coral heads and soft corals.

The Bells ② is located north of Dahab in depths from 25–50 m (80–160 ft). This is a site for experienced divers only, who descend into a 5-m (16-ft) wide chimney that extends into the open sea at 30 m (100 ft). As well as plenty of marine life, you are likely to see black and white coral, and plate and cabbage coral.

The Blue Hole ④ is a shore-entry dive close to Dahab. On a good day, the 102-m (335-ft) deep hole should yield jacks, barracuda and reef sharks. The outer slope of the reef enclosing the lagoon offers corals, fissures and shoals of numerous fish species. The Blue Hole also attracts snorkellers.

The Islands ③, a shore-entry, shallow-water dive near Dahab, is a great beginners' dive, in depths of 12–16 m (40–50 ft), with superbly preserved coral, spectacular scenery and wide-ranging marine life from turtles to barracuda. One of the most rewarding dives on this coast.

GETTING TO THE DIVE SITES

Dive centres offer boat trips to inshore reefs and wrecks, or minibus rides to walk-in dive sites. Some of the Red Sea's best dive sites can be reached only on a live-aboard dive cruise. Currents can be strong, and diving with a guide who knows the area well is highly recommended.
Getting there: Hurghada, Sharm el-Sheikh and Marsa Alam airports receive flights from Europe and Cairo, Luxor and Alexandria. Access to Nuweiba and Dahab is by bus, minibus or taxi from Sharm el-Sheikh; Safaga is reached by road from Hurghada.

Snorkelling off the beach at Dahab

Shark's Bay ⑤, just north of Na'ama Bay near Sharm el-Sheikh, is a novice-friendly dive in just 20 m (65 ft) of water. Superb soft corals line a sandy underwater canyon haunted by lyre-tail coralfish; eagle rays, barracuda and sharks are sometimes seen in the deeper water. Angelfish, parrot fish, grouper, wrasse and moray eels also inhabit the reef, while rays favour the sandy bottom.

Octopus found off the shores of the Sinai

The Brothers ⑦ is one of Egypt's most impressive dive sites. These two rocky islets are the tops of twin deep-water reefs, covered by magnificent corals, that attract huge numbers of reef and open-water fish, including large sharks. Features include a vertical wall, shallow reefs and two shipwrecks. Accessible only by live-aboard boat, the Brothers is never crowded; some cruises allow up to a week's diving here.

Turtle in a swim-through

NILE CRUISES

Nothing beats sitting on the deck of a slow-moving boat as it glides elegantly along the Nile. Cruising combines transport and accommodation to provide the most relaxing way of exploring the major cultural sites, as well as those that are otherwise difficult to get to. The on-board guides, many of them qualified Egyptologists, are on

Hathor, Cow God, Temple of Dendara

hand to explain the history of each site and outline their most important architectural features.

The Nile is home to hundreds of cruise boats and feluccas. Many tour operators offer cruises as part of a package holiday to the region. Flights arrive at Luxor and Aswan airports, and direct transfers are laid on to get you to your cruise ship.

View of the Nile from the deck of a cruise ship

WHEN TO GO

The best time for a Nile cruise is from November to February, when it is not too hot. However, this means that resorts like Luxor and Aswan tend to become unpleasantly overcrowded. It also means that prices are higher than at other times of the year, and the opportunities for bargains greatly reduced. From March to April and from October to early November, the weather is still pleasant, but there are fewer visitors, and prices drop. From May to October is the hottest season and not the best time to enjoy cruising. Having said that, if you are not bothered by the heat, this is when the best bargains can be found. At this time the Nile is at its lowest level because of the need to conserve water at the Aswan Dam; this can make it difficult for the boats to navigate. If locks on the Nile are closed, operators arrange boats on either side of the locks and you then transfer between them.

NILE CRUISING AS A PACKAGE DEAL

Romanticized by countless films and novels, cruising on the Nile has been a popular tourist pastime since the 19th century, when visiting Egypt's ancient sights was a highlight of the Grand Tour. Since then, cruising has developed into a hugely profitable industry, with an incredible selection of boats plying the river between Aswan and Luxor. The simplest way of organizing a Nile cruise is to book an inclusive

The elegant, luxurious interior of a cruise ship on the Nile

package holiday from home. This will include flights to Egypt, where you will join your cruise boat. Trips vary in length and may be one way from Luxor to Aswan or include the return journey.

A typical trip will start in Luxor and Thebes (*see pp182–203*), with visits to the Luxor Temple and the Temple of Amun at Karnak. Following a night on board the cruise ship, an organized excursion leaves the next morning for the Valley of the Kings and a few of the more famous tombs, including that of Tutankhamun and possibly those of Ramses VI and Tuth-mosis III. Some tours may also include a visit to the Ramesseum, the mortuary Temple of Ramses II. On your way back to the boat, you will stop at the two huge statues known as the Colossi of Memnon.

The cruise ship then leaves Luxor heading south towards Aswan and stopping en route to visit various ancient temples and settlements. As the boat sails slowly along the river, you can unwind by sitting under a sun shade on deck, reading a book or joining some of the many activities that are included in the price. Or you can just relax while Egypt moves slowly past you. Fishermen in feluccas, old men on donkeys and small children on the river bank will all wave to you in much the same way as their ancestors would have done to the Pharaohs several millennia ago.

Since your accommodation, transport and meals are included in the price – as are on-board entertainment, entrance fees to the sites and the services of professional guides – most trips offer good value for money. There are always some excellent deals available on Nile cruising holidays, and it does pay to shop around. Before booking, check carefully exactly what is included in the price.

Cruises offered as part of package holidays are generally reliable and of a consistent standard. **Sonesta Nile Cruises** is a tried and trusted American-based operator with offices in Cairo. Its modern fleet consists of five ships built between 1989 and 2006, ranging in size from 33 suites to 65 cabins. Depending on which vessel you choose, facilities include swimming pools, lounge bars and restaurants. Evening entertainment is provided in the form of discos, belly dancers and Nubian shows. Air-conditioned cabins are en suite and come with satellite television, video players, mini bars and safety deposit boxes. On the more luxurious ships, you might also find a jogging track or a spa with gym, massage, sauna and Jacuzzi, and extras in the cabins like private telephones, wireless Internet access with laptop and private dining until midnight.

During your cruise down the Nile, you are likely to visit the Temple of Dendara *(see pp178–9)* in Qena, the Temple of Horus in Edfu *(see p204)*

The Temple of Kom Ombo at sunset

and the Temple of Kom Ombo *(see p205)*. In Aswan *(see pp 208–11)* the shore-based itinerary includes visits to the Aga Khan Mausoleum, the High Dam granite quarries and the Temple of Philae *(see p212)*. For cruising on a more intimate and luxurious scale, **dahabiya** boats hark back to the glory days of the 19th century, when travellers to Egypt spent weeks or months drifting down the Nile. Several companies now offer these wooden boats for trips between Esna and Aswan, hosting small groups of guests and exploring interesting sites along the way. As the boats are smaller than the cruise ships, they can moor in quiet locations and time visits to temples in order to avoid crowds. The decor is often colonial, meals are taken on deck and tranquility reigns. **Nour el-Nil**'s fleet of four

Falcon statue at the Temple of Horus, Edfu

boats has attentive crews and gorgeous decor and has trips between Esna and Aswan. Another attractive option is the Lake Nasser cruises run by **Belle Epoque**, between Aswan and Abu Simbel, which offer as intimate an atmosphere as a dahabiya but on slightly larger vessels.

CAIRO-BASED NILE CRUISING

It is no longer possible to cruise from Cairo to Aswan. If you are based in the capital but still want to enjoy the rest of the Nile, you can fly from Cairo or book a sleeper on the overnight train to Luxor or Aswan and join a cruise ship there.

River buses travel regularly up and down the Nile and are good for day trips to Qanater *(see p169)*. However, if you are based in Cairo, Alexandria or the Sinai Peninsula and want to visit the ancient monuments of the Nile Valley, you may decide that a cruise is the best way of doing this. Because of the proliferation of boats offering such excursions, cruises are easy to arrange through the major hotels, including the Sheraton, Oberoi and Hilton *(see pp268–71)*. The best deals, however, are generally found through local agents or by dealing directly with the boatmen in Luxor or Aswan. Prices vary greatly, depending on the level of luxury offered. Shop around and check out the facilities on board before confirming the booking. Always ensure that you know what is included in the fare.

The hustle and bustle of a port on the banks of the Nile

Enjoying a felucca trip on the Nile

FELUCCA TRIPS

No holiday in Egypt would be complete without a trip in a felucca, a working boat of a design that has been used by Nile fishermen for hundreds of years. These vessels are available for short trips or longer cruises. Most felucca trips, however, are fairly short and cannot be compared in any way to the luxurious cruises on what are really floating hotels.

Facilities on feluccas range between the primitive and the non-existent. You won't have a cabin and will have to sleep on the open deck, under the stars. This is an excellent way to get a true appreciation of the Nile.

The most popular felucca trips are between Aswan and Edfu. Travellers can sail from Aswan to Kom Ombo or Edfu, and continue on to Luxor by road. In winter, when the weather is most favourable, the journey to Kom Ombo takes one night, while the trip to Edfu takes at least two nights. Since the journey upstream from Luxor to Aswan depends heavily on the wind, most travellers start the journey in Aswan and travel downstream. To arrange a day trip, simply walk along the banks of the Nile at Aswan and Luxor. You'll be hailed by boat skippers all looking for work. Decide on a felucca you like

the look of, tell the skipper what you want, and then haggle over the price.

Another option in Luxor is to hire a felucca to take you across the Nile and pick up a taxi to tour the sites. The skipper may offer to make a taxi arrangement on your behalf. It is probably best to turn down all such offers politely but firmly – as soon as you dock, you will be besieged by waiting taxi drivers, so you can negotiate your own deal. Do not ask the skipper to wait until you return or to come back for you at a pre-arranged time either. That might prove costly, and there are plenty of boats about, or you can take the ferry.

Felucca trips from Aswan are best arranged with the help of the tourist office, who can recommend good captains and quote official

A member of the crew washing up onboard a felucca

rates, whereas hotels will add on a commission.

Prices vary according to the season and demand, so these rates should be taken as a starting point for negotiation. Note that, in some cases, "all inclusive" may not guarantee that water, or even food, is included, so always check.

Ensure that your felucca is stocked with the following: a water container (such as a jerry can); a shade awning; a kerosene stove and lamp; utensils and cutlery; and a luggage hold with a lock. Nights are very cold on the river, so make sure that the felucca has plenty of blankets. Better still, take a sleeping bag with you. Also take some water and some back-up food with you just in case. Three litres of drinking water per person per day is the minimum; this does not include water for cooking. To ensure that you have a pleasant experience, hats, sunscreen and insect repellent are also essential.

Hygiene can be a serious issue on feluccas. Treat the Nile water used for washing up with sterilizing tablets and take extra care to wash your hands before handling food. Bear in mind that you will be going to the toilet on the riverbank, so take sufficient supplies of toilet paper for the duration of your trip. It is also wise to take a torch for possible night time excursions to the riverbank. Burn all rubbish, and bury bodily waste to avoid polluting the banks of the Nile.

You can take a dip in the Nile between Aswan and Luxor, where it is still blue and welcoming, as the only crocodiles are above the High Dam in the waters of Lake Nasser. The Nile is, however, infested with parasitic worms, the larvae of which penetrate the skin causing bilharzia, an infection also known as snail fever or swimmer's itch. The mortality rate is very low, but the disease is debilitating. Locals insist you will be fine in fast-moving waters but the sluggish banks are best avoided.

DIRECTORY

NILE CRUISE TOUR OPERATORS

IN EGYPT

Abercrombie & Kent
18 Sharia Yusuf al-Gindi, Cairo. **Map** 5 C4.
Tel (02) 2393 6255.
www.abercrombiekent. com

Airlink Travel
6A Sharia Fouah, Mohandiseen, Cairo.
Tel (02) 3302 6243/4.
www.airlinktravelegypt. com

Belle Epoque Travel Bureau
17 Sharia Tunis, Maadi, Cairo.
Tel (02) 2516 9649.
www.dahabiya.com

Blue Sky Travel
44 Sharia Shehab, Mohandiseen, Cairo.
Tel (02) 3305 9797.
www.blueskygroup.com

Five Star Travel Group
49 Sharia Mohiel Din Abul Ezz, Mohandiseen, Cairo.
Tel (02) 3336 0244.
www.fivestar-egypt.com

KT Travel
15 Lebanon St, Mohandiseen, Cairo.
Tel (02) 3302 8486.
www.kt-travel.com

Memphis Tours Egypt
1st Qorh Ibn Sherik, off Sharia Morad, Midan Giza, Giza, Cairo.
Tel (02) 3571 6050.
www.memphistours.net

Nile Melody
3 El Khadrawi Street, El Tahrir Square, Cairo.
Tel (02) 2578 3127.
www.egyptmelody.com

Nour Einil
Tel 010 6578 322.
www.nourelnil.com

Safari Egypt
43 Sharia Abdel Khalek Tharwat, Cairo.
Tel (02) 2393 6722 or (02) 2393 6728.
www.safariegypt.com

Select Egypt
28 Street 269, Maadi, Cairo.
Tel (02) 2517 5492.
www.selectegypt.com

Sonesta Nile Cruises
3 Sharia El Ta yaran, Nasr City, Cairo.
Tel (02) 2262 8111.
www.sonesta.com/ nilecruises

Spring Tours
3 Sharia al-Sayed al-Bakry, Zamalek, Cairo.
Map 1 A3.
Tel (02) 2736 5972.
www.springtours.com

Suneast Tours
El-Nasr Road, Nasr City, Cairo.
PO Box 78, Cairo Airport.
Tel (02) 2415 3687.
www.suneasttours.com

Thomas Cook
17 Sharia Mahmoud Bassiouni, Cairo.
Map 3 B3.
Tel (02) 2576 3687.
www.thomascook egypt.com

Travcotels
19 Yehia Ibrahim St, Zamalek, 11211 Cairo.
Tel (02) 2735 4890/4895.
www.travcotels.com

IN THE UK

Acacia Adventure Holidays Ltd
23A Craven Terrace, Lancaster Gate, London W2 3QH.
Tel (020) 7706 4700.
www.acacia-africa.com

Amoun Travel & Tours Ltd
56 Kendal Street, London W2 2BP.
Tel (020) 7402 3100.
www.amountravel.co.uk

Archers Direct
Ground Floor, Dale House, Tiviot Dale, Stockport, Cheshire SK1 1TB.
Tel 0844 573 4806.
www.archersdirect.co.uk

Audley Travel
New Mill, New Mill Lane, Witney, Oxfordshire OX29 9SX.
Tel (01993) 838 400.
www.audleytravel.com

Bales Worldwide Ltd
Bales House, Junction Road, Dorking, Surrey RH4 3HL. *Tel* 0845 057 1819.
www.balesworldwide.com

Blue Water Holidays
The Old Mill, Firth Street, Skipton, North Yorkshire BD23 2PT. *Tel* (01756) 639 609. **www**. bluewaterholidays.com

Cox & Kings Travel Ltd
6th Floor, 30 Millbank, London SW1P 4EE.
Tel (020) 7873 5000.
www.coxandkings.co.uk

Discover Egypt
80 Borough High Street, London SE1 1LL.
Tel 0844 880 0462.
www.discoveregypt.co.uk

Exodus Travels Ltd
Grange Mills, Weir Road, London SW12 0NE.
Tel (020) 8675 5550.
www.exodus.co.uk

Explore Worldwide Ltd
Nelson House, 55 Victoria Road, Farnborough, Hampshire GU14 7PA.
Tel 0845 013 1537.
www.explore.co.uk

Hayes & Jarvis Worldwide
The Atrium, London Road, Crawley RH10 9SR. *Tel* 0844 855 4488. **www**. hayesandjarvis.co.uk

Kuoni
Kuoni House, Dorking, Surrey RH5 4AZ.
Tel (01306) 747 002.
www.kuoni.co.uk

Planet Holidays
Castle House, 21 Station Road, New Barnet EN5 1PA.
Tel 0871 871 2234.
www.planet-holidays. co.uk

Soliman Travel UK
113 Earl's Court Road, London SW5 9RL.
Tel 0207 244 6855.
www.solimantravel.co.uk

Voyages Jules Verne
21 Dorset Square, London NW1 6QG.
Tel 0845 166 7003.
www.vjv.co.uk

IN THE USA

Exodus Travels/ Explore Worldwide
Adventure Center, 1311 63rd Street, Suite 200, Emeryville CA 94608.
Tel 1 800 843 4277 or 1 800 228 8747 (toll free). **www**.exodus.co.uk **www**.explore.co.uk

Misr Travel Company
Suite 604, 1270 Avenue of the Americas, New York.
Tel (212) 332 2600.
www.egypt-vacation.com

Sonesta Nile Cruises
116 Huntington Avenue, Boston, MA 02116.
Tel 800 766 3782; UK: 0800 898 410.
www.sonesta

Travel Egypt Inc
4015 Nine McFarland Dr, Suite 150, Alpharetta, GA 30004.
Tel toll free (877) 778 3497.
www.pharaohsnile.com

SURVIVAL
GUIDE

PRACTICAL INFORMATION

Egypt has made significant progress in improving its tourist infrastructure and the provision of services and security to visitors. Nevertheless certain obstacles remain. Major cities usually have adequate signposting, but most of the monuments still lack proper on-site information panels, signs and labelling. One of ancient Egypt's gifts to the world was bureaucracy and modern-day

Sign for the Temple of Amun, Siwa

visitors must now contend with a sometimes bewildering and frustrating number of formal and informal procedures. With six millennia of history behind them, Egyptians are not in as much of a hurry as the rest of the world. Problems can often be avoided by allowing extra time for even the most minor tasks. However, patience and a good sense of humour are definite assets on a trip to Egypt.

A tourist sign providing general information at Saqqara

PASSPORTS AND VISAS

Visitors to Egypt should possess a passport valid for six months beyond their planned date of entry. All North Americans, Australians, New Zealanders and most Europeans need a tourist visa to enter the country. These can be obtained in advance from Egyptian consulates abroad, but can also be bought on arrival at Cairo, Hurghada or Luxor airport. It is worth bringing $15 dollars with you to pay for the visa. Note that general visas cannot be bought at the overland crossing of Taba, nor can they be obtained at Aswan, Suez or Nuweiba.

Both the single-visit and multiple-entry types of visa allow visitors to stay in Egypt for one month; multiple-entry visas allow the bearer to go in and out of the country three times during that period.

Visas that are valid only for Sinai can be purchased at the border crossing at Taba,

at Sharm el-Sheikh airport and at the ports of Sharm el-Sheikh and Nuweiba. These visas last for only two weeks and restrict visitors to the Aqaba coastline as far as the main resort of Sharm el-Sheikh and the vicinity of St Catherine's Monastery.

Be prepared for individual officials to be generally obstructive. In such an event, try to keep calm and friendly.

CUSTOMS AND DUTY-FREE ALLOWANCES

If you wish to bring personal supplies of cigarettes and alcohol into Egypt, it is best to purchase them when you arrive at either Cairo or Luxor airport. Both have duty-free shops, before and after the Customs checkpoint. The shops before Customs are generally better stocked and less crowded than those after.

Semiramis Hotel on the banks of the Nile, Cairo

Upon arrival, visitors can purchase 4 litres of alcohol, or 3 litres and a case of beer, and 200 cigarettes. If visitors elect not to purchase these items upon arrival, they have 48 hours to get to a duty-free shop elsewhere, where they can purchase 3 litres of alcohol and 200 cigarettes.

There are duty-free shops in Cairo at the Giza Sheraton, the Stars City Center at Ahmed Fakhry Street in Nasr City, and at the end of Sharia Gamiat ad-Dowal al-Arabiyya in Mohandiseen. There are also duty-free shops in the centre of Luxor and Hurghada. Bring your passport, as you will be asked for it. You may also be approached by Egyptians asking if you will use your passport to buy duty-free items on their behalf.

The allowance for visitors bringing cigarettes or alcohol that have been purchased in another country is 1 litre of alcohol and 200 cigarettes.

If you bring a video camera or computer into Egypt, it must be declared on "Form D" upon arrival. If either of those items is stolen, be sure to obtain a police report. If not, when you leave, it will be assumed that you have sold them and a duty of 100 per cent will be levied.

LANGUAGE

Most urban and professional Egyptians speak a little English and sometimes some French as well. Egyptians working in the tourist sector are accustomed to visitors who cannot speak Arabic and will speak enough English to

◁ **Feluccas on the Nile at Luxor at sunset, with a camel standing on the shore**

Typical ticket kiosk at Philae – vendors usually understand some English

take care of your needs. It is still worth mastering a few Arabic words and phrases. Recognizing Arabic numerals can help in getting around and dealing with money, while being able to convey a polite greeting will inevitably delight the recipient. If you are planning to travel off the beaten tourist track, a little knowledge of basic Arabic can be useful, if not essential.

PUBLIC CONVENIENCES

Public toilets are rare in Egypt, although major tourist sites often have some type of provision. Facilities in petrol stations, bus and train terminals and cafés in the poorer quarters are likely to be unpleasant, squat toilets. Toilet paper is unlikely to be provided, so it is a good idea to carry tissues with you. Small packets are available from kiosks, stores and street vendors everywhere. Better hotels and restaurants usually have flush toilets. These are often staffed by an attendant who will provide toilet paper and turn on the tap for you. *Baksheesh* of 25–50 piastres is customary for this service.

Electric plug adaptor with two round pins

ELECTRICAL ADAPTORS

The electric current is 220V and sockets take two-pin plugs. A travel converter will enable you to use appliances from abroad. Brief power cuts are common, so it is a good idea to carry a torch with you.

TIME

Egypt is two hours ahead of the standard GMT, and often uses its own concept of time – what Egyptians and foreigners alike call "IBM" time, which stands for *Inshallah, Bokra, Maalesh.*

Inshallah (God willing) is a way of remembering Allah in every action, but sometimes, in the context of tourism, it suggests that something might or might not happen. *Bokra* literally means "tomorrow", but it might be used to mean two days, two weeks or perhaps never. It definitely means "not today". *Maalesh* means "Never mind, don't worry, forget about it."

Egyptians do not like to say no or disappoint guests, so you must be persistent and good-humoured in trying to establish when, or if, a desired outcome is likely to occur.

CONVERSION CHART

Imperial to Metric
1 inch = 2.54 centimetres
1 foot = 30 centimetres
1 mile = 1.6 kilometres
1 ounce = 28 grams
1 pound = 454 grams
1 pint = 0.6 litre
1 gallon = 4.6 litres

Metric to Imperial
1 millimetre = 0.04 inch.
1 centimetre = 0.4 inch
1 metre = 3 feet 3 inches
1 kilometre = 0.6 mile
1 gram = 0.04 ounce
1 kilogram = 2.2 pounds
1 litre = 1.8 pints

DIRECTORY

EGYPTIAN EMBASSIES ABROAD

Australia
241 Commonwealth Street, Surrey Hills, Sydney. **Tel** *(612) 9281 4844.* **www**.egypt.org.au

United Kingdom
2 Lowndes Street, London SW1X 9ET. **Tel** *(020) 7235 9719.* **www**.egypt. embassaryhomepage.com

Canada
454 Laurier Avenue East, Ottawa, ON, K1N 6R3. **Tel** *(613) 234 4931.*

Ireland
12 Clyde Road, Dublin 4. **Tel** *(01) 6606 566.*

Israel
54 Rehov Basel, Tel Aviv. **Tel** *(03) 546 4151.*

Egyptian Consulate 68 Efroni Street, Eilat. **Tel** *(972) 6376 882.*

Jordan
14 Riyad Mefleh Street, Amman. **Tel** *(26) 5605 176.*

Egyptian Consulate, Aqaba. **Tel** *(26) 2016 181.*

United States
3521 International Court, NW Washington, DC 20008. **Tel** *(202) 966 6342.*

Egyptian Consulate 1110 Second Ave, New York, NY 10022. **Tel** *(212) 759 7120.*

EGYPTIAN TOURIST OFFICES

In the UK
170 Piccadilly, London W1V 9DD. **Tel** *(020) 7493 5283.*

In the US
630 Fifth Avenue, Suite 1706, New York, NY 10111. **Tel** *(212) 332 2570.*

In Canada
1253 McGill College Ave, Suite 250, Montreal, Quebec, H3B 2Y5. **Tel** *(514) 861 4420.*

Tips for Visitors

Although practical information is sometimes hard to obtain from the Egyptian tourist board, the major offices are worth visiting as some of the staff usually speak good English and are knowledgeable about the sites. Travel agencies and hotel receptionists are often more helpful and can usually offer up-to-date advice on accommodation, transport and other practicalities.

Tourist information office at Aswan with Nubian-style domes

OPENING HOURS

The major historic sites and museums are open daily from 9am until 5pm (6pm in summer). In Luxor, most monuments open at 6am. During Ramadan, they may open a little later than the advertised time and close around 3pm.

Government and administrative offices generally close on Fridays, while shops and stores sometimes close on Sundays. Most stores are open from 9am until 2 or 3pm, then again from 5 to 9pm. However, shops in tourist areas usually stay open all day and late into the night.

During Ramadan, offices and shops open later than normal and close around 3pm. They re-open around 8 or 9pm, and remain open until quite late.

VISITING RELIGIOUS SITES

Egypt generally welcomes non-Muslim visitors to its mosques (see pp32–3). It is, however, advisable to seek permission before visiting any mosque outside Cairo and Alexandria, where residents may be less accustomed to seeing tourists.

With the exception of the mosques of Al-Hussein and Sayyida Zeinab, most religious sites in Cairo are seen as historic monuments, open to non-Muslims from 9am until 4pm. However, tourists should not intrude in any way on worshippers and avoid visiting at prayer times.

Modest dress is essential at all mosques. In some places, women may be asked to cover their hair (a scarf will be provided). You must also remove your shoes before entering the mosque. There is sometimes a shoe custodian (who will expect a small *baksheesh*) or you can leave them outside the door. If you want to climb the minaret, carry your shoes, with the two soles pressed together.

Similar rules apply when visiting monasteries, though you will not have to remove your shoes. With the exception

Modestly dressed women visiting a mosque

of St Catherine's, which is Greek Orthodox, monasteries in Egypt are Coptic. All the monasteries quite readily admit visitors during the day, except during Lent.

DISABLED TRAVELLERS

Few tourist sites in Egypt are equipped for disabled visitors. Steep flights of stairs, deep sand and the poor condition of streets combine to make life difficult for those who are less able. On a more positive note, Egyptians are not embarrassed by disability and museum and hotel staff are always willing to help.

The Egyptian national travel company, **Misr Travel**, has tours and accommodation suited for disabled travellers and now has branches worldwide. For those who wish to experience the magic of swimming and diving in the Red Sea, the **Camel Dive Club**, based in Sharm el-Sheikh, has facilities and training geared towards travellers with special needs.

STUDENTS

Full-time students can enjoy discounts at museums and historical sites, and reduced air, rail and bus fares with an International Student Identity Card (ISIC). If you arrive in Cairo without one, you can obtain a card at the Egyptian Scientific Centre, 23 Sharia al-Manial on Rhoda Island. A student card can also be purchased at several downtown hotels, but beware of shops offering forgeries.

International Student Identity Card

ETIQUETTE

Egypt is one of the most liberal Muslim countries in the Middle East, and its citizens are justifiably famous for their tolerance, generosity and warmth. However, the presence of five-star hotels,

Visitor about to engage in the ancient art of haggling in Aswan's souk

beach resorts, casinos and other trappings of Western culture, such as mobile phones, luxury cars and bars serving alcohol, may lead the casual visitor to conclude that Egypt is more open and liberal than it really is. At its heart, Egypt is still a deeply conservative country and the dominant values are Islamic. To get closer to a truly welcoming people, visitors need to be aware of these values and modify their dress and behaviour accordingly.

Modest dress is essential if one wishes to avoid giving offence or, for women, attracting undue attention. Shorts and swimwear are really only acceptable at beach resorts, primarily along the Aqaba coast on the Red Sea, and the private beaches of certain hotels in Hurghada. In other areas, use your discretion, but remember that, for both sexes, bare shoulders are considered offensive.

Boorish behaviour, such as arrogance or bluntness, can create problems, so remain patient and polite when confronted with bureaucratic hassles or persistent touts. A gentle sense of humour helps to ameliorate difficult circumstances, and is the approach most often deployed by Egyptians themselves.

Egyptians of the same sex frequently hold hands and kiss in public, but open displays of affection between the sexes are rare and can cause deep offence.

If invited to someone's home, a small gift of flowers or sweets is appropriate. For men, sitting with legs crossed and showing the sole of your foot is seen as rude. Shopkeepers will offer tea or soft drinks during negotiations, but this incurs no obligation to buy. When bargaining, however, once you have agreed a price, it is rude to refuse to purchase the item.

Egyptians are aware of their country's weaknesses but do not appreciate it when foreigners point them out. Avoid criticizing religion or the president, and issues such as *baksheesh* or the condition of the streets or buildings.

PHOTOGRAPHY

Museums and major tourist sites sometimes charge for the use of video and still cameras. The use of a flash is often forbidden. Always ask permission before taking someone's photograph, especially of women or religious figures and in rural areas. Taking photographs that show Egypt as backward or poor may also cause offence. Visitors should remember that it is always forbidden to take pictures of army bases, airports, government buildings, dams, bridges or anything considered vital to security.

Tourists photographing the Sphinx near the Pyramids of Giza

DIRECTORY

TOURIST OFFICES

Alexandria
Midan Saad Zaghloul.
🕐 8am–6pm daily (till 8pm in summer).
Tel (03) 485 1556.

Masr railway station.
🕐 8am–8pm daily.
Tel (03) 392 5985.

Aswan
Aswan railway station.
🕐 9am–3pm, 6–8pm daily; 9am–3pm, 7–9pm in summer.
Tel (097) 2312 811.

Cairo
5 Sharia Adly.
🕐 9am–6pm daily.
Tel (02) 2391 3454.

Terminal 1, Cairo airport.
🕐 8am–9pm daily.
Tel (02) 2265 5000-1.

Ramses railway station.
🕐 8:30am–8pm daily.
Tel (02) 2579 0767.

Giza Pyramids.
🕐 8:30am–5pm daily.
Tel (02) 3383 8823.

Luxor
Opposite railway station (main office).
🕐 8am–8pm daily.
Tel (095) 2373 294.
Inside railway station.
🕐 8am–8pm daily.
Tel (095) 2370 259.
Luxor airport.
🕐 24 hours daily.
Tel (095) 2372 306.

DISABLED TRAVELLERS

Camel Dive Club
Sharm el-Sheikh, Sinai.

Tel (069) 3600 700.
www.cameldive.com

Misr Travel
1 Sharia Talaat Harb, Cairo.
Tel (02) 3393 0010.
www.misrtravel.net

In the UK
Misr Travel UK,
Old Inn House, Suite D,
Carshalton Road, Sutton,
SM1 4LE.
Tel (020) 8643 2429.

Egypt For All
www.egyptforall.net

Security

In spite of the size and population density of its cities, Egypt is one of the safest countries in the world for travellers. The most serious crime that most visitors are likely to encounter is minor theft, which is rare, especially away from congested tourist areas. Visitors should, of course, take the usual precautions of wearing a money belt and keeping a close watch on cameras and bags. In fact, tales abound of taxi drivers, hotel personnel and ordinary citizens returning lost property and keeping a look-out for the welfare of guests.

POLICE

Visitors to Egypt are often surprised by the numbers of police posted on street corners, at intersections and outside government buildings and historic sites. This is not a sign of imminent or recent trouble, but has simply been the status quo since the 1960s.

Different police forces deal with different aspects of law and order. The Municipal Police handle crime and are recognizable by their uniforms – khaki in winter and tan or white in summer. Traffic Police wear similar uniforms, with the addition of striped cuffs. Both forces deal with accidents and can help in emergencies, but few speak English.

The Tourist Police are the agency visitors should turn to in times of trouble. Ordinary ranks wear khaki uniforms, while officers wear black in winter, white in summer. Easily identified by "Tourist Police" armbands, they are stationed at ports, airports, stations, tourist sites and museums and usually speak some English.

The Central Security Police guard embassies, banks and highways. Dressed in black uniforms and armed with Kalashnikovs, their appearance can be very intimidating. In general they are no cause for concern, but if you do find yourself caught up in a demonstration, get right away immediately.

Sign for police guarding antiquities

Unless drugs or espionage are suspected, foreigners are usually treated with politeness by the police.

PETTY CRIME

Egypt is proud of its low crime rate and in general visitors should have little trouble as long as they take sensible precautions and avoid travelling alone when away from tourist areas. As in any large city, crowded areas, such as the Khan al-Khalili, provide the ideal conditions for pickpockets and petty thieves. Keep your money and passport in a money belt or pouch and your camera and other valuables out of sight. Security on camp sites, hostels and cheap hotels is likely to be poor, so leave valuables at the reception desk, or take them with you. If travelling by car, do not leave anything of value visible or accessible.

Crowded street near Khan al-Khalili, where it is wise for visitors to mind their valuables

TRAVEL AND TERRORISM

Following demonstrations in 2011, it is sensible to be cautious when in large cities, listen to local advice and obey curfews. Get up-to-date advice from your ministry of foreign affairs before travelling. In the UK, call the Foreign and Commonwealth Office or visit their website. US citizens should check the US State Department's website for current advice for travellers. Middle Egypt – which includes the cities of Minya, Asyut and Sohag and the historic sites of the Tombs of Beni Hassan, Tell al-Amarna, Abydos, Dendara and several monasteries – is a potential hot spot for trouble (see p176). Because of this, the Egyptian authorities are vigilant over visitors to the area. There is heavy security and the movements of tourists are tightly controlled.

It is possible to arrange day trips as part of a group from Cairo and Luxor, but only under strict security. If you go alone by local bus or by service taxi, police at checkpoints may ask to see your passport and might even give you an escort into the sites, depending on the situation. Information about the causes and extent of the unrest is hard to come by and often conflicting. The threat is not always directed at tourists, but visitors do run the risk of being caught up in local violence.

Terrorist attacks on tourists in general have ceased since the massacre at the Temple of Hatshepsut in Luxor, on 17 November 1997. Since then, the Egyptian government has tried to prevent further attacks on tourists and has increased security, particularly at the major historical sites.

IN CASE OF FIRE

Hostels, cheap hotels and even some of the more expensive establishments are unlikely to have adequate fire exits or even fire extinguishers. Therefore, it is a good idea at

Distinctive Egyptian fire engine, equipped for the rough terrain

least to familiarize yourself with the layout of the building and possible escape routes in case a fire does occur.

WOMEN TRAVELLERS

Egypt has become more conservative in recent years, as witnessed by the increasing numbers of women wearing the *hijab* or head-scarf. Women tourists are not expected to wear scarves, but may feel more at ease doing so in mosques or rural areas.

The social norms for women in Egypt are very different from those in the West and this, combined with images of women in Hollywood films, creates misconceptions. For example, women travellers unaccompanied by a man are often regarded as morally loose. While serious sexual assaults are rare, verbal harass-ment and groping does occur. The risk of harassment can be reduced by dressing modestly. Wear long, loose, opaque

clothes that cover your chest, shoulders, upper arms and your legs below the knees. Many single women wear wedding rings, which signal respectability. Sit with other women on trains and buses and in the Cairo Metro, where there are cars reserved for women. Avoid eye contact and smiling at strange men as these can be misconstrued. If you are harassed, the best response is to ignore the offender. Using phrases such as *haram* (shame), or *sibnee le wahdi* (leave me alone) may bring help. Women in Islam are highly respected and help is frequently extended to female travellers in distress.

EMBASSIES

If you find yourself in trouble, contact your embassy or consulate who will give legal advice and replace lost pass-ports. They are unsympathetic to drug offenders and will not lend you money to get home,

although, as a last resort, they will arrange repatriation. It is as well to remember that although you are a welcome visitor to the country, you are still subject to Egyptian laws.

DIRECTORY

EMERGENCY SERVICES

Fire *Tel 180.*
Tourist Police *Tel 126.*
Emergency *Tel 123.*

TRAVEL ADVICE

www.fco.gov.uk (in UK) or
Tel (020) 7008 1500.
http://travel.state.gov (in US).

EMBASSIES

Australia
World Trade Centre (11th floor), Corniche el-Nil, Bulaq, Cairo. **Map** 1 A3. *Tel (02) 2575 0444.*

Canada
26 Sharia Kamel el Shenawi, Garden City, Cairo. **Map** 5 A5. *Tel (02) 2791 8700.*

Ireland
22 Hassan Assem, Zamalek, Cairo. **Map** 1 A3. *Tel (02) 2735 8264.*

UK
7 Sharia Ahmed Ragheb, Garden City, Cairo. **Map** 5 A4. *Tel (02) 2791 6000.*

USA
5 Sharia Amerika al-Latineya, Garden City, Cairo. **Map** 5 B4. *Tel (02) 2797 3300.*

A police escort accompanying tourists taking a camel ride at Aswan

Health and Insurance

Distinctive Egyptian pharmacy logo

Although travelling in Egypt might be thought to pose serious health risks, these can be minimized by careful pre-planning, taking sensible precautions while in the country and by the reassurance offered by taking out appropriate travel insurance before leaving home. The most common problems are mild gastric disturbances – simply caused by bacteria in food and drink to which the traveller has yet to acquire immunity – plus the range of ailments induced by a careless attitude to extreme heat and sunshine.

Egyptian pharmacy shop front, with name in Arabic and English

GENERAL ADVICE

For most visitors to Egypt, stomach upsets and over-exposure to the sun constitute the greatest health risks. It is a good idea, however, to pack a first-aid kit with plasters, bandages, antiseptic ointment and some painkillers. Insect repellent is vital, especially in the Western Desert oases, on the Sinai coast, in the Delta, and for felucca rides at sunset. Include some oral rehydration salts in your kit: these will help replace lost minerals if you do suffer a bad bout of diarrhoea.

Check the current requirements regarding prescription medicines with the Egyptian embassy before you travel; you may need to carry a letter from your GP. It's a good idea to bring your own supply of contact lens solution.

The sun is strong throughout Egypt, even in winter, and particularly in Upper Egypt, where there is very little shade. Wear a sunhat and sunglasses and use a sunscreen with a protection factor of at least 30.

VACCINATIONS

Visitors to Egypt do not require any vaccinations unless they are coming from an infected area. However you may like to ask your GP for the current World Health Organization (WHO) health bulletin on Egypt before travelling. As well as ensuring that your polio and tetanus cover is up to date, the most common recommendations include vaccinations against typhoid and Hepatitis A and B. A meningitis vaccination may also be advised.

Rabies is a problem throughout the country. Avoid touching any stray animals, including cats, dogs, bats and monkeys. If you think you have been exposed to the disease, seek help urgently.

PHARMACIES

Egyptian pharmacists are a good source of help for minor health complaints. They generally speak English and can be trusted to advise on remedies for most common ailments. Pharmacies carry a wide range of drugs, which are cheap and can often be dispensed without a doctor's prescription. Pharmacists can also help you find a doctor.

A dive trip in the Red Sea, with fierce sun, intense heat and lack of shade posing potential health hazards

STOMACH UPSETS

Mild diarrhoea is a common ailment for visitors to Egypt. However, a few simple precautions can reduce your chances of falling ill, or at least lessen the effects.

While tap water is generally safe, it is heavily chlorinated and rather unpleasant tasting. Bottled water is available everywhere – but make sure that the seal is unbroken when you buy it. Avoid raw vegetables and unpeeled fruit, or wash them thoroughly in purified water. Do not buy food from a street stall that has no running water, and beware of ice-cream that may have melted, then been refrozen. Choose budget restaurants with care and always check that meat has been cooked thoroughly.

If you do feel unwell, bottled water with a little added fresh lime juice can help settle an upset stomach.

Local brand of Egyptian bottled water

OTHER HAZARDS

Dehydration, sunburn and heat exhaustion are of particular concern, especially in Upper Egypt. Lack of shade at archaeological sites, plus wind-blown sand and dust, can make for an uncomfortable experience. Sweat evaporates quickly in these dry conditions and you may become de-hydrated without realizing it. Drink plenty of bottled water and add a little extra salt to your food to replace salts lost in sweat. Wear a sunhat and loose-fitting clothes made of natural fibres, and wear a T-shirt when swimming.

Heatstroke is a potentially fatal condition that occurs when the body temperature rises to dangerous levels. Symptoms include flushed skin, severe headaches and confusion. Immediate medical attention is essential.

Bilharzia, or schistosomiasis, is another hazard in Egypt. This disease is transmitted by water-borne flukes that infest the stagnant water found in canals or in slower-moving stretches of the Nile. Do not wade or bathe in such water or walk barefoot on the muddy banks. Never drink water from such a source.

HOSPITALS AND EMERGENCIES

Private hospitals provide the best medical care in Egypt, but they still fall short of standards found in the West. The most reliable private hospitals are in Cairo and Alexandria, and those attached to universities are generally competent and well equipped. Irrespective of whether the patient is insured, both private and state-run hospitals will probably ask for a cash payment before providing treatment of any kind. If you do not have sufficient funds to cover this, contact your embassy who may be able to arrange for relatives or your insurance company to cover the fees in advance of your claim. Be sure to obtain receipts for all the expenses you incur, since these will be required by your insurance company to support your claim for reimbursement.

With the exception of the private service run by As-Salaam Hospital in Cairo, ambulances do not carry paramedics or life-support equipment. Since telephone lines in Egypt are seriously overloaded, it is best, in a real emergency, to take a taxi to the nearest hospital rather than trying to call an ambulance.

A typical red and white Egyptian ambulance

TRAVEL INSURANCE

Most travel policies cover you for lost belongings and cancellation as well as medical emergencies, and are strongly recommended. Be sure to inform the insurance company if you intend to take part in any dangerous sports, such as diving, otherwise your cover may be invalid. Keep the documents with you so that you can readily contact the company if necessary.

Communications & Media

Egyptian telephone and Internet services have improved dramatically in recent years. Internet cafés are widely available in the more tourist-orientated areas and almost all hotels have a wireless connection. Unfortunately the same cannot be said of the postal service. Overseas letters sent from Egypt can still take weeks to arrive, if they do at all. Egypt has eight television channels and many satellite channels, as well as several English-language newspapers and magazines.

USEFUL DIALLING CODES

- To dial locally:
  dial the 7- or 8-digit telephone number.
- To dial within Egypt:
  dial 0 + area code + telephone number.
- Area codes: Cairo and Giza: 2; Alexandria: 3; Aswan: 97; Fayoum: 84; Luxor: 95; Ismailia: 64; Hurghada: 65; Sharm el-Sheikh: 69.
- To dial internationally:
  dial 00 + country code + telephone number.
- Country codes: US and Canada: 1; France: 33; Germany: 49; Italy: 39; Netherlands: 31; Spain: 34; Switzerland: 41; UK: 44; South Africa: 27; Australia: 61.
- Mobile phone numbers are prefixed by 010; 012; 016; 017; 018; or 019.

PUBLIC TELEPHONES

Menatel, identified by its green-and-yellow half-booths, is the most widespread of the public card phone services.

Man using a mobile phone whilst on a camel, in front of a pyramid

Phonecards can be obtained from pharmacies, newspaper stands, tobacco shops and kiosks displaying the green-and-yellow Menatel sign. The LE 10 cards are for local calls and the LE 30 cards for international calls. Cheaper rates are available from 8pm–8am. All booths have instructions in Arabic and English.

Phonebooths are gradually being phased out, however as the use of mobile phones is endemic in Egypt. The phone system as a whole remains overloaded and it can take numerous attempts to reach the person you are calling. Numbers change often and in such cases, a recorded message both in Arabic and English will provide you with the new number.

MOBILE PHONES

Not all networks provide roaming services in Egypt so if you are planning to use your mobile phone frequently, you can buy a SIM card from a local provider such as Mobinil, Vodafone or Etisalat. On some SIM cards incoming calls are free. All providers have shops in most towns and cities. SIM cards can be bought for about LE 50 and top-up cards for phone credit can be bought easily from kiosks and grocery shops.

MAIL SERVICES

Most post offices in Egypt are open from 9am to 3pm daily, except Friday and Saturday, although the central Cairo post office remains open 24 hours a day. Post offices are often overcrowded and difficult to use if you don't speak Arabic. It is probably simpler therefore to buy stamps and send mail from hotels. To send important letters or packages, it is strongly advised to use one of the international courier services, such as Federal Express or DHL. Both companies have several offices in Cairo. This is a more expensive option but the only way of guaranteeing that items will reach their intended recipient quickly.

A typical postbox in Egypt

Receiving letters *poste restante* at the post office is not always reliable and it is a better idea to have letters sent to your hotel. In addition, the main American Express office in Cairo at 15 Sharia Qasr el-Nil holds mail for people who have American Express cards or Amex traveller's cheques. Receiving packages or over-stuffed envelopes from overseas is best avoided as all such parcels are inspected by customs and censors. Items such as compact discs, DVDs and computer games arrive very late or not at all. If they do arrive, expect to pay duty worth more than the package's contents.

TELEVISION AND RADIO

Television channels 1 and 2 are the national channels, with the latter broadcasting news in English and French. Channel 3 is the local Cairo channel. Channels 4 to 8 are broadcast from Ismailia, Alexandria, Tanta, Minya and Aswan respectively. All the channels broadcast foreign language programmes with Arabic subtitles, and the better hotels provide cable or

Newspaper stand selling foreign papers in Mahattat Ramla, Alexandria

satellite television. Increasing numbers of private television channels broadcast mainly entertainment programmes.

Foreign-language radio programmes are rare outside Cairo and Alexandria. In Cairo, FM 95 broadcasts programmes in English and French and a few other stations mix Western classical and pop music with Arabic music and news. Check the *Egyptian Gazette* for TV and radio schedules or *Egypt Today* magazine for satellite and cable TV highlights.

A selection of English-language newspapers and magazines

NEWSPAPERS AND MAGAZINES

The daily *Egyptian Gazette* and the weekly *Middle East Times* and *Al-Ahram Weekly* cover international and domestic news; the latter two provide good coverage of television, films and cultural events. The weekly *Cairo Times* is a mix of local and regional news, features and reviews. Outside Cairo, the *Egyptian Gazette* is the only local English-language paper.

There are a number of English-language magazines. The monthly *Egypt Today* contains comprehensive cultural and restaurant listings. Other English-language magazines include *Egypt Today*'s sister publications *Business Today* and *Sports and Fitness*, which is

useful for health clubs, sports and recreation listings. A broad range of Western newspapers is usually on sale the day after publication at streetside newspaper stands in affluent areas of large cities and at major hotels. *Time, Newsweek* and *The Economist* are also available.

INTERNET AND WI-FI

Internet access is widespread in Egypt and Internet cafés and Wi-Fi technology are fast-growing phenomena, especially in the tourist centres of Cairo, Alexandria and Luxor. Major hotels also offer Internet access and Wi-Fi. Some hotels charge for use, costs are usually LE 5–10 per hour, although five-star hotels can charge considerably more for access.

DIRECTORY

MAIN POST OFFICES

Cairo
Midan Ataba. **Map** 6 E2.

Luxor
Sharia al-Mahatta.

INTERNATIONAL COURIER SERVICES

Federal Express
1079 Corniche el-Nil, Garden City, Cairo. **Map** 5 A5.
Tel (02) 2795 2803.

DHL
16 Sharia Lebanon, Mohandiseen, Cairo. **Map** 1 A2.
Tel (02) 3302 9811/16345.

INTERNET CAFÉS

Internet Egypt
Ground floor, 2 Midan Simon Bolivar, Garden City, Cairo.
Map 5 B4.
Tel (02) 2796 2882.

Mohandiseen Cybercafé
Sharia Gamiat ad-Dowal al-Arabiyya, Cairo.
Tel (02) 3305 0493.

Sun Café
Between Sharia Souq el-Tawfiqa and Sharia 26th July, Downtown, Cairo.

Zamalek Center
25a Sharia Ismail Mohammed, Zamalek. **Map** 5 B3.
Tel (02) 2736 4004.

One of many Internet cafés in Cairo

Banking and Currency

Egypt is still very much a cash economy. Both banks and exchange offices will change cash and traveller's cheques, but exchange offices usually offer better hours, shorter queues and more favourable rates. Credit cards, while accepted at most major hotels and some tourist shops, are not much use anywhere else. Automated Teller Machines (ATMs) are now often found outside many banks and can be used for cash withdrawals, although

Logo of Banque de Caire

some credit cards charge heavily for this service. Egypt prohibits the exportation of its currency, which, in any case, is useless outside the country.

Standard ATM with instructions in a range of languages

BANKS

The usual opening hours for banks in Egypt are Sunday to Thursday 8:30am to 2pm. Exchange offices are also open in the evenings from 6:00pm to 9:00pm. Most banks are closed on Friday and Saturday. As well as Egyptian banks, which include Banque Misr, there are a few well-known international names such as Barclays and Citibank. The best time to go is just as the bank opens – to avoid crowds.

EXCHANGE OFFICES

Exchange offices can be found throughout major cities and tourist areas and are preferable to banks, shops and hotels for changing money. The black market for hard

currency is now in decline and scarcely worth the risk.

It is a good idea to change some money on arrival; both terminals at Cairo Airport have 24-hour exchange offices.

TRAVELLER'S CHEQUES AND CREDIT CARDS

Most banks and exchange offices accept American Express, Barclays, Citibank and Travelex traveller's cheques. Eurocheques are not recommended for use in Egypt. A passport is required to change traveller's cheques. Always keep the receipt and a record of the serial numbers separate from the cheques in case they are lost or stolen. It is often difficult outside tourist areas to use either traveller's cheques or debit and credit cards. The most commonly accepted credit cards are Visa, MasterCard and American Express.

BAKSHEESH AND TIPPING

People demanding *baksheesh* without rendering a service can be irritating, but calm and good-humoured refusals will eventually meet with success. Most Egyptians are paid such low salaries that *baksheesh*, in the form of a tip for service, is a vital part of their income. It is usual, in restaurants, to round up the bill or give an extra 10 per

cent directly to the waiter. Small tips, in the 25 pt to LE 1 range, should be given to people who help you in some small way, such as lavatory

DIRECTORY

BANKS

Banque Misr
151 Sharia Mohammed Farid, Cairo. **Map** 2 D5, 6 D4.
Tel (02) 2792 1856.

Barclays International
12 Midan al-Sheikh Yusuf, Garden City, Cairo. **Map** 3 B1, 5 A5.
Tel (02) 2366 2600.

Citibank
4 Sharia Ahmed Pasha, Garden City, Cairo. **Map** 3 B1, 5 A5.
Tel (02) 2795 1873.

EXCHANGE OFFICES

American Express
15 Sharia Qasr el-Nil, Cairo.
Map 1 C5, 5 C3.
Tel (02) 2480 1530.

Winter Palace Arcade, Luxor.
Tel (095) 237 8333.

Thomas Cook
17 Sharia Mahmoud Bassiouni, Cairo. **Map** 5 B5.
Tel (02) 2576 6982.

Corniche el Nile, Aswan.
Tel (097) 230 6839.

Midan Saad Zaghloul, Alexandria.
Tel (03) 484 7830.

Winter Palace Arcade, Luxor.
Tel (095) 237 2402.

LOST OR STOLEN CREDIT CARDS

American Express
Tel (02) 2480 1530 (24 hours).

Visa/MasterCard
Tel (001) 410 581 9994 (reverse charge call).

Thomas Cook exchange office on the Corniche, Luxor

attendants, and the people who park cars, carry luggage or unlock tombs. Offers to bend the rules a bit, such as letting you into a site after hours or opening one supposedly closed, will cost a little more. However, don't assume money will buy you everything. Do not risk offence by refusing to pay small sums for even minor assistance, but also do not throw money at people to get your way.

CURRENCY

The basic unit of currency in Egypt is the Egyptian pound or *ginee*, written as £E or LE. The Egyptian pound is divided into 100 piastres (pt) or *irsh*.

The 50, 100 and 200 LE notes can sometimes be difficult to change, so always carry some smaller notes. It is also advisable to keep a separate supply of lower denomination notes for *baksheesh* and for taxis who invariably have no change. Do not accept ragged or mutilated notes because taxi drivers and vendors will also refuse them.

Banknotes
Banknotes are issued in 1, 5, 10, 20, 50, 100 and 200 pound denominations as well as 50 and 25 piastres. Smaller in size than pound notes, they are often refused by vendors and taxi drivers alike. Most smaller shops round prices up.

5 Egyptian pounds (LE 5)

10 Egyptian pounds (LE 10)

20 Egyptian pounds (LE 20)

50 Egyptian pounds (LE 50)

100 Egyptian pounds (LE 100)

200 Egyptian pounds (LE 200)

Coins
Coins come in denominations of 1 LE and 5, 10, 20, 25 and 50 piastres. Different versions of the same value can be found in circulation.

5 piastres (5 pt)

10 piastres (10 pt)

20 piastres (20 pt)

25 piastres (25 pt)

50 piastres (50 pt)

1 pound (LE 1)

TRAVEL INFORMATION

Most visitors to Egypt fly to Cairo, but flights are also available to Luxor, Alexandria, Hurghada and Sharm el-Sheikh. A holiday in Egypt can also be combined with a visit to another Middle Eastern or North African country, but flying within the region is comparatively more expensive than flying direct from the US or Europe.

EgyptAir logo

Another popular method of entry into Egypt is overland from Jordan, via Israel, although this entails some extra effort and time because of having to cross two borders on the way. An easier route from Jordan is on the regular ferry or catamaran service that runs between Aqaba and Nuweiba on the Gulf of Aqaba coast of Sinai.

Cairo International Airport, to the northeast of the city

ARRIVING BY AIR

Direct flights to Egypt are regularly available from most European capitals. Both British Airways and EgyptAir fly daily from Heathrow (with a flight time of approximately 5 hours) while Air France flies daily from Paris (4.5 hours). Other daily flights include CSA from Prague, KLM from Amsterdam, Lufthansa from Frankfurt, Malev from Budapest, Olympic from Athens, TAROM from Bucharest and Turkish Airlines from Istanbul. Charter flights are available to both domestic and international destinations.

EgyptAir flies daily direct to Cairo from New York's JFK airport. The flight time is approximately 12 hours. Delta flies direct to and from New York four times a week. There are no direct flights to Egypt from Canada.

Travellers from Australia and New Zealand usually get to Egypt via London, or add on Cairo as part of a Round the World Ticket. However, EgyptAir offers daily flights to Bangkok (with a flight time of approximately 9 hours). Fares vary according to the time of year.

TRANSPORT FROM CAIRO AIRPORT

Cairo International Airport is 20 km (12 miles) to the northeast of the city and has three terminals. The latest addition, Terminal 3, will serve all domestic and international EgyptAir flights, and all international flights from fellow Star Alliance airlines, such as Lufthansa. Terminal 2 (undergoing renovation and due for completion in 2013) serves non-Star Alliance airlines, such as British Airways, and also Saudi and Gulf state airlines. All other international flights land at Terminal 1.

All terminals are connected to the city

centre by bus, but the fastest and most comfortable transfer is by taxi. (For more general information regarding buses and taxis, see pp343–7.)

There is no difficulty in finding a taxi at the airport, as drivers descend on new arrivals the minute they have cleared Customs. The time of day, number, gender and appearance of the passengers, amount of luggage, volume of traffic and bargaining skills all factor into the fare. A trip from the airport to downtown Cairo typically costs between LE 60 and 80 per car load, not per person. New arrivals may also be offered a "limousine" service – the fixed rate for the trip in a decent saloon is around LE 80.

TRANSPORT FROM OTHER AIRPORTS

The airport in Alexandria is 5 km (3 miles) south of the city, however, until 2012, flights into Alexandria are instead using Borg El-Arab airport, 40 km (24 miles) west of the city, whilst El-Nouzha airport is upgraded. Buses connect Borg El-Arab to the centre of town, but a taxi is easier, costing about LE 80–100. Most visitors arriving at Luxor are met at the airport by

Black and yellow taxi serving Alexandria airport

representatives from their hotels or cruise boats. If not, a taxi into town costs around LE 30. Similarly, most visitors to Sharm el-Sheikh are met by hotel transportation. Taxis from the airport, located north of Naama Bay, test the skills of the best bargainers. Expect to pay around LE 30 to 50 per trip. The situation at Hurghada airport is similar, but a taxi into town should cost only LE 40.

ARRIVING BY LAND FROM ISRAEL AND JORDAN

Buses run twice a week on Sundays and Thursdays at 8am, from Tel Aviv and Jerusalem to Egypt, crossing at Taba, the gateway to the Sinai coast. The journey between Jerusalem and Cairo takes 12–14 hours, depending on how long it takes to cross the border. The process has been streamlined slightly at the Taba crossing, which serves both the Israeli resort of Eilat and Egyptian resorts on the Gulf of Aqaba and the rest of the Sinai.

It is also possible to enter Egypt by land from Jordan through Israel. The journey involves a 5-km (3-mile) taxi or "service" taxi from Aqaba to the border, followed by a short walk to the Israeli side. From there, visitors can take a taxi into Eilat. Buses and taxis

Cruise ship passing through the Suez Canal

run from the centre of Eilat to the border with Egypt at Taba. Departure taxes must be paid when leaving Jordan and Israel, even if one is just passing through the latter.

Bear in mind that having Israeli stamps in your passport may preclude you from visiting other Arab countries.

ARRIVING BY SEA

Although Egypt is served by several ports on both its Mediterranean and Red Sea coasts, the advent of cheap air fares and package holidays has inevitably seen the decline of passenger ferries bringing travellers to the country. There

is one exception to this – the crossing from Aqaba, in Jordan, to Nuweiba, in the Sinai. This route is served by both a ferry, which takes 3–5 hours, depending on the weather, and a high-speed catamaran service that does the trip in an hour.

There are no longer any direct ferries from Greece or Cyprus, but two cruise ships sail from Limassol to Port Said, taking passengers on a two-day group visa to Egypt.

Otherwise the only other arrivals by sea are passengers from the cruise ships in the surrounding waters, who come ashore on daytrips to visit some of the sights.

DIRECTORY

AIRPORTS

Alexandria
Tel (03) 459 1486.

Cairo
Tel (02) 2265 5000 (Terminal 1).
Tel (02) 2265 2222 (Terminal 2).
www.cairo-airport.com

Hurghada
Tel (085) 3442 831.

Luxor
Tel (095) 2374 655.

Marsa Alam
Tel (065) 3700 026.

Sharm el-Sheikh
Tel (069) 3601 141.

AIRLINE OFFICES IN CAIRO

Air France
2 Midan Talaat Harb.
Map 5 C3.
Tel (02) 2770 6260.
www.airfrance.com

British Airways
InterContinental Residence Suites, Citystars Complex, Heliopolis, Cairo.
Tel (02) 2480 0380.
www.britishairways.com

Czech Airlines
9 Sharia Talaat Harb, Cairo. **Map** 5 C3.
Tel (02) 2393 0395.
www.csa.cz

Delta
Jeddah Tower, 15 Shakia Ismail Mohammed Zamalek, Cairo.
Tel (02) 2736 2030/9.
www.delta.com

EgyptAir
9 Sharia Talaat Harb.
Map 5 C3.
Tel (02) 2393 0381.
www.egyptair.com
Cairo International Airport.
Tel (02) 2267 7010.

Lufthansa & Swiss
6 Sharia al-Sheikh al-Marsafi, Zamalek.
Map 1 A4.
Tel (02) 19380.

Cairo International Airport.
Tel (02) 2269 5210.

Singapore Airlines
Cairo International Airport.
Tel (02) 2690 0798.

BUSES TO AND FROM ISRAEL

Mazada Tours
Cairo Sheraton, 11 Midan Gala, Cairo.
Tel (02) 3348 8600.

Travelling in Egypt

Egyptian tour bus logo

The overall standards of plane and train travel in Egypt are pretty good, but both services can be frustrating in terms of booking and scheduling. The rail network links the Nile Valley, the Delta and the Canal Zone, while EgyptAir and Air Sinai, the national carriers, serve the major cities. Costs for air travel, however, are substantially higher than trains and long-distance buses, so it is not an option for budget travellers. The bus service in Egypt is extensive and, for short trips, often preferable to trains, both in cost and transit time. For longer journeys, night buses are often available.

Train bound for Aswan departing from Ramses station in Cairo

Sign for the Abu Simbel airport in the Nile Valley

DOMESTIC FLIGHTS

Flying within Egypt entails flying with EgyptAir as the company has a monopoly on air travel within the country. Air Sinai is part of the same company and was formed to serve Israel and the Sinai, thus protecting the mother carrier from losing its landing rights in other Arab countries. EgyptAir operates frequent daily flights between Cairo, Luxor, Hurghada and Aswan, and a slightly reduced service to Alexandria. All domestic flights leave from Terminal 1, the Old Airport, in Cairo. There are several flights a day between Aswan and Abu Simbel. Air Sinai offers daily flights between Cairo, Luxor, Hurghada and Sharm el-Sheikh.

FLIGHT RESERVATIONS

Fares are average by international standards and are calculated in US dollars. It is possible to pay in Egyptian pounds, backed up by an exchange receipt. Reservations should be made as far in advance as possible, especially during winter or if travelling at the time of important Muslim festivals such as Eid

al-Adha and Eid al-Fitr *(see p39)*. Overbooking is common on EgyptAir and Air Sinai: always confirm your flight reservation and make a note of the confirmation reference number. Delays are also common. It is a good idea to have something to read or to otherwise fill the time you may spend waiting. The baggage allowance for domestic flights is 20 kg (44 lb), but this rule is often flouted, especially with regard to hand luggage. It is important to arrive at the airport at least one hour before domestic flights and two hours before international flights.

TRAINS

Trains are the best option for long trips between major cities, offering a much more pleasant alternative to buses and taxis. For short journeys, however, trains tend to be slower and less reliable. Trains in Egypt fall into two categories:

air conditioned (A/C), which includes the more luxurious sleeping trains, and non-A/C, or local stopping trains. A/C trains usually offer first-and second-class cars. First-class cars are less crowded and the seats are more comfortable. Second-class travel is not significantly worse and costs quite a bit less. Seats can be reserved up to a week in advance and it is best to book for the return journey at the same time. There are ten A/C trains a day between Cairo and Alexandria and five daily between Cairo and Luxor and Aswan, but tourists are only officially allowed on the night train, which departs from Ramses station at 10pm. It is impossible to buy advance tickets for the other trains.

Sleeping trains provide a fast, comfortable, but expensive overnight service between Cairo and Luxor and Aswan.

Façade of the Masr train station in central Alexandria

One of the buses used by the West Delta Bus Company

Carpeted compartments have two bunks and a washbasin. There is a lounge car, and breakfast and dinner are served in the compartments. The meals are included in the price. The company that operates the sleeping trains, has ticket offices at both Ramses and Giza railway stations. Tickets should be booked well in advance.

Non-A/C trains have only second-and third-class seats, the latter with open doors and windows for ventilation. Both classes are very dirty and crowded and cannot be used by foreign travellers.

Logo of the Superjet bus run by the Arab Union Transport Company

LONG-DISTANCE BUSES

There are three main bus operators in Egypt. The Upper Egypt Bus Company operates services to the Nile Valley, Al-Fayoum, the Western Desert oases and towns along the Red Sea Coast down to Quesir. It also runs a luxury bus service every evening to Luxor and to Aswan. The East Delta Bus Company covers services to the Sinai beach towns of Sharm el-Sheikh, Dahab, Nuweiba and Taba, as well as to St Catherine's Monastery and the Suez Canal towns of Port Said, Ismailia and Suez. Alexandria, Marsa Matruh, Siwa Oasis and the Delta towns are served by the West Delta Bus Company. Travellers have a choice between air-conditioned (A/C) buses, which are usually newer, and non-A/C vehicles which are generally in worse shape and can take much longer to arrive at their destination. Be aware that just because a bus is advertised as having air-conditioning does not mean that it will actually work; nor will passengers necessarily obey the "no smoking" signs.

The Arab Union Transport Company operates the super-comfortable Superjet and Golden Arrow buses along the main Cairo to Alexandria, Luxor, Hurghada, Sharm el-Sheikh and Aswan routes. Superjet buses also serve Port Said with around nine trips a day. The buses are air-conditioned, with toilets, videos and hostesses offering highly priced snacks.

All long-distance buses from Cairo now depart from the Cairo Gateway bus terminal near Ramses train station. Bus schedules, usually posted in Arabic, are erratic and change frequently so it is advisable to ask travel agencies, hotels and tourist offices to help check the departure times. Tickets are sold from small kiosks at city terminals, up to 24 hours in advance for A/C and long-haul services. In smaller towns, tickets may only be available an hour or so before departure. Prices vary with the type of service and time of travel. For popular trips, book as early as possible to be sure of a seat and to catch the bus at the main departure terminal.

DIRECTORY

AIRPORTS

Alexandria
Tel (03) 459 1486.

Aswan
Tel (097) 3480 333.

Cairo
Tel (02) 2265 5000 (Terminal 1).
Tel (02) 2265 2222 (Terminal 2).

Hurghada
Tel (065) 3462 722/3.

Luxor
Tel (095) 2374 655.

Marsa Alam
Tel (065) 3700 026.

Sharm el-Sheikh
Tel (069) 3601 141.

BUS COMPANIES

East Delta
Tel (02) 2577 8347.

Superjet
Tel (02) 2579 8181.

Upper Egypt
Tel (02) 2576 0261.

West Delta
Tel (02) 2575 2157.

TRAIN STATIONS

Alexandria
Sidi Gaber Station.
Tel (03) 4274 423.

Cairo
Ramses Station, Midan Ramses.
Map 2 D3. *Tel (02) 2575 3555.*

Imposing entrance to Ramses train station, on Midan Ramses, Cairo

Road Travel in Egypt

Driving in Egypt is not for the faint-hearted. Traffic in Cairo is continually busy and horrendous and the main roads out of the metropolis are hazardous. In Alexandria, traffic is no more orderly than in Cairo, but it is less dense, except for summer when millions of Egyptians relocate to Alexandria and the Mediterranean coast. Service (pronounced *servees*) taxis go just about anywhere in the country, providing a fast, cheap form of transport. However their relative discomfort and lack of safety limit their usefulness on all but a few routes. For day-trips, hiring a driver with car may be the best option.

Typical petrol pump

SERVICE TAXIS

As in other Middle-Eastern countries, service taxis form an important part of Egypt's internal transport system, providing a fast and cheap method of getting around the country. Drivers congregate at recognized locations – usually near bus and train stations – and tout for passengers by shouting out their destination. They leave when their vehicle is full. They will not leave before unless the passengers are prepared to pay the extra fares. There is no need to book a seat: just show up at the "terminal" and look for a vehicle that goes to your destination.

Because the vehicles are always full to capacity, the ride can be hot and uncomfortable, especially over long distances. There is little room for luggage, though there is usually a roofrack where luggage can be stowed. More worryingly, the drivers are notorious for their reckless driving and their vehicles are often in poor condition.

Alternatively, you may like to hire a whole service taxi for your group if you wish to undertake a day trip to a destination that is not easily accessed by other means. This can be a cheaper option than hiring a car to drive yourself or using other forms of public transport.

Parking sign for international car rental agencies in Egypt

In Cairo, Giza and Alexandria, a taxi service called Yellow Cabs allows you to order a private car with a driver at any time of the day or night.

CAR RENTAL

International vehicle rental companies such as Hertz, Budget and Avis have offices at the airports and in major hotels in tourist areas. To rent a car, you must be between 25 and 70 years old and hold a valid International Driver's Licence. Cairo and the larger towns are well served by petrol stations but in rural and desert areas long distances can separate them, so always fill the tank to the limit. If driving off-road, always carry spare fuel, water and tools. Most petrol stations can perform minor repairs and Egyptian mechanics are quite good at solving problems, sometimes resorting to more creative or less orthodox measures.

DRIVING IN EGYPT

There are few fixed rules for driving in Egypt and in the cities anarchy prevails. Drivers ignore lane markings, drive the wrong way up one-way streets, back up in the face of oncoming traffic if they miss a turn and ignore red lights and non-signposted intersections. Drivers' intentions are often communicated by hand gestures rather than by conventional signals. A common gesture of drivers

Large estate car operating as a service taxi for longer trips

Minibus holding up to 12 passengers, operating as a service taxi

and pedestrians alike is raised fingers, tips pinched together. This means "Wait". A flip of the hand forward means "Pass". Drivers will sometimes signal turns by pointing with their whole arm out of the window. However, drivers and front passengers must wear seat belts, and indiscriminate honking of horns is now forbidden. Failure to observe either rule is an offence that will incur a fine.

Other hazards in the cities include people jumping from moving buses, overloaded motorbikes, donkey carts and flocks of sheep, and pedestrians who also do not follow any rules of road etiquette.

Hazards on roads between cities are even more serious and numerous. Cars and trucks routinely overtake in the face of oncoming traffic or on the hard shoulder. Roads are in poor condition, with potholes, rough patches and drifting sand. Children often play alongside and in the road, and all manner of livestock, including camels, wander across. Motorists will stack rocks or construction

Typical heavy traffic near Midan Ramses in Cairo

debris in the road in lieu of hazard warning signs when they have pulled in because of a breakdown.

Driving at night is best avoided. Egyptians tend not use their lights at night, except to flash them at oncoming vehicles. Off-road driving without a local guide in the Sinai, along the North Coast near El-Alamein and in the Canal Zone can be especially dangerous because of the presence of land mines, left over from World War II and the Arab-Israeli wars.

Police checkpoints are a frequent occurrence. Foreign drivers are usually waved through, but be prepared to show your passport.

Hiring a private car with a driver can work out cheaper than renting a car. Check with travel agencies and hotels. Regular taxis can also be hired for the day at negotiable rates.

MAPS

The best general map of Egypt is one published by Freytag & Berndt, which is available in most major tourist areas. Mobil's *Motoring Guide to Egypt* is a good choice if you are going to drive. It is sold in Mobil stations and tourist bookstores. Egyptians themselves seldom refer to maps and map coverage of cities other than Cairo is poor.

Stop sign

Uneven road

No car horns

DIRECTORY

TAXI SERVICE

Yellow Cabs
Tel 16516.

CAR RENTAL

Avis
Cairo International Airport.
Tel (02) 2265 2429.
Behind Semiramis
InterContinental Hotel,
Garden City, Cairo.
Tel (02) 2793 2400.
www.avisegypt.com

Budget Rent-a-Car
Cairo International Airport.
Tel (02) 2265 2395.
22 Sharia el Mathaf el
Zeraey, Agouza, Cairo.
Tel (02) 3762 0518.

Hertz
Cairo International
Airport.
Tel (02) 2265 2430.
Ramses Hilton,
Corniche el-Nil, Cairo.
Map 5 A3.
Tel (02) 2575 8914.
195 Sharia 26th July,
Agouza, Cairo.
Tel (02) 3347 2238.
www.hertzegypt.com

**MOTORING
ORGANIZATIONS**

**Automobile
Association (AA)**
Lambert House, Stockport
Road, Cheadle SK8 2DY.
Tel (0161) 495 8945.
www.theaa.com

**Automobile and
Touring Club of
Egypt**
10 Sharia Qasr el-Nil,
Cairo. **Map** 1 C5.
Tel (02) 2574 3355.

**Royal Automobile
Club (RAC)**
8 Surrey Street, Norwich,
NR1 3NG. *Tel* (01922)
727 313.
www.rac.co.uk

MAP OUTLETS

**In UK
Stanfords**
12–14 Long Acre,
London WC2E LP.
Tel (020) 7836 1321.

**In Egypt
AUC Bookshop**
AUC Hostel, 16 Sharia
Mohammed Thakeb,
Zamalek, Cairo.
Tel (02) 2739 7045.

Getting Around Cairo and Alexandria

Metro sign at Midan Opera

The traffic in Cairo is notorious, both for its congestion and its chaos. Driving in the city is impractical for the visitor and many areas, such as the narrow streets and alleys of Islamic and Coptic Cairo, are best explored on foot. The city's public transport includes an extensive bus system, which is cheap but extremely overcrowded, and an efficient metro, although it is of limited use to visitors. Taxis are the easiest way to get around and are plentiful, inexpensive and simple to use once the fare system is understood.

Alexandria's main form of transport is its tram system which covers most areas around the city centre. Downtown is compact enough to negotiate on foot, and minibuses run constantly east and west along the Corniche.

Tram in front of the Basilica in Heliopolis (see pp136–7)

WALKING

Walking in Cairo is the best way to experience the richness and diversity of this vibrant city. Tackling the streets for the first time, however, can be an intimidating prospect and care should be taken. Drivers do not obey lane markings, road signs or traffic lights. They will slow down to give you time to cross the street, but do not hesitate partway across as this confuses the dodge-and-dash flow of traffic and pedestrians and can increase the chances of an accident. Where possible, cross with groups of other people. Walking in the poorer quarters is remarkably safe, but be wary of petty thieves in crowded areas like the Khan al-Khalili.

Women may also encounter verbal harassment and gropers downtown, on the bridges and in the Khan al-Khalili.

TAXIS

To hail one of Cairo's taxis, stand on the side of the road and signal with your hand. State your destination by district or landmark and be prepared for the driver to pick up other people travelling in the same direction.

Black-and-white taxis do not have meters, so it is best to agree on a price beforehand. White cabs, which all have meters that start at LE 2.50, have made it much easier for locals and tourists alike. In general, most trips within the Downtown-Dokki-Mohandiseen-Zamalek area cost between LE 7–10. From Downtown to Heliopolis or Maadi charges are LE 25–30 and from Downtown to the airport, LE 40. Expect to

pay a little more late at night. Taxis at five-star hotels charge higher fares but are good for day hire as they are in better condition and the drivers speak some English. Yellow Cabs (see p344) is also a useful service for tourists.

Taxis are generally cheaper in Alexandria than in Cairo, however, and journeys around the city centre cost no more than LE 3, while a ride to the bus station is LE 15.

Single women passengers are generally safe, but should ride in the back of cabs and not talk or make eye contact with the driver, as both of these actions can attract unwanted attention.

RIVER BUSES AND FELUCCAS

An alternative means of getting around is by river bus. These are inexpensive and run approximately every half-hour from near Coptic Cairo to the Arab Television Building north of the Egyptian Museum, stopping at Rhoda Island (see pp124–5). At weekends, the buses are full of revellers heading for the Nile Barrages (see p169) north of the city. River buses only run until 4pm.

Feluccas (sailing boats) are found along the river and can be hired out for short cruises (about LE 60 per hour). This is a great way to see Cairo from the Nile and cruises at sunset are particularly popular. One of the main departure points for felucca cruises is in Garden City by the Meridien Hotel.

One of Cairo's ubiquitous black-and-white taxis

Felucca on the Nile in Central Cairo – a sedate mode of travel

METRO

The Cairo Metro is clean, safe and inexpensive but visitors will find it useful for only a few stops, the most prominent of which is the Mar Girgis station opposite Coptic Cairo. There are two lines, identified by direction. The al-Marg to Helwan line follows the east bank of the Nile for most of its length and the Shubra to Giza line runs north to southwest, via Midan Tahrir. The last stop on the line is displayed on the front of each train and maps of the network can be found at each station.

Local bus providing an authentic Cairo experience for the visitor

Tickets are available at all stations and are valid for one trip, including transfers. A trip costs a flat rate of LE 1 to any destination. Ticket-operated turnstiles control access to all platforms so you will need to keep your ticket in order to exit at your destination. The metro is extremely crowded during the morning and evening rush hours.

The middle one or two carriages on each train is reserved for women only, but women can and do choose to ride on any car.

BUSES

City buses are usually green, with route numbers displayed in Arabic on the front. The buses are often overcrowded and are not really recom-

mended. However, they do cover almost all destinations and are very cheap. The city-run minibuses (usually white or green) are a slightly more pleasant experience and are still very inexpensive. These have fixed routes and charge a flat fare, which is paid as you board. Buses leave from Midan Abdel Moneim Riad, next to Midan Tahir, or from where you see metal shelters, signs posted on lamp posts, or more commonly, crowds of people waiting alongside the road.

Air-conditioned buses (No.356 and No.799) travel to and from the airport and Tahrir and Ramses respectively. The city also has microbuses and service taxis that operate on fixed routes and stop on request. Like the local buses, they are overcrowded and used mainly by workers and residents.

GETTING AROUND ALEXANDRIA

Alexandria has an aged tram system. The cars are worn and the pace is slow, but fares are cheap. The service runs from 5:30am to midnight, and to 1am during the summer months. Ramla is the main downtown terminal, located east of the bus depot on Midan Saad Zaghloul. Trams headed east from Ramla are blue, while those travelling west are yellow. Note that on trams that are made up of three cars the middle car is normally reserved for women.

Useful tram routes for visitors include No.15 and No.36 (yellow) for the Mosque of Abu al-Abbas Mursi (*see pp244–5*) and Fort Qaitbey (*see p245*). Heading east, route No.2 (blue) travels two-thirds of the way to Montazah Palace (*see p247*). All tram and route numbers are in Arabic script only.

As in Cairo, buses are old and overcrowded. Minibuses are a better option, following most of the same routes and operating hours as the tram. City minibuses are white while private ones are blue or grey. Both cost under LE 1.

The minibuses that travel along the Corniche day-and-night are convenient.

City taxis are black and orange, or yellow, and the rules that apply to taxis in Cairo (*see p346*) apply here.

Horse-drawn carriages ply the Corniche and Masr Station and can be a relaxing way of getting around the city, providing the traffic is light. The price is negotiable. An hourly rate of LE 25 is reasonably equitable to all involved.

A westbound tram on a busy thoroughfare in Alexandria

General Index

Page numbers in **bold** type refer to main entries.

Acknowledgments

Dorling Kindersley would like to thank the following people whose contributions and assistance have made the preparation of this book possible.

Publishing Manager
Jane Ewart.

Managing Editor
Anna Streiffert.

Director of Publishing, Travel Guides
Gillian Allan.

Publisher
Douglas Amrine.

Production
Joanna Bull, Sarah Dodd.

Main Contributors
Jane Dunford, Dr Joann Fletcher, Carole French, Robin Gauldie, Andrew Humphreys, Kyle Pakka, Richard Williams.

Additional Contributors and Consultants
Mohammed Saad El-Essawy, David Stone, Hugh Taylor, Wendy Wrangham.

Additional Illustrations
Rebecca Milner.

Additional Photography
Vanessa Bell, Jo Doran, Minesh Modha, Ian O'Leary, Rough Guides/Eddie Gerald, Clive Streeter, Wendy Wrangham.

Design and Editorial Assistance
Claire Baranowski, Vanessa Bell, Helen Foulkes, Dale Harris, Victoria Heyworth-Dunne, Juliet Kenny, Jude Ledger, Carly Madden, Samira Mahmoud, Nicola Malone, Sonal Modha, Marisa Renzullo, Collette Sadler, Rada Radojicic, Ellen Root, Sands Publishing Solutions, Kareen Sharawy, Meredith Smith, Conrad Van Dyk.

Proof Reader
Stewart J Wild.

Indexer
Helen Peters.

Special Assistance
Ben Faulks, Gamal, Peter Sheehan, Shehad, Hisham Youssif.

Additional Picture Research
Nicole Kaczynski.

Photography Permissions
The publisher would like to thank all the churches, museums, hotels, restaurants, shops, galleries and sights too numerous to thank individually, for their co-operation and contribution to this publication.

Picture Credits
a=above; b=below/bottom; c =centre; f=far; l=left; r=right; t=top.

The publisher would like to thank the following individuals, companies and picture libraries for permission to reproduce their photographs:

4CORNERS IMAGES: SIME/Fantuz Olimpio 10cla.

AFP, LONDON: Amr Mammoud-STR 309cr; Manoocher Deghati-STF 39clb; Marwan Naamani-STF 38cr; Mohammed al-Sihiti-STR 40bl, 38t, 41t, 313tr; Narwan Naamani-STR 40b; Patrick Hertzog-STF 42b; STR 39tr; STR-STR 41b.

AKG LONDON: 55tc; 183t, 240bl, 245ca; François Guenet 174b; Erich Lessing 24tl, 83cl, 175tr, 183t, 197bl, 238tr; Gilles Mermet 110bl.

ALAMY IMAGES: Peter Bowater 318bl; Adam Butler 321cb; Peter Chadwick 318c; Gary Cook 11br; Dennis Cox 11cl; Ian Dagnall 226tl; dbimages/Amanda Ahn 340cla; Dacorum Gold 323c; Nick Hanna 321ca; 321cr; Peter Horree 10br, 150cla; imagebroker/Manfred Bail 321br; Paul Ives 316br; Stan Kujawa 318tr, 344b; Celia Mannings 324bc; Barry Mason 322bc; Michele Molinari 289c; Patrick Syder Images 322tc; Wolfgang Pölzer 320tr; Profimedia International s.r.o./Jaroslav Hejzlar 320cl; SAS 289tl; Gordon Sinclair 317cl; travelpixs 244tl; WaterFrame 320crb; Andrew Woodley 323bl; WoodyStock/ McPhoto 324tl.

ANCIENT ART & ARCHITECTURE COLLECTION: 22tr, 24cl, 26–27, 26br, 28tr, 29cl, 31tl, 45ca, 48br, 49b, 50crb, 51b, 52clb, 52bc, 56bc, 70cb, 77tl, 105tl, 132br, 168cr, 174tr, 175cl, 190br, 193cr, 193br, 195br; Dr. S Coyne 211tr, 211cl, 211br;

Muhammed al-Agsarai 56crb; R Sheridan 20tl, 22br, 34br, 246b.

THE ANCIENT EGYPT PICTURE LIBRARY: 30bl, 74cl, 174cr, 175br, 177tr, 194cra, 194bl, 239cl.

JON ARNOLD: 1c.

THE ART ARCHIVE: Egyptian Museum of Cairo 10tc; Mander & Mitcheson Theatre Col/ Eileen Tweedy 61ca; Museo Civico Revoltella Trieste/Dagli Orti 60–61c; Museum Correr, Venice/Dagli Orti 58cb, 215cra; Dagli Orti 58t; Museum of Islamic Art Cairo/Dagli Orti 79c; The Egyptian Museum, Cairo/Dagli Orti 3c, 27tr, 74clb, 76tl, 76br, 77bc.

AXIOM: Heidi Grassley 215bl, James Morris 31crb, 164br, 177cb, 177bl, 215tc, 239br, 260cb.

BILDARCHIV PREUSSISCHER KULTURBESITZ: Johannes Laurentius 54cl.

BRIDGEMAN ART LIBRARY, LONDON/ NEW YORK: 30tr, 30cr, 32ca, 55tr, 57br, 59bc, *The Flight into Egypt* by Jean-Leon Gerome 123t, 128tr; Bargello, Florence 57bc; Magdelen College, Oxford 57br; Musée des Beaux-Arts, Beziers 54–5 c; Musée du Louvre 22cl, 22–23, 26bl, 178br; Stapleton Collection 24b, 65inset, 132bl, 214tr, 309bl; The British Library, London 58bc; The British Museum, London 46bl; Whitford & Hughes 123t.

ROB DEN BRAASEM: photographersdirect. com 152cla.

JEAN-LOUP CHARMET: 53bl.

CITYSTARS: 303br.

BRUCE COLEMAN LTD: Franco Banfi 37bl; Charles and Sandra Hood 227br, 316br.

THOMAS COOKE ARCHIVE: 191cr.

CORBIS: 60tr; Yann Arthus-Bertrand 15b; Bettman 55ca; Bettmann 18c; Hulton Deutsch Collection 20br; Jose Fuste Raga 323tr; Carmen Redondo 199 cl; Reuters New Media Inc, 54c, 257cl; Galen Rowell

261cbr; Stephane Compoint/Sygma 19t; Sygma 20/21c; Vanni Archive 118–119; Vanni Archive/Gian Berto Vanni 198cra, 198tl; Sandro Vannini 262–3; KM Westermann 64–5, 314cl

G. DAGLI ORTI: 110cl; Graeco-Roman Museum, Alexandria 55tl, 242tl, 242clb, 243cra; Graeco-Roman Museum, Alexandria.

CM DIXON: 24tr.

DK PICTURE LIBRARY: 60b, 306tr, 306br; Alan Hills 306bl; Alistair Duncan 21t, 25b, 25cra; British Museum 23cb, 31br; British Museum/ Peter Hayman 122t, 122tr; Dave King 307br; Frank Greenaway 55cb; Geoff Brightling 21br, 31clb; Peter Hayman 30cbl; Philip Dowell 307br; Philip Enticknap 191cl.

DK PICTURE LIBRARY/BRITISH MUSEUM, LONDON: 28cla, 28cl, 28cr, 28crb, 28br, 28bcl, 29tl, 29tr, 29cla, 29ca, 29crb, 29bl, 48t, 55bl.

JO DORAN: 115b, 201t.

EDIMEDIA FRANCE: 34c.

EGYPTAIR: 340c.

MARY EVANS PICTURE LIBARY: 56tc, 57tl, 59tr, 59cr, 59clb, 59br, 60cl, 191crb, 191br, 309cbl.

WERNER FORMAN ARCHIVE: 51ca, 134cr, 163tc, 164cl, 192tr, 195cb; British Museum London 26tl, 30ca; Dr. E Strouhal 31bl, 31c, 199tc, 199bc, 203tl; Graeco-Roman Museum, Alexandria 53tc, 242cl, 242bl, 243bl; J Paul Getty Museum, Malibu 169bc; Metropolitan Museum of Art, New York 77c, Musée du Louvre 31cla; Schimmel Collection New York 23tl, 122cl; The Egyptian Museum, Cairo 20clb, 50ca, 51cb, 74tl, 74bc, 75tr, 75cra, 75cr, 75cb, 76cr, 76cla.

KENNETH GARRETT: 194b.

GENESIS SPACE PHOTO LIBRARY: 10bl.

GETTY IMAGES: AFP/Cris Bouroncle 42bl; Photographer's Choice/Georgette Douwma 11tr; The Image Bank/Stuart Westmorland 288cl.

PATRICK GODEAU, EGYPT: 14fp, 114b.

RONALD GRANT ARCHIVE: 55b.

HILTON ALEXANDRIA GREEN PLAZA: 265b.

HEMISPHERE IMAGES: Arnaud Chicurel 316tc; Luis Orteo 317tr.

© MICHAEL HOLFORD: 23tr, 25crb, 117tc, 197br, 206–207.

ANGELO HORNAK LIBRARY: 34tl, 35ca, 93cr.

HULTON GETTY: Hulton Getty 54tr.

HUTCHISON LIBRARY: Liba Taylor 166–167.

KATAMEYA HEIGHTS GOLF & TENNIS RESORT: 317br.

JURGEN LIEPE: 5bl, 45bl, 46tl, 47tc, 47crb, 47bl, 49cb, 122bl, 132tc, 309cla.

MAGNUM: Bruno Barbey 63bc.

LEONARDO MEDIA LTD: 240cr; 284bl.

NILE CITY INVESTMENTS: 18bl.

RICHARD T NOWITZ: 110tr, 114ca, 116bl, 125c, 184b, 185b, 187cr, 187br, 316c.

ORONOZ ARCHIVO FOTOGRAFICO: British Museum 22bl.

LESLEY ORSEN: 237cla.

CHRISTINE OSBORNE: 25tl, 31cra, 35cb, 92bl, 103br, 106tr, 106cl, 107t, 111bl, 114cb, 120bl, 121bl, 123b, 176tl, 176c.

OXFORD SCIENTIFIC FILMS: Mark Webster 216; Mike Brown 261tc.

PA PHOTOS: 61br; EPA European Press Agency 63cb, 63t.

PHOTOLIBRARY: JTB Photo 322cl.

POPPERFOTO: 20tr, 20cla, 20cl, 21cr, 60tl, 61bl, 62tl, 62cb, 63br, 122br, 125br, 135bc; Donald McLeish 73tr.

RANA EL NEMR PHOTOGRAPHY: photographersdirect.com 152bc.

RETROGRAPH ARCHIVE LTD: 191bl.

SCALA GROUP S.P.A.: 30tl, 116cr; Archaeological Museum, Palestine 44a; Coptic Museum, Cairo 114t, 116t; The Egyptian Museum, Cairo 15t, 45bc, 66crb.

STA TRAVEL GROUP: 330crb.

SUPERSTOCK: Caroline Von Tuempling 336bl.

THOMAS COOK EGYPT: 338bl.

TOPHAM PICTUREPOINT: 20bl.

WAWSON WOOD: 227t, 227cra, 227clb, 227bl.

JACKET
Front: PHOTOLIBRARY: Aflo Foto Agency/ Yoshio Tomii Photo Studio.
Back: DORLING KINDERSLEY: Max Alexander tl; Eddie Gerald bl; David Peart clb; Rough Guides/Eddie Gerald cla.
Spine: Aflo Foto Agency/Yoshio Tomii Photo Studio t.

All other images © Dorling Kindersley. For further information see:
www.dkimages.com

SPECIAL EDITIONS OF DK TRAVEL GUIDES

DK Travel Guides can be purchased in bulk quantities at discounted prices for use in promotions or as premiums. We are also able to offer special editions and personalized jackets, corporate imprints, and excerpts from all of our books, tailored specifically to meet your own needs.

To find out more, please contact:
(in the United States) **SpecialSales@dk.com**
(in the UK) **Travelspecialsales@uk.dk.com**
(in Canada) DK Special Sales at
general@tourmaline.ca
(in Australia)
business.development@pearson.com.au

Phrase Book

The official language of Egypt is Arabic. While
it is not an easy language for newcomers to
learn, it is well worth taking the time to
practise and memorize a few key words and
phrases. Most urban Egyptians speak a little
English but they will greet any attempt to
speak Arabic with delight and encouragement.

The Arabic given here is the Modern
Standard Arabic. This is the Arabic written in
newspapers, spoken on the radio and recited
in prayers in the mosque. This varies somewhat
from the language spoken on the street
(Egyptian Colloquial Arabic), which is in fact a
dialect of the standard language. Nevertheless
if you speak slowly and clearly, you should
have no difficulty being understood.

Transliteration from Arabic script to the
Roman alphabet is a difficult task. Although
many attempts have been made, there is no
satisfactory system and you will repeatedly
come across contradictory spellings in Egypt.

In this phrase book we have given a simple
phonetic transcription only. The underlined
letter indicates the stressed syllable.

Pronunciation

a,-ah	as in "mad"
aa	as in "far"
aw	as in "law"
ay	as in "day"
e	as in "bed"
ee	as in "keen"
i	as in "bit"
o	as in "rob"
oo	as in "food"
u	as in "book"
A	pronounced as an emphasised "a" as in "both of us – you And me!"
D	a heavily pronounced "d"
gh	like a French "r" – from the back of the throat
H	a heavily pronounced "h"
kh	as in the Scottish pronunciation of "loch"
q	a "k" sound from the back of the mouth as in "caramel"
S,T	heavily pronounced "s", "t"
th	as in "thin"
Z	heavily pronounced "z"
'	this sounds like a small catch in the breath

When two different vowels occur together, for example Ae-
and aA- each is pronounced separately.

In Emergency

Help!	an-najdah!
Stop!	qeff!
I want to go to a doctor	oreed al zehab lel tabeeb
I want to go to a pharmacist	oreed al zehab lel saydaliya
Where is the nearest telephone?	ayn yoogad aqrab telifoon?
Where is the hospital?	ayn toogad al mostashfa?
I'm allergic to… …penicillin/aspirin	Andee Hasaaseeyah men… penicillin/aspirin

Communication essentials

Yes/No	naAm/laa
Thank you	shokran
No, thank you	laa shokran
Please (asking for something)	min faDlak
Please (offering)	tafaDal
Good morning	sabaaH al-khayr
Good afternoon	as-salaam Alaykum
Good evening	masa' al-khayr
Good night (when going to bed)	teSbaH Ala khayr
Good night (leaving group early)	maA as-salaamah or as-salaam Alaykum
Goodbye	maA as-salaamah
Excuse me, please	min faDlak, law samaHt
today	al-yawm
yesterday	al-ams
tomorrow	ghadan
this morning	haza aS-sabaaH
this afternoon	al-yawm baAd aZ-Zohr
this evening	haza al-masa'
here	hona
there	honaak
what?	maza?
which?	ay?
when?	mata?
who?	man?
where?	ayn?

Useful Phrases

I don't understand	la afham
Do you speak English/French?	hal tatakalam engleezee/faransee?
I can't speak Arabic	la ataklam al Arabeya
I don't know	la aAref
Please speak more slowly	men faDlak tahadath bebote'
Please write it down for me	men faDlak ektob ala hazeehee al-waraqah
My name is…	esmee…
How do you do, pleased to meet you	kayf Haalak, tasharafna be-meArefatak
How are you?	kayf Haalak?
Sorry!	aasef
I'm really sorry	aasef jeddan
Can you help me, please?	min faDlak, momken tosaAednee?
Can you tell me…?	men faDlak qol lee…?
I would like….?	oreed…
Is there…here?	yugad…hona?
Where can I get…?	ayn ajed…?
How much is it?	kam thaman haza (m) hazeehee (f)?
What time is it?	as-saAH kam
I must go now	labod an azhab al-a'n
Do you take credit cards?	hal taqbal Visa, Access?
Where is the toilet?	ayn ajed al-hamam?
Go away! (for children only)	emshee!
Excellent!	momtaaz!
left	yasaar
right	yameen
up	fawq
down	asfal

Travel

I want to go to…	oreed al zehab le…
How do you get to…	kayef tazhab le…?
I'd like to rent a car	oreed asta'jer sayaarah
driver's licence	rokhSat qiyaadah
I've lost my way	ana Dalayt aT-Tareeq

Where is the nearest garage?	ayn yoogad aqrab warshet sayarat?	single room	ghorfa be-sareer waaHed
garage (for repairs)	garaaj meekaaneekee	shower	dosh
petrol/gas	banzeen	toilet	towaaleet
petrol/gas station	maHaTTat banzeen	toilet paper	waraq towaleet
When is there a flight to...?	mata toogad reHalat tayaran ela...?	key	meftaaH
What is the fare to...?	kam thaman al tazkarah le...?	lift/elevator	mesAd
A ticket to...please	law samaHt, tazkarat zehaab le...	breakfast	foToor
		restaurant	maTAm
airport	maTaar	bill	faatoorah
ticket	tazkarah		
passport	jawaaz safar		

Shopping

visa	veeza
airport shuttle	baaS al-maTaar
When do we arrive in...?	mata nasel ela...?
When is the next train to...?	mata yaqoom al-qeTaar alzaheb le...?
What station is this?	hazehe ay maHaTTah?

train	qeTaar	I'd like...	oreed...
first-class (train)	darajah oolah	Do you have...?	hal Andak...?
second-class	darajah thaaneeyah	How much is this?	be-kam haza?
sleeping car	Arabat nawm	I'll give you...	ha aAteek...
bus	otobees	Two for...	ethnayn be...
bus station	mahatet el-otobees	Where do I pay?	ayn adfaA?
boat	markeb	to buy	yashtaree
cruise	jawlah baHareeyah	to go shopping	yatasawwaq
ferry	Abaarah		
taxi	taaksee		

Sightseeing

mosque	jaamea

Making a Telephone Call

may I use your telephone?	momken astaAmel teleefoonak	street, road	shaareA
How much is a call to...?	be-kam al-mokaalamah le...?	house	bayt
Can I call abroad from here?	momken ataSel bel-khaarej men hona?	square	midan
		beach	shaaTee'
Hello, this is...speaking	alloo, ...yatakalam	museum	matHaf
I would like to speak to...	oreed atakalam maA...	church	kaneesah
Could you leave him a message?	momken tatrok laho resaalah?	castle, palace	qasr

Eating Out (see also pp280–81)

My number is...	raqamee...	A table for...one/two, please	ma'eda le-shakhS waHed/le-shakhSayn, law samaHt
telephone call	mokaalamah		
emergency	Tawaare'	I'd like...	oreed...
operator	sentraal	May we have the bill, please?	momken al-Hesaab, law samaHt?

Post Offices and Banks

		May we have some more...?	momken al-mazeed mendfadlak...?
How much is a letter to...?	kam taklefat ersal kheTab ela....?	My compliments to the chef!	taheyaty le-Tahy!
This is to go airmail	erselha bel-bareed al-jawee	beer	beerah
I'd like to change this into...	oreed oghayyer haza ela	bottle	zojaajah
bank	bank	cake	kayk
dollar (US)	dollar	coffee	qahwah
exchange rate	seAr at-taghyeer	– no sugar	– saadah
letter	kheTaab	– medium	– maZbooT
postbox	sondooq bareed	– sweet	– sukkar zeyaadah
package	tard	– with milk	– bel-Haleeb
post	boosTah	cup	fenjaan
postcard	beTaaqah bareedeeyah	glass	koob
post office	maktab al-bareed	plate	Tabaq
stamp	TaabeA bareed	sandwich	sandwetsh
traveller's cheque	sheek siyaaHee	snack	wajbah khafeefah
		sugar	sukkar
		table	ma'eda

Staying in a Hotel

		tea	shaay
Have you got any vacancies?	hal yoogad ghoraf khaaleeyah?	mint	neAnaA
I have a reservation	Andee Hajz	(mineral) water	miyaah (maAdaneeyah)
I'd like a room with a bathroom	oreed ghorfah be-Hammam	wine	nabeez

Food and Drink

May I have the bill please?	momken al-hesab law samaHt	soup	shorbah
I'll pay by credit card	sa-asfaA al-fatoorah law Visa, Access	fish	samak
		aubergine salad	salaaTat baazenjaan
I'll pay by cash	sa-adfaA naqdan	melon	shammaam
hotel	fondoq	pickles	mekhallalaat
air-conditioning	takyeef	hummus	Hommos
double room	ghorfa mozdawajah	falafel - fried balls of ground fava beans or chickpeas	falaafel
		fried balls of ground fava beans with herbs	taAmeeyah
		olives	zaytoon
		stuffed vine leaves	waraq Aenab maHsee

aubergine and tahina paté	baaba ghanooj
cheese	jebnah
curd cheese	labnah
egg	bayDah
macaroni	makaroonah
noodles	sheAreeyah

Fish

grilled fish	samak mashwee
fried fish	samak maqlee
fish with rice	samak sayaadeeyah
smoked fish	samak medakhan
shrimp	jambaree
squid	Habaar
tuna	toonah

Meat and Poultry

beef	laHm baqaree
chicken	firaakh
chicken pieces	koftat dajaaj
duck	baTT
grilled lamb kebab	kebaab
lamb	laHm Daanee
meat	laHm
meatballs	koftah
mixed grilled meats	luHoom mashweeyah
pigeon	Hamaam
roast beef	roosbeef
sliced spit-roast lamb	shaawerma
steak	boftayk

Vegetables

aubergine	baazenjaan
avocado	abookaado
cabbage	koronb
celery	karafs
chillies	felfel Haamee
cucumber	khiyaar
lentils	Adas
lettuce	khass
okra	baamyah
onions	baSal
potatoes	baTaaTes
rice	rozz
tomatoes	TamaaTem
vegetables	khoDaar

Fruit and Nuts

almonds	looz
apricots	meshmesh
bananas	mooz
dried fruits	fawaakeh mojaffafah
figs	teen
fruits	fawaakeh
lemon	laymoon HaameD
pistachio nuts	fostoq
watermelon	baTeekh

Desserts

cake	kayk
baclava	baqlaawah
biscuits	baskooweet
dessert	Halawiyaat
fritters in syrup	zalaabeeyah
fruit salad	salaatet fawaakeh
ice cream	aays kreem
"Mother of Ali"	omm Alee
milk pudding with raisins	
pastry with nuts and syrup	konaafah
yoghurt	zabaadee

Methods of Cooking

baked	feel-forn
barbecued	mashwee Ala al-faHm
boiled	maslooq
fried	maqlee
grilled	mashwee
pickled	mekhaalil
spiced	metabbel
stewed	mesabbek
stuffed	maHshee

Numbers

0	sefr	30	thalaatheen
1	waaHed	31	waaHed wa thalaatheen
2	ethnayn	32	ethnayn wa thalaatheen
3	thalaathah	40	arbaAeen
4	arbaAh	50	khamseen
5	khamsah	60	setteen
6	settah	70	sabAeen
7	sabAh	80	thamaaneen
8	thamaaneeyah	90	tesAeen
9	tesAh	100	me'ah
10	Asharah	110	me'ah wa Asharah
11	Hedaash	200	me'tayn
12	etnaash	300	thalaathme'ah
13	thalaathaash	400	arbaAme'ah
14	arbaAtaash	500	khamsme'ah
15	khamastaash	600	setme'ah
16	settaash	700	sabAme'ah
17	sabaAtaash	800	thamaanme'ah
18	thamaantaash	900	tesAme'ah
19	tesAtaash	1,000	alf
20	Aeshreen	2,000	alfayn
21	waaHed wa Aeshreen	10,000	Asharat aalaaf
22	ethnayn wa Aeshreen	1,000,000	malyoon

Days, Months and Seasons

Sunday	yawm al-aHad
Monday	yawm al-ethnayn
Tuesday	yawm ath-tholatha'
Wednesday	yawm al-arbeAa'
Thursday	yawm al-khamees
Friday	yawm al-jomAh
Saturday	yawm as-sabt
January	yanaayer
February	febraayer
March	Maars
April	ebreel
May	maayo
June	yoonyo
July	yoolyo
August	aghosTos
September	sebtember
October	oktoober
November	noofember
December	deesember
spring	al-ar-rabeeA
summer	aS-Sayf
autumn	al-khareef
winter	ash-sheta'

Things You'll Hear

enshaallah	God (Allah) willing
tasharafna	you're welcome
esmak eh?	What is your name?
bel-hanaa' wash-shefaa'	Enjoy your meal